THE DAY PHONICS KICKED IN

Other *Baby Blues*® Books from Andrews McMeel Publishing

Guess Who Didn't Take a Nap?
I Thought Labor Ended When the Baby Was Born
We Are Experiencing Parental Difficulties . . . Please Stand By
Night of the Living Dad
I Saw Elvis in My Ultrasound
One More and We're Outnumbered!
Check, Please . . .
threats, bribes & videotape
If I'm a Stay-at-Home Mom, Why Am I Always in the Car?
Lift and Separate
I Shouldn't Have to Scream More Than Once!
Motherhood Is Not for Wimps
Baby Blues®: Unplugged
Dad to the Bone
Never a Dry Moment
Two Plus One Is Enough
Playdate: Category 5
Our Server Is Down
Something Chocolate This Way Comes
Briefcase Full of Baby Blues
Night Shift

Treasuries
The Super-Absorbent Biodegradable Family-Size Baby Blues®
Baby Blues®: Ten Years and Still in Diapers
Butt-Naked Baby Blues®
Wall-to-Wall Baby Blues®
Driving Under the Influence of Children
Framed!
X-Treme Parenting

THE DAY PHONICS KICKED IN

BABY BLUES® GOES BACK TO SCHOOL

SELECTED CARTOONS BY RICK KIRKMAN & JERRY SCOTT

Andrews McMeel
Publishing, LLC

Kansas City

Baby Blues® is syndicated internationally by King Features Syndicate, Inc. For information, write King Features Syndicate, Inc., 300 West Fifty-Seventh Street, New York, New York 10019.

08 09 10 11 12 BAM 10 9 8 7 6 5 4 3 2 1

ISBN-13: 978-0-7407-7738-7
ISBN-10: 0-7407-7738-6

Library of Congress Control Number: 2008926291

www.andrewsmcmeel.com

Find *Baby Blues*® on the Web at
www.babyblues.com.

Many thanks to all the great teachers at Heritage Elementary for guiding our girls through their first few years of school.
And thanks to all my teachers as well—especially Helen Wichowsky at Upper Heyford,
and team-teachers Mr. Adams and Mr. Burges at Cortez, wherever you are.
—R.K.

To Marylou Gooden, Debbie Farmer, Jackie Kirk-Martinez, Mishele Sneed, Kristine Maas, Jennifer Truesdell,
Marilyn Requarth, and Coach Dan. Thanks for making Cady's kindergarten experience a huge success.
—J.S.

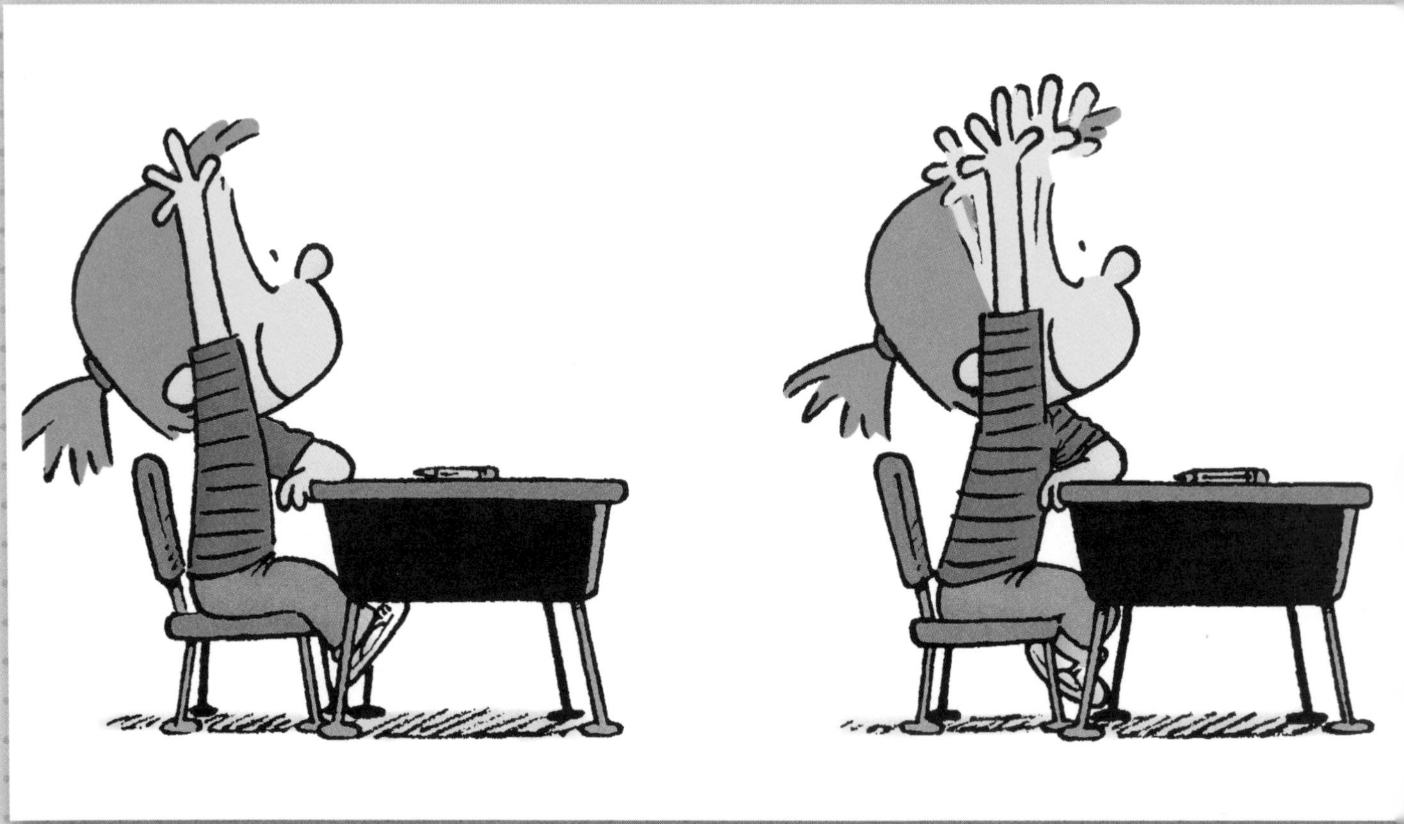

KIRKMAN & SCOTT

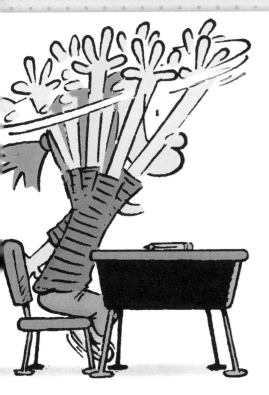

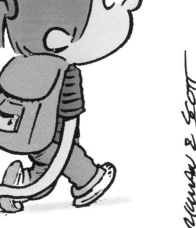

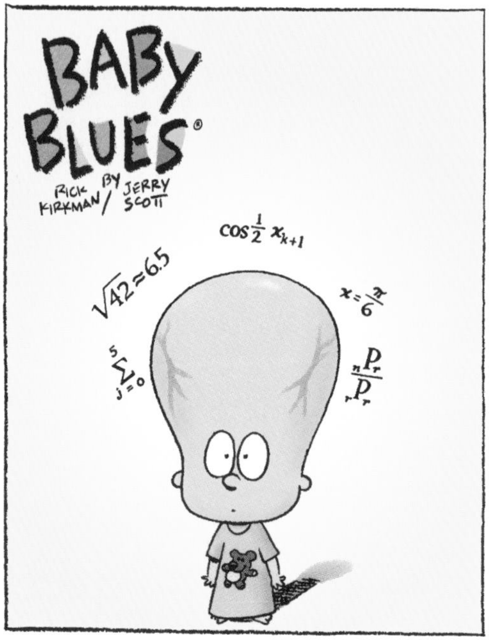
BABY BLUES®
RICK KIRKMAN / BY JERRY SCOTT
cos 1/2 x k+1
√42=6.5
x=π/6
Σ j=0 5
nPr / rPr

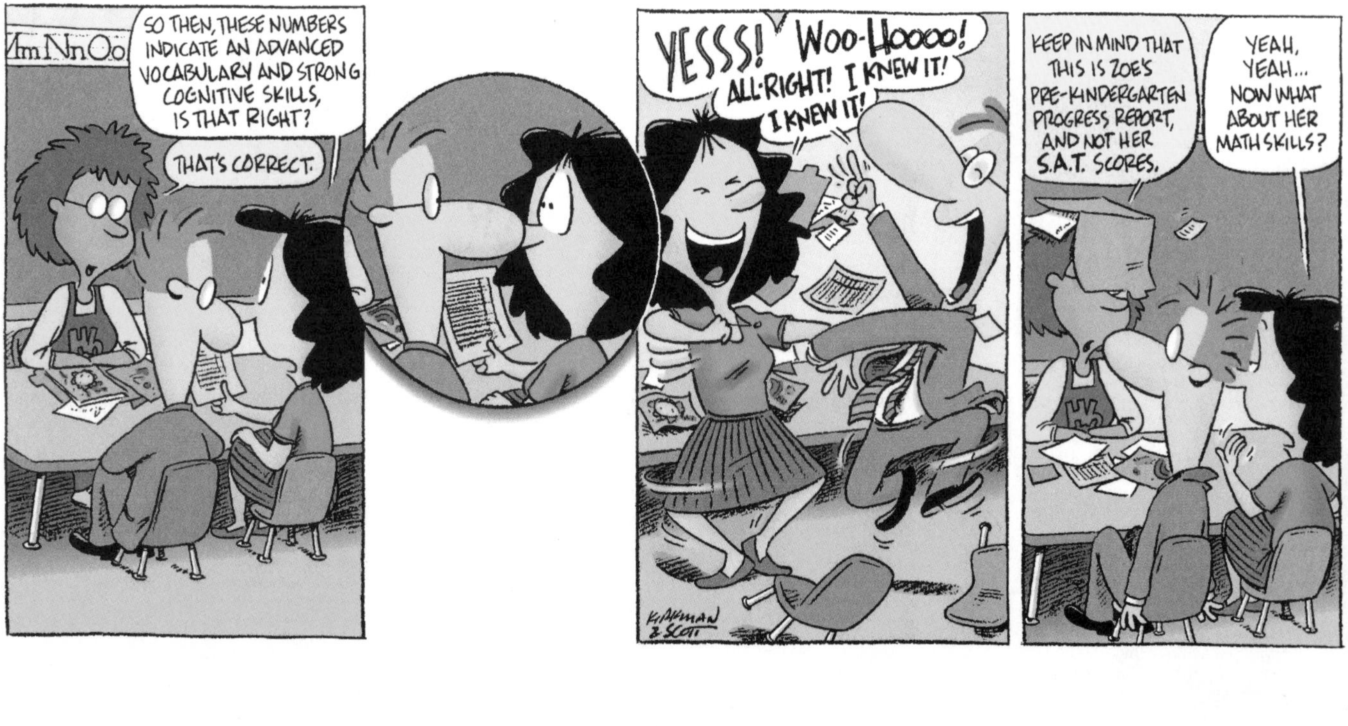
MmNnOo
SO THEN, THESE NUMBERS INDICATE AN ADVANCED VOCABULARY AND STRONG COGNITIVE SKILLS, IS THAT RIGHT?
THAT'S CORRECT.
YESSS!
WOO-HOOOO!
ALL-RIGHT! I KNEW IT! I KNEW IT!
KIRKMAN & SCOTT
KEEP IN MIND THAT THIS IS ZOE'S PRE-KINDERGARTEN PROGRESS REPORT, AND NOT HER S.A.T. SCORES.
YEAH, YEAH... NOW WHAT ABOUT HER MATH SKILLS?

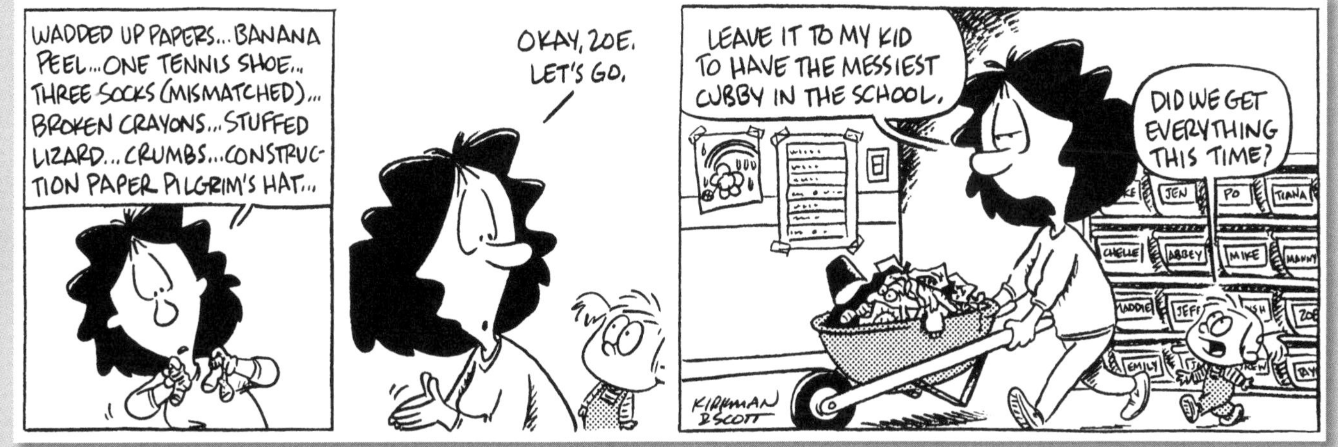
WADDED UP PAPERS... BANANA PEEL... ONE TENNIS SHOE... THREE SOCKS (MISMATCHED)... BROKEN CRAYONS... STUFFED LIZARD... CRUMBS... CONSTRUCTION PAPER PILGRIM'S HAT...
OKAY, ZOE. LET'S GO.
LEAVE IT TO MY KID TO HAVE THE MESSIEST CUBBY IN THE SCHOOL.
DID WE GET EVERYTHING THIS TIME?
JEN
PO
TIANA
CHELLE
ABBEY
MIKE
MANNY
MADDIE
JEFF
ZOE
EMILY
KIRKMAN & SCOTT

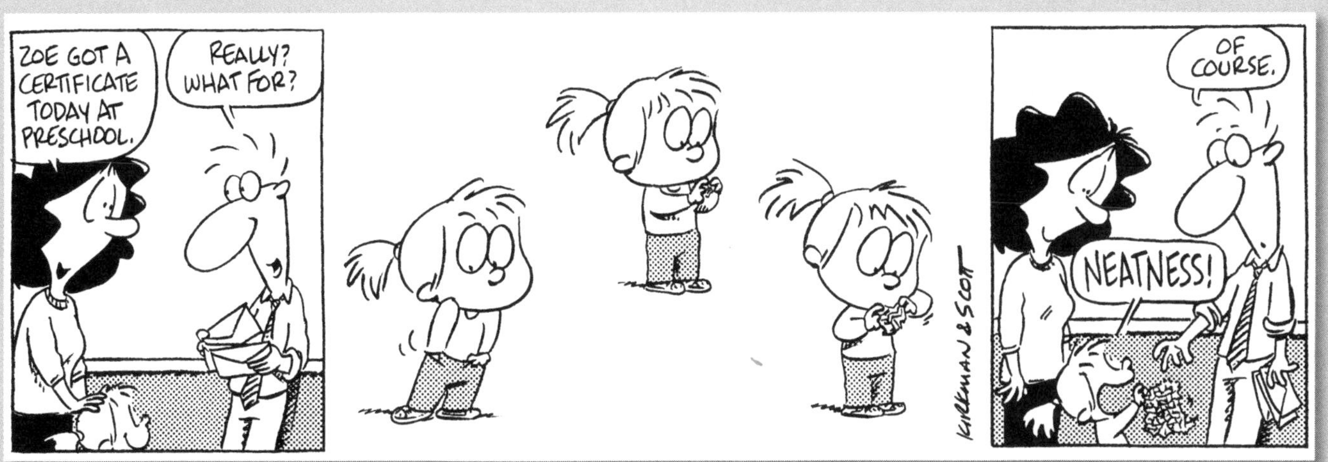
ZOE GOT A CERTIFICATE TODAY AT PRESCHOOL.
REALLY? WHAT FOR?
KIRKMAN & SCOTT
OF COURSE.
NEATNESS!

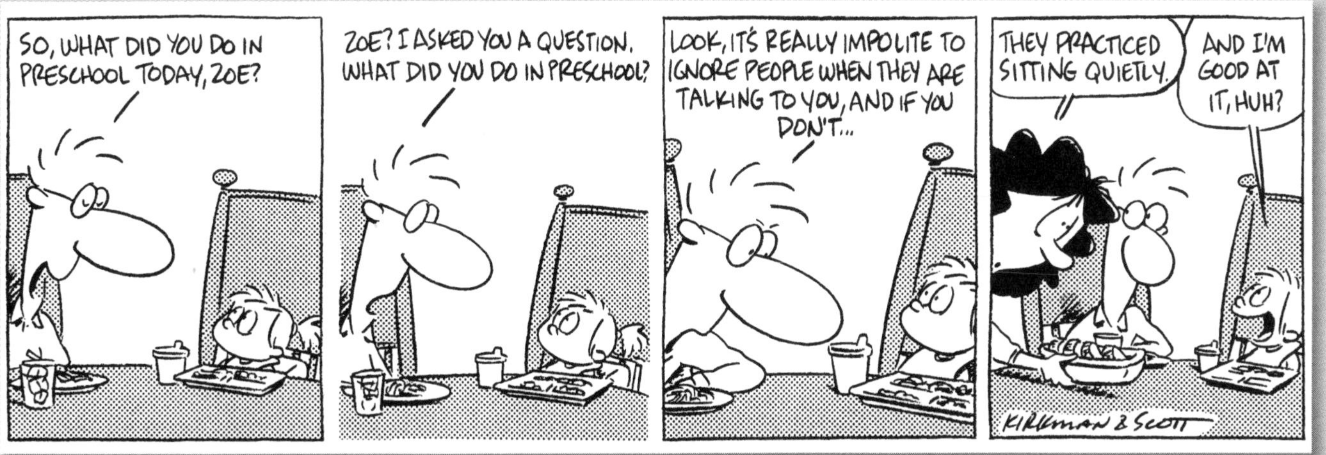
SO, WHAT DID YOU DO IN PRESCHOOL TODAY, ZOE?
ZOE? I ASKED YOU A QUESTION. WHAT DID YOU DO IN PRESCHOOL?
LOOK, IT'S REALLY IMPOLITE TO IGNORE PEOPLE WHEN THEY ARE TALKING TO YOU, AND IF YOU DON'T...
THEY PRACTICED SITTING QUIETLY.
AND I'M GOOD AT IT, HUH?
KIRKMAN & SCOTT

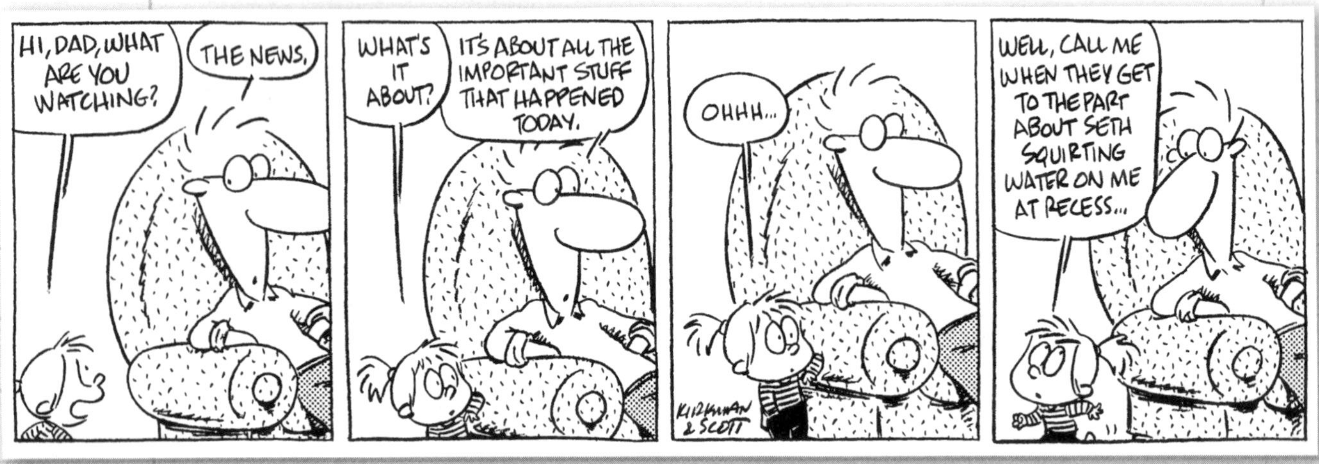
HI, DAD, WHAT ARE YOU WATCHING?
THE NEWS.
WHAT'S IT ABOUT?
IT'S ABOUT ALL THE IMPORTANT STUFF THAT HAPPENED TODAY.
OHHH...
WELL, CALL ME WHEN THEY GET TO THE PART ABOUT SETH SQUIRTING WATER ON ME AT RECESS...
KIRKMAN & SCOTT

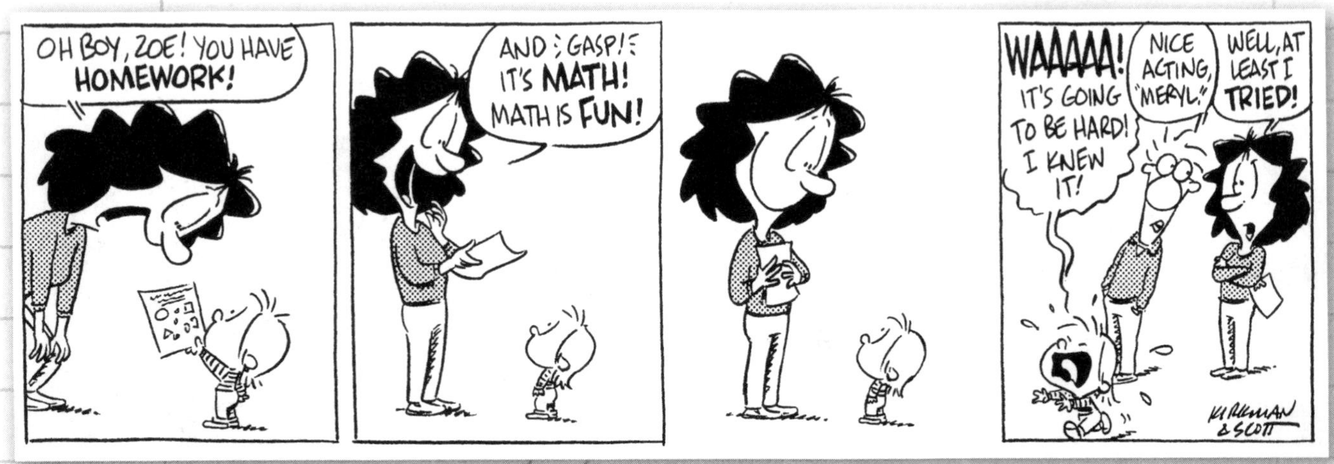
OH BOY, ZOE! YOU HAVE HOMEWORK!
AND *GASP!* IT'S MATH! MATH IS FUN!
WAAAAA! IT'S GOING TO BE HARD! I KNEW IT!
NICE ACTING, "MERYL."
WELL, AT LEAST I TRIED!
KIRKMAN & SCOTT

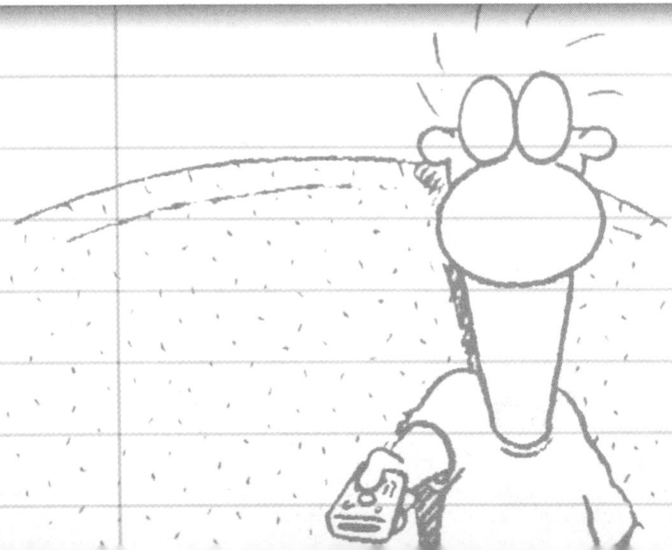

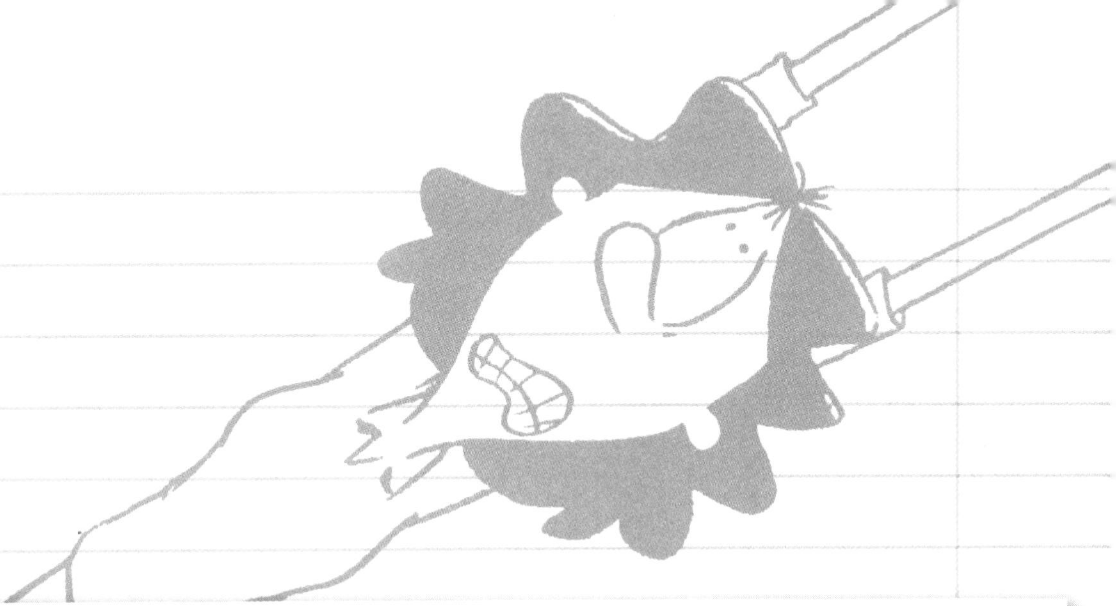

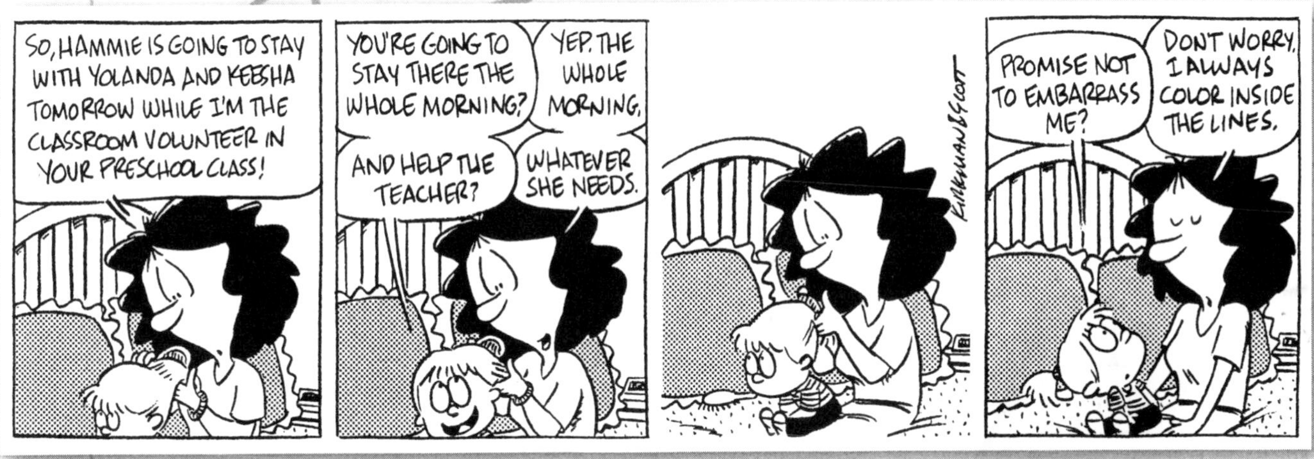
SO, HAMMIE IS GOING TO STAY WITH YOLANDA AND KEESHA TOMORROW WHILE I'M THE CLASSROOM VOLUNTEER IN YOUR PRESCHOOL CLASS!
YOU'RE GOING TO STAY THERE THE WHOLE MORNING?
YEP. THE WHOLE MORNING.
AND HELP THE TEACHER?
WHATEVER SHE NEEDS.
KIRKMAN & SCOTT
PROMISE NOT TO EMBARRASS ME?
DON'T WORRY. I ALWAYS COLOR INSIDE THE LINES.

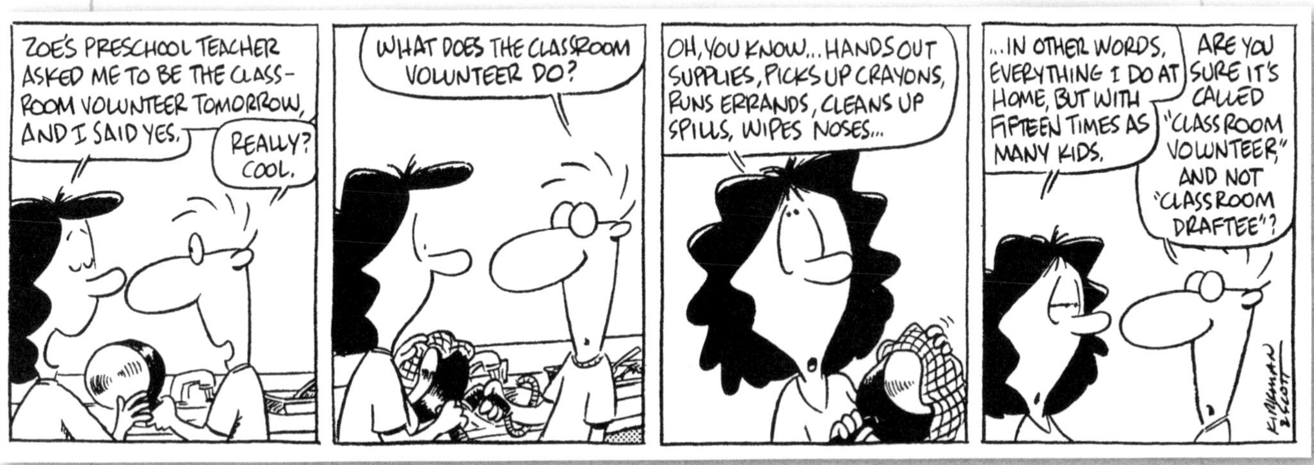
ZOE'S PRESCHOOL TEACHER ASKED ME TO BE THE CLASSROOM VOLUNTEER TOMORROW, AND I SAID YES.
REALLY? COOL.
WHAT DOES THE CLASSROOM VOLUNTEER DO?
OH, YOU KNOW... HANDS OUT SUPPLIES, PICKS UP CRAYONS, RUNS ERRANDS, CLEANS UP SPILLS, WIPES NOSES...
...IN OTHER WORDS, EVERYTHING I DO AT HOME, BUT WITH FIFTEEN TIMES AS MANY KIDS.
ARE YOU SURE IT'S CALLED "CLASSROOM VOLUNTEER," AND NOT "CLASSROOM DRAFTEE"?
KIRKMAN & SCOTT

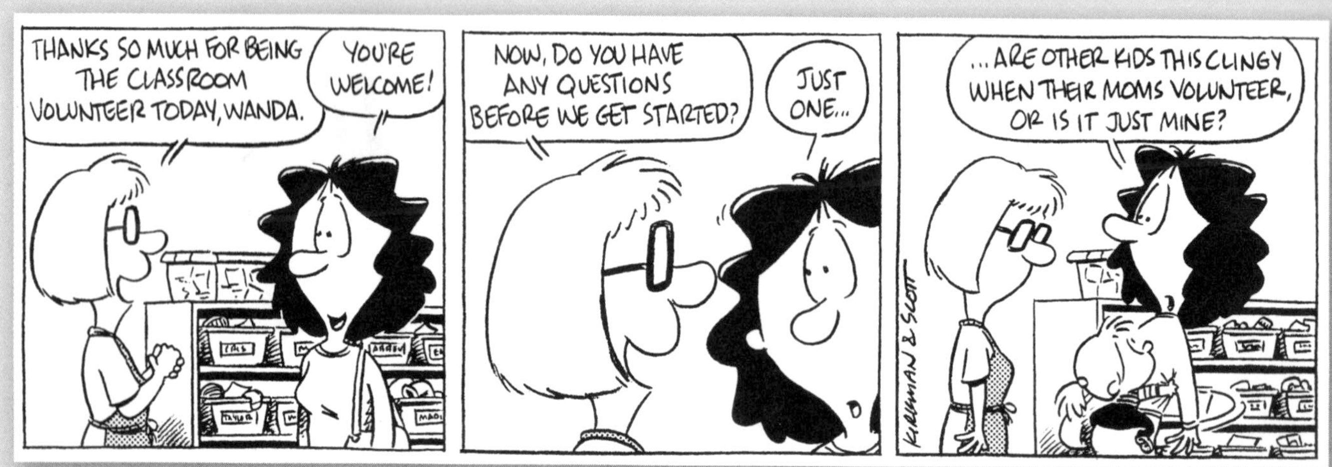
THANKS SO MUCH FOR BEING THE CLASSROOM VOLUNTEER TODAY, WANDA.
YOU'RE WELCOME!
NOW, DO YOU HAVE ANY QUESTIONS BEFORE WE GET STARTED?
JUST ONE...
...ARE OTHER KIDS THIS CLINGY WHEN THEIR MOMS VOLUNTEER, OR IS IT JUST MINE?
KIRKMAN & SCOTT

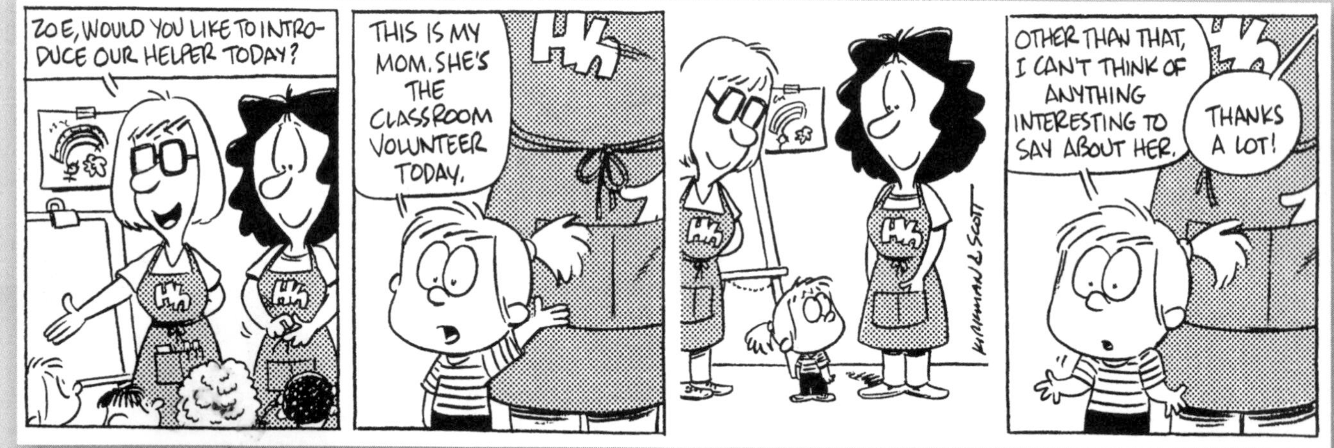
ZOE, WOULD YOU LIKE TO INTRODUCE OUR HELPER TODAY?
THIS IS MY MOM. SHE'S THE CLASSROOM VOLUNTEER TODAY.
KIRKMAN & SCOTT
OTHER THAN THAT, I CAN'T THINK OF ANYTHING INTERESTING TO SAY ABOUT HER.
THANKS A LOT!

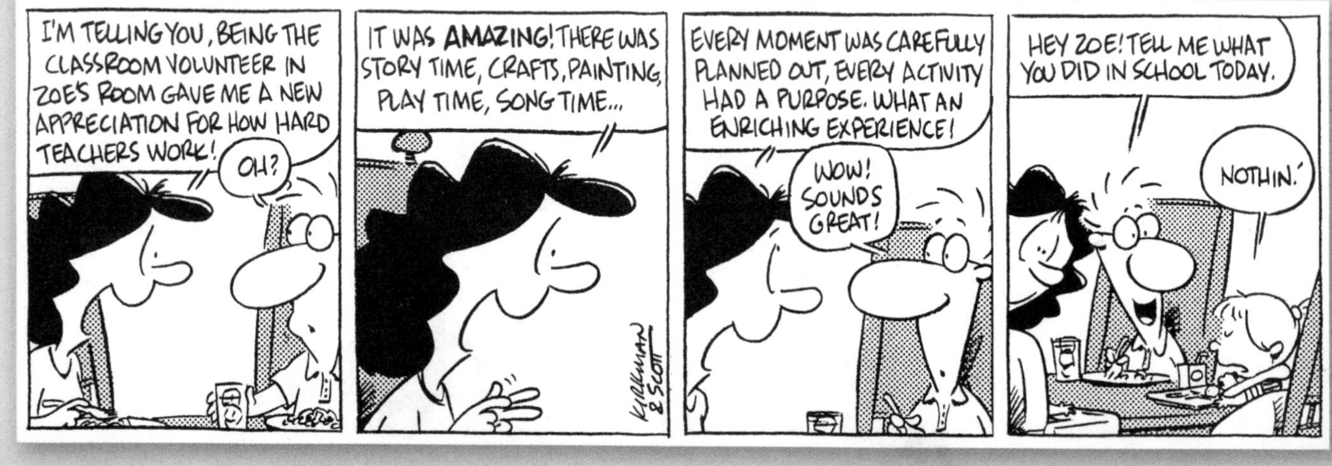
I'M TELLING YOU, BEING THE CLASSROOM VOLUNTEER IN ZOE'S ROOM GAVE ME A NEW APPRECIATION FOR HOW HARD TEACHERS WORK!
OH?
IT WAS **AMAZING**! THERE WAS STORY TIME, CRAFTS, PAINTING, PLAY TIME, SONG TIME...
KIRKMAN & SCOTT
EVERY MOMENT WAS CAREFULLY PLANNED OUT, EVERY ACTIVITY HAD A PURPOSE. WHAT AN ENRICHING EXPERIENCE!
WOW! SOUNDS GREAT!
HEY ZOE! TELL ME WHAT YOU DID IN SCHOOL TODAY.
NOTHIN'.

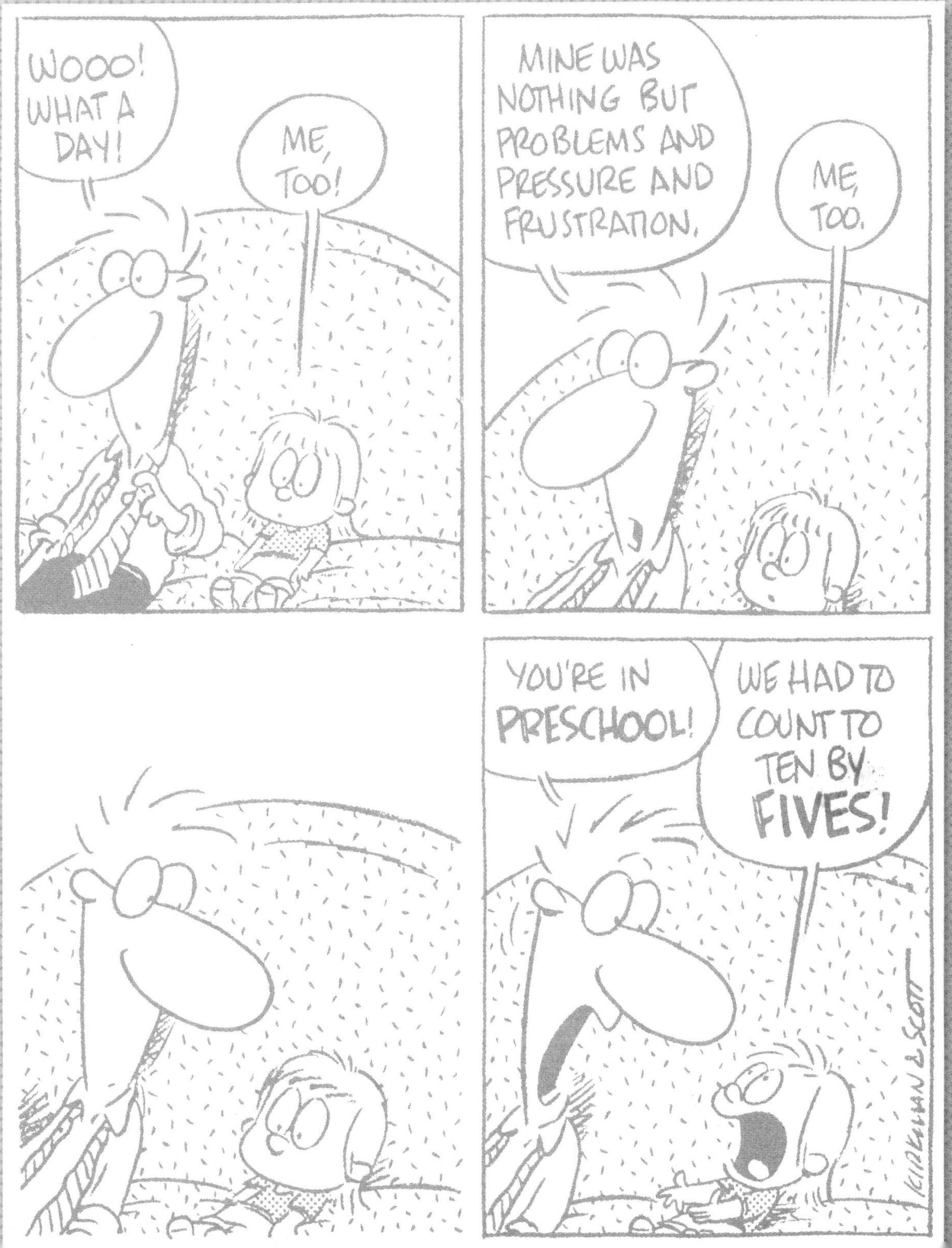
WOOO! WHAT A DAY!
ME, TOO!
MINE WAS NOTHING BUT PROBLEMS AND PRESSURE AND FRUSTRATION.
ME, TOO.
YOU'RE IN PRESCHOOL!
WE HAD TO COUNT TO TEN BY FIVES!
KIRKMAN & SCOTT

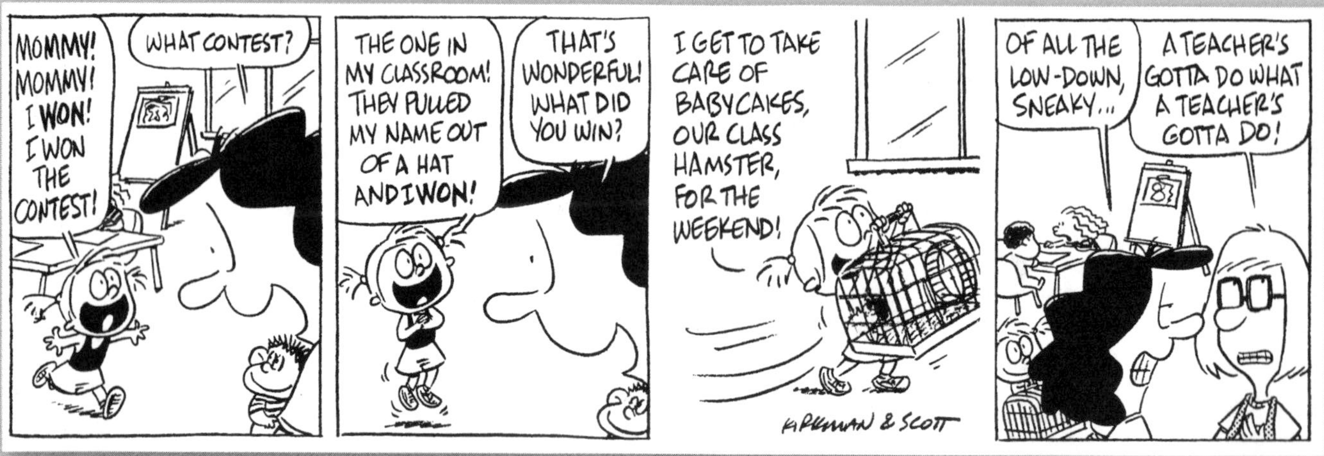
MOMMY! MOMMY! I **WON**! I WON THE CONTEST!
WHAT CONTEST?
THE ONE IN MY CLASSROOM! THEY PULLED MY NAME OUT OF A HAT AND I **WON**!
THAT'S WONDERFUL! WHAT DID YOU WIN?
I GET TO TAKE CARE OF BABYCAKES, OUR CLASS HAMSTER, FOR THE WEEKEND!
KIRKMAN & SCOTT
OF ALL THE LOW-DOWN, SNEAKY...
A TEACHER'S GOTTA DO WHAT A TEACHER'S GOTTA DO!

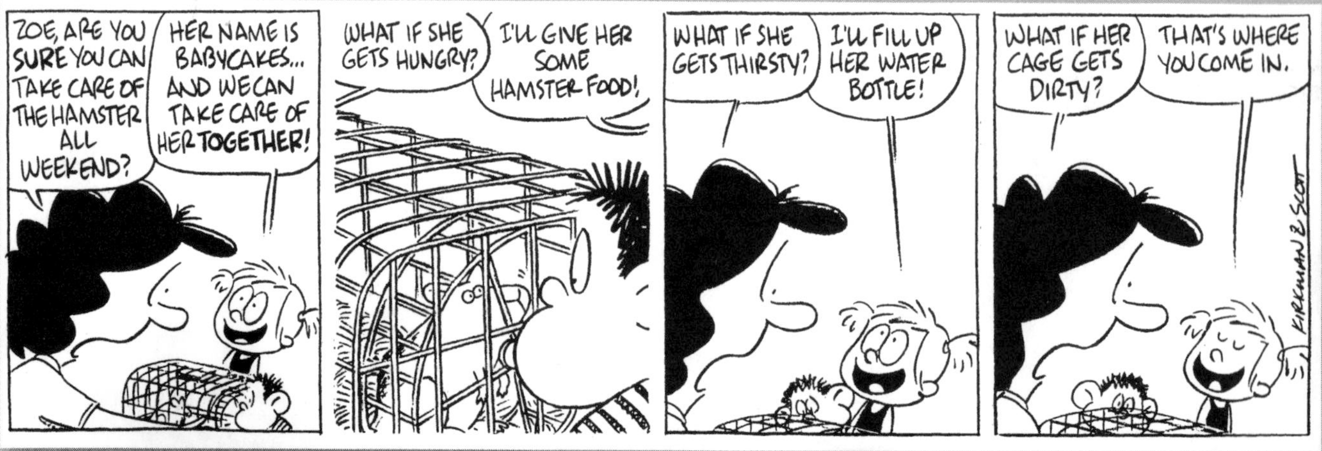
ZOE, ARE YOU **SURE** YOU CAN TAKE CARE OF THE HAMSTER ALL WEEKEND?
HER NAME IS BABYCAKES... AND WE CAN TAKE CARE OF HER **TOGETHER**!
WHAT IF SHE GETS HUNGRY?
I'LL GIVE HER SOME HAMSTER FOOD!
WHAT IF SHE GETS THIRSTY?
I'LL FILL UP HER WATER BOTTLE!
WHAT IF HER CAGE GETS DIRTY?
THAT'S WHERE YOU COME IN.
KIRKMAN & SCOTT

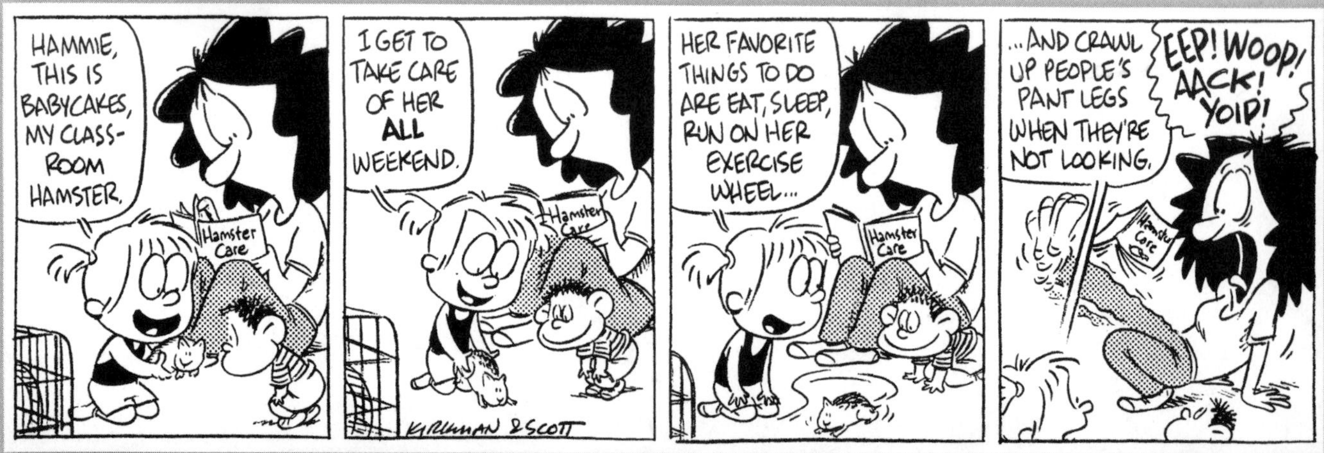
HAMMIE, THIS IS BABYCAKES, MY CLASS-ROOM HAMSTER.
Hamster Care
I GET TO TAKE CARE OF HER **ALL** WEEKEND.
KIRKMAN & SCOTT
HER FAVORITE THINGS TO DO ARE EAT, SLEEP, RUN ON HER EXERCISE WHEEL...
...AND CRAWL UP PEOPLE'S PANT LEGS WHEN THEY'RE NOT LOOKING.
EEP! WOOP! AACK! YOIP!

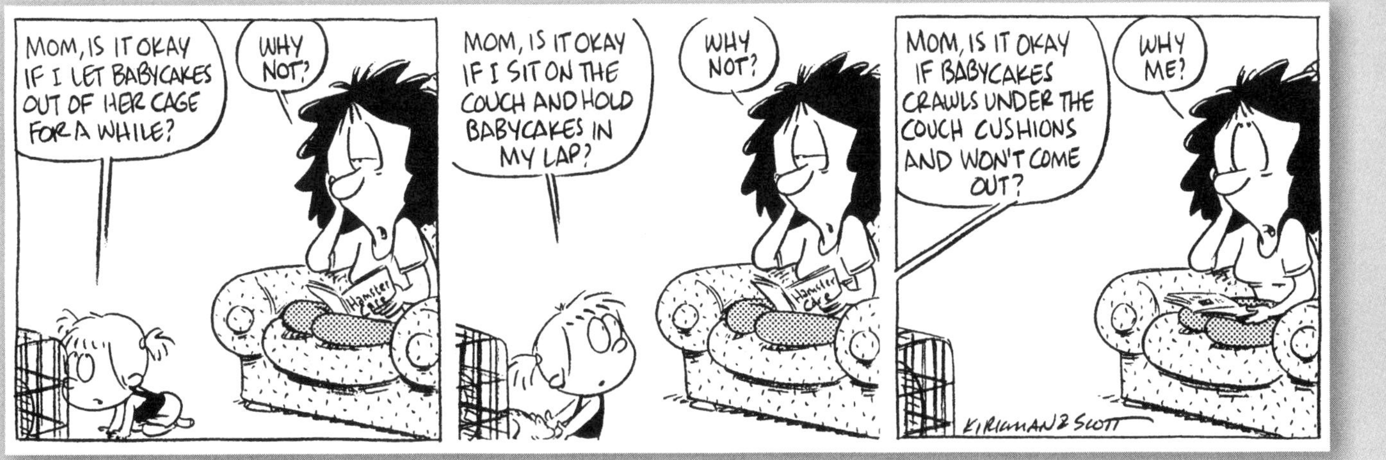
MOM, IS IT OKAY IF I LET BABYCAKES OUT OF HER CAGE FOR A WHILE?
WHY NOT?
MOM, IS IT OKAY IF I SIT ON THE COUCH AND HOLD BABYCAKES IN MY LAP?
WHY NOT?
Hamster Care
MOM, IS IT OKAY IF BABYCAKES CRAWLS UNDER THE COUCH CUSHIONS AND WON'T COME OUT?
WHY ME?
KIRKMAN & SCOTT

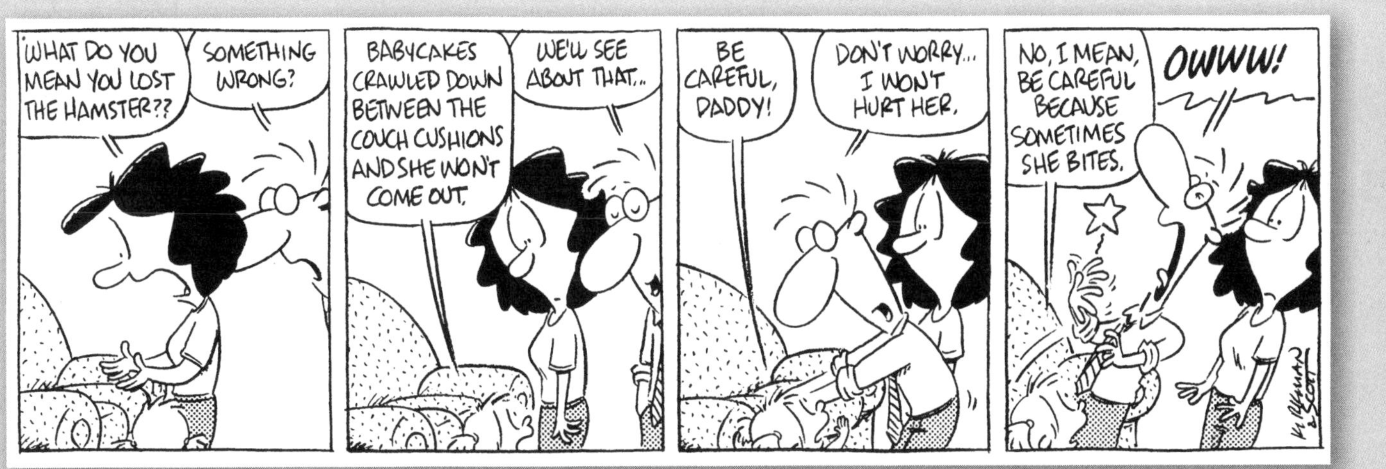
WHAT DO YOU MEAN YOU LOST THE HAMSTER??
SOMETHING WRONG?
BABYCAKES CRAWLED DOWN BETWEEN THE COUCH CUSHIONS AND SHE WON'T COME OUT.
WE'LL SEE ABOUT THAT...
BE CAREFUL, DADDY!
DON'T WORRY... I WON'T HURT HER.
NO, I MEAN, BE CAREFUL BECAUSE SOMETIMES SHE BITES.
OWWW!
KIRKMAN & SCOTT

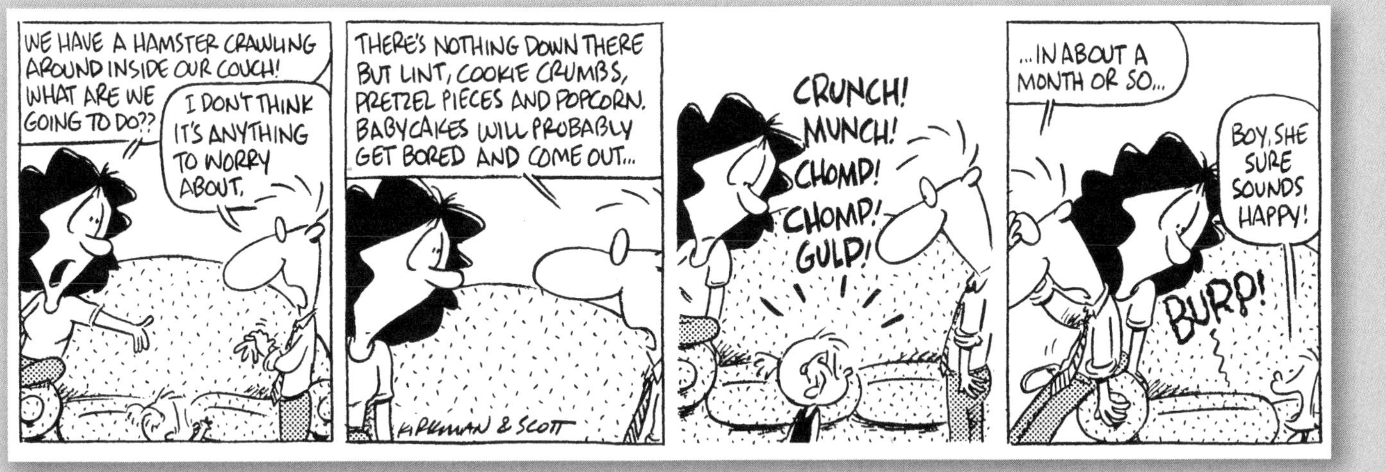
WE HAVE A HAMSTER CRAWLING AROUND INSIDE OUR COUCH! WHAT ARE WE GOING TO DO??
I DON'T THINK IT'S ANYTHING TO WORRY ABOUT.
THERE'S NOTHING DOWN THERE BUT LINT, COOKIE CRUMBS, PRETZEL PIECES AND POPCORN. BABYCAKES WILL PROBABLY GET BORED AND COME OUT...
KIRKMAN & SCOTT
CRUNCH! MUNCH! CHOMP! CHOMP! GULP!
...IN ABOUT A MONTH OR SO...
BOY, SHE SURE SOUNDS HAPPY!
BURP!

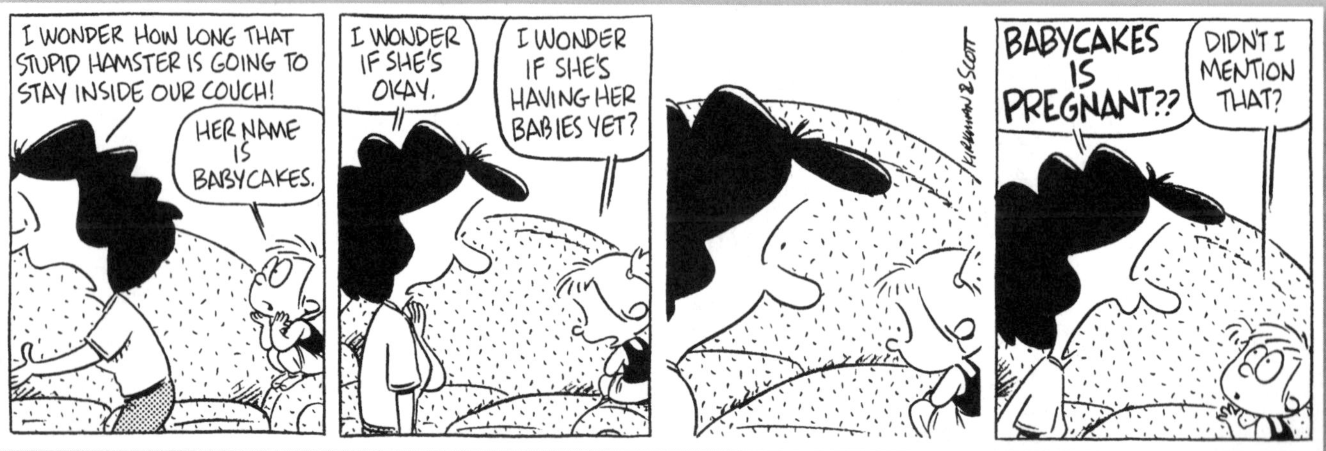
I WONDER HOW LONG THAT STUPID HAMSTER IS GOING TO STAY INSIDE OUR COUCH!
HER NAME IS BABYCAKES.
I WONDER IF SHE'S OKAY.
I WONDER IF SHE'S HAVING HER BABIES YET?
KIRKMAN & SCOTT
BABYCAKES IS PREGNANT??
DIDN'T I MENTION THAT?

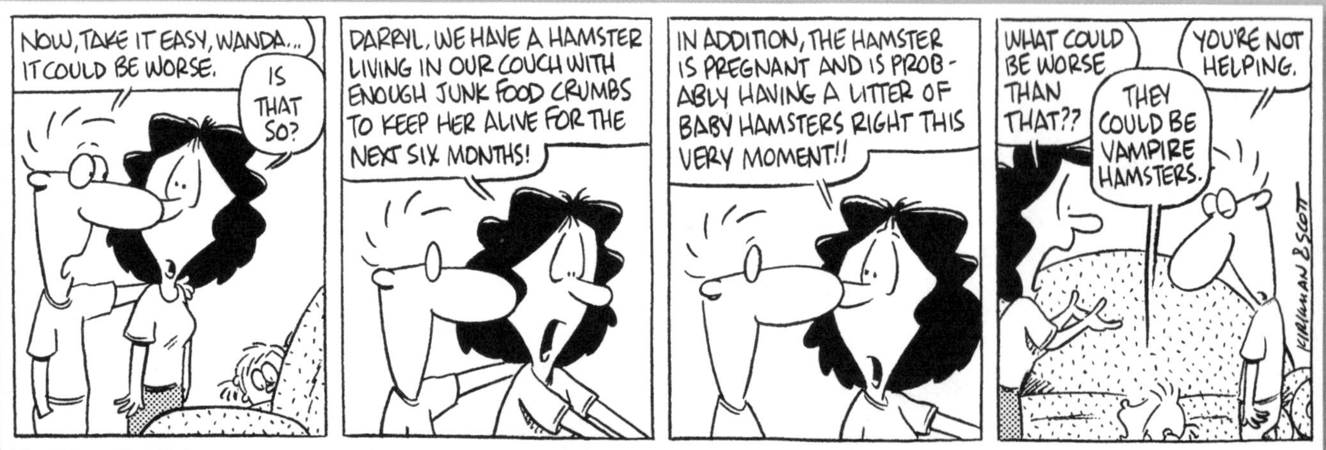
NOW, TAKE IT EASY, WANDA... IT COULD BE WORSE.
IS THAT SO?
DARRYL, WE HAVE A HAMSTER LIVING IN OUR COUCH WITH ENOUGH JUNK FOOD CRUMBS TO KEEP HER ALIVE FOR THE NEXT SIX MONTHS!
IN ADDITION, THE HAMSTER IS PREGNANT AND IS PROB-ABLY HAVING A LITTER OF BABY HAMSTERS RIGHT THIS VERY MOMENT!!
WHAT COULD BE WORSE THAN THAT??
THEY COULD BE VAMPIRE HAMSTERS.
YOU'RE NOT HELPING.
KIRKMAN & SCOTT

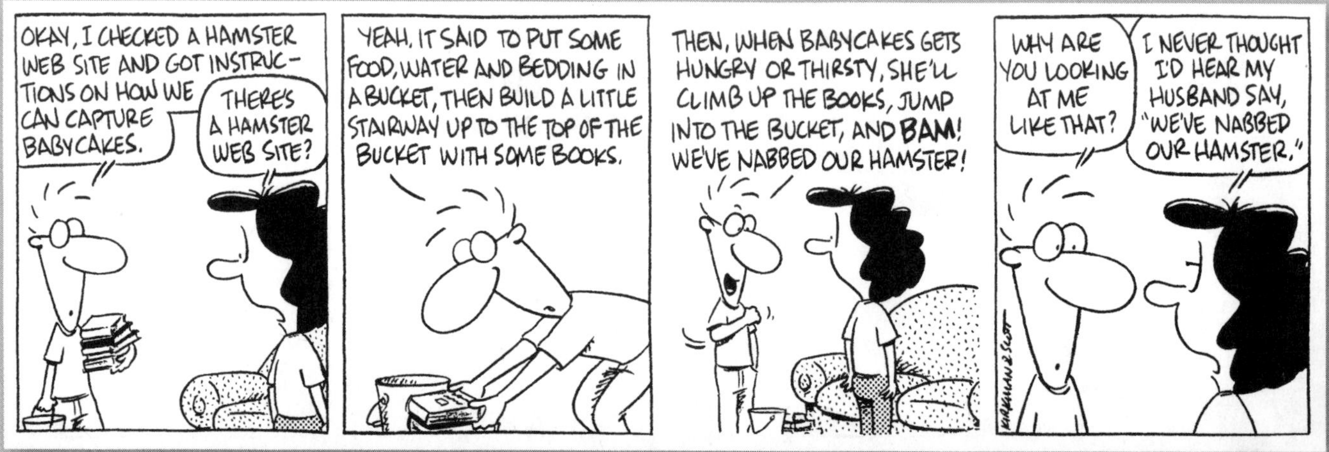
OKAY, I CHECKED A HAMSTER WEB SITE AND GOT INSTRUC-TIONS ON HOW WE CAN CAPTURE BABYCAKES.
THERE'S A HAMSTER WEB SITE?
YEAH. IT SAID TO PUT SOME FOOD, WATER AND BEDDING IN A BUCKET, THEN BUILD A LITTLE STAIRWAY UP TO THE TOP OF THE BUCKET WITH SOME BOOKS.
THEN, WHEN BABYCAKES GETS HUNGRY OR THIRSTY, SHE'LL CLIMB UP THE BOOKS, JUMP INTO THE BUCKET, AND BAM! WE'VE NABBED OUR HAMSTER!
WHY ARE YOU LOOKING AT ME LIKE THAT?
I NEVER THOUGHT I'D HEAR MY HUSBAND SAY, "WE'VE NABBED OUR HAMSTER."

WE GOT HER!
REALLY?
BABY-CAKES, YOU NAUGHTY LITTLE HAMSTER!
I'M SO GLAD THAT I CAN STOP OBSESSING ABOUT HAVING A HAMSTER LIVING IN OUR COUCH...
HEY! COME BACK HERE!
KIRKMAN & SCOTT
ZIP!
...AND START OBSESSING ABOUT A HAMSTER LIVING IN OUR CHAIR, INSTEAD.
I'LL PUT SOME MORE HAMSTER CHOW IN THE BUCKET.
OOPS.

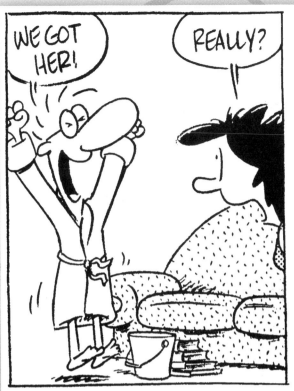

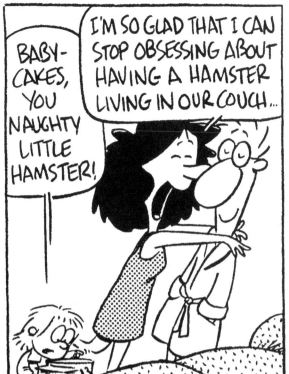

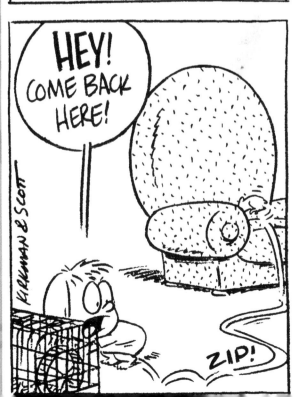

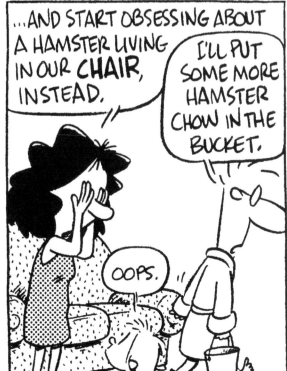

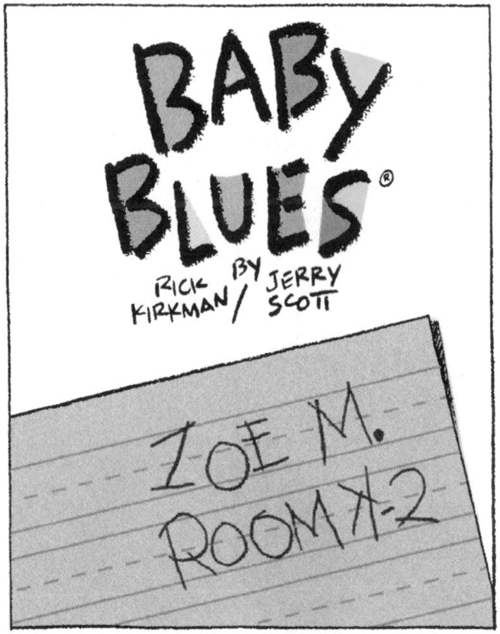
BABY BLUES®
BY RICK KIRKMAN / JERRY SCOTT
ZOE M.
ROOM K-2

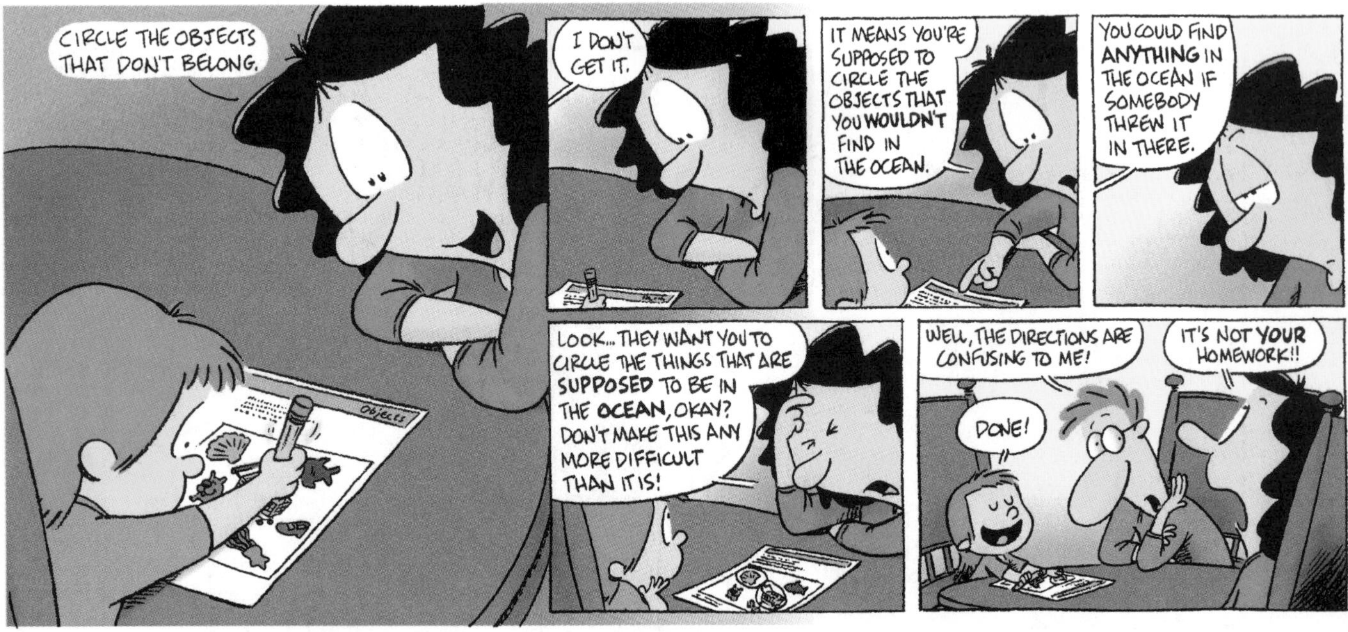
CIRCLE THE OBJECTS THAT DON'T BELONG.
Objects
I DON'T GET IT.
IT MEANS YOU'RE SUPPOSED TO CIRCLE THE OBJECTS THAT YOU **WOULDN'T** FIND IN THE OCEAN.
YOU COULD FIND **ANYTHING** IN THE OCEAN IF SOMEBODY THREW IT IN THERE.
LOOK... THEY WANT YOU TO CIRCLE THE THINGS THAT ARE **SUPPOSED** TO BE IN THE **OCEAN**, OKAY? DON'T MAKE THIS ANY MORE DIFFICULT THAN IT IS!
WELL, THE DIRECTIONS ARE CONFUSING TO ME!
IT'S NOT **YOUR** HOMEWORK!!
DONE!

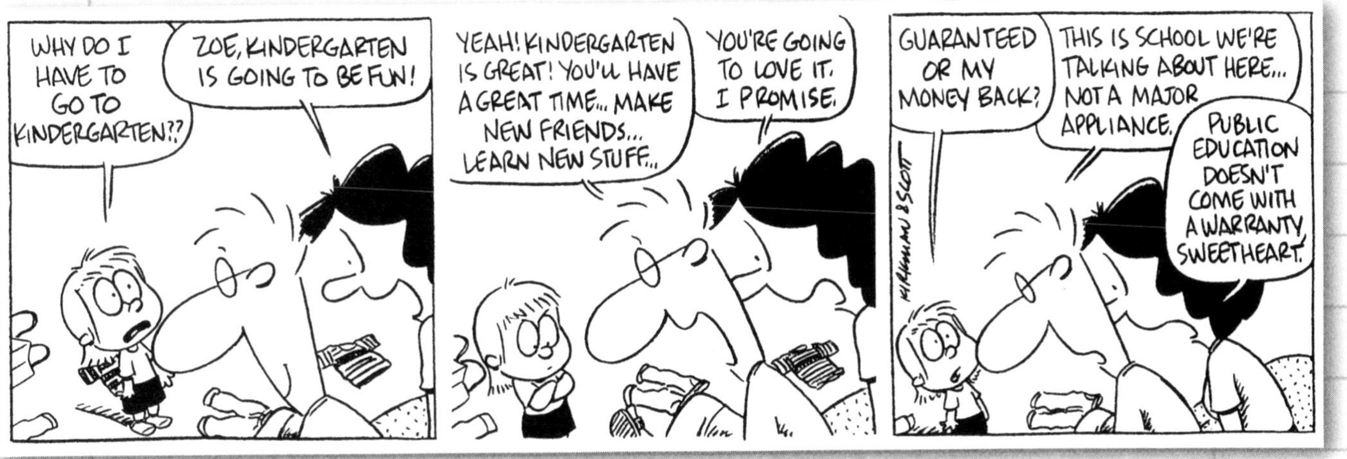
WHY DO I HAVE TO GO TO KINDERGARTEN??
ZOE, KINDERGARTEN IS GOING TO BE FUN!
YEAH! KINDERGARTEN IS GREAT! YOU'LL HAVE A GREAT TIME... MAKE NEW FRIENDS... LEARN NEW STUFF...
YOU'RE GOING TO LOVE IT. I PROMISE.
GUARANTEED OR MY MONEY BACK?
THIS IS SCHOOL WE'RE TALKING ABOUT HERE... NOT A MAJOR APPLIANCE.
PUBLIC EDUCATION DOESN'T COME WITH A WARRANTY, SWEETHEART.
KIRKMAN & SCOTT

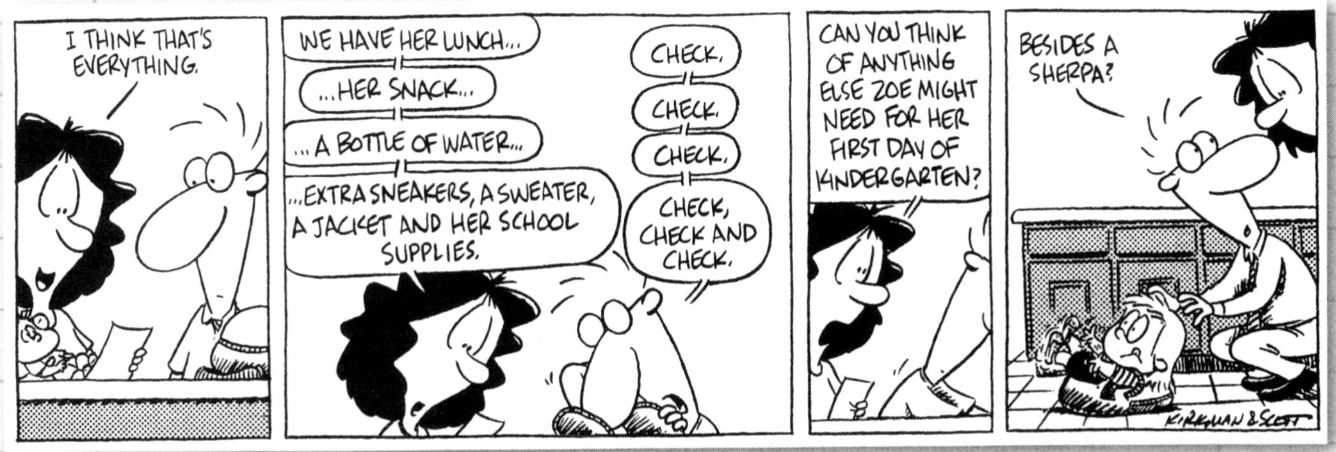
I THINK THAT'S EVERYTHING.
WE HAVE HER LUNCH...
CHECK.
...HER SNACK...
CHECK.
...A BOTTLE OF WATER...
CHECK.
...EXTRA SNEAKERS, A SWEATER, A JACKET AND HER SCHOOL SUPPLIES.
CHECK, CHECK AND CHECK.
CAN YOU THINK OF ANYTHING ELSE ZOE MIGHT NEED FOR HER FIRST DAY OF KINDERGARTEN?
BESIDES A SHERPA?
KIRKMAN & SCOTT

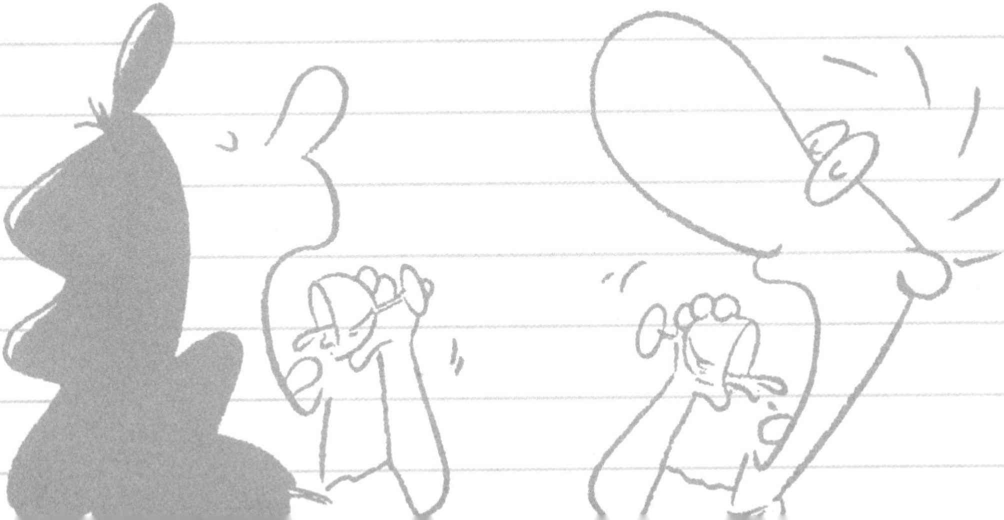

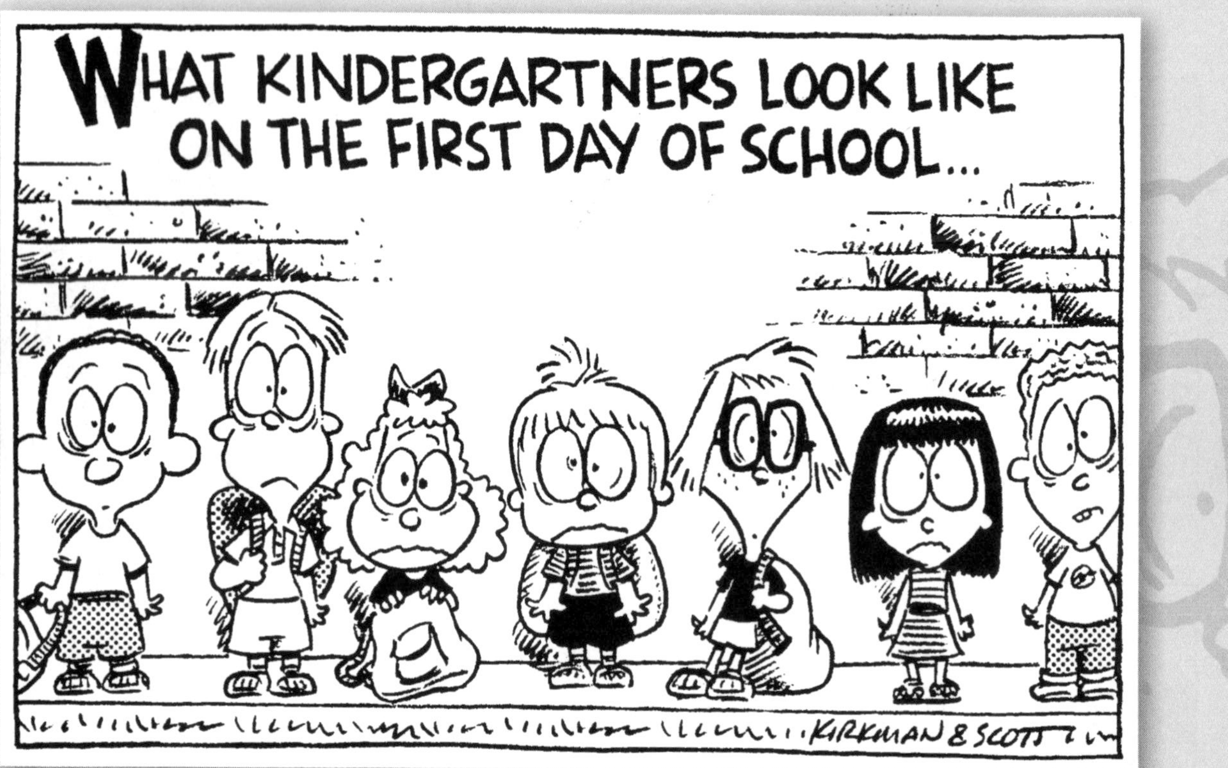
WHAT KINDERGARTNERS LOOK LIKE ON THE FIRST DAY OF SCHOOL...
KIRKMAN & SCOTT

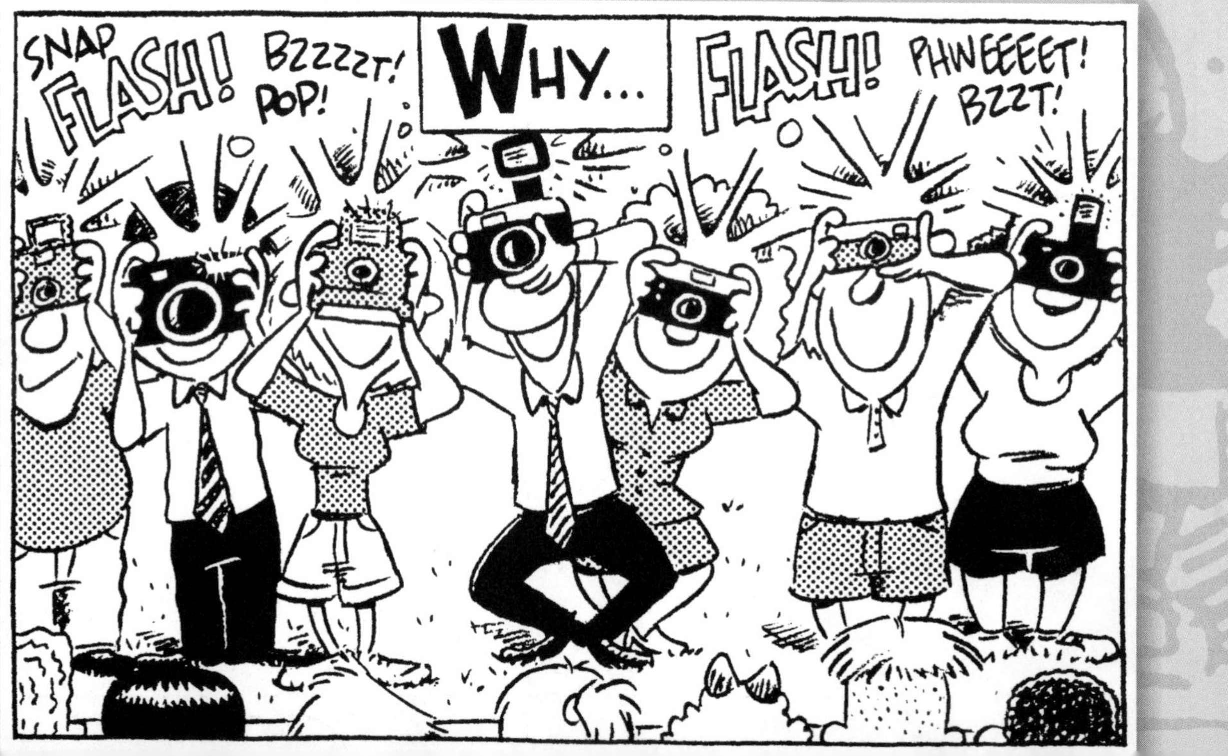
SNAP
FLASH!
BZZZZT!
POP!
WHY...
FLASH!
PHWEEEET!
BZZT!

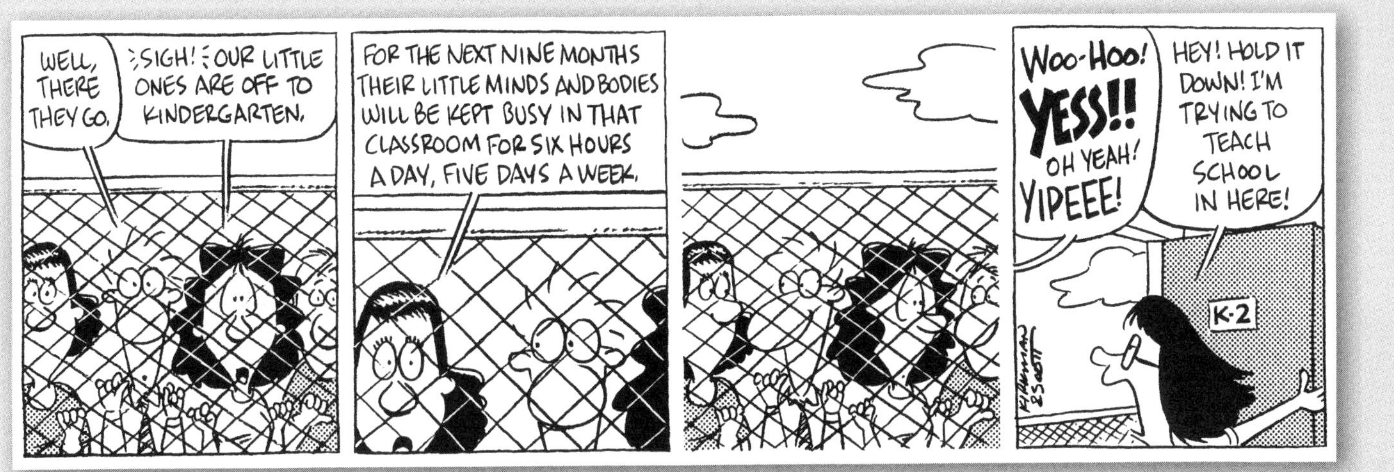
WELL, THERE THEY GO.
SIGH! OUR LITTLE ONES ARE OFF TO KINDERGARTEN.
FOR THE NEXT NINE MONTHS THEIR LITTLE MINDS AND BODIES WILL BE KEPT BUSY IN THAT CLASSROOM FOR SIX HOURS A DAY, FIVE DAYS A WEEK.
WOO-HOO! YESS!! OH YEAH! YIPEEE!
HEY! HOLD IT DOWN! I'M TRYING TO TEACH SCHOOL IN HERE!
K-2
KIRKMAN & SCOTT

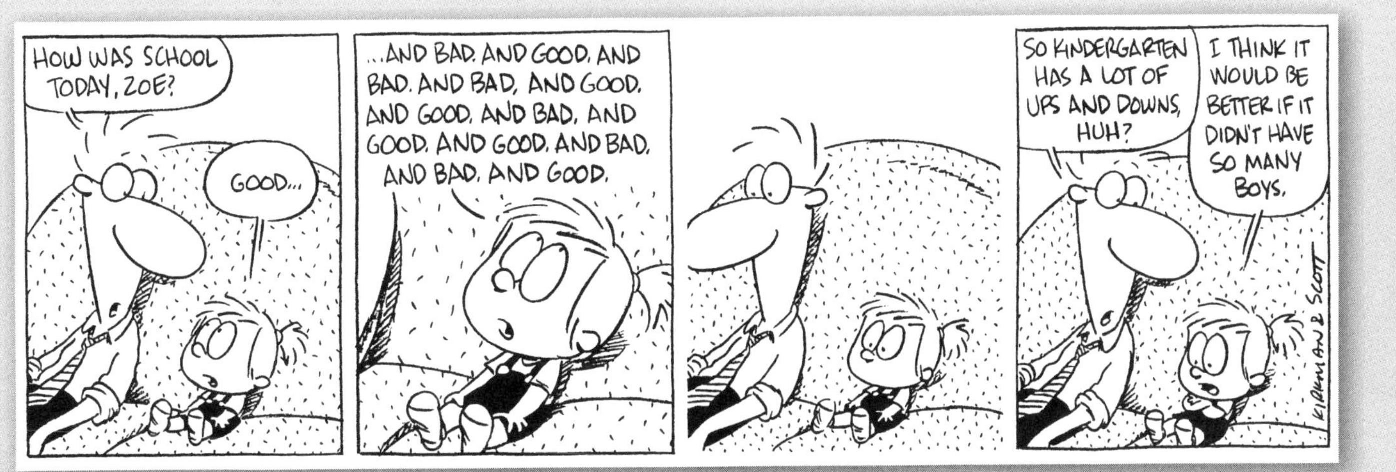
HOW WAS SCHOOL TODAY, ZOE?
GOOD...
...AND BAD. AND GOOD. AND BAD. AND BAD, AND GOOD. AND GOOD. AND BAD, AND GOOD. AND GOOD. AND BAD, AND BAD. AND GOOD.
SO KINDERGARTEN HAS A LOT OF UPS AND DOWNS, HUH?
I THINK IT WOULD BE BETTER IF IT DIDN'T HAVE SO MANY BOYS.
KIRKMAN & SCOTT

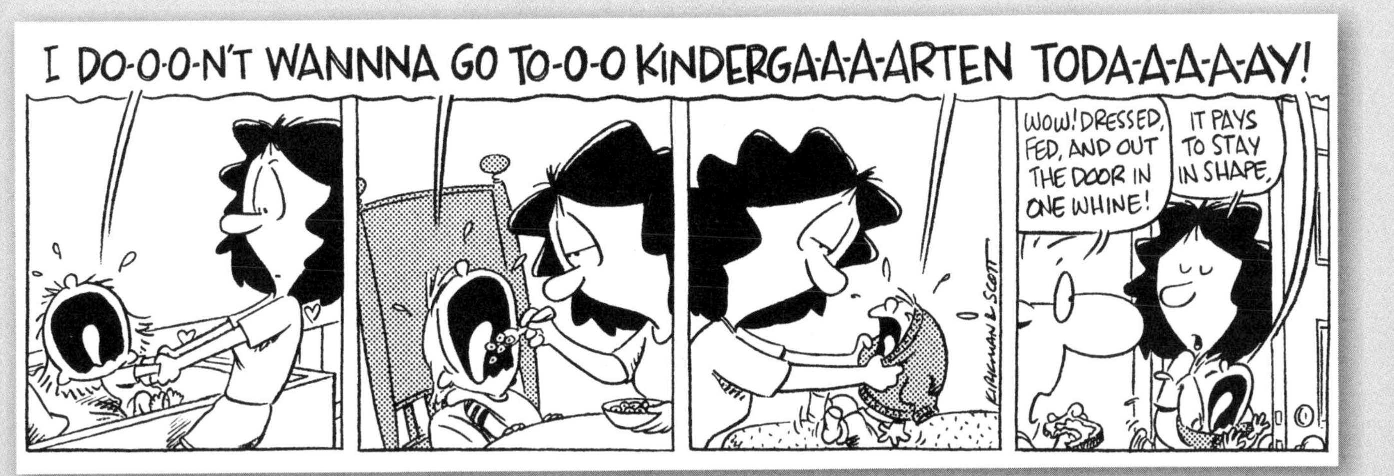
I DO-O-O-N'T WANNNA GO TO-O-O KINDERGA-A-A-ARTEN TODA-A-A-A-AY!
KIRKMAN & SCOTT
WOW! DRESSED, FED, AND OUT THE DOOR IN ONE WHINE!
IT PAYS TO STAY IN SHAPE.

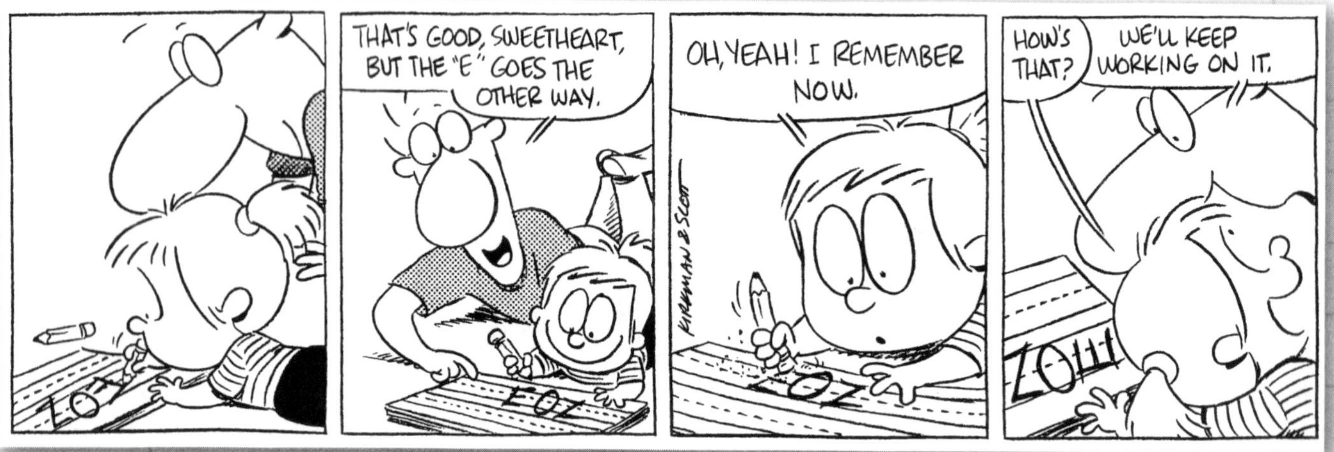
THAT'S GOOD, SWEETHEART, BUT THE "E" GOES THE OTHER WAY.
OH, YEAH! I REMEMBER NOW.
HOW'S THAT?
WE'LL KEEP WORKING ON IT.
KIRKMAN & SCOTT

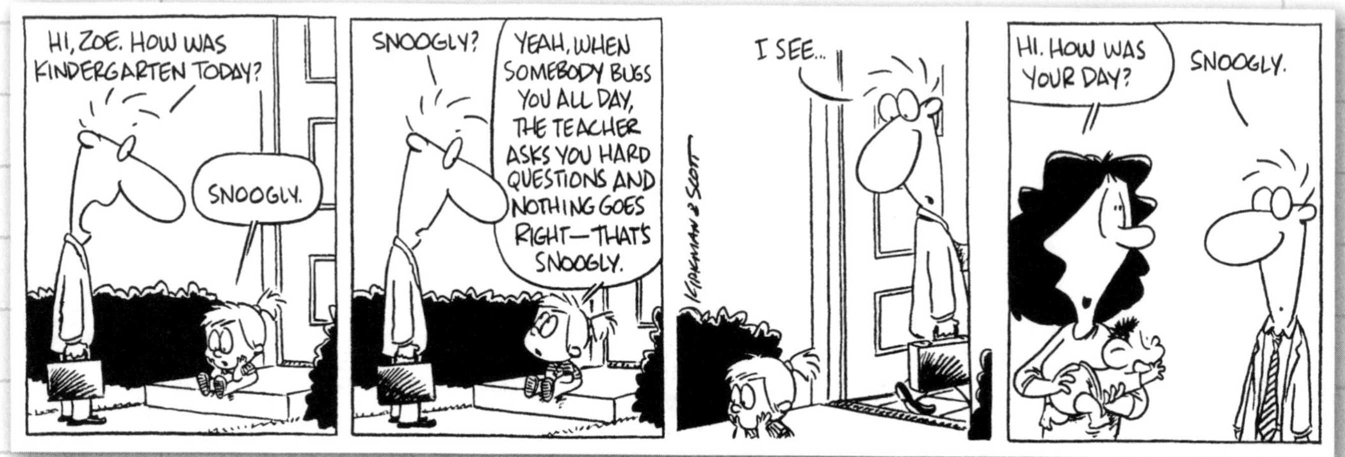
HI, ZOE. HOW WAS KINDERGARTEN TODAY?
SNOOGLY.
SNOOGLY?
YEAH, WHEN SOMEBODY BUGS YOU ALL DAY, THE TEACHER ASKS YOU HARD QUESTIONS AND NOTHING GOES RIGHT—THAT'S SNOOGLY.
KIRKMAN & SCOTT
I SEE...
HI. HOW WAS YOUR DAY?
SNOOGLY.

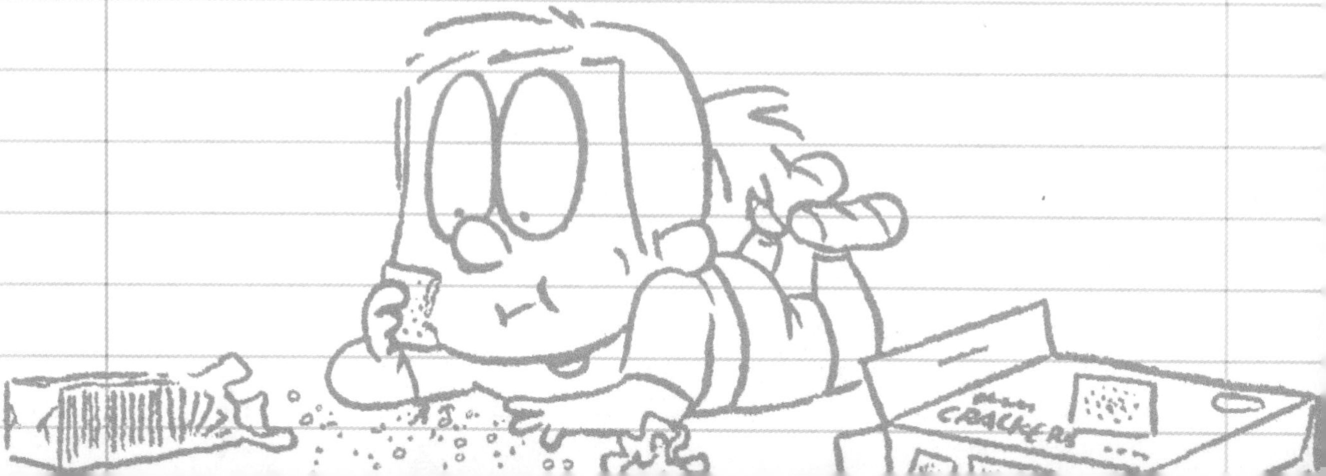
CRACKERS

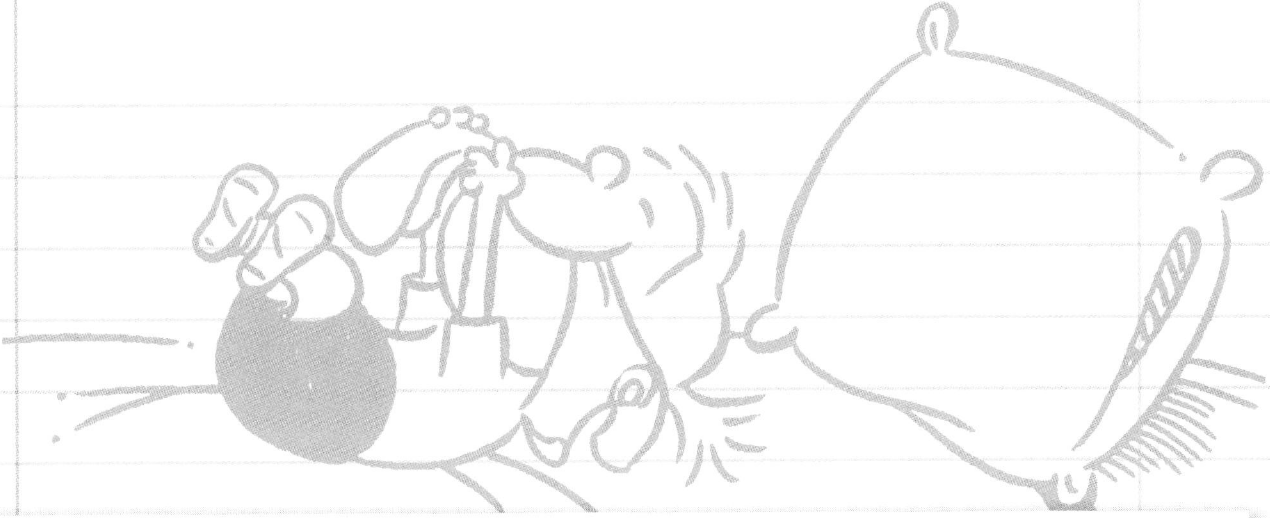

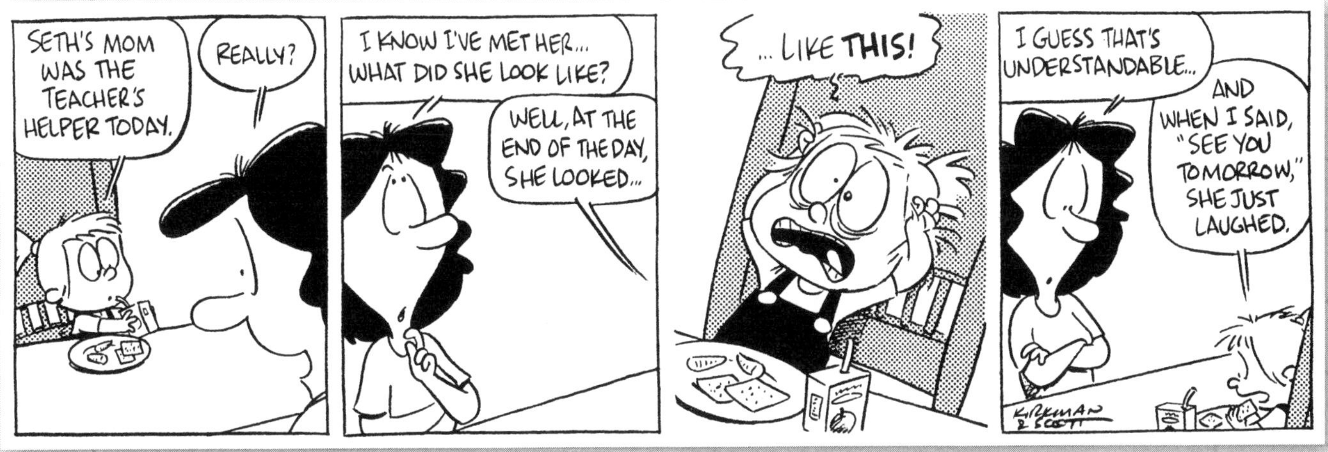
SETH'S MOM WAS THE TEACHER'S HELPER TODAY.
REALLY?
I KNOW I'VE MET HER... WHAT DID SHE LOOK LIKE?
WELL, AT THE END OF THE DAY, SHE LOOKED...
... LIKE **THIS**!
I GUESS THAT'S UNDERSTANDABLE...
AND WHEN I SAID, "SEE YOU TOMORROW," SHE JUST LAUGHED.
KIRKMAN & SCOTT

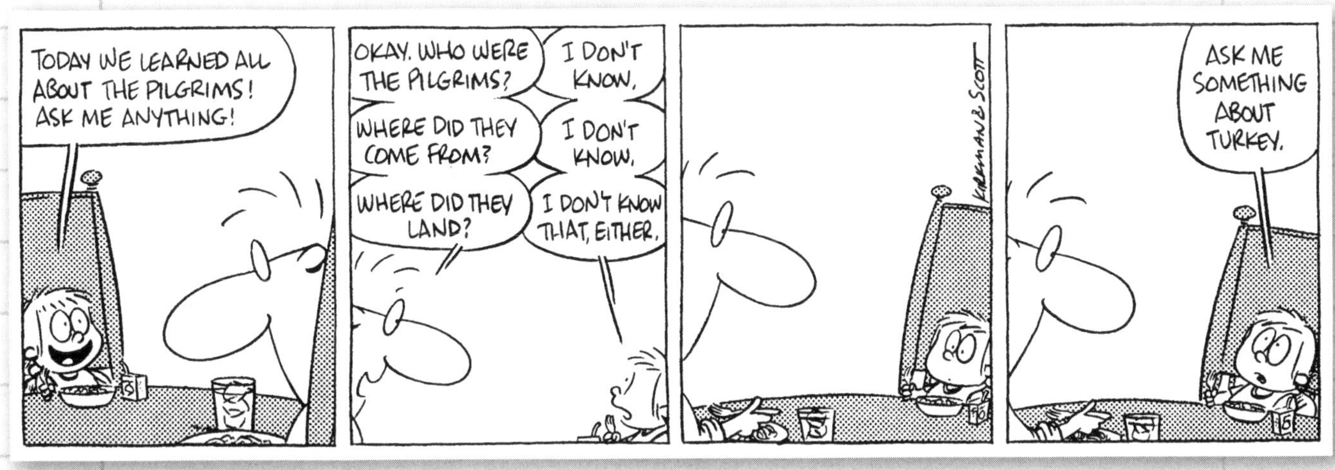
TODAY WE LEARNED ALL ABOUT THE PILGRIMS! ASK ME ANYTHING!
OKAY. WHO WERE THE PILGRIMS?
I DON'T KNOW.
WHERE DID THEY COME FROM?
I DON'T KNOW.
WHERE DID THEY LAND?
I DON'T KNOW THAT, EITHER.
KIRKMAN & SCOTT
ASK ME SOMETHING ABOUT TURKEY.

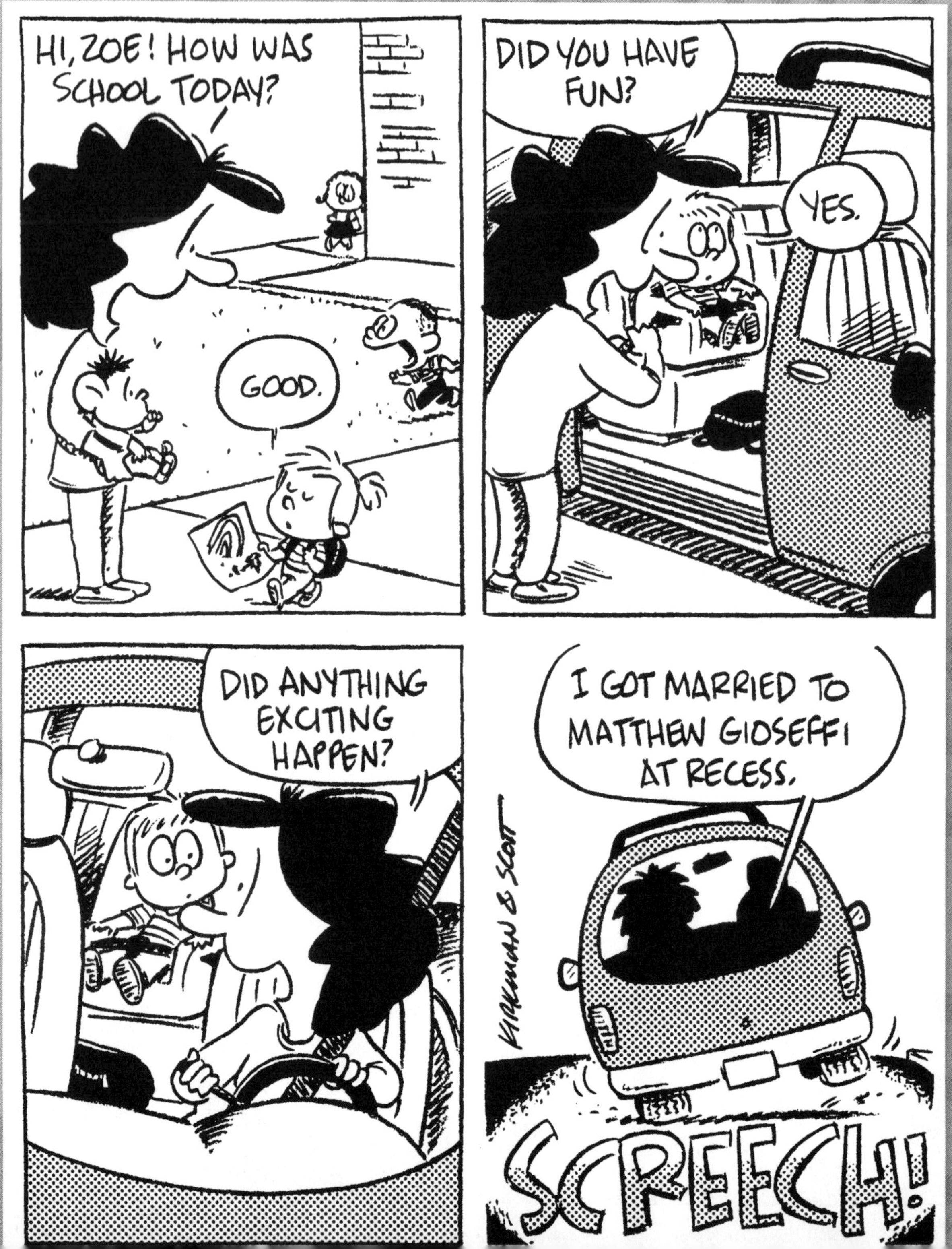
HI, ZOE! HOW WAS SCHOOL TODAY?
GOOD.
DID YOU HAVE FUN?
YES.
DID ANYTHING EXCITING HAPPEN?
KIRKMAN & SCOTT
I GOT MARRIED TO MATTHEW GIOSEFFI AT RECESS.
SCREECH!

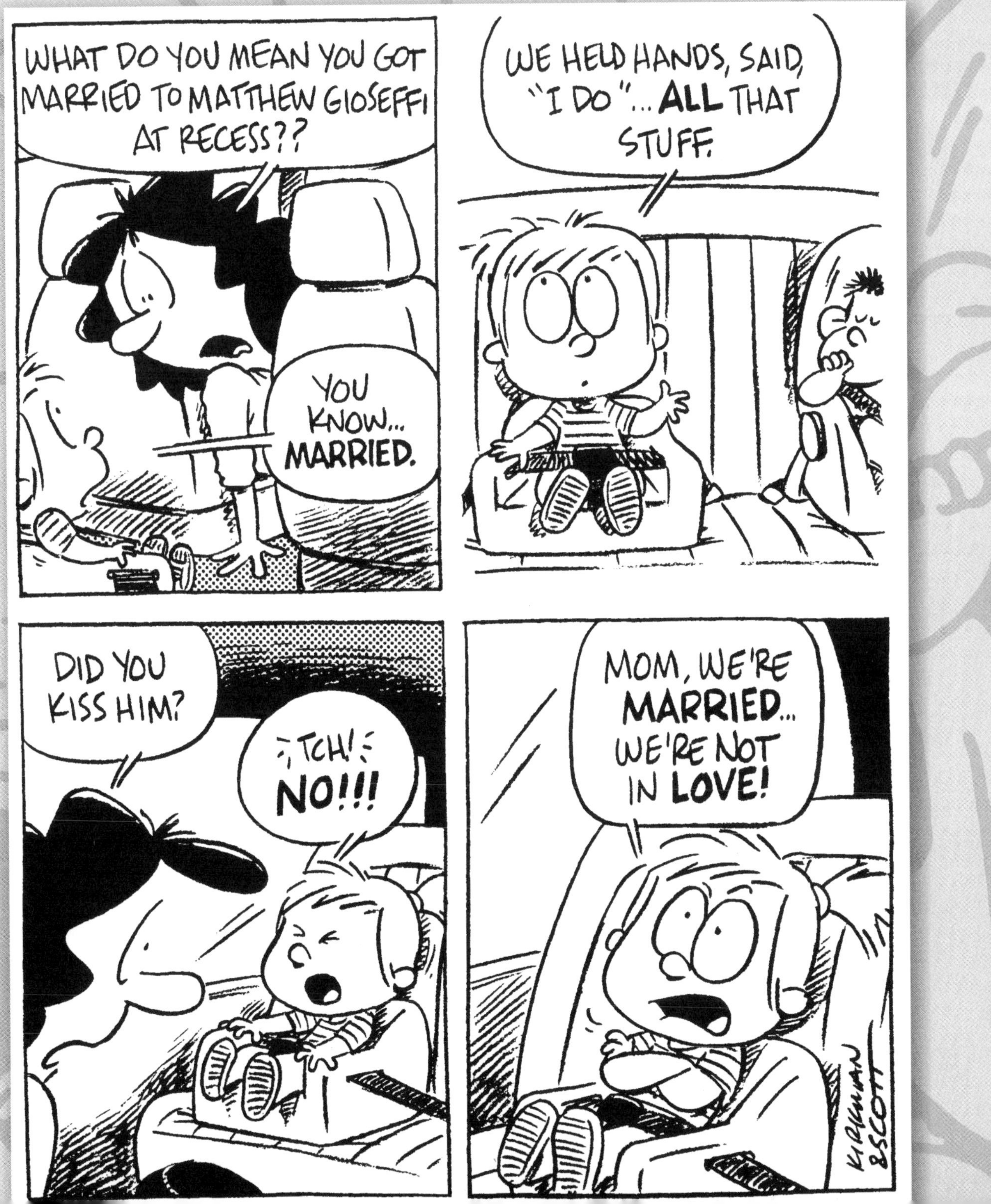
WHAT DO YOU MEAN YOU GOT MARRIED TO MATTHEW GIOSEFFI AT RECESS??
YOU KNOW... **MARRIED.**
WE HELD HANDS, SAID, "I DO"... **ALL** THAT STUFF.
DID YOU KISS HIM?
TCH! **NO!!!**
MOM, WE'RE **MARRIED**... WE'RE NOT IN **LOVE!**
KIRKMAN & SCOTT

KINDERGARTEN: WEEK 1
DADDY, WILL YOU HELP ME WITH MY HOMEWORK?
SURE, ZOE!
KINDERGARTEN: WEEK 2
DADDY, WILL YOU HELP ME WITH MY HOMEWORK?
YEAH. SURE. OKAY.

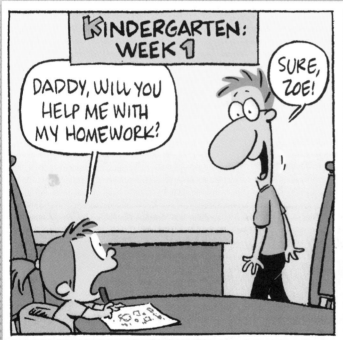

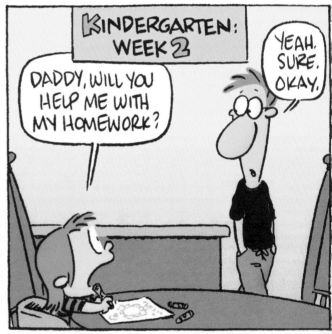

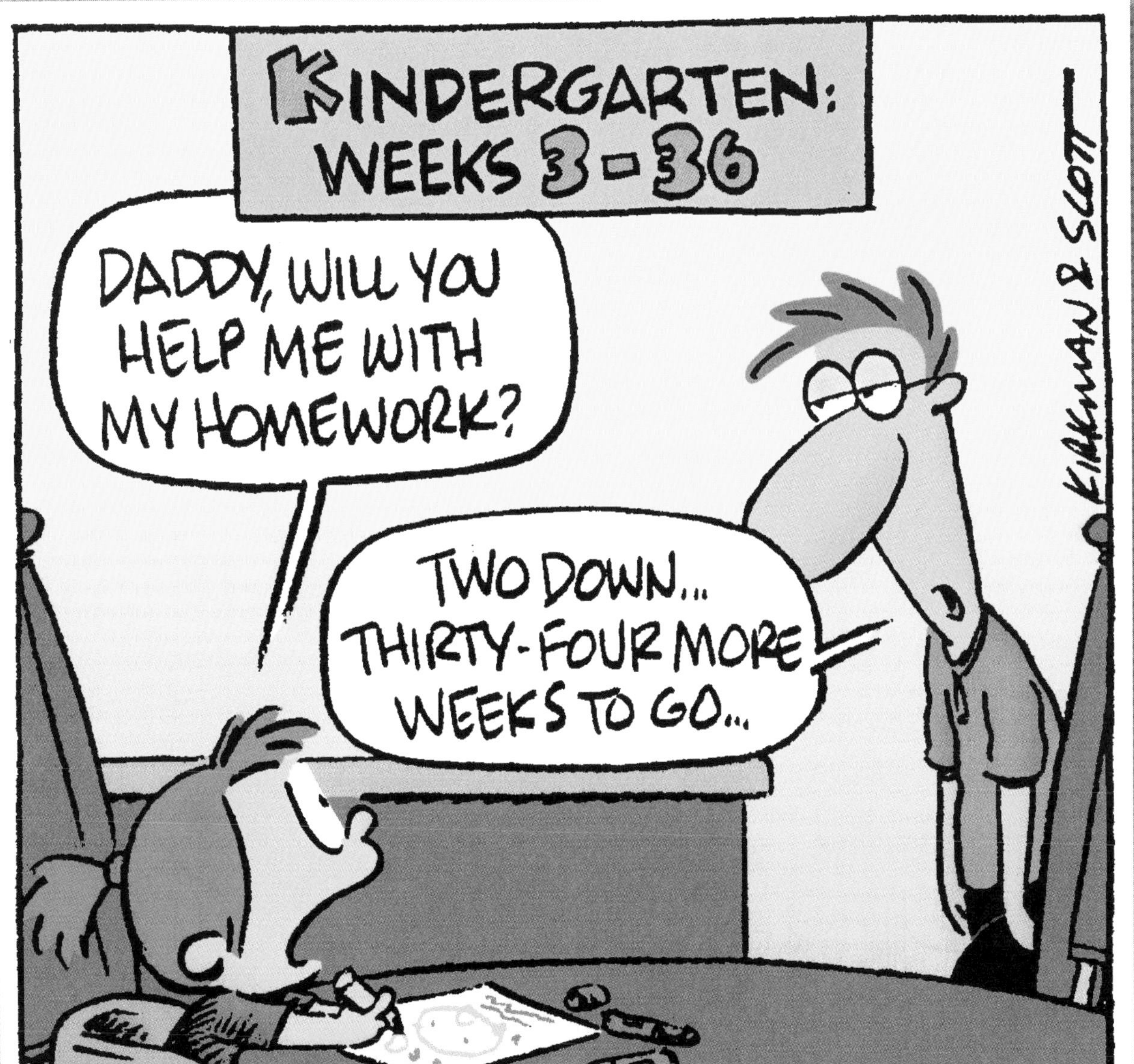
KINDERGARTEN: WEEKS 3 - 36
DADDY, WILL YOU HELP ME WITH MY HOMEWORK?
TWO DOWN... THIRTY-FOUR MORE WEEKS TO GO...
KIRKMAN & SCOTT

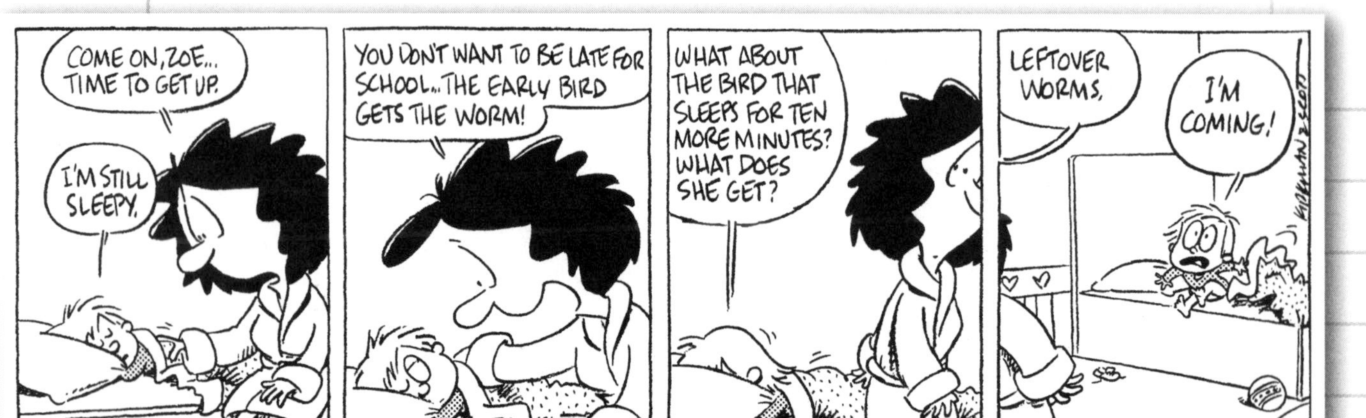
COME ON, ZOE... TIME TO GET UP.
I'M STILL SLEEPY.
YOU DON'T WANT TO BE LATE FOR SCHOOL... THE EARLY BIRD GETS THE WORM!
WHAT ABOUT THE BIRD THAT SLEEPS FOR TEN MORE MINUTES? WHAT DOES SHE GET?
LEFTOVER WORMS.
I'M COMING!
KIRKMAN & SCOTT

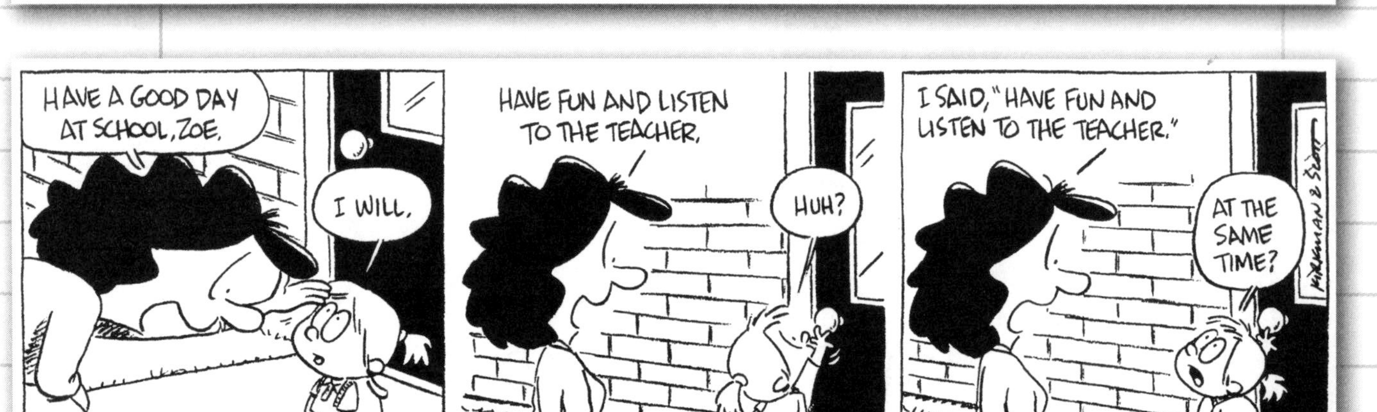
HAVE A GOOD DAY AT SCHOOL, ZOE.
I WILL.
HAVE FUN AND LISTEN TO THE TEACHER.
HUH?
I SAID, "HAVE FUN AND LISTEN TO THE TEACHER."
AT THE SAME TIME?
KIRKMAN & SCOTT

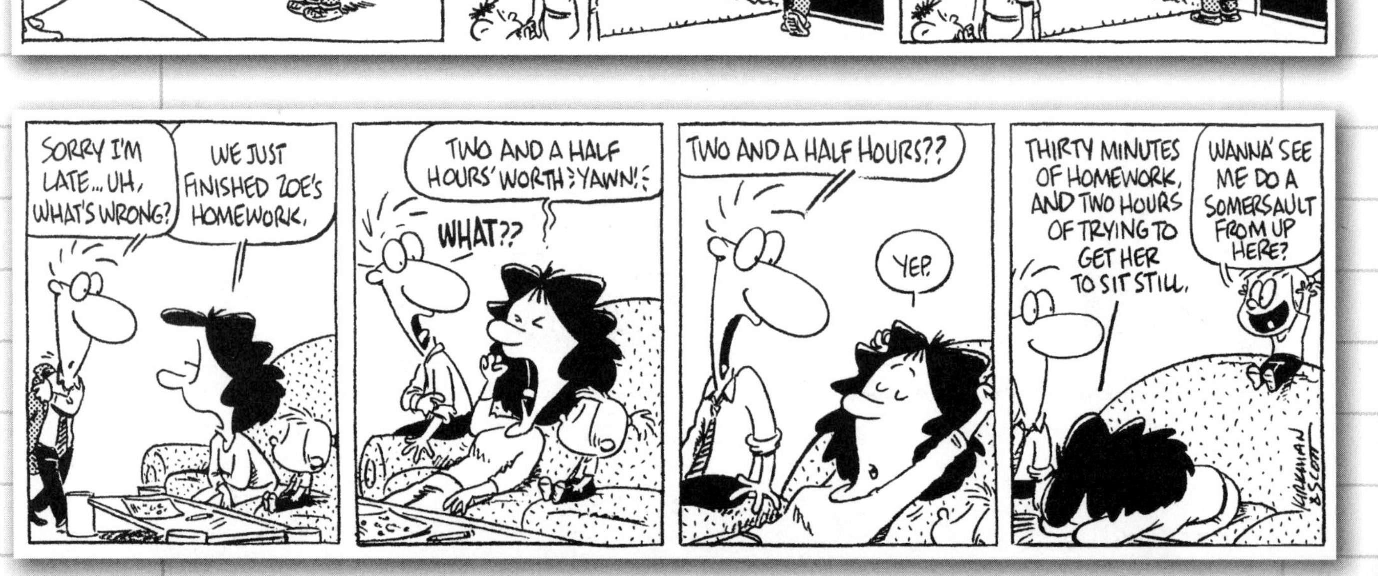
SORRY I'M LATE... UH, WHAT'S WRONG?
WE JUST FINISHED ZOE'S HOMEWORK.
TWO AND A HALF HOURS' WORTH ~YAWN!~
WHAT??
TWO AND A HALF HOURS??
YEP.
THIRTY MINUTES OF HOMEWORK, AND TWO HOURS OF TRYING TO GET HER TO SIT STILL.
WANNA' SEE ME DO A SOMERSAULT FROM UP HERE?
KIRKMAN & SCOTT

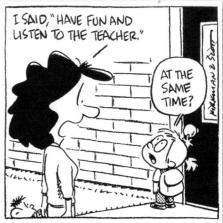

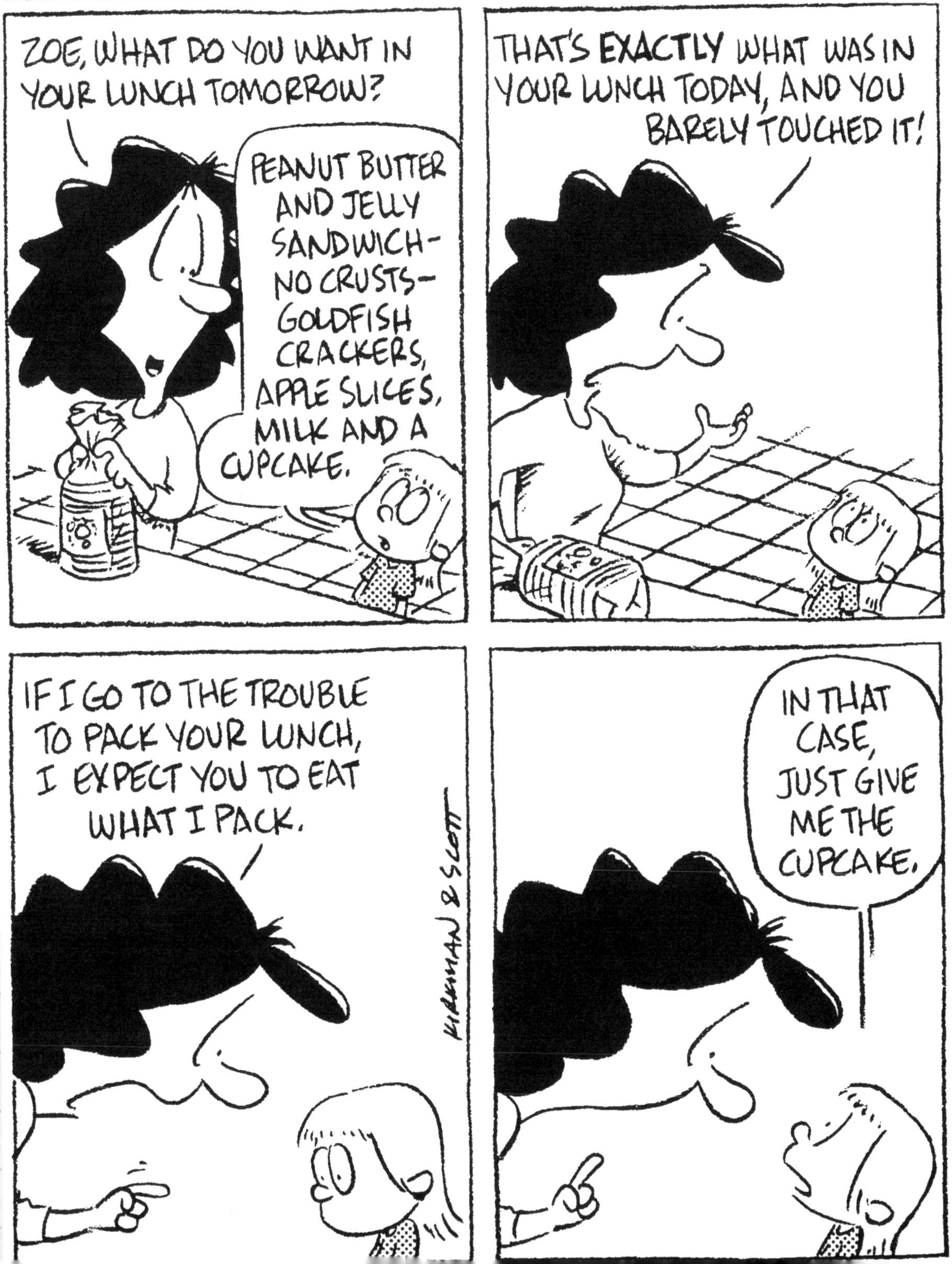
ZOE, WHAT DO YOU WANT IN YOUR LUNCH TOMORROW?
PEANUT BUTTER AND JELLY SANDWICH- NO CRUSTS- GOLDFISH CRACKERS, APPLE SLICES, MILK AND A CUPCAKE.
THAT'S **EXACTLY** WHAT WAS IN YOUR LUNCH TODAY, AND YOU BARELY TOUCHED IT!
IF I GO TO THE TROUBLE TO PACK YOUR LUNCH, I EXPECT YOU TO EAT WHAT I PACK.
KIRKMAN & SCOTT
IN THAT CASE, JUST GIVE ME THE CUPCAKE.

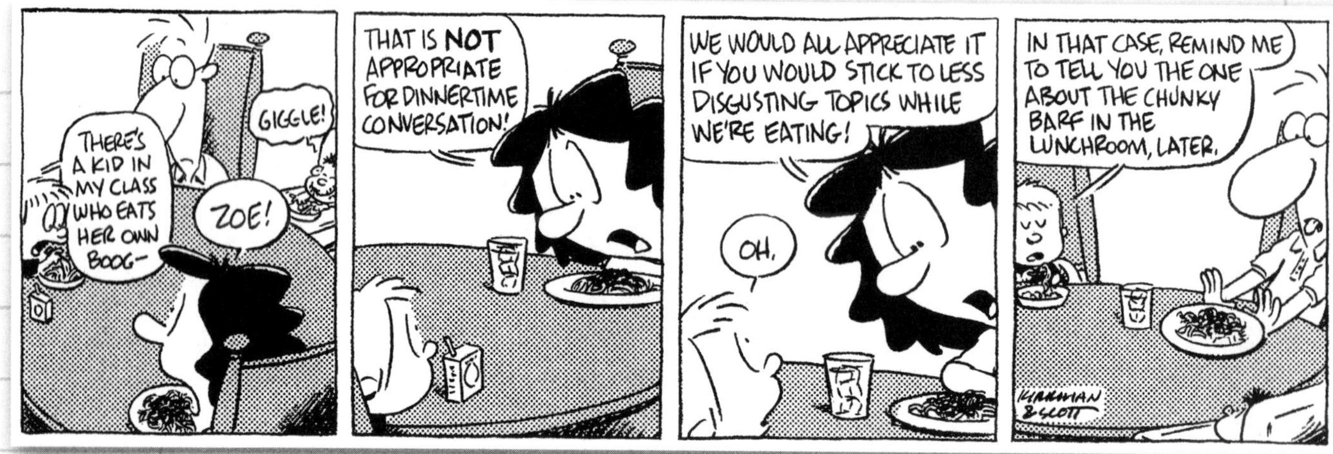
THERE'S A KID IN MY CLASS WHO EATS HER OWN BOOG-
GIGGLE!
ZOE!
THAT IS **NOT** APPROPRIATE FOR DINNERTIME CONVERSATION!
WE WOULD ALL APPRECIATE IT IF YOU WOULD STICK TO LESS DISGUSTING TOPICS WHILE WE'RE EATING!
OH.
IN THAT CASE, REMIND ME TO TELL YOU THE ONE ABOUT THE CHUNKY BARF IN THE LUNCHROOM, LATER.
KIRKMAN & SCOTT

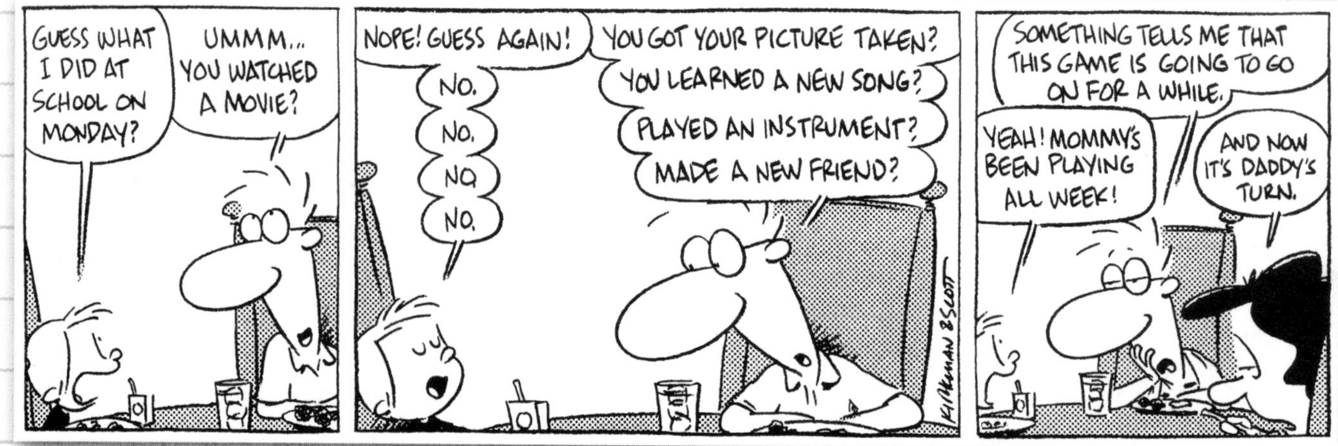
GUESS WHAT I DID AT SCHOOL ON MONDAY?
UMMM... YOU WATCHED A MOVIE?
NOPE! GUESS AGAIN!
YOU GOT YOUR PICTURE TAKEN?
NO.
YOU LEARNED A NEW SONG?
NO.
PLAYED AN INSTRUMENT?
NO.
MADE A NEW FRIEND?
NO.
KIRKMAN & SCOTT
SOMETHING TELLS ME THAT THIS GAME IS GOING TO GO ON FOR A WHILE.
YEAH! MOMMY'S BEEN PLAYING ALL WEEK!
AND NOW IT'S DADDY'S TURN.

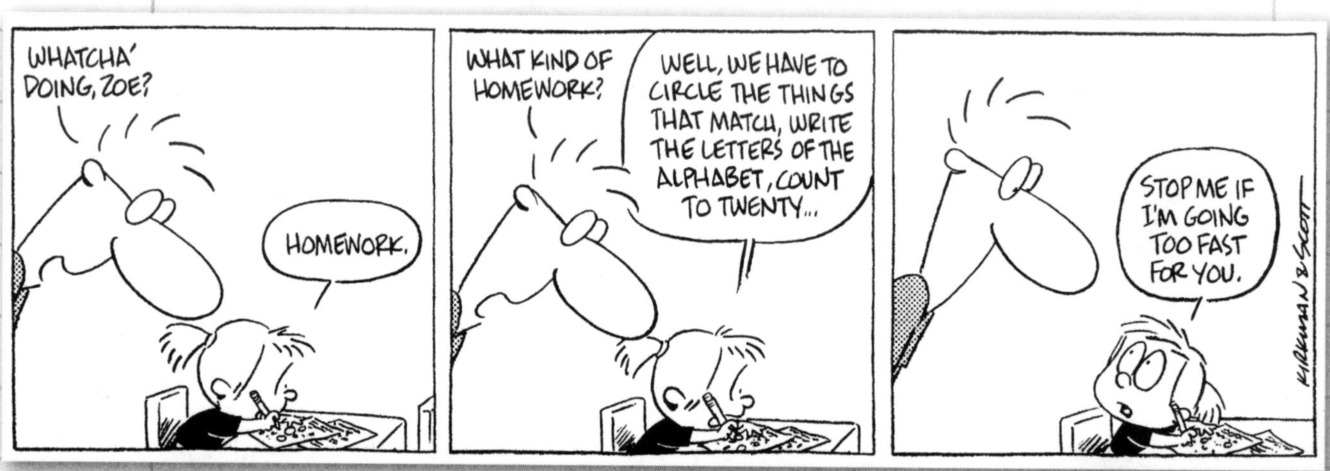
WHATCHA' DOING, ZOE?
HOMEWORK.
WHAT KIND OF HOMEWORK?
WELL, WE HAVE TO CIRCLE THE THINGS THAT MATCH, WRITE THE LETTERS OF THE ALPHABET, COUNT TO TWENTY...
STOP ME IF I'M GOING TOO FAST FOR YOU.
KIRKMAN & SCOTT

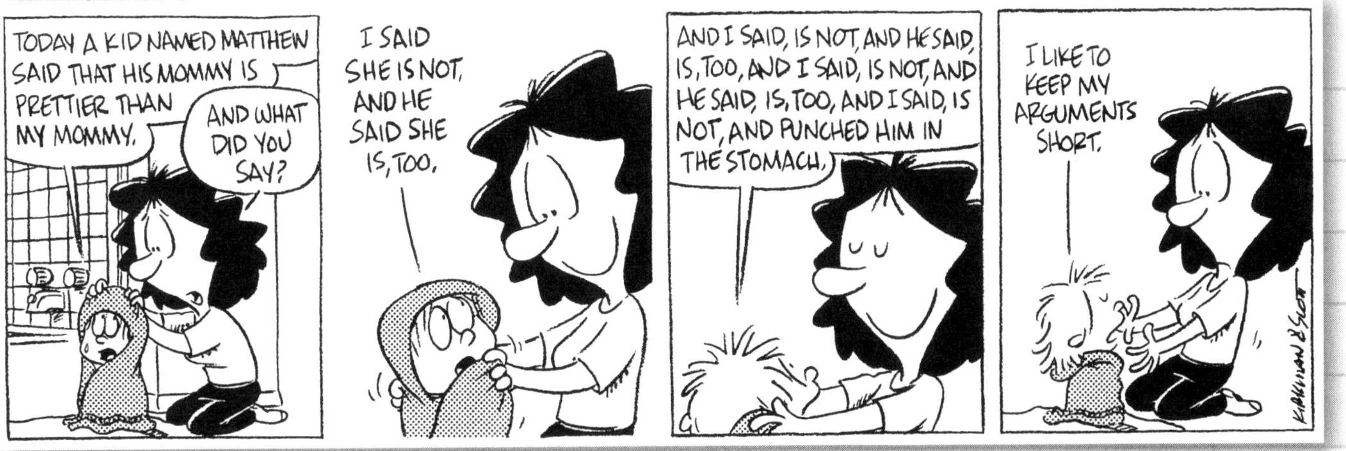
TODAY A KID NAMED MATTHEW SAID THAT HIS MOMMY IS PRETTIER THAN MY MOMMY.
AND WHAT DID YOU SAY?
I SAID SHE IS NOT, AND HE SAID SHE IS, TOO.
AND I SAID, IS NOT, AND HE SAID, IS, TOO, AND I SAID, IS NOT, AND HE SAID, IS, TOO, AND I SAID, IS NOT, AND PUNCHED HIM IN THE STOMACH.
I LIKE TO KEEP MY ARGUMENTS SHORT.
KIRKMAN & SCOTT

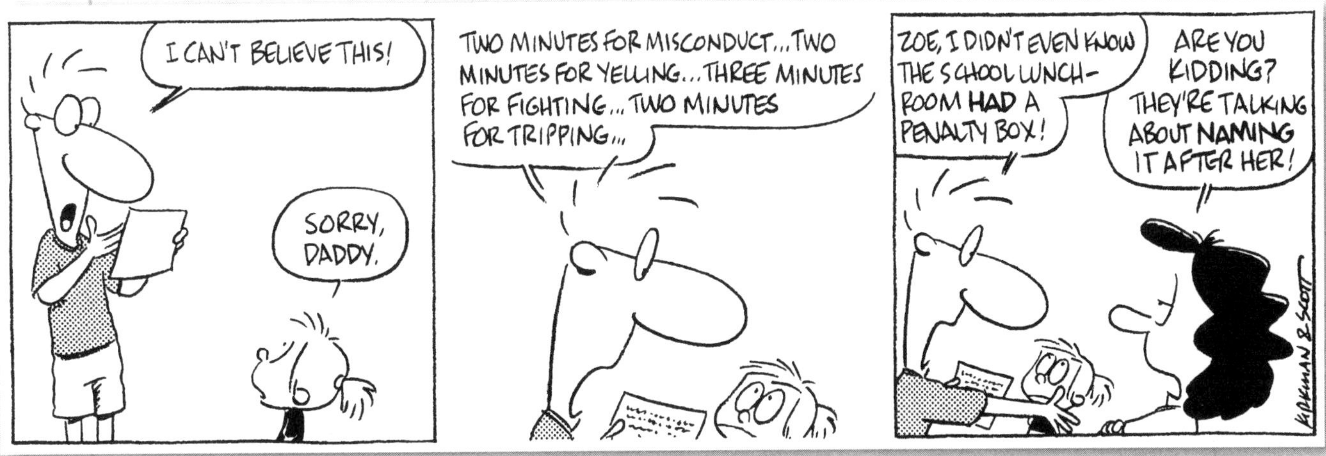
I CAN'T BELIEVE THIS!
SORRY, DADDY.
TWO MINUTES FOR MISCONDUCT... TWO MINUTES FOR YELLING... THREE MINUTES FOR FIGHTING... TWO MINUTES FOR TRIPPING...
ZOE, I DIDN'T EVEN KNOW THE SCHOOL LUNCH-ROOM **HAD** A PENALTY BOX!
ARE YOU KIDDING? THEY'RE TALKING ABOUT **NAMING** IT AFTER HER!
KIRKMAN & SCOTT

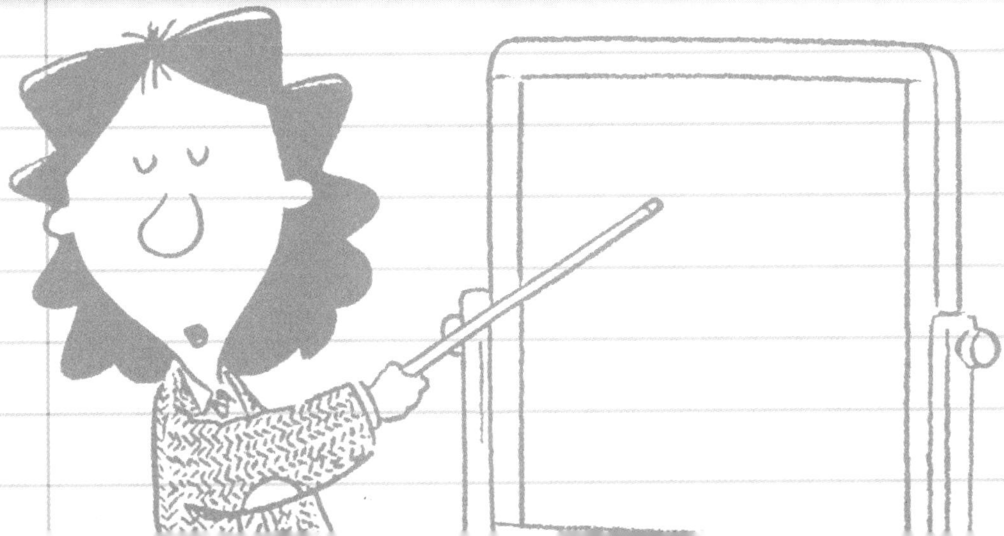

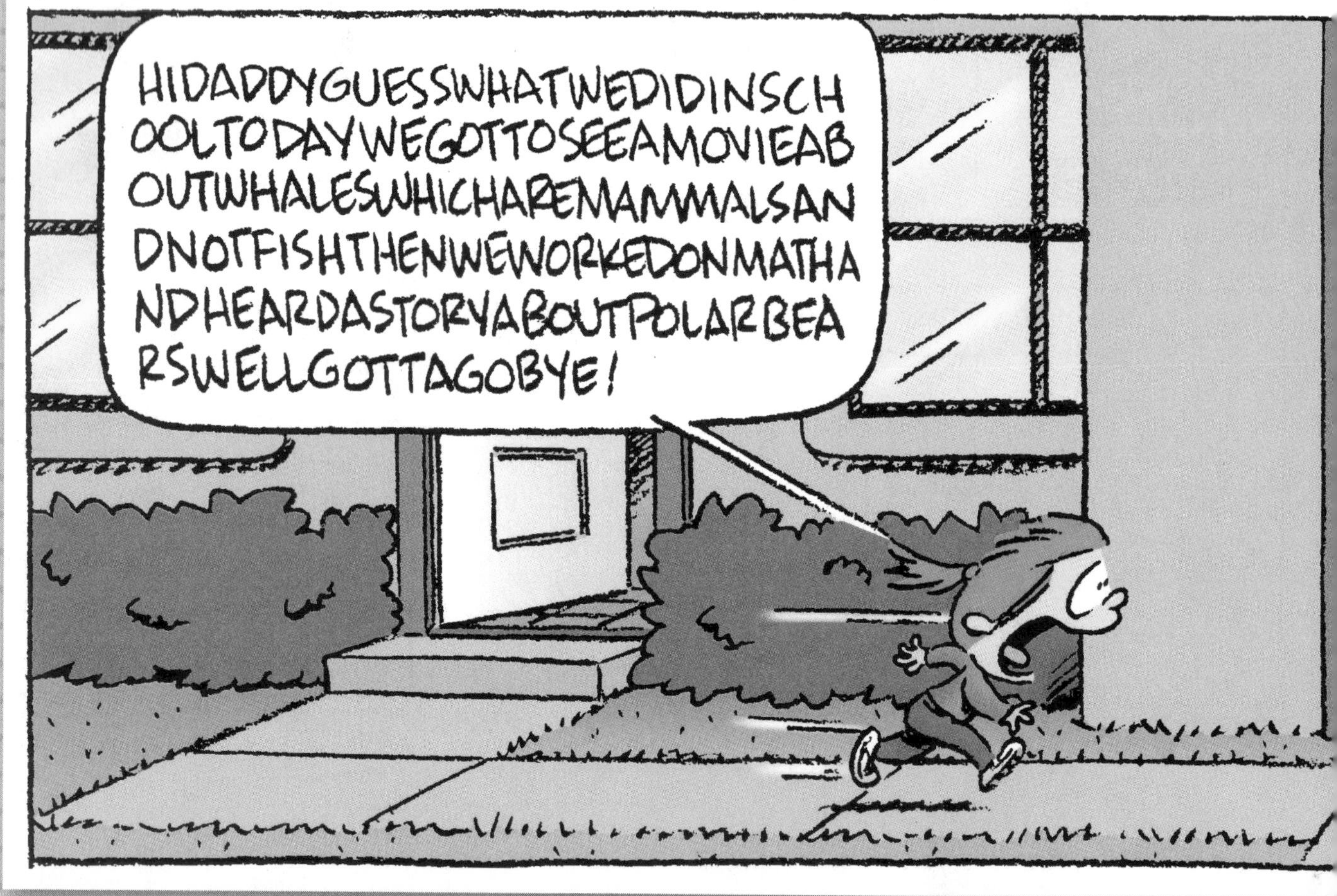
HIDADDYGUESSWHATWEDIDINSCHOOLTODAYWEGOTTOSEEAMOVIEABOUTWHALESWHICHAREMAMMALSANDNOTFISHTHENWEWORKEDONMATHANDHEARDASTORYABOUTPOLARBEARSWELLGOTTAGOBYE!

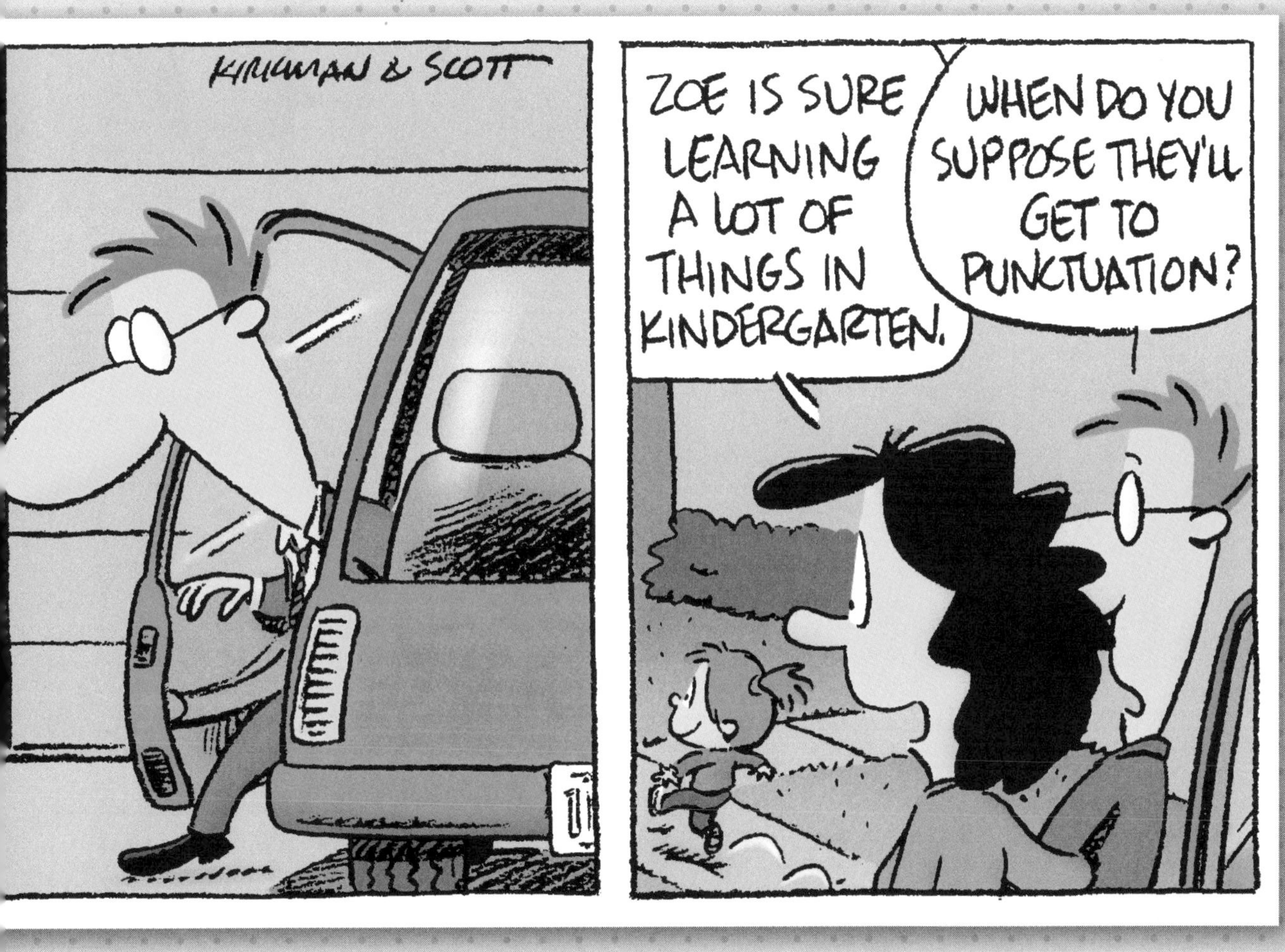
KIRKMAN & SCOTT
ZOE IS SURE LEARNING A LOT OF THINGS IN KINDERGARTEN.
WHEN DO YOU SUPPOSE THEY'LL GET TO PUNCTUATION?

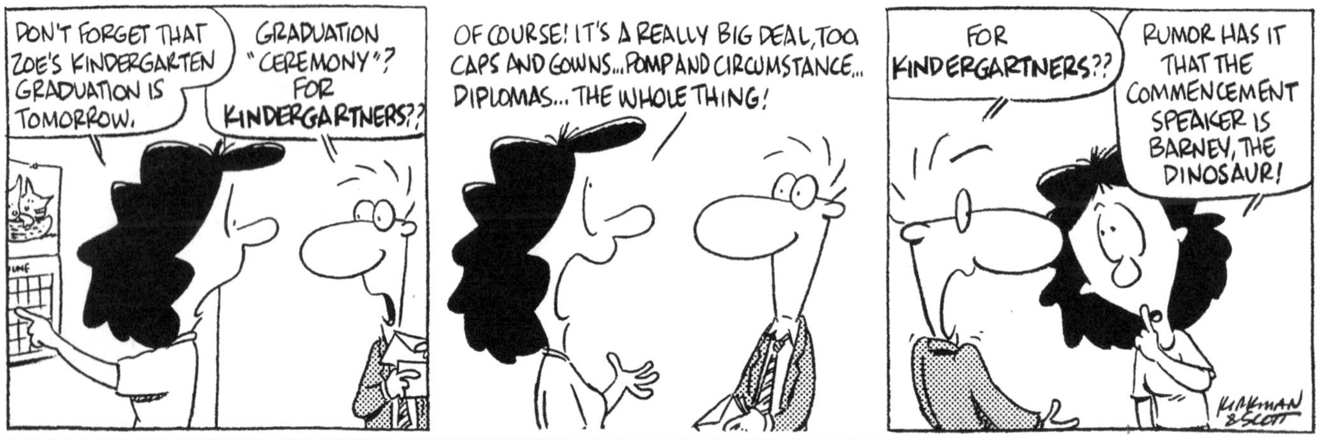
DON'T FORGET THAT ZOE'S KINDERGARTEN GRADUATION IS TOMORROW.
GRADUATION "CEREMONY"? FOR KINDERGARTNERS??
OF COURSE! IT'S A REALLY BIG DEAL, TOO. CAPS AND GOWNS... POMP AND CIRCUMSTANCE... DIPLOMAS... THE WHOLE THING!
FOR KINDERGARTNERS??
RUMOR HAS IT THAT THE COMMENCEMENT SPEAKER IS BARNEY, THE DINOSAUR!
KIRKMAN & SCOTT

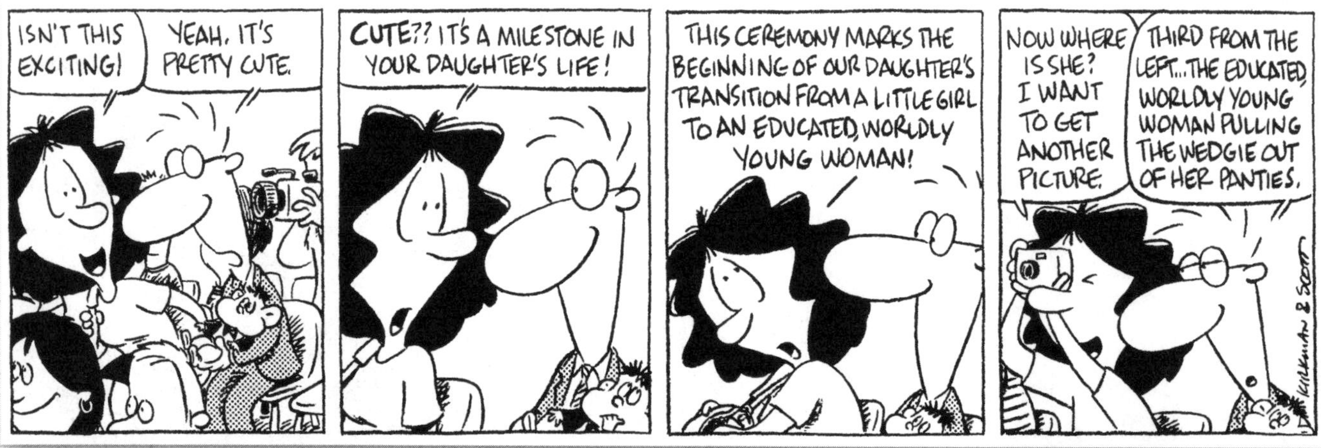
ISN'T THIS EXCITING!
YEAH. IT'S PRETTY CUTE.
CUTE?? IT'S A MILESTONE IN YOUR DAUGHTER'S LIFE!
THIS CEREMONY MARKS THE BEGINNING OF OUR DAUGHTER'S TRANSITION FROM A LITTLE GIRL TO AN EDUCATED, WORLDLY YOUNG WOMAN!
NOW WHERE IS SHE? I WANT TO GET ANOTHER PICTURE.
THIRD FROM THE LEFT... THE EDUCATED, WORLDLY YOUNG WOMAN PULLING THE WEDGIE OUT OF HER PANTIES.
KIRKMAN & SCOTT

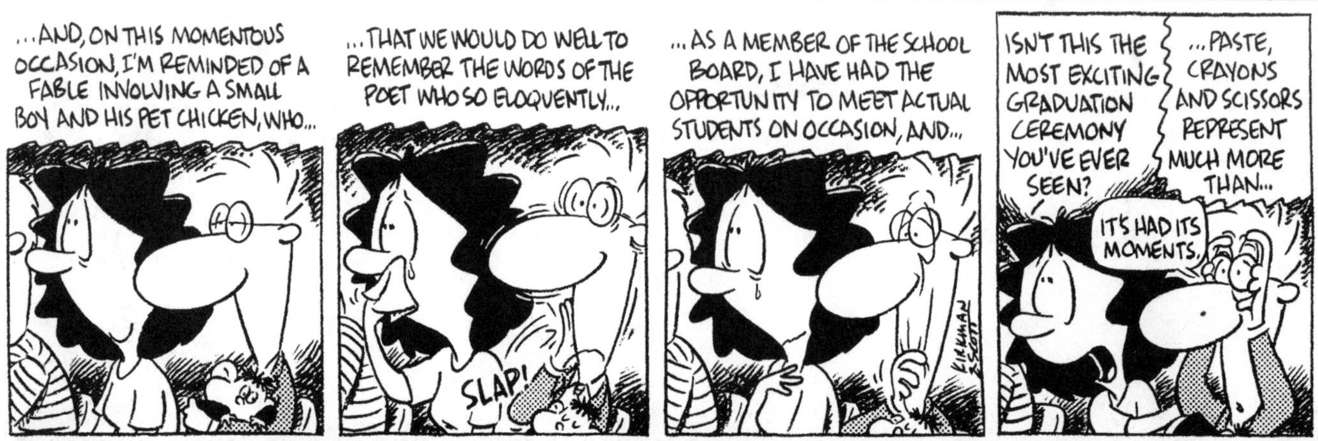
...AND, ON THIS MOMENTOUS OCCASION, I'M REMINDED OF A FABLE INVOLVING A SMALL BOY AND HIS PET CHICKEN, WHO...
...THAT WE WOULD DO WELL TO REMEMBER THE WORDS OF THE POET WHO SO ELOQUENTLY...
SLAP!
...AS A MEMBER OF THE SCHOOL BOARD, I HAVE HAD THE OPPORTUNITY TO MEET ACTUAL STUDENTS ON OCCASION, AND...
KIRKMAN & SCOTT
ISN'T THIS THE MOST EXCITING GRADUATION CEREMONY YOU'VE EVER SEEN?
...PASTE, CRAYONS AND SCISSORS REPRESENT MUCH MORE THAN...
IT'S HAD ITS MOMENTS.

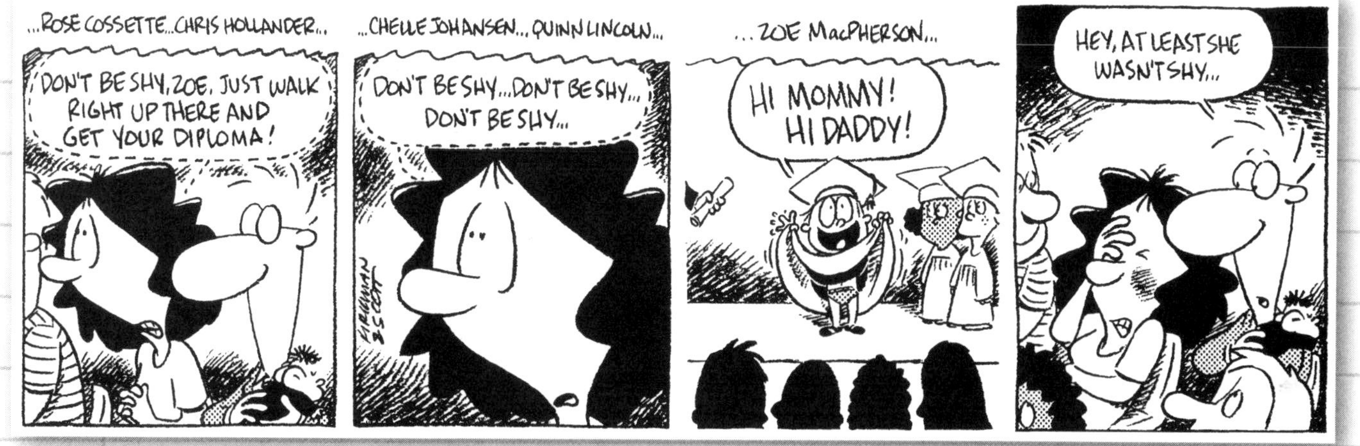
...ROSE COSSETTE...CHRIS HOLLANDER...
DON'T BE SHY, ZOE. JUST WALK RIGHT UP THERE AND GET YOUR DIPLOMA!
...CHELLE JOHANSEN... QUINN LINCOLN...
DON'T BE SHY...DON'T BE SHY... DON'T BE SHY...
KIRKMAN & SCOTT
...ZOE MacPHERSON...
HI MOMMY! HI DADDY!
HEY, AT LEAST SHE WASN'T SHY...

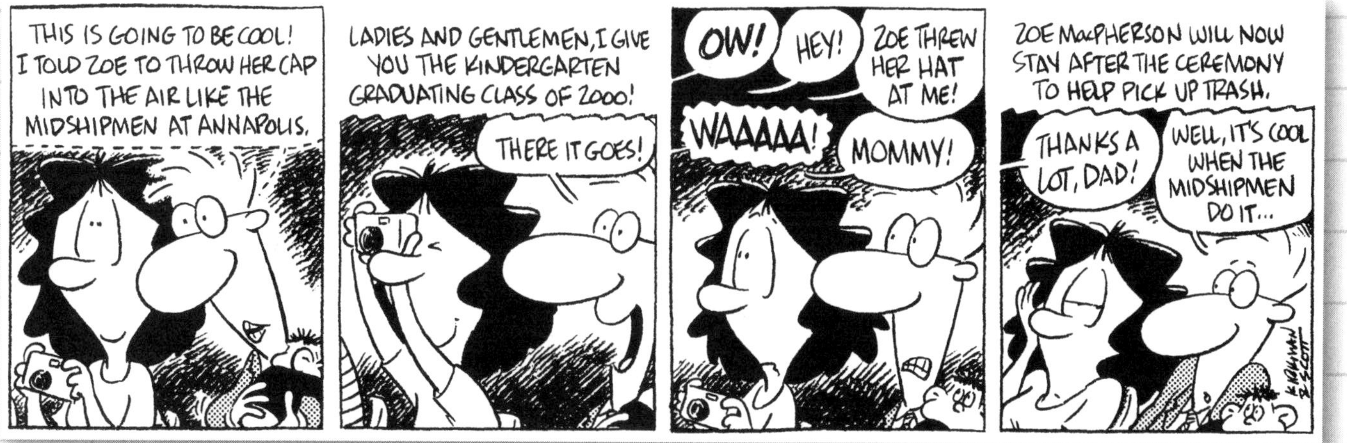
THIS IS GOING TO BE COOL! I TOLD ZOE TO THROW HER CAP INTO THE AIR LIKE THE MIDSHIPMEN AT ANNAPOLIS.
LADIES AND GENTLEMEN, I GIVE YOU THE KINDERGARTEN GRADUATING CLASS OF 2000!
THERE IT GOES!
OW!
HEY!
ZOE THREW HER HAT AT ME!
WAAAAA!
MOMMY!
ZOE MacPHERSON WILL NOW STAY AFTER THE CEREMONY TO HELP PICK UP TRASH.
THANKS A LOT, DAD!
WELL, IT'S COOL WHEN THE MIDSHIPMEN DO IT...
KIRKMAN & SCOTT

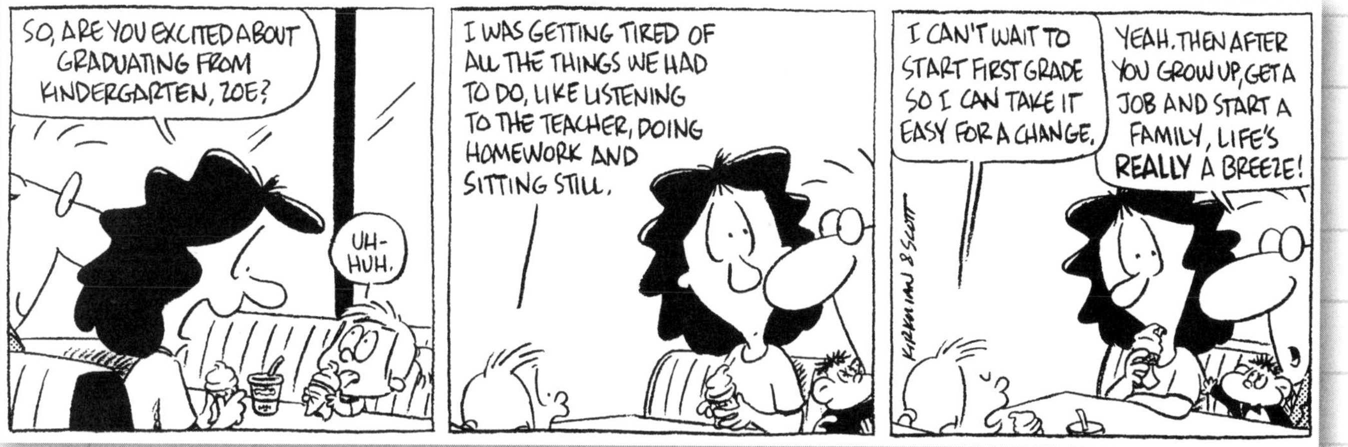
SO, ARE YOU EXCITED ABOUT GRADUATING FROM KINDERGARTEN, ZOE?
UH-HUH.
I WAS GETTING TIRED OF ALL THE THINGS WE HAD TO DO, LIKE LISTENING TO THE TEACHER, DOING HOMEWORK AND SITTING STILL.
KIRKMAN & SCOTT
I CAN'T WAIT TO START FIRST GRADE SO I CAN TAKE IT EASY FOR A CHANGE.
YEAH. THEN AFTER YOU GROW UP, GET A JOB AND START A FAMILY, LIFE'S REALLY A BREEZE!

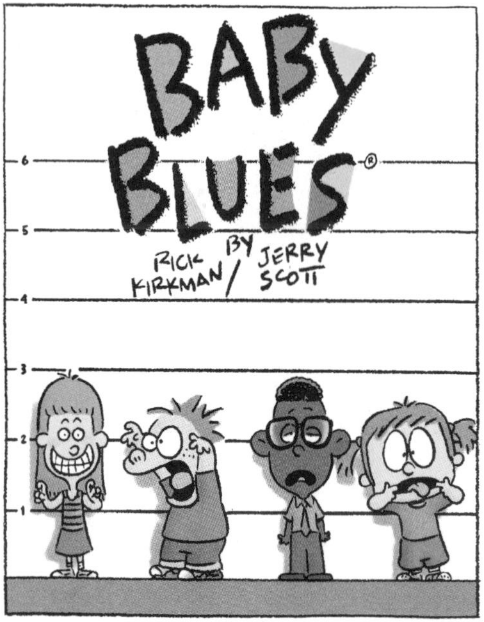
BABY BLUES®
BY
RICK KIRKMAN / JERRY SCOTT
6
5
4
3
2
1

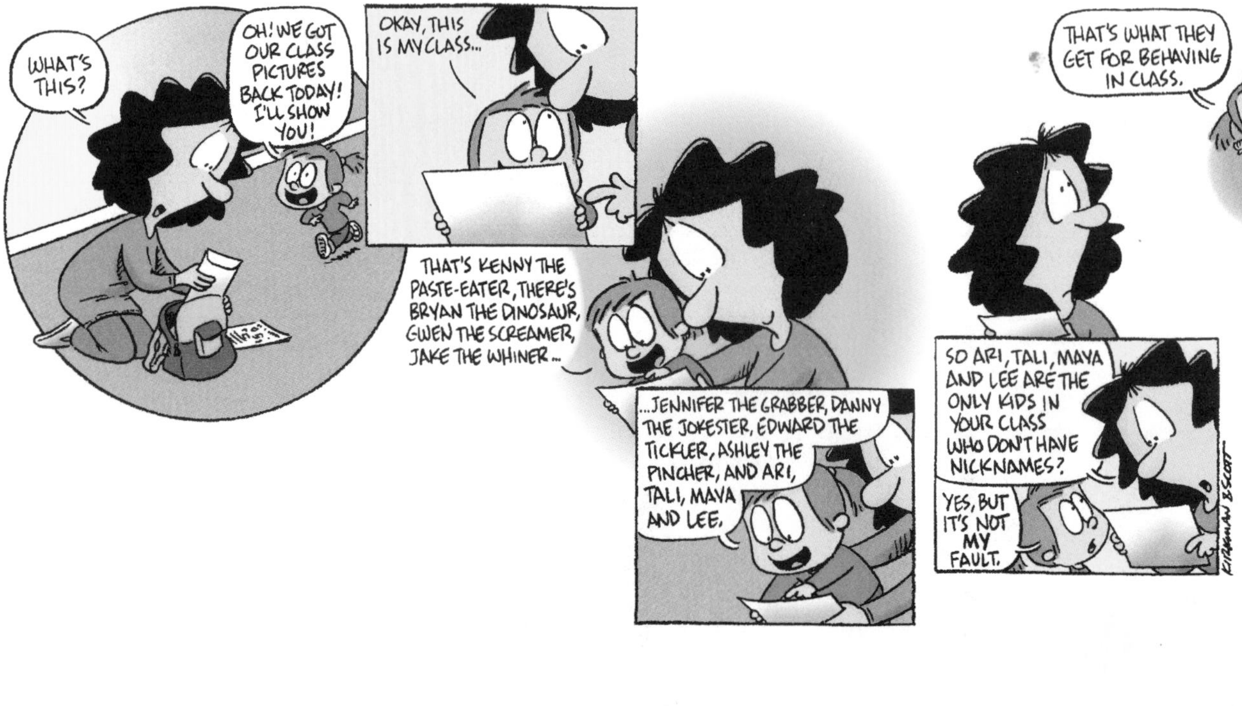
WHAT'S THIS?
OH! WE GOT OUR CLASS PICTURES BACK TODAY! I'LL SHOW YOU!
OKAY, THIS IS MY CLASS...
THAT'S KENNY THE PASTE-EATER, THERE'S BRYAN THE DINOSAUR, GWEN THE SCREAMER, JAKE THE WHINER...
...JENNIFER THE GRABBER, DANNY THE JOKESTER, EDWARD THE TICKLER, ASHLEY THE PINCHER, AND ARI, TALI, MAYA AND LEE.
SO ARI, TALI, MAYA AND LEE ARE THE ONLY KIDS IN YOUR CLASS WHO DON'T HAVE NICKNAMES?
YES, BUT IT'S NOT MY FAULT.
THAT'S WHAT THEY GET FOR BEHAVING IN CLASS.
KIRKMAN & SCOTT

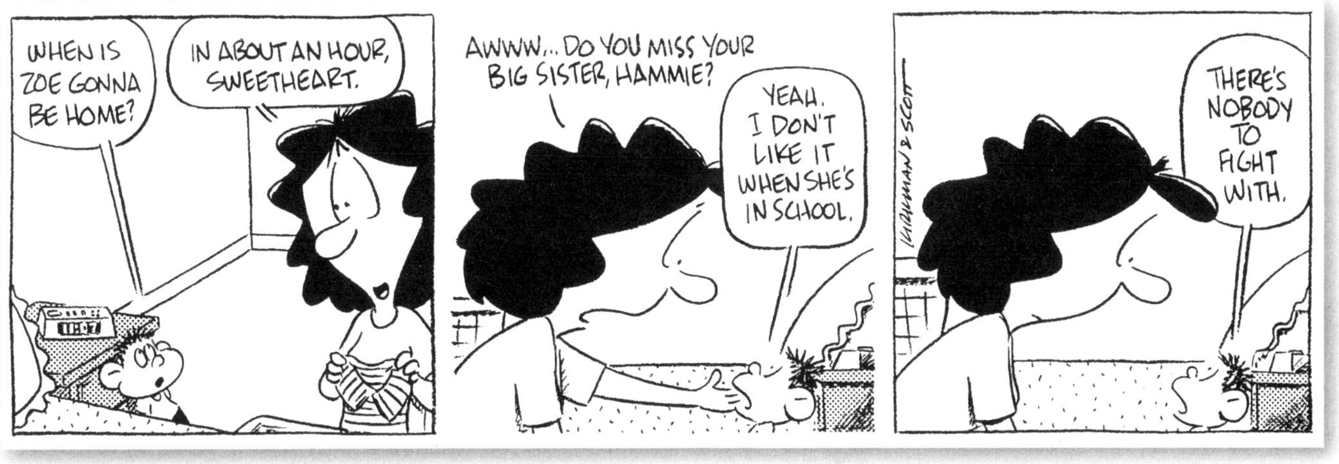
WHEN IS ZOE GONNA BE HOME?
IN ABOUT AN HOUR, SWEETHEART.
AWWW... DO YOU MISS YOUR BIG SISTER, HAMMIE?
YEAH. I DON'T LIKE IT WHEN SHE'S IN SCHOOL.
KIRKMAN & SCOTT
THERE'S NOBODY TO FIGHT WITH.

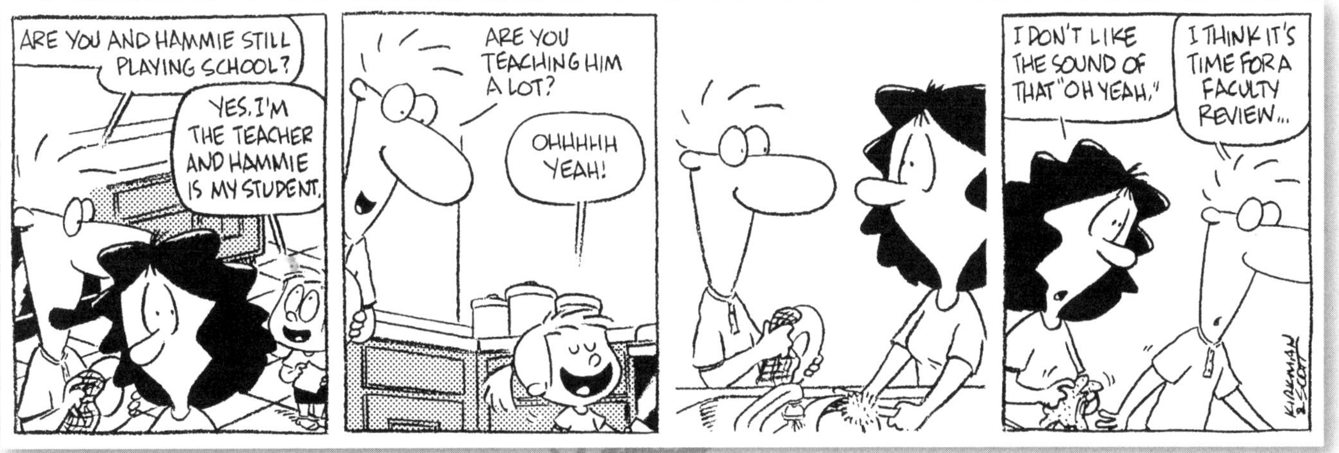
ARE YOU AND HAMMIE STILL PLAYING SCHOOL?
YES. I'M THE TEACHER AND HAMMIE IS MY STUDENT.
ARE YOU TEACHING HIM A LOT?
OHHHHH YEAH!
I DON'T LIKE THE SOUND OF THAT "OH YEAH."
I THINK IT'S TIME FOR A FACULTY REVIEW...
KIRKMAN & SCOTT

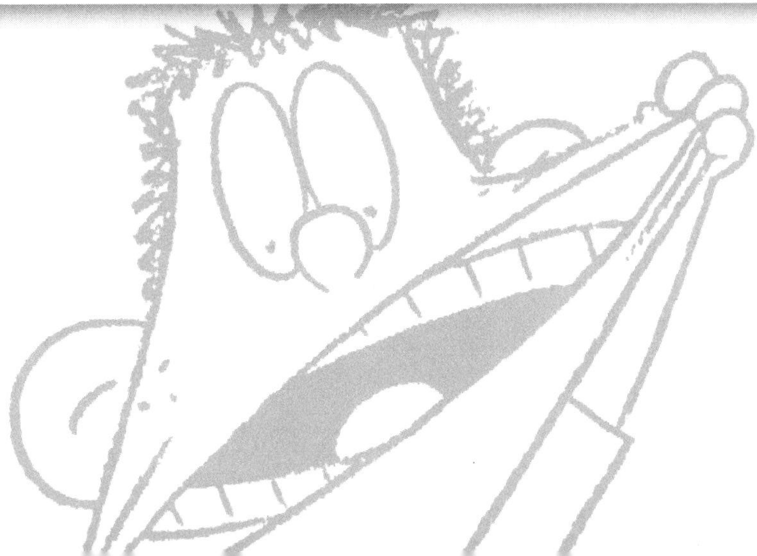

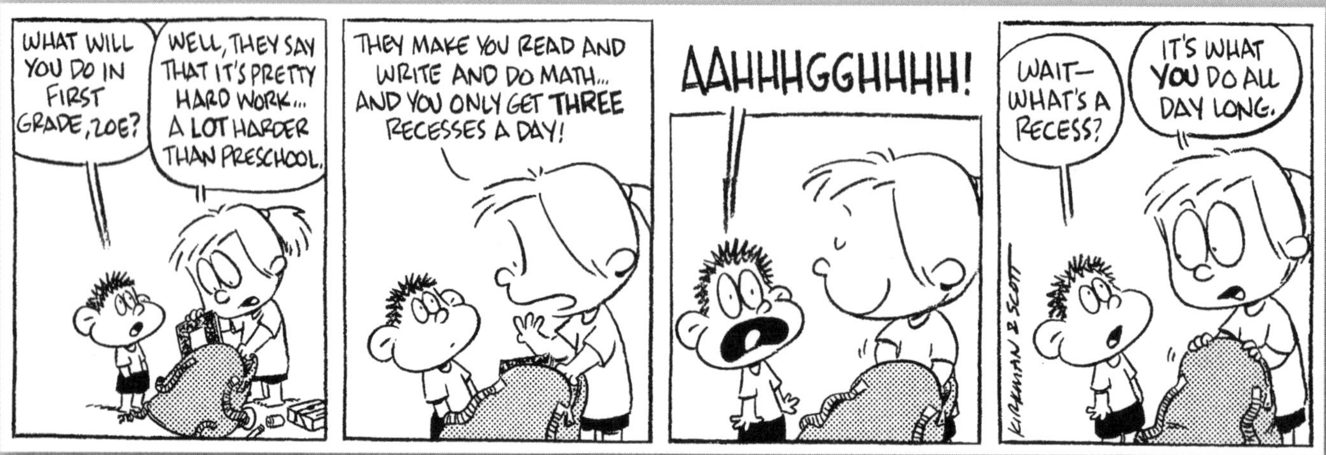
WHAT WILL YOU DO IN FIRST GRADE, ZOE?
WELL, THEY SAY THAT IT'S PRETTY HARD WORK... A LOT HARDER THAN PRESCHOOL.
THEY MAKE YOU READ AND WRITE AND DO MATH... AND YOU ONLY GET THREE RECESSES A DAY!
AAHHHGGHHHH!
WAIT— WHAT'S A RECESS?
IT'S WHAT YOU DO ALL DAY LONG.
KIRKMAN & SCOTT

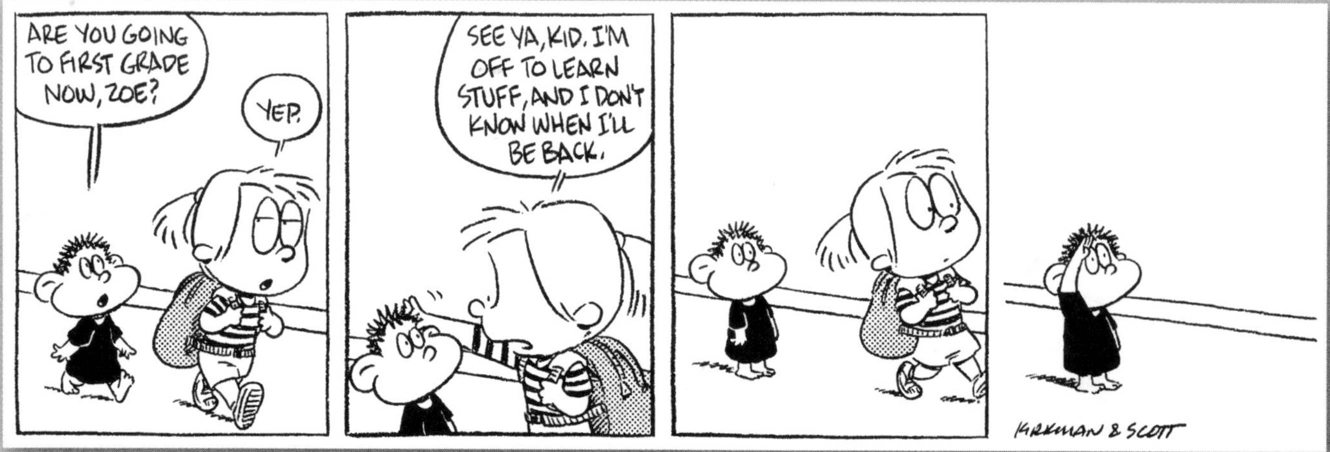
ARE YOU GOING TO FIRST GRADE NOW, ZOE?
YEP.
SEE YA, KID. I'M OFF TO LEARN STUFF, AND I DON'T KNOW WHEN I'LL BE BACK.
KIRKMAN & SCOTT

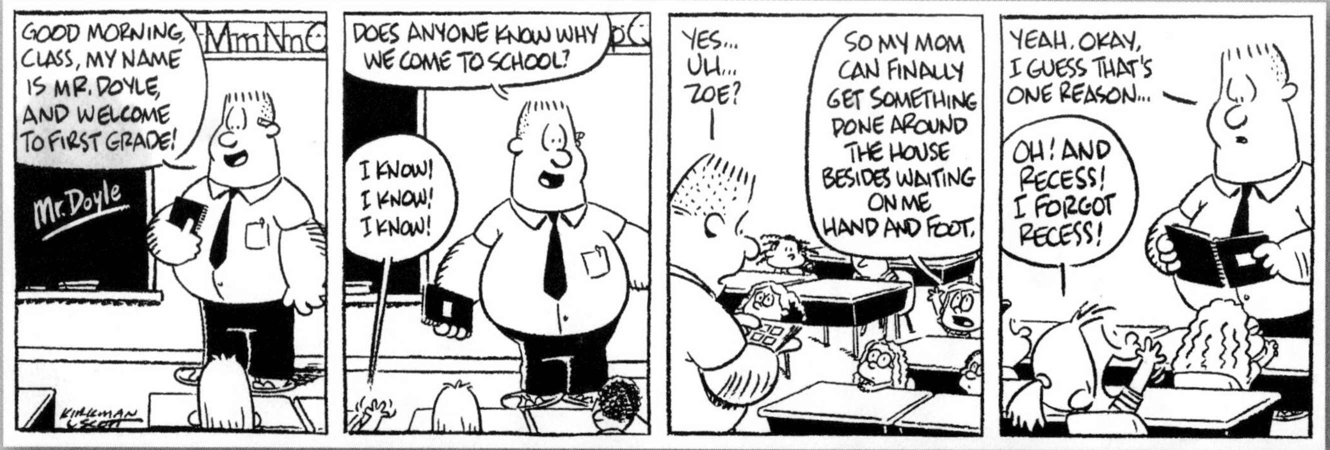
GOOD MORNING, CLASS, MY NAME IS MR. DOYLE, AND WELCOME TO FIRST GRADE!
Mr. Doyle
KIRKMAN & SCOTT
DOES ANYONE KNOW WHY WE COME TO SCHOOL?
I KNOW! I KNOW! I KNOW!
YES... UH... ZOE?
SO MY MOM CAN FINALLY GET SOMETHING DONE AROUND THE HOUSE BESIDES WAITING ON ME HAND AND FOOT.
YEAH. OKAY, I GUESS THAT'S ONE REASON...
OH! AND RECESS! I FORGOT RECESS!

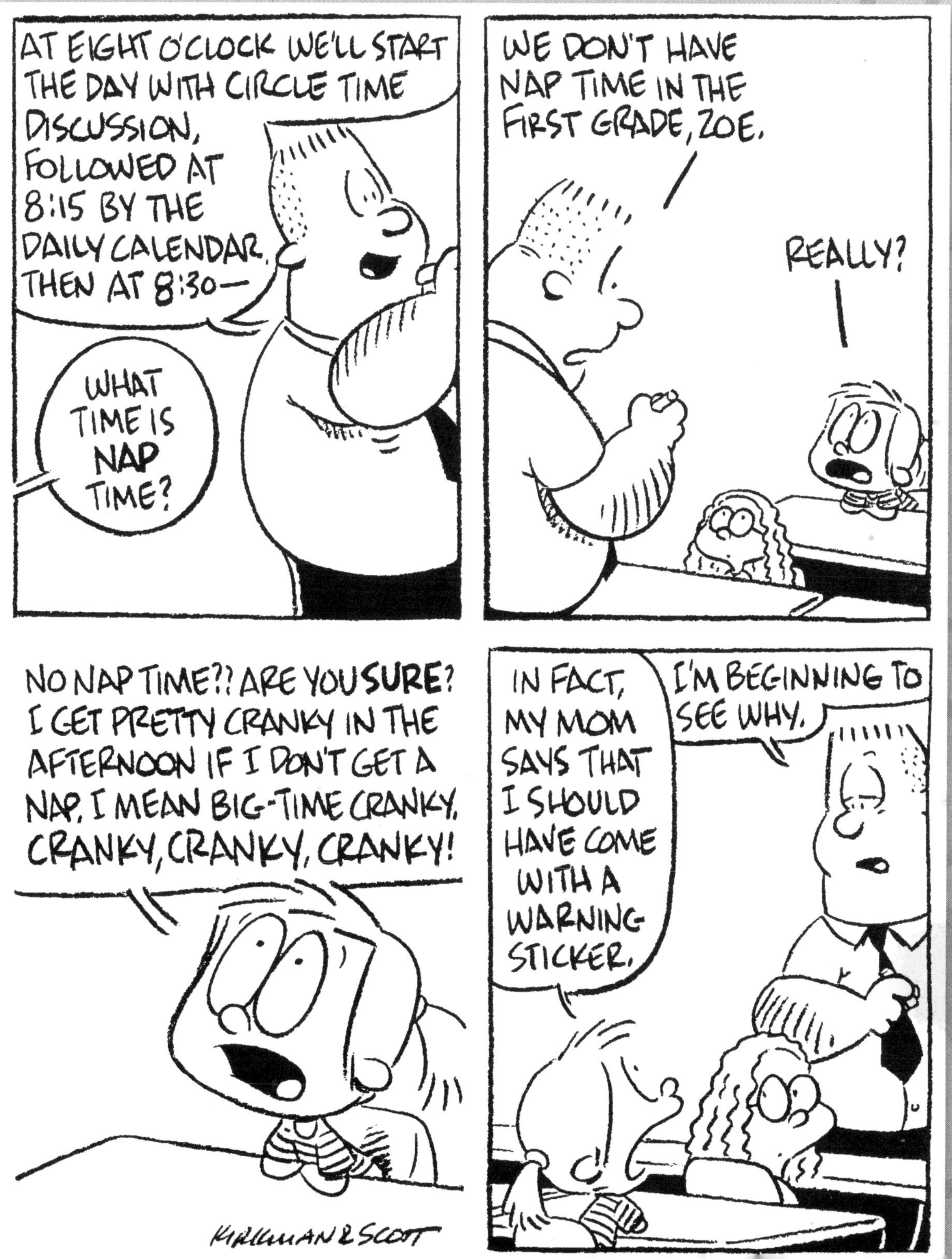
AT EIGHT O'CLOCK WE'LL START THE DAY WITH CIRCLE TIME DISCUSSION, FOLLOWED AT 8:15 BY THE DAILY CALENDAR. THEN AT 8:30—
WHAT TIME IS NAP TIME?
WE DON'T HAVE NAP TIME IN THE FIRST GRADE, ZOE.
REALLY?
NO NAP TIME?? ARE YOU SURE? I GET PRETTY CRANKY IN THE AFTERNOON IF I DON'T GET A NAP. I MEAN BIG-TIME CRANKY. CRANKY, CRANKY, CRANKY!
IN FACT, MY MOM SAYS THAT I SHOULD HAVE COME WITH A WARNING STICKER.
I'M BEGINNING TO SEE WHY.
KIRKMAN & SCOTT

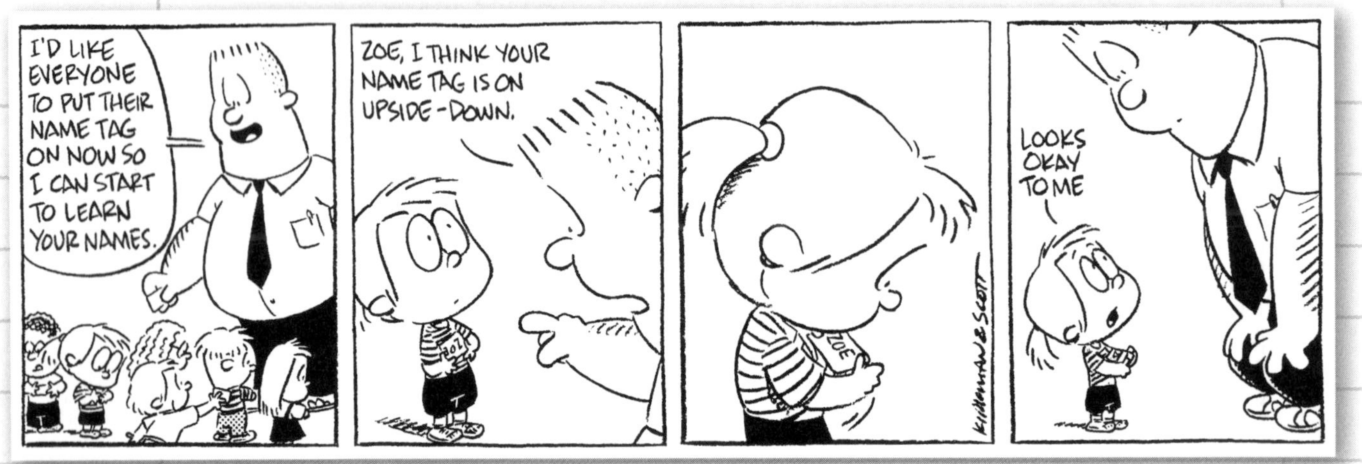
I'D LIKE EVERYONE TO PUT THEIR NAME TAG ON NOW SO I CAN START TO LEARN YOUR NAMES.
ZOE, I THINK YOUR NAME TAG IS ON UPSIDE-DOWN.
ZOE
KIRKMAN & SCOTT
LOOKS OKAY TO ME

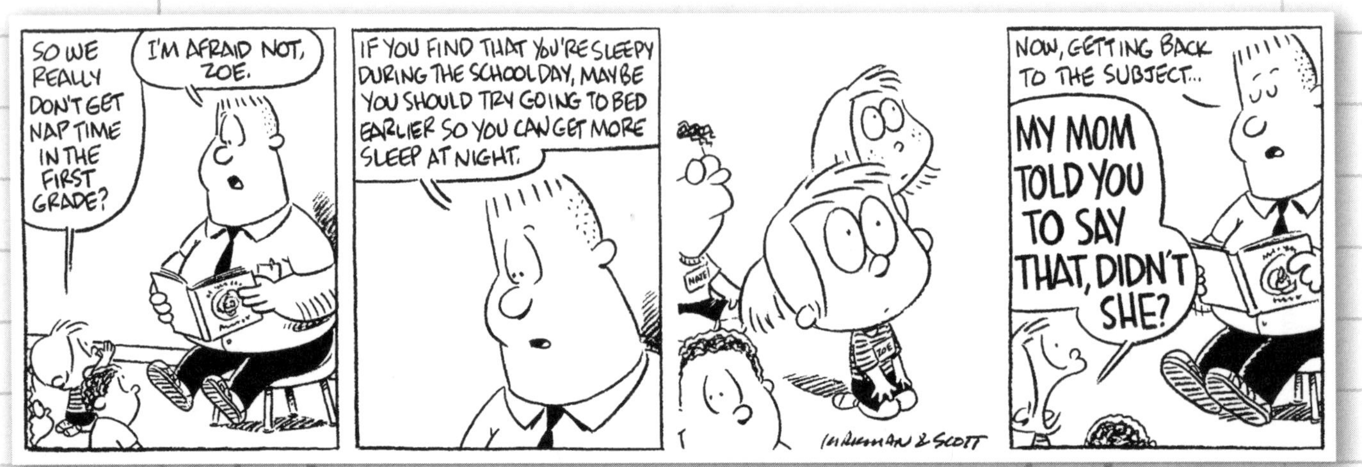
SO WE REALLY DON'T GET NAP TIME IN THE FIRST GRADE?
I'M AFRAID NOT, ZOE.
IF YOU FIND THAT YOU'RE SLEEPY DURING THE SCHOOL DAY, MAYBE YOU SHOULD TRY GOING TO BED EARLIER SO YOU CAN GET MORE SLEEP AT NIGHT.
ZOE
KIRKMAN & SCOTT
NOW, GETTING BACK TO THE SUBJECT...
MY MOM TOLD YOU TO SAY THAT, DIDN'T SHE?

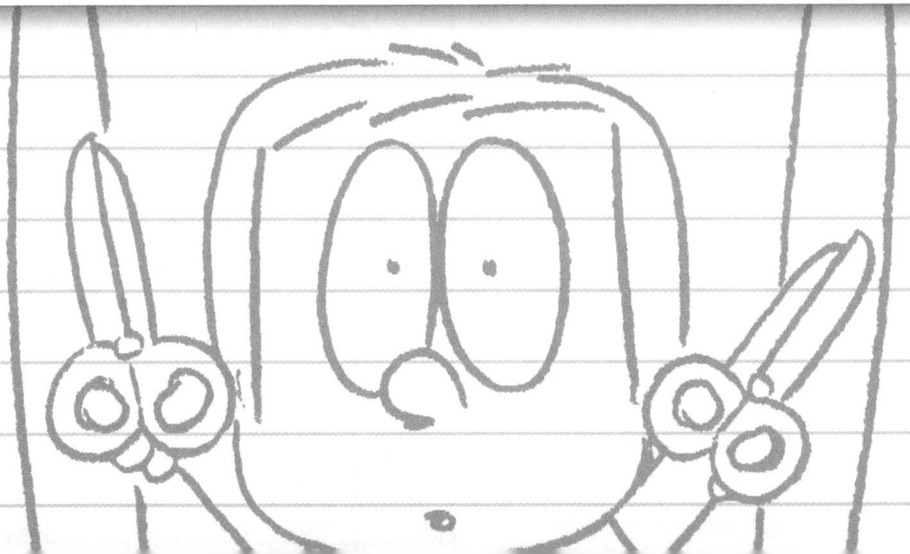

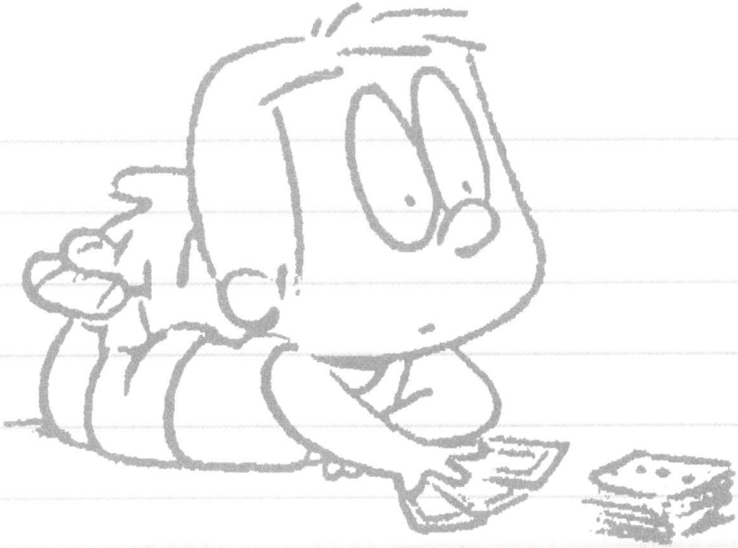

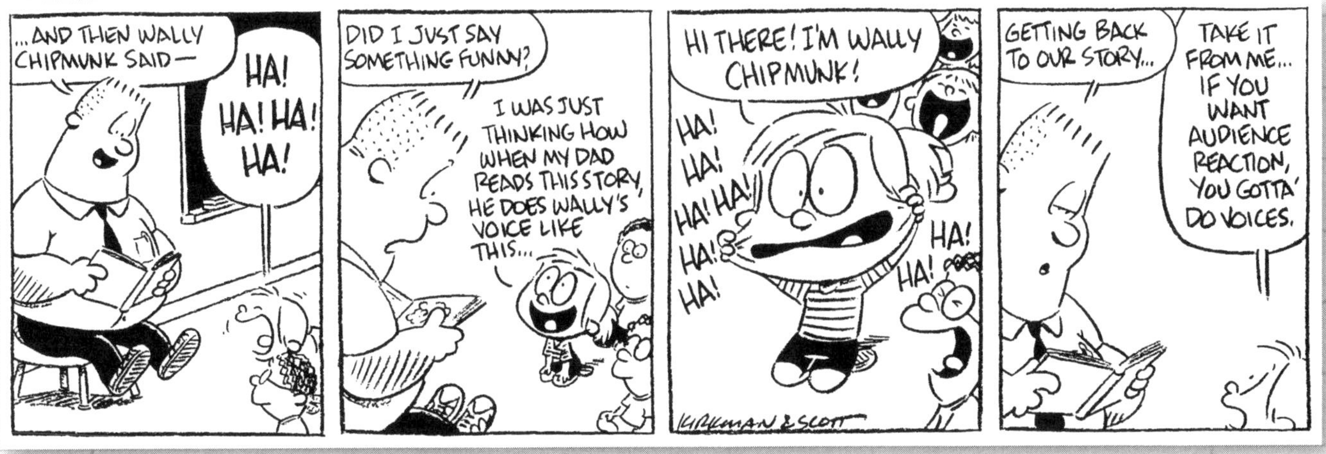
...AND THEN WALLY CHIPMUNK SAID—
HA! HA! HA! HA!
DID I JUST SAY SOMETHING FUNNY?
I WAS JUST THINKING HOW WHEN MY DAD READS THIS STORY, HE DOES WALLY'S VOICE LIKE THIS...
HI THERE! I'M WALLY CHIPMUNK!
HA! HA! HA! HA! HA! HA!
HA! HA!
KIRKMAN & SCOTT
GETTING BACK TO OUR STORY...
TAKE IT FROM ME... IF YOU WANT AUDIENCE REACTION, YOU GOTTA' DO VOICES.

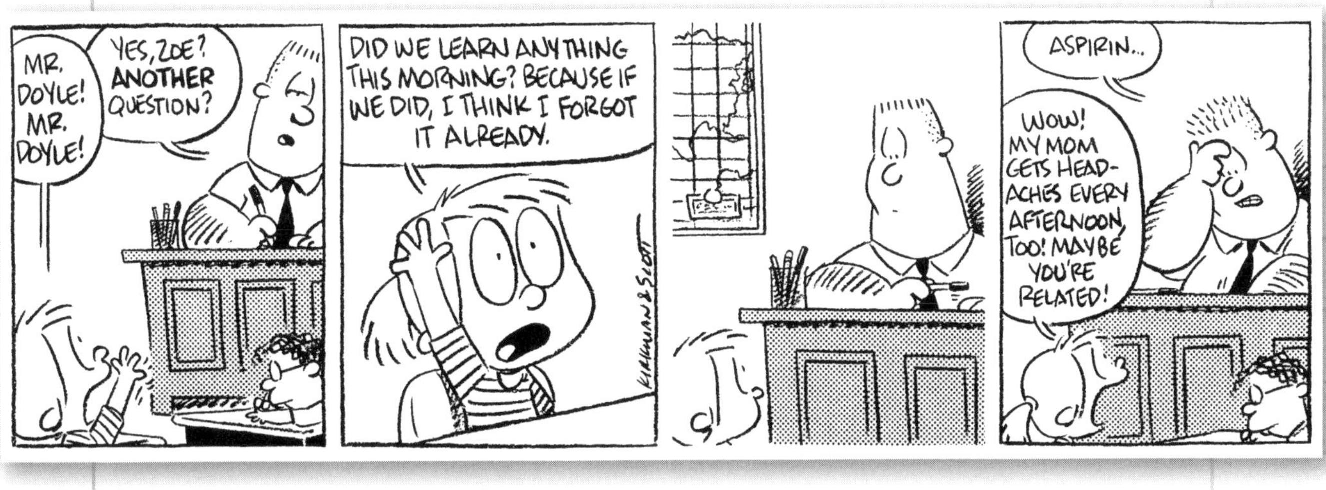
MR. DOYLE! MR. DOYLE!
YES, ZOE? ANOTHER QUESTION?
DID WE LEARN ANYTHING THIS MORNING? BECAUSE IF WE DID, I THINK I FORGOT IT ALREADY.
KIRKMAN & SCOTT
ASPIRIN...
WOW! MY MOM GETS HEAD-ACHES EVERY AFTERNOON, TOO! MAYBE YOU'RE RELATED!

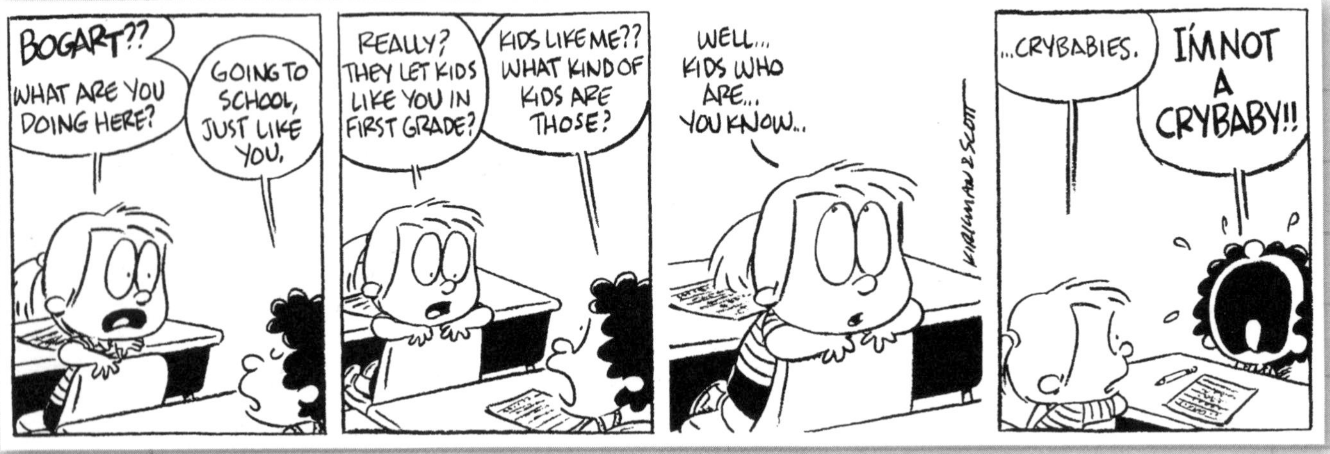
BOGART?? WHAT ARE YOU DOING HERE?
GOING TO SCHOOL, JUST LIKE YOU.
REALLY? THEY LET KIDS LIKE YOU IN FIRST GRADE?
KIDS LIKE ME?? WHAT KIND OF KIDS ARE THOSE?
WELL... KIDS WHO ARE... YOU KNOW...
KIRKMAN & SCOTT
...CRYBABIES.
I'M NOT A CRYBABY!!

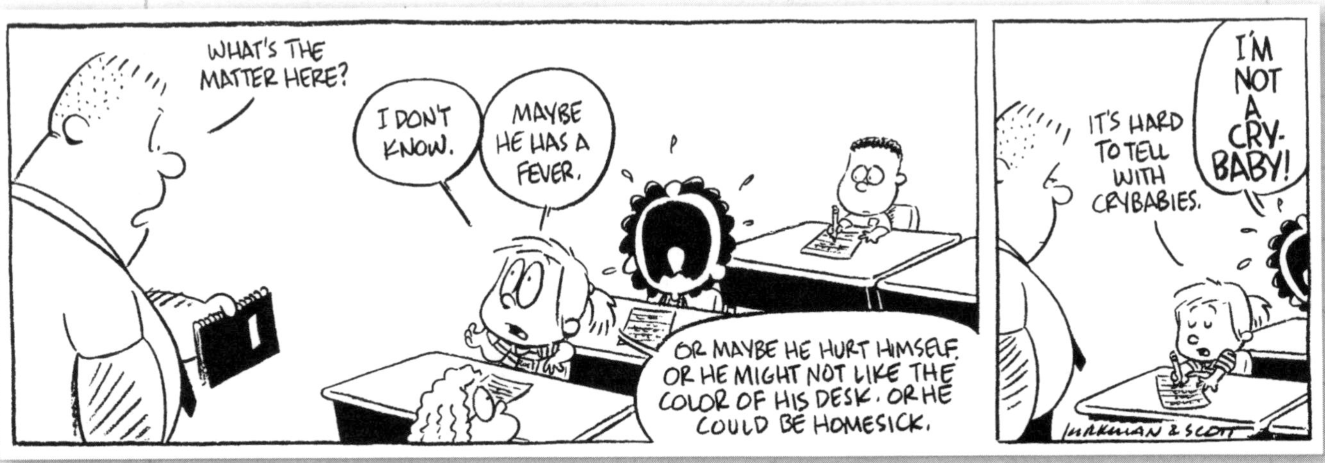
WHAT'S THE MATTER HERE?
I DON'T KNOW.
MAYBE HE HAS A FEVER.
OR MAYBE HE HURT HIMSELF. OR HE MIGHT NOT LIKE THE COLOR OF HIS DESK. OR HE COULD BE HOMESICK.
IT'S HARD TO TELL WITH CRYBABIES.
I'M NOT A CRY-BABY!
KIRKMAN & SCOTT

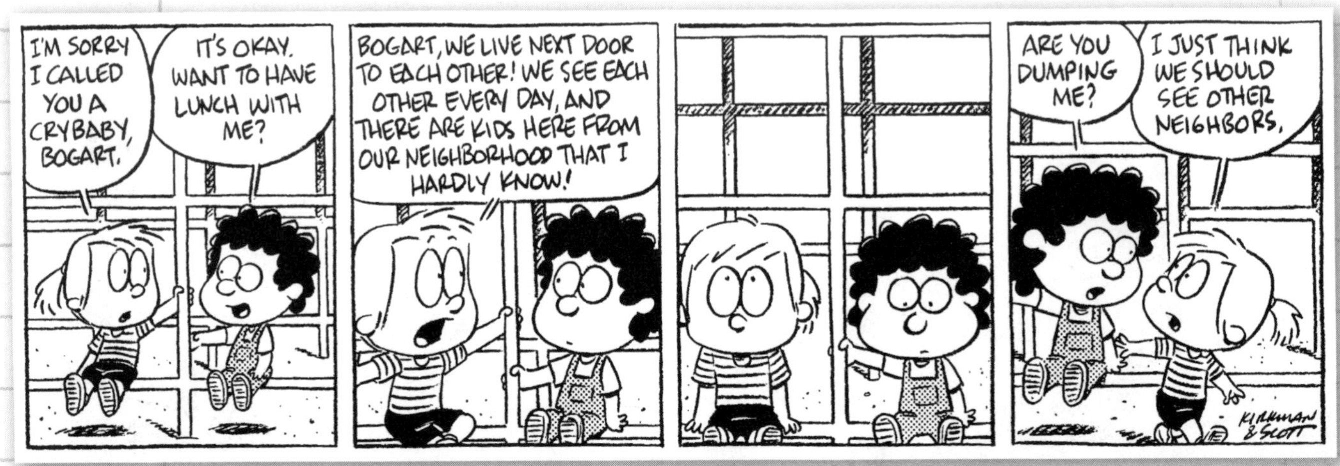
I'M SORRY I CALLED YOU A CRYBABY, BOGART.
IT'S OKAY. WANT TO HAVE LUNCH WITH ME?
BOGART, WE LIVE NEXT DOOR TO EACH OTHER! WE SEE EACH OTHER EVERY DAY, AND THERE ARE KIDS HERE FROM OUR NEIGHBORHOOD THAT I HARDLY KNOW!
ARE YOU DUMPING ME?
I JUST THINK WE SHOULD SEE OTHER NEIGHBORS.
KIRKMAN & SCOTT

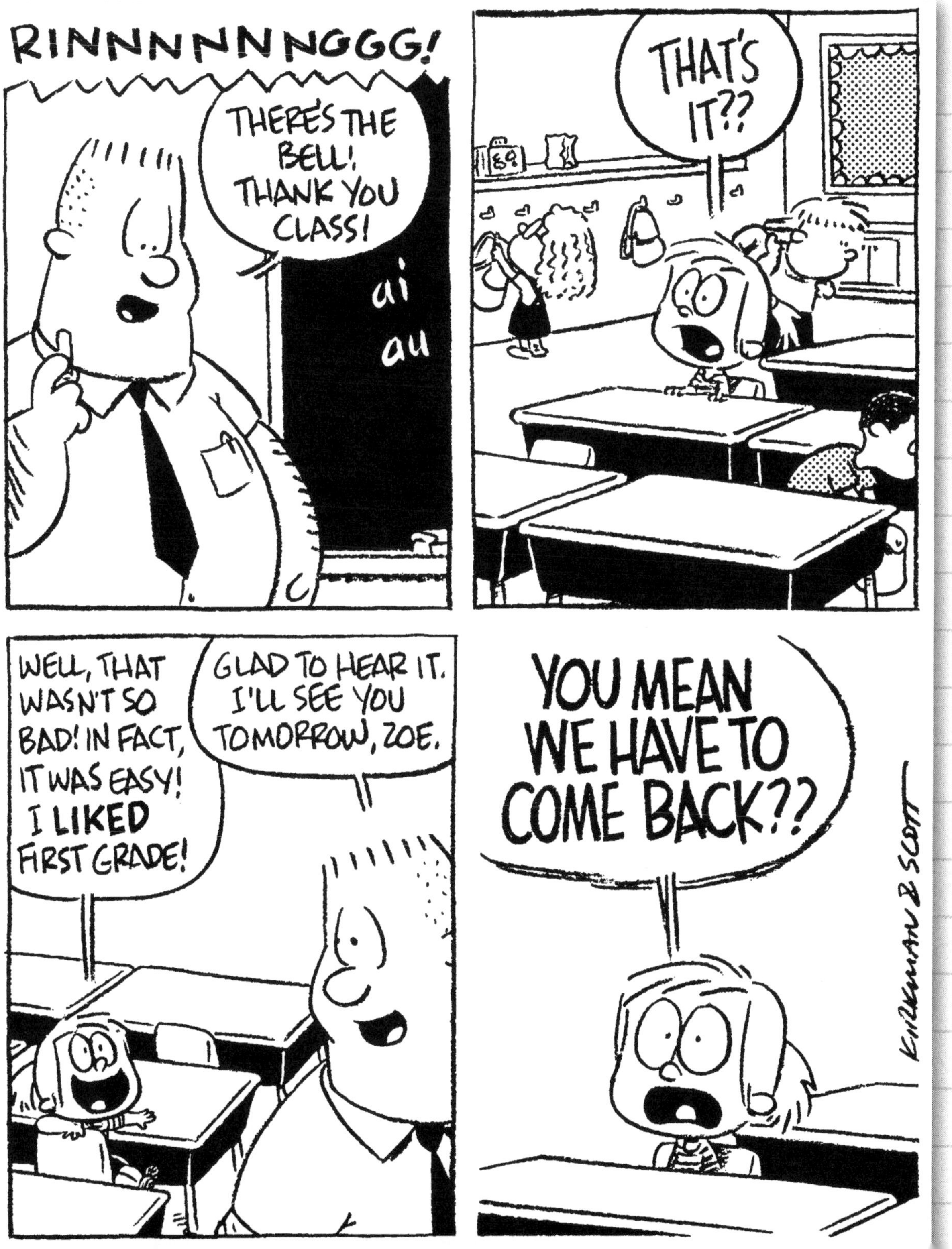
RINNNNNNNGGG!
THERE'S THE BELL! THANK YOU CLASS!
ai
au
THAT'S IT??
WELL, THAT WASN'T SO BAD! IN FACT, IT WAS EASY! I LIKED FIRST GRADE!
GLAD TO HEAR IT. I'LL SEE YOU TOMORROW, ZOE.
YOU MEAN WE HAVE TO COME BACK??
KIRKMAN & SCOTT

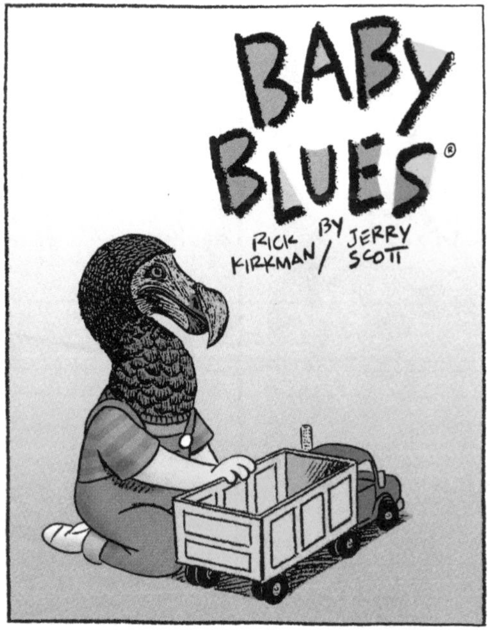
BABY BLUES®
BY RICK KIRKMAN / JERRY SCOTT

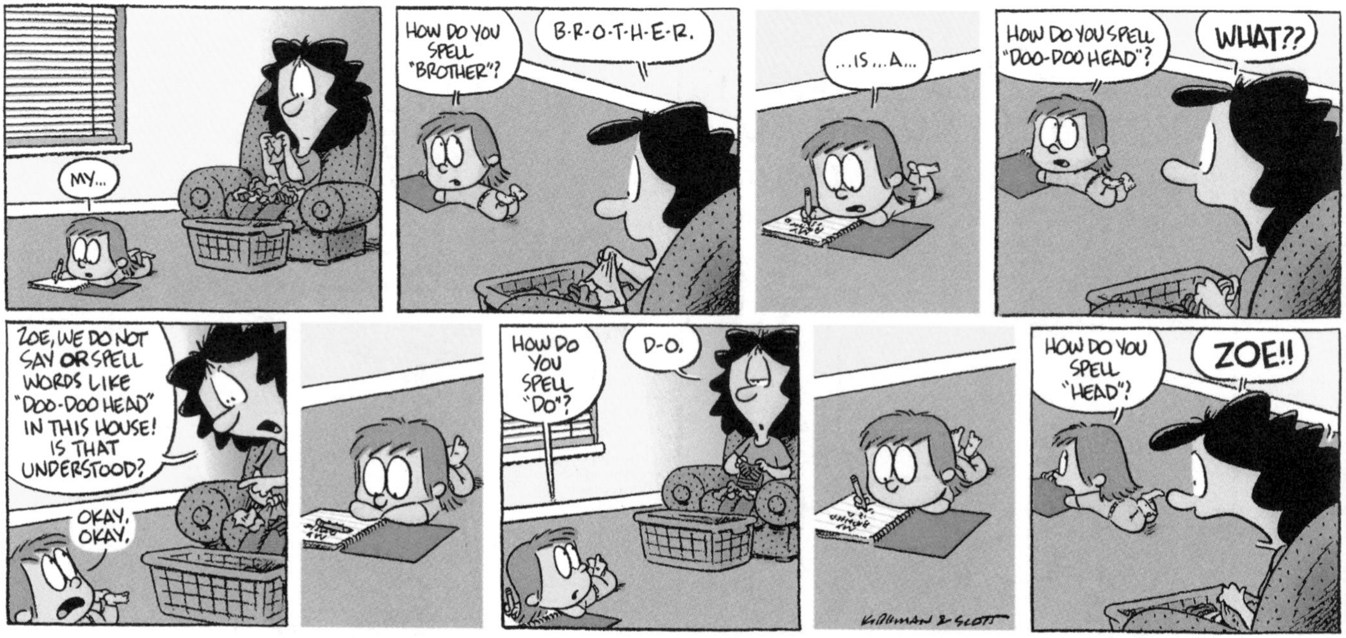
MY...
HOW DO YOU SPELL "BROTHER"?
B-R-O-T-H-E-R.
...IS...A...
HOW DO YOU SPELL "DOO-DOO HEAD"?
WHAT??
ZOE, WE DO NOT SAY OR SPELL WORDS LIKE "DOO-DOO HEAD" IN THIS HOUSE! IS THAT UNDERSTOOD?
OKAY, OKAY.
HOW DO YOU SPELL "DO"?
D-O.
HOW DO YOU SPELL "HEAD"?
ZOE!!
KIRKMAN & SCOTT

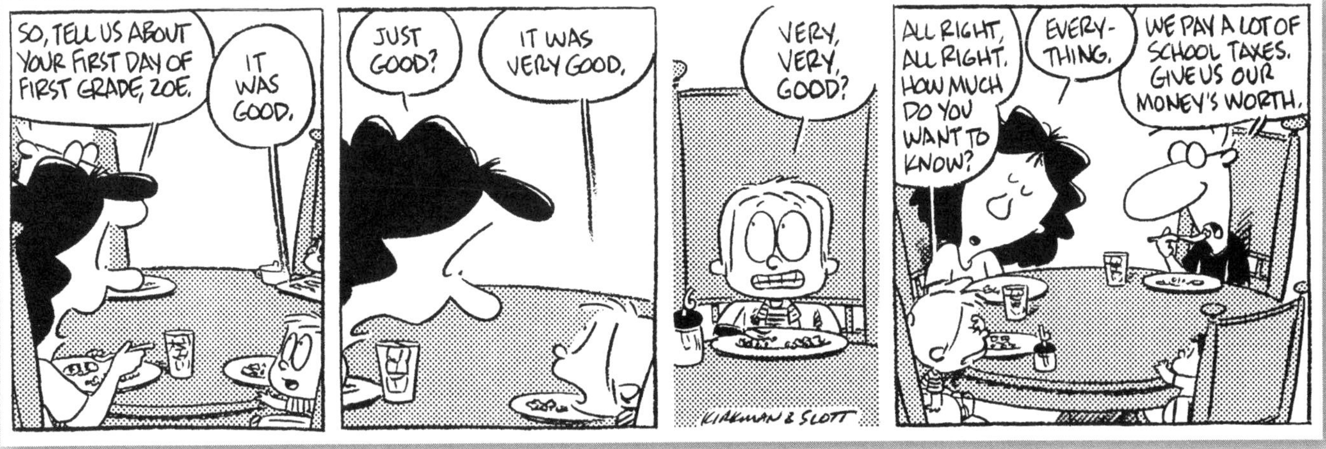
SO, TELL US ABOUT YOUR FIRST DAY OF FIRST GRADE, ZOE.
IT WAS GOOD.
JUST GOOD?
IT WAS VERY GOOD.
VERY, VERY, GOOD?
KIRKMAN & SCOTT
ALL RIGHT, ALL RIGHT. HOW MUCH DO YOU WANT TO KNOW?
EVERY-THING.
WE PAY A LOT OF SCHOOL TAXES. GIVE US OUR MONEY'S WORTH.

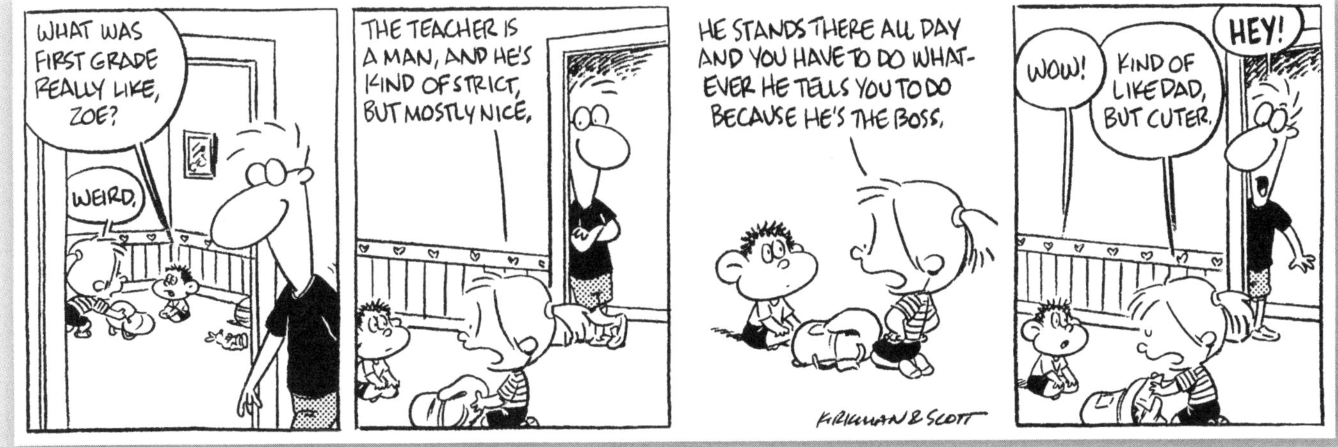
WHAT WAS FIRST GRADE REALLY LIKE, ZOE?
WEIRD.
THE TEACHER IS A MAN, AND HE'S KIND OF STRICT, BUT MOSTLY NICE.
HE STANDS THERE ALL DAY AND YOU HAVE TO DO WHAT-EVER HE TELLS YOU TO DO BECAUSE HE'S THE BOSS.
KIRKMAN & SCOTT
WOW!
KIND OF LIKE DAD, BUT CUTER.
HEY!

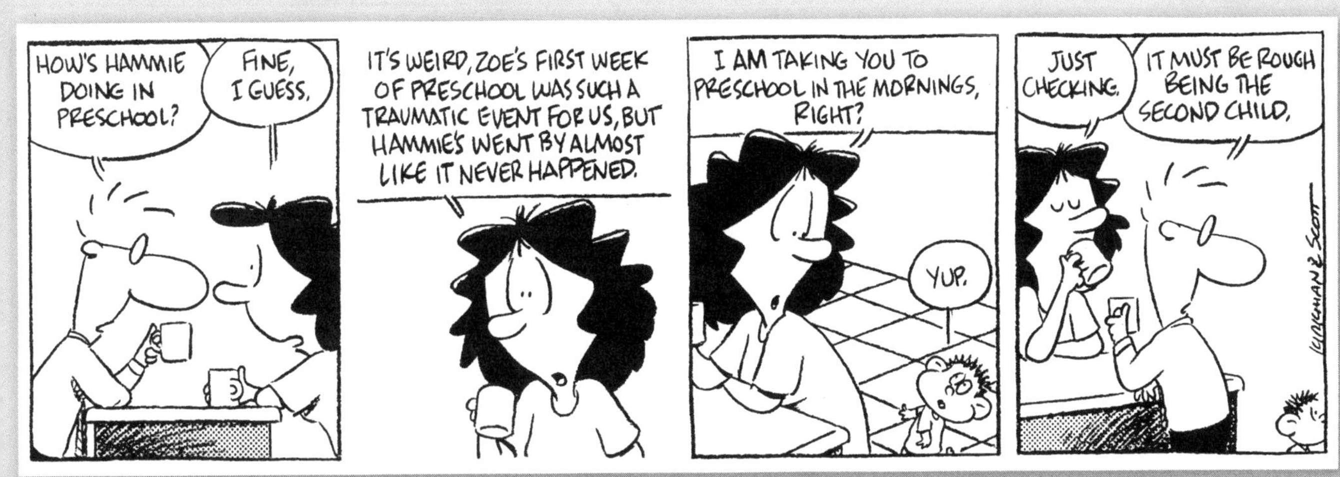
HOW'S HAMMIE DOING IN PRESCHOOL?
FINE, I GUESS.
IT'S WEIRD, ZOE'S FIRST WEEK OF PRESCHOOL WAS SUCH A TRAUMATIC EVENT FOR US, BUT HAMMIE'S WENT BY ALMOST LIKE IT NEVER HAPPENED.
I AM TAKING YOU TO PRESCHOOL IN THE MORNINGS, RIGHT?
YUP.
JUST CHECKING.
IT MUST BE ROUGH BEING THE SECOND CHILD.
KIRKMAN & SCOTT

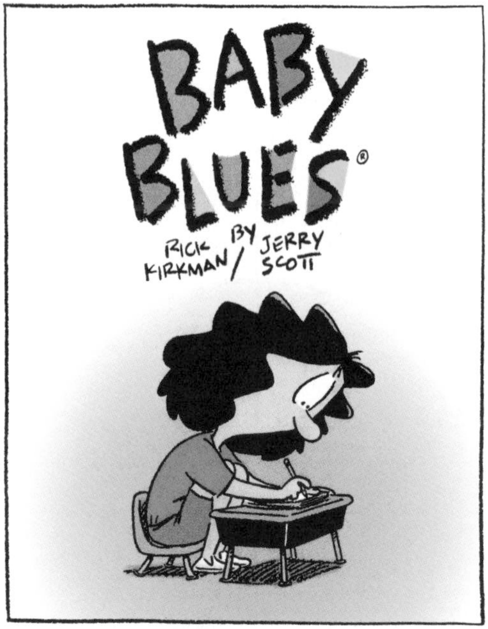
BABY BLUES®
BY
RICK KIRKMAN / JERRY SCOTT

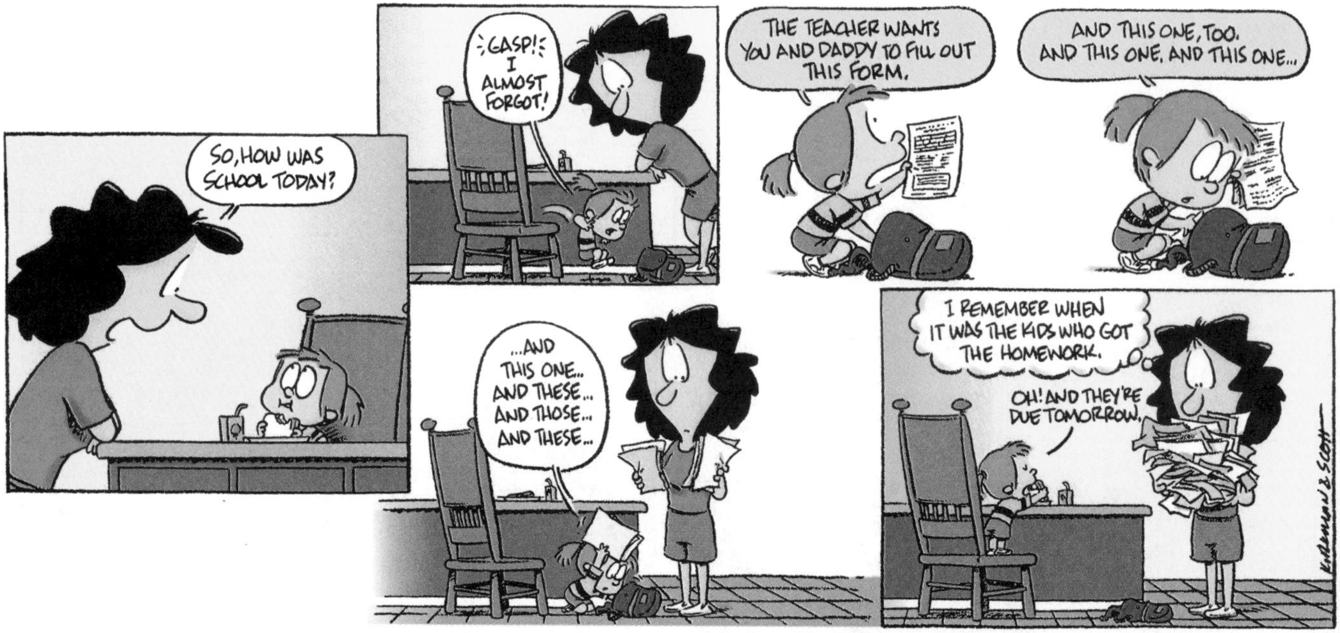
SO, HOW WAS SCHOOL TODAY?
GASP! I ALMOST FORGOT!
THE TEACHER WANTS YOU AND DADDY TO FILL OUT THIS FORM.
AND THIS ONE, TOO. AND THIS ONE. AND THIS ONE...
...AND THIS ONE... AND THESE... AND THOSE... AND THESE...
I REMEMBER WHEN IT WAS THE KIDS WHO GOT THE HOMEWORK.
OH! AND THEY'RE DUE TOMORROW.
KIRKMAN & SCOTT

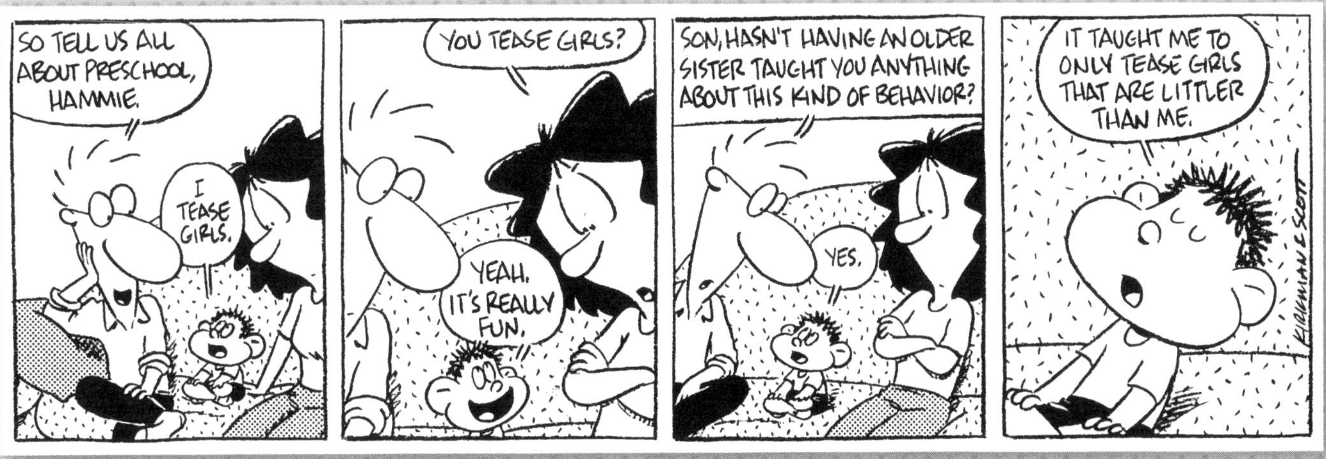
SO TELL US ALL ABOUT PRESCHOOL, HAMMIE.
I TEASE GIRLS.
YOU TEASE GIRLS?
YEAH. IT'S REALLY FUN.
SON, HASN'T HAVING AN OLDER SISTER TAUGHT YOU ANYTHING ABOUT THIS KIND OF BEHAVIOR?
YES.
IT TAUGHT ME TO ONLY TEASE GIRLS THAT ARE LITTLER THAN ME.
KIRKMAN & SCOTT

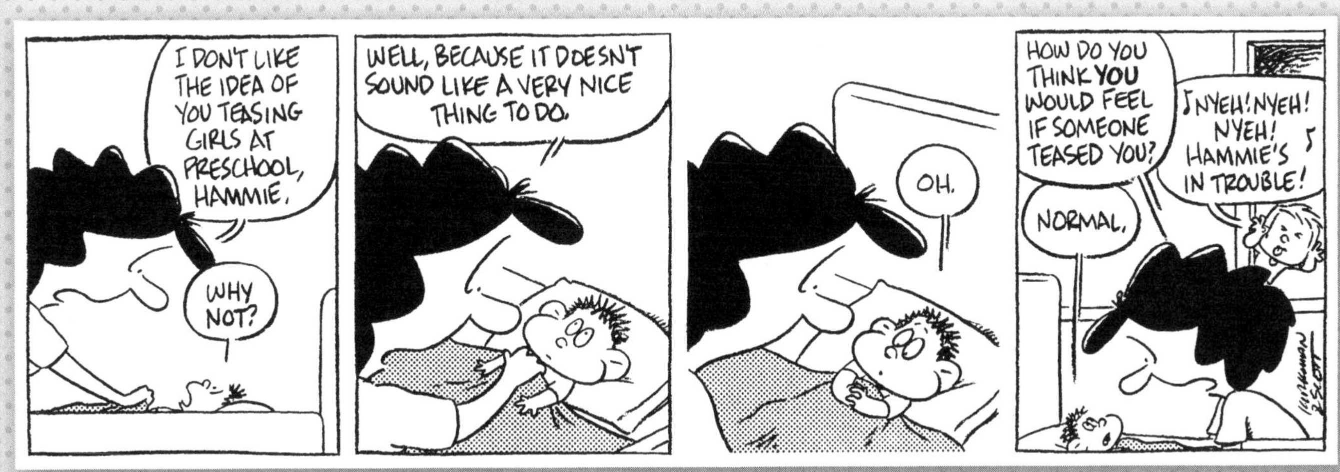
I DON'T LIKE THE IDEA OF YOU TEASING GIRLS AT PRESCHOOL, HAMMIE.
WHY NOT?
WELL, BECAUSE IT DOESN'T SOUND LIKE A VERY NICE THING TO DO.
OH.
HOW DO YOU THINK **YOU** WOULD FEEL IF SOMEONE TEASED YOU?
NORMAL.
♪ NYEH! NYEH! NYEH! HAMMIE'S IN TROUBLE! ♪
KIRKMAN & SCOTT

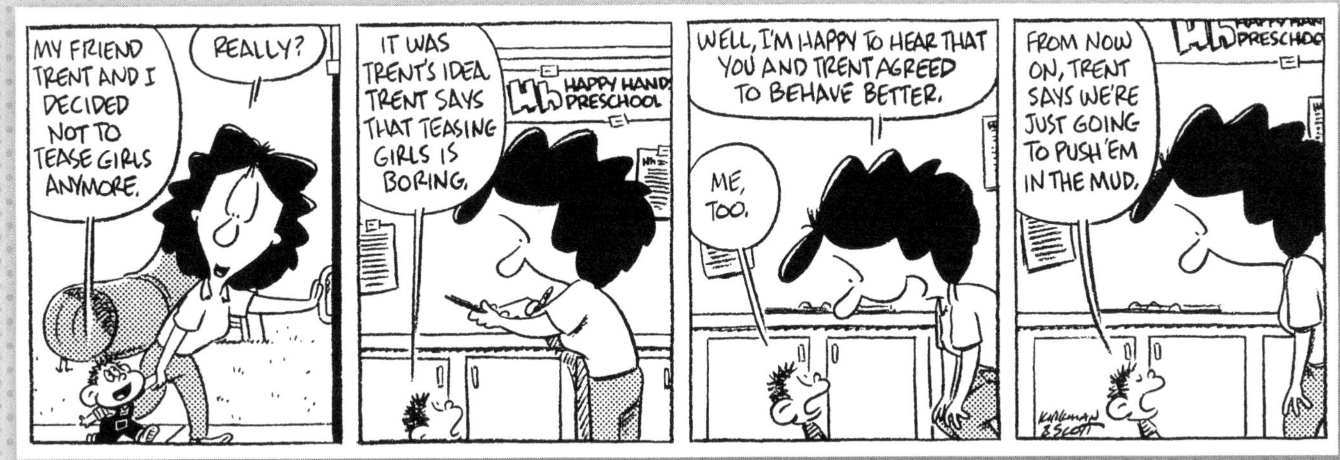
MY FRIEND TRENT AND I DECIDED NOT TO TEASE GIRLS ANYMORE.
REALLY?
IT WAS TRENT'S IDEA. TRENT SAYS THAT TEASING GIRLS IS BORING.
HAPPY HAND PRESCHOOL
WELL, I'M HAPPY TO HEAR THAT YOU AND TRENT AGREED TO BEHAVE BETTER.
ME, TOO.
FROM NOW ON, TRENT SAYS WE'RE JUST GOING TO PUSH 'EM IN THE MUD.
KIRKMAN & SCOTT

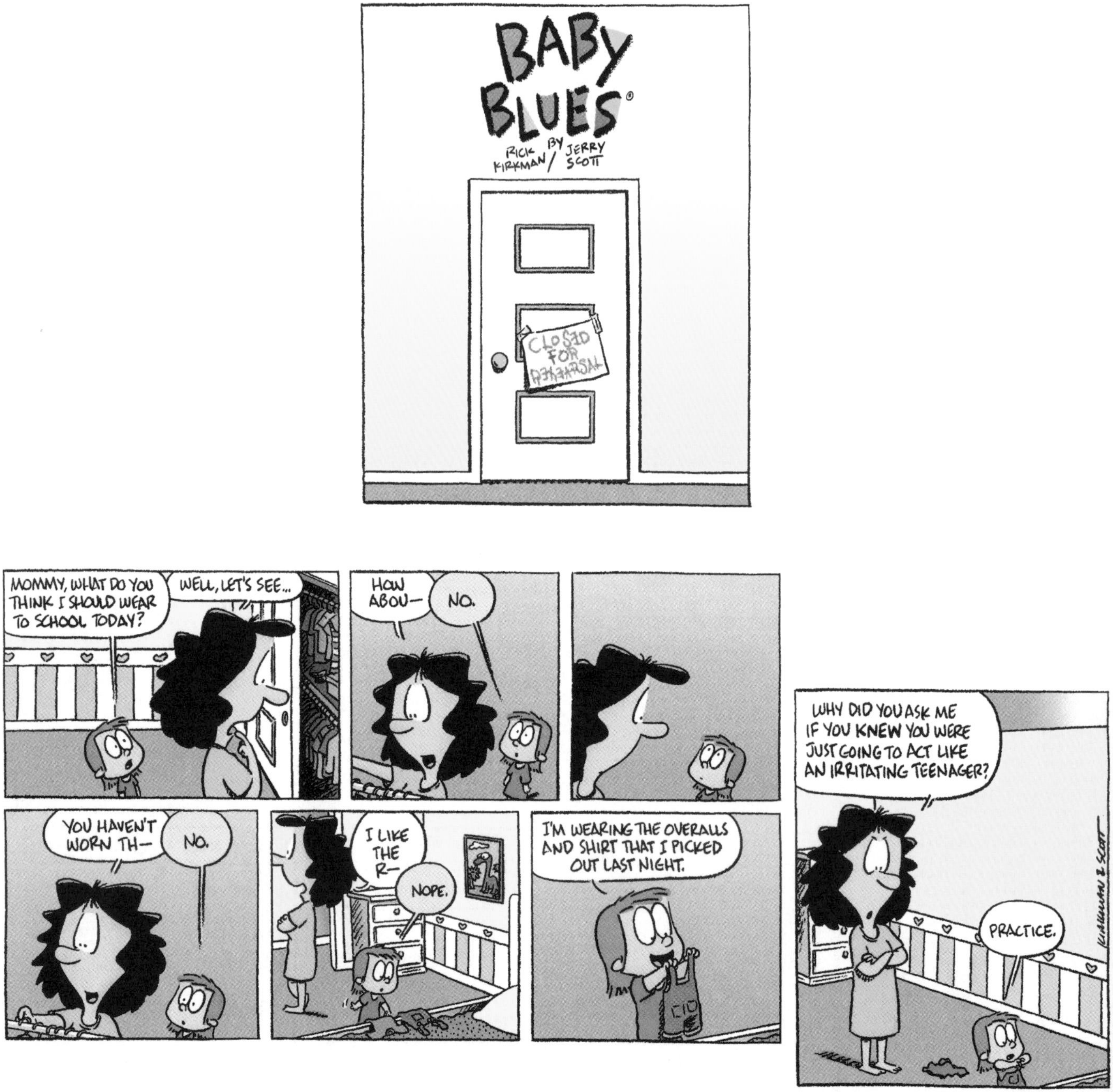
BABY BLUES®
BY RICK KIRKMAN / JERRY SCOTT
CLOSED FOR
MOMMY, WHAT DO YOU THINK I SHOULD WEAR TO SCHOOL TODAY?
WELL, LET'S SEE...
HOW ABOU—
NO.
YOU HAVEN'T WORN TH—
NO.
I LIKE THE R—
NOPE.
I'M WEARING THE OVERALLS AND SHIRT THAT I PICKED OUT LAST NIGHT.
WHY DID YOU ASK ME IF YOU KNEW YOU WERE JUST GOING TO ACT LIKE AN IRRITATING TEENAGER?
PRACTICE.
KIRKMAN & SCOTT

BABY BLUES®
BY RICK KIRKMAN / JERRY SCOTT

WHAT'S THE MATTER WITH OUR PUNKINS?
NOTHING. THEY'RE JUST SHRIVELING UP.
WHY?
BECAUSE THEY'RE OLD. I LEARNED IT IN SCIENCE CLASS.
ALL THINGS GET MOOSHY AND DROOPY AND STINKY WHEN THEY GET OLD.
NO, THEY DON'T.
YES, THEY DO.
NO, THEY DON'T.
YES, THEY DO.
NO, THEY DON'T.
YES, THEY DO.
WHEW! I'M NOT AS YOUNG AS I USED TO BE!
PLOP!
MOOSH! MOOSH!
SNIFF! SNIFF!
OKAY. TELL ME SOME MORE STUFF YOU LEARNED IN SCIENCE CLASS!
KIRKMAN & SCOTT

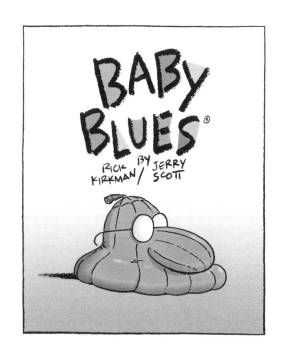

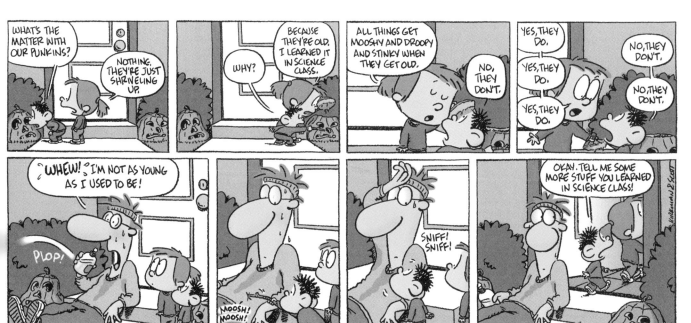

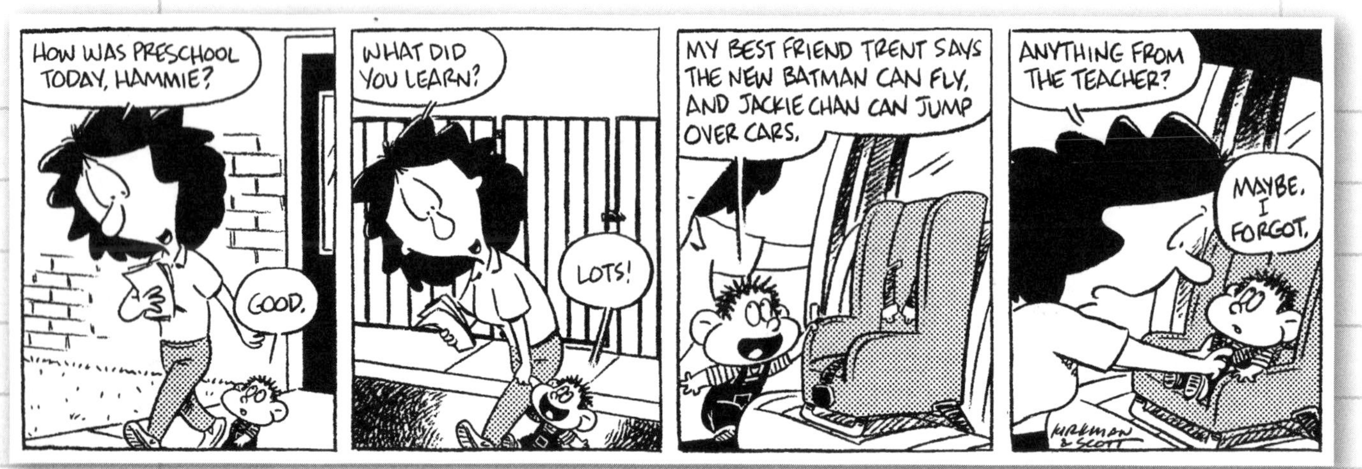
HOW WAS PRESCHOOL TODAY, HAMMIE?
GOOD.
WHAT DID YOU LEARN?
LOTS!
MY BEST FRIEND TRENT SAYS THE NEW BATMAN CAN FLY, AND JACKIE CHAN CAN JUMP OVER CARS.
ANYTHING FROM THE TEACHER?
MAYBE. I FORGOT.
KIRKMAN & SCOTT

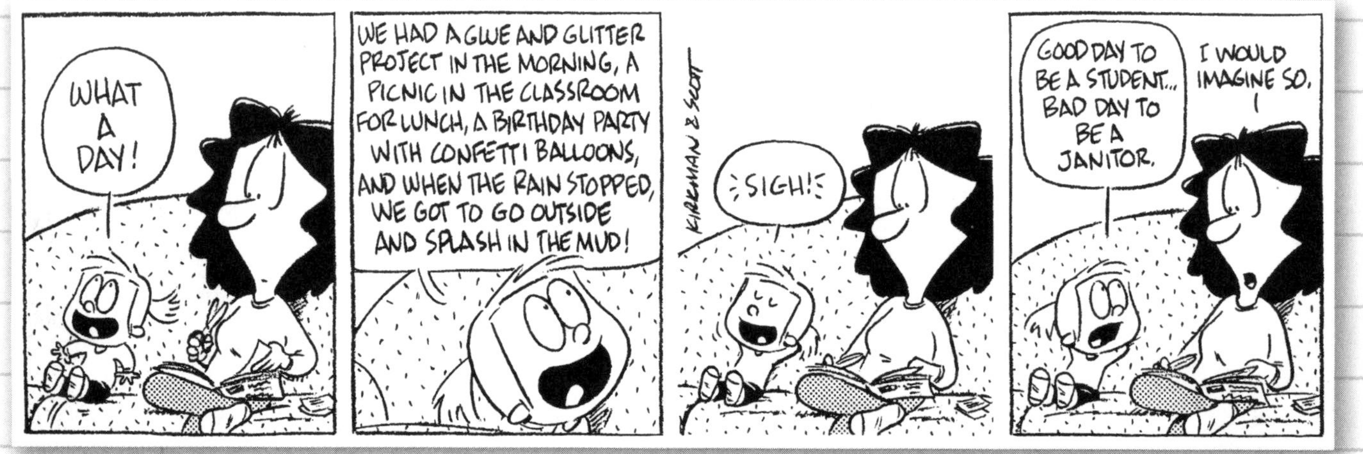
WHAT A DAY!
WE HAD A GLUE AND GLITTER PROJECT IN THE MORNING, A PICNIC IN THE CLASSROOM FOR LUNCH, A BIRTHDAY PARTY WITH CONFETTI BALLOONS, AND WHEN THE RAIN STOPPED, WE GOT TO GO OUTSIDE AND SPLASH IN THE MUD!
KIRKMAN & SCOTT
SIGH!
GOOD DAY TO BE A STUDENT... BAD DAY TO BE A JANITOR.
I WOULD IMAGINE SO.

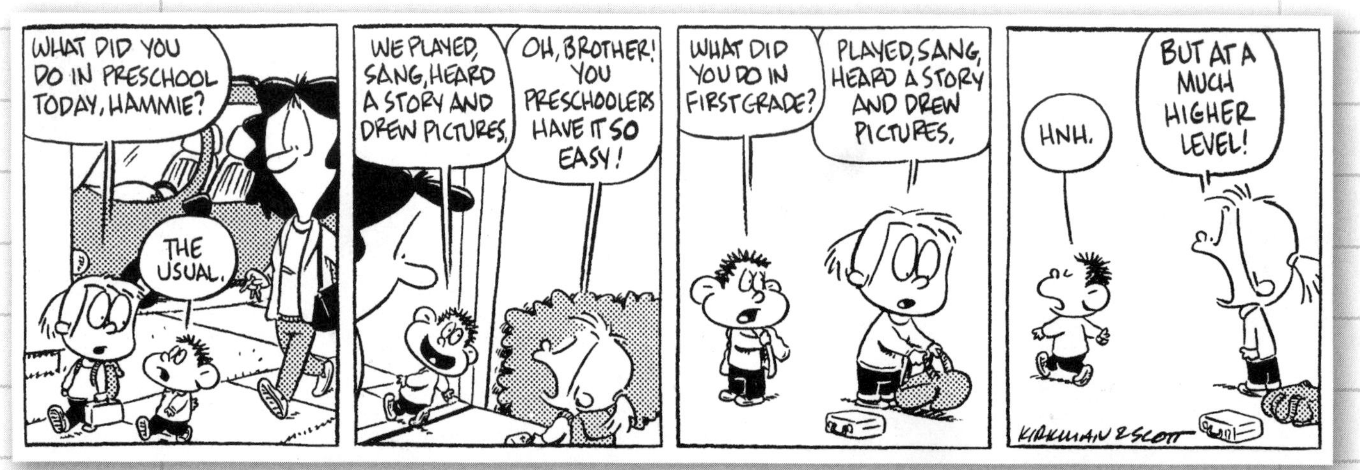
WHAT DID YOU DO IN PRESCHOOL TODAY, HAMMIE?
THE USUAL.
WE PLAYED, SANG, HEARD A STORY AND DREW PICTURES.
OH, BROTHER! YOU PRESCHOOLERS HAVE IT SO EASY!
WHAT DID YOU DO IN FIRST GRADE?
PLAYED, SANG, HEARD A STORY AND DREW PICTURES.
HNH.
BUT AT A MUCH HIGHER LEVEL!
KIRKMAN & SCOTT

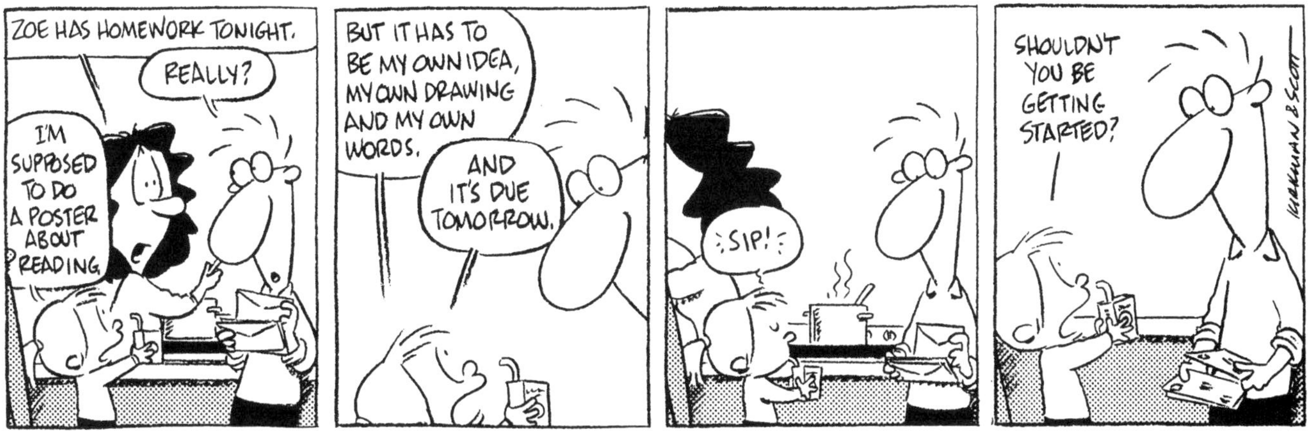
ZOE HAS HOMEWORK TONIGHT.
REALLY?
I'M SUPPOSED TO DO A POSTER ABOUT READING.
BUT IT HAS TO BE MY OWN IDEA, MY OWN DRAWING AND MY OWN WORDS.
AND IT'S DUE TOMORROW.
SIP!
SHOULDN'T YOU BE GETTING STARTED?
KIRKMAN & SCOTT

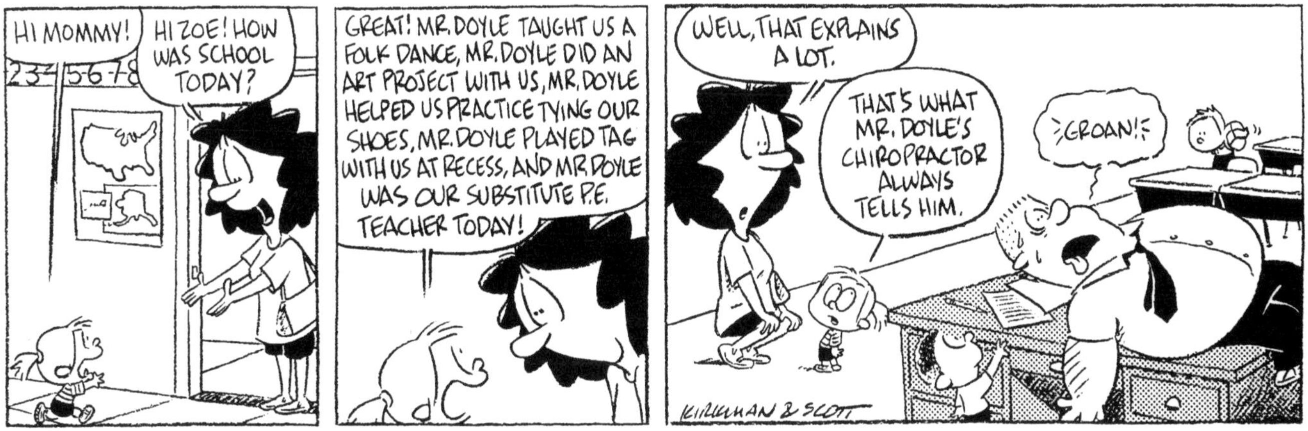
HI MOMMY!
HI ZOE! HOW WAS SCHOOL TODAY?
GREAT! MR. DOYLE TAUGHT US A FOLK DANCE, MR. DOYLE DID AN ART PROJECT WITH US, MR. DOYLE HELPED US PRACTICE TYING OUR SHOES, MR. DOYLE PLAYED TAG WITH US AT RECESS, AND MR. DOYLE WAS OUR SUBSTITUTE P.E. TEACHER TODAY!
WELL, THAT EXPLAINS A LOT.
THAT'S WHAT MR. DOYLE'S CHIROPRACTOR ALWAYS TELLS HIM.
GROAN!
KIRKMAN & SCOTT

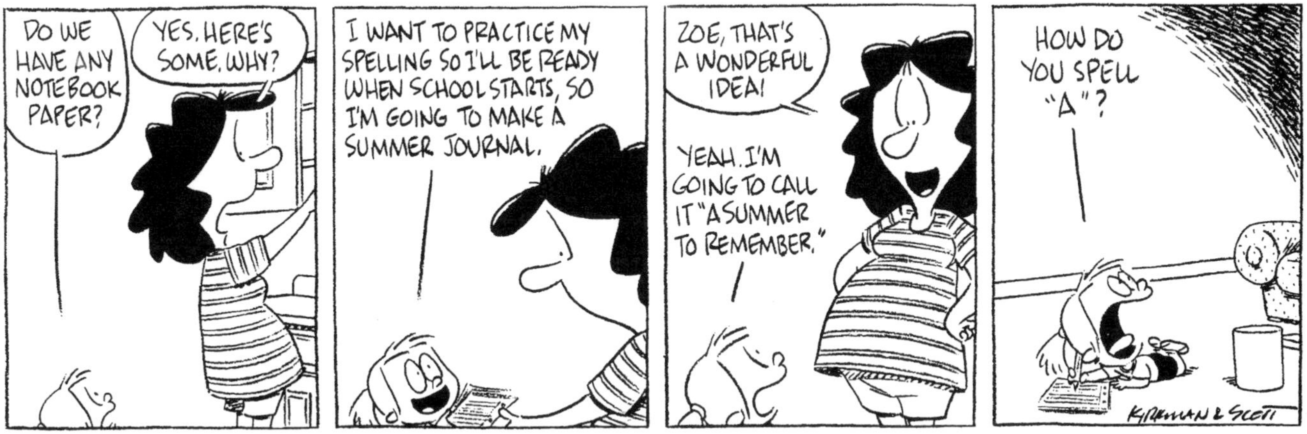
DO WE HAVE ANY NOTEBOOK PAPER?
YES. HERE'S SOME. WHY?
I WANT TO PRACTICE MY SPELLING SO I'LL BE READY WHEN SCHOOL STARTS, SO I'M GOING TO MAKE A SUMMER JOURNAL.
ZOE, THAT'S A WONDERFUL IDEA!
YEAH. I'M GOING TO CALL IT "A SUMMER TO REMEMBER."
HOW DO YOU SPELL "A"?
KIRKMAN & SCOTT

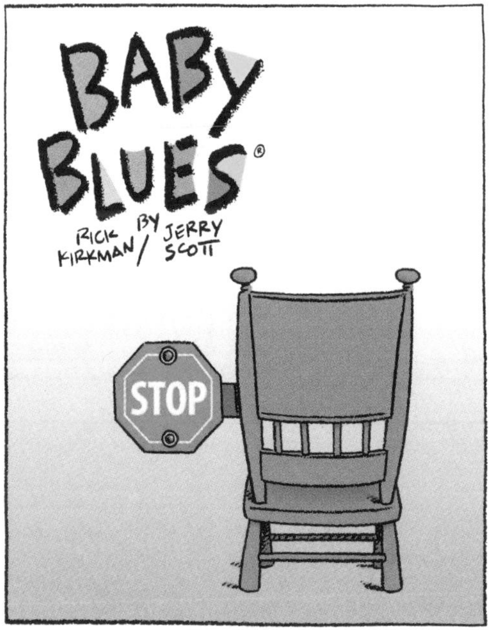
BABY BLUES®
BY RICK KIRKMAN / JERRY SCOTT
STOP

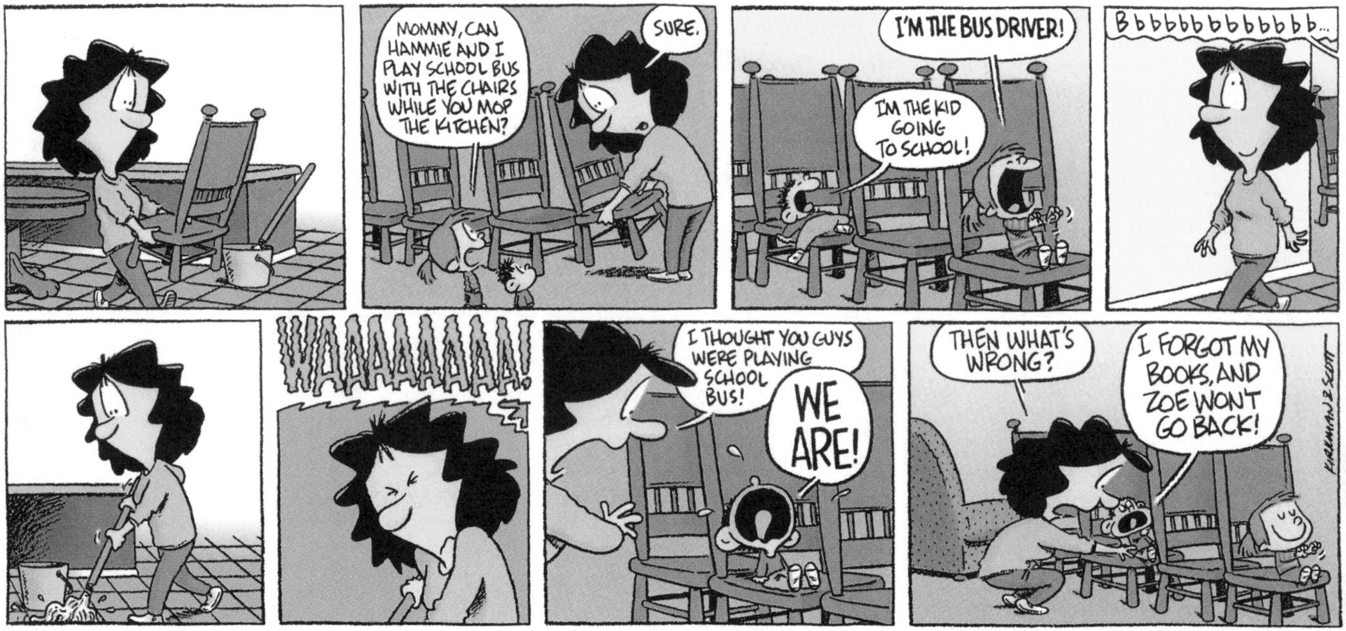
MOMMY, CAN HAMMIE AND I PLAY SCHOOL BUS WITH THE CHAIRS WHILE YOU MOP THE KITCHEN?
SURE.
I'M THE BUS DRIVER!
I'M THE KID GOING TO SCHOOL!
Bbbbbbbbbbbbb...
WAAAAAAAA!
I THOUGHT YOU GUYS WERE PLAYING SCHOOL BUS!
WE ARE!
THEN WHAT'S WRONG?
I FORGOT MY BOOKS, AND ZOE WON'T GO BACK!
KIRKMAN & SCOTT

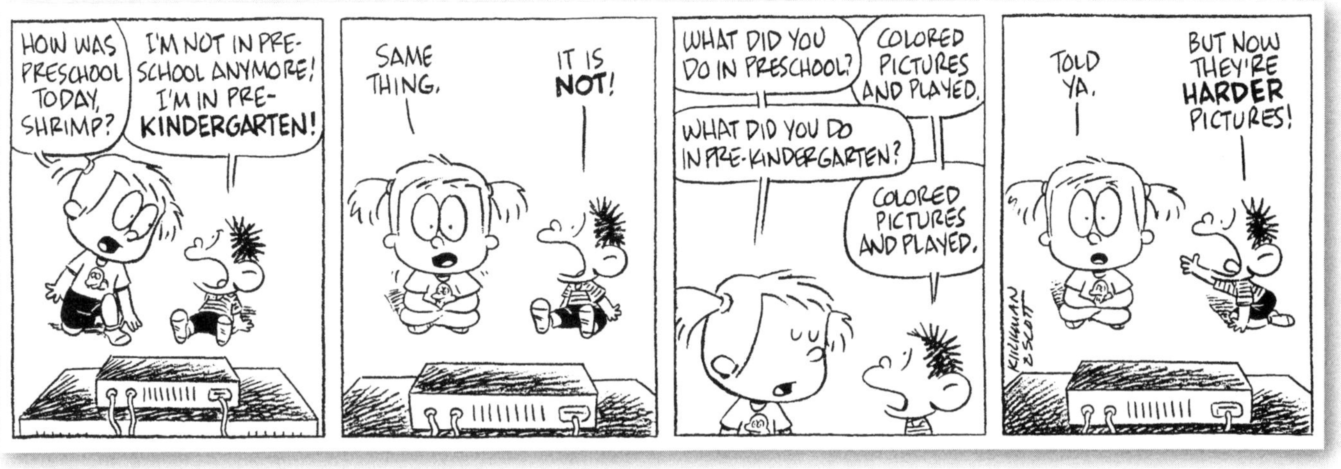
HOW WAS PRESCHOOL TODAY, SHRIMP?
I'M NOT IN PRE-SCHOOL ANYMORE! I'M IN PRE-**KINDERGARTEN!**
SAME THING.
IT IS **NOT**!
WHAT DID YOU DO IN PRESCHOOL?
COLORED PICTURES AND PLAYED.
WHAT DID YOU DO IN PRE-KINDERGARTEN?
COLORED PICTURES AND PLAYED.
TOLD YA.
BUT NOW THEY'RE **HARDER** PICTURES!
KIRKMAN & SCOTT

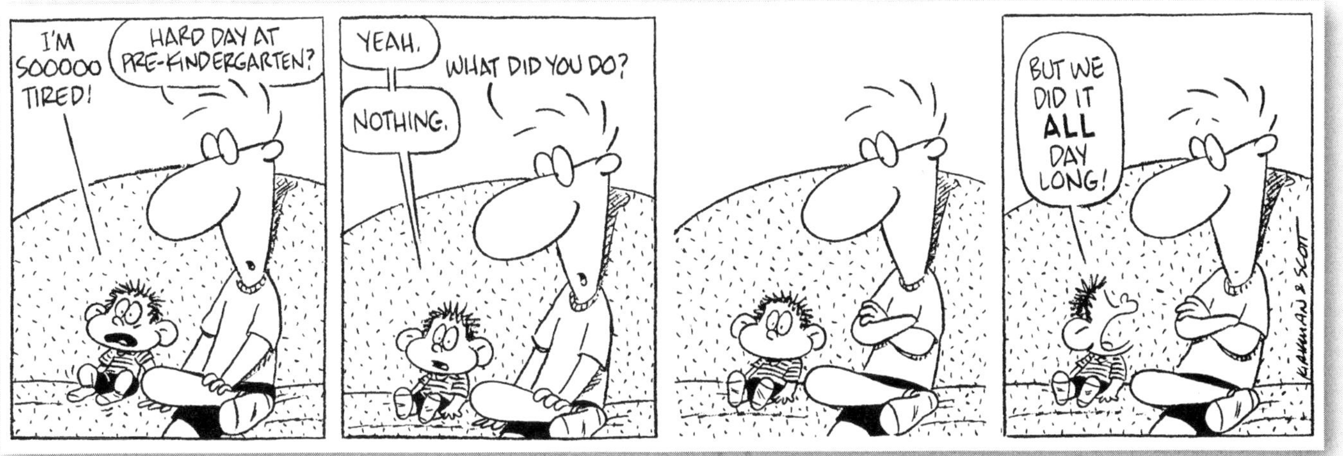
I'M SOOOOO TIRED!
HARD DAY AT PRE-KINDERGARTEN?
YEAH.
WHAT DID YOU DO?
NOTHING.
BUT WE DID IT **ALL** DAY LONG!
KIRKMAN & SCOTT

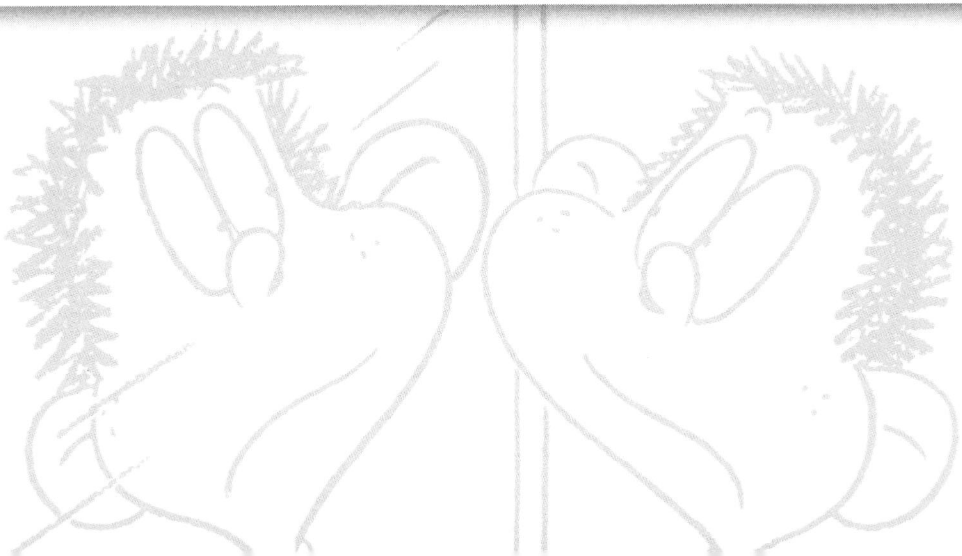

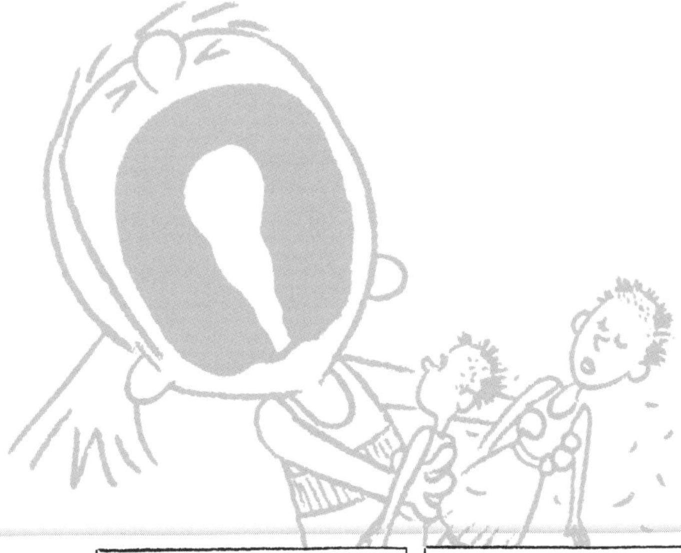

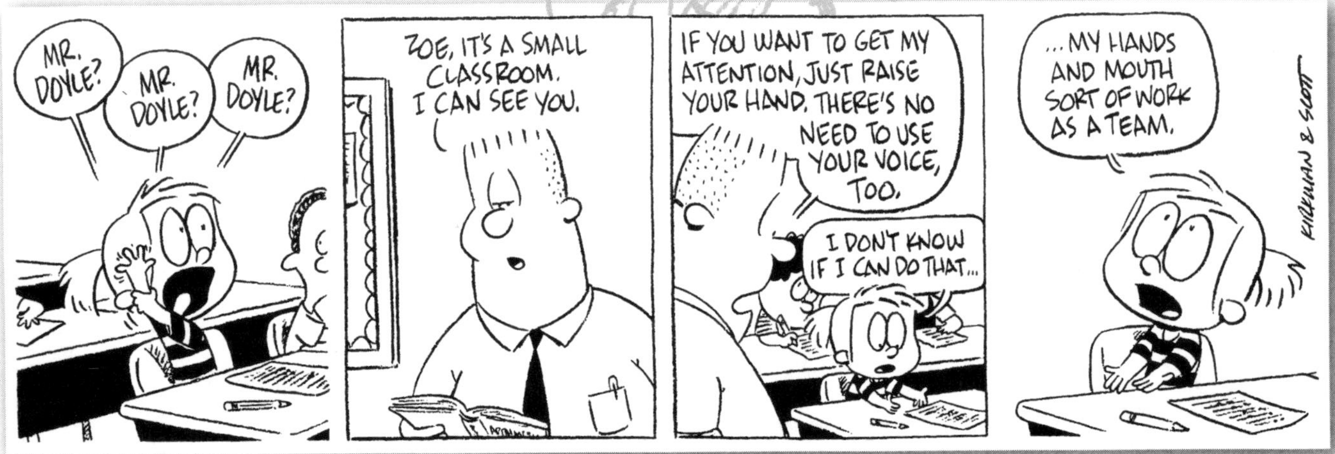

MR. DOYLE?
MR. DOYLE?
MR. DOYLE?
ZOE, IT'S A SMALL CLASSROOM. I CAN SEE YOU.
IF YOU WANT TO GET MY ATTENTION, JUST RAISE YOUR HAND. THERE'S NO NEED TO USE YOUR VOICE, TOO.
I DON'T KNOW IF I CAN DO THAT...
...MY HANDS AND MOUTH SORT OF WORK AS A TEAM.
KIRKMAN & SCOTT

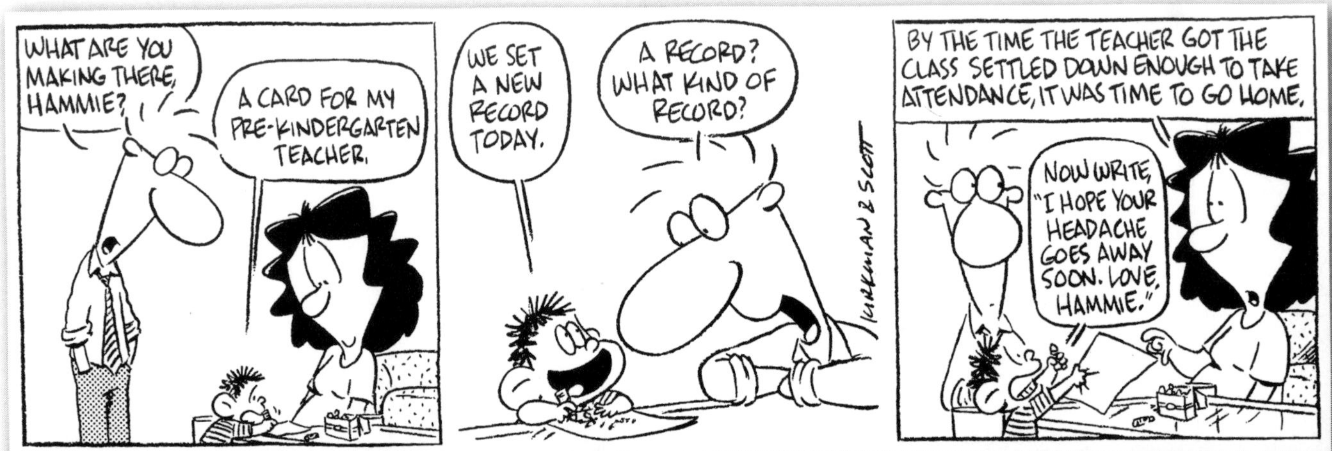

WHAT ARE YOU MAKING THERE, HAMMIE?
A CARD FOR MY PRE-KINDERGARTEN TEACHER.
WE SET A NEW RECORD TODAY.
A RECORD? WHAT KIND OF RECORD?
KIRKMAN & SCOTT
BY THE TIME THE TEACHER GOT THE CLASS SETTLED DOWN ENOUGH TO TAKE ATTENDANCE, IT WAS TIME TO GO HOME.
NOW WRITE, "I HOPE YOUR HEADACHE GOES AWAY SOON. LOVE, HAMMIE."

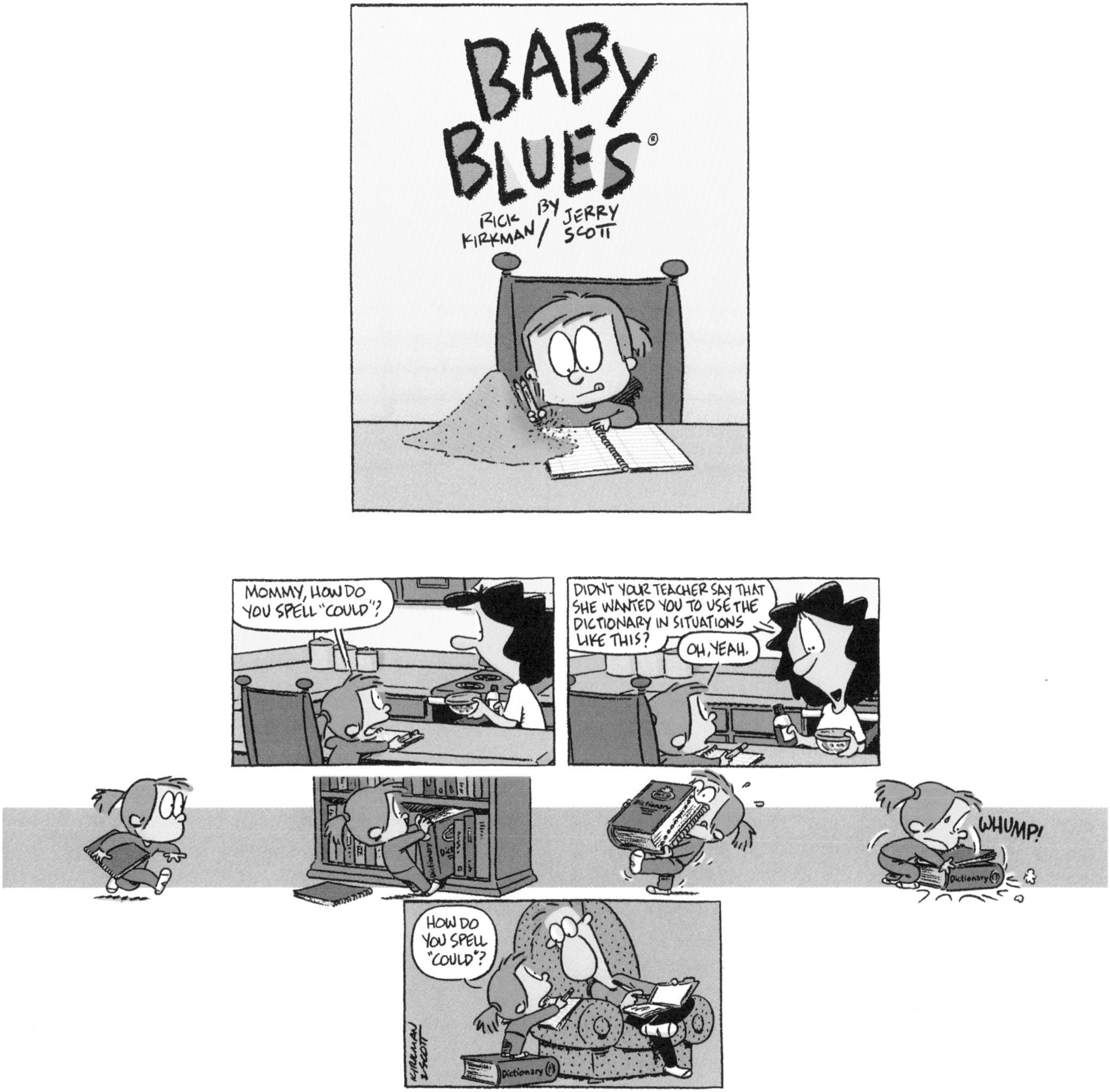
BABY BLUES®
BY RICK KIRKMAN / JERRY SCOTT
MOMMY, HOW DO YOU SPELL "COULD"?
DIDN'T YOUR TEACHER SAY THAT SHE WANTED YOU TO USE THE DICTIONARY IN SITUATIONS LIKE THIS?
OH, YEAH.
Dictionary
WHUMP!
HOW DO YOU SPELL "COULD"?
Dictionary

T-T-T-T
h-u-u-h-h

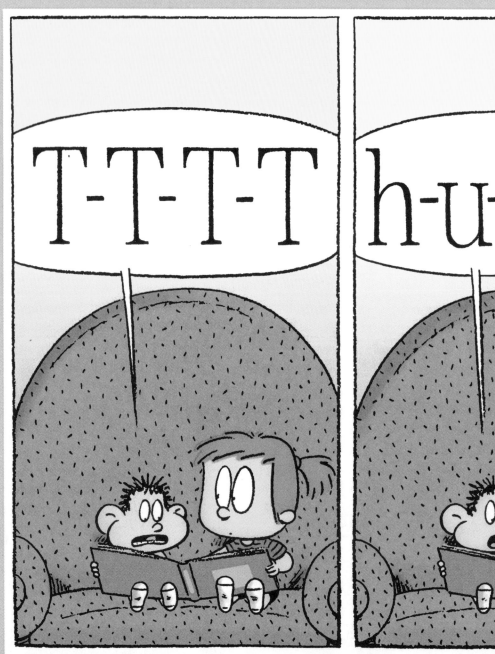

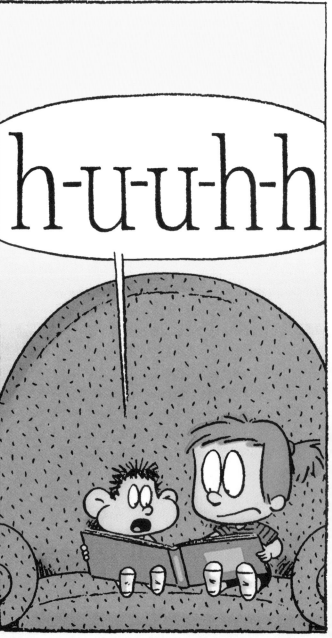

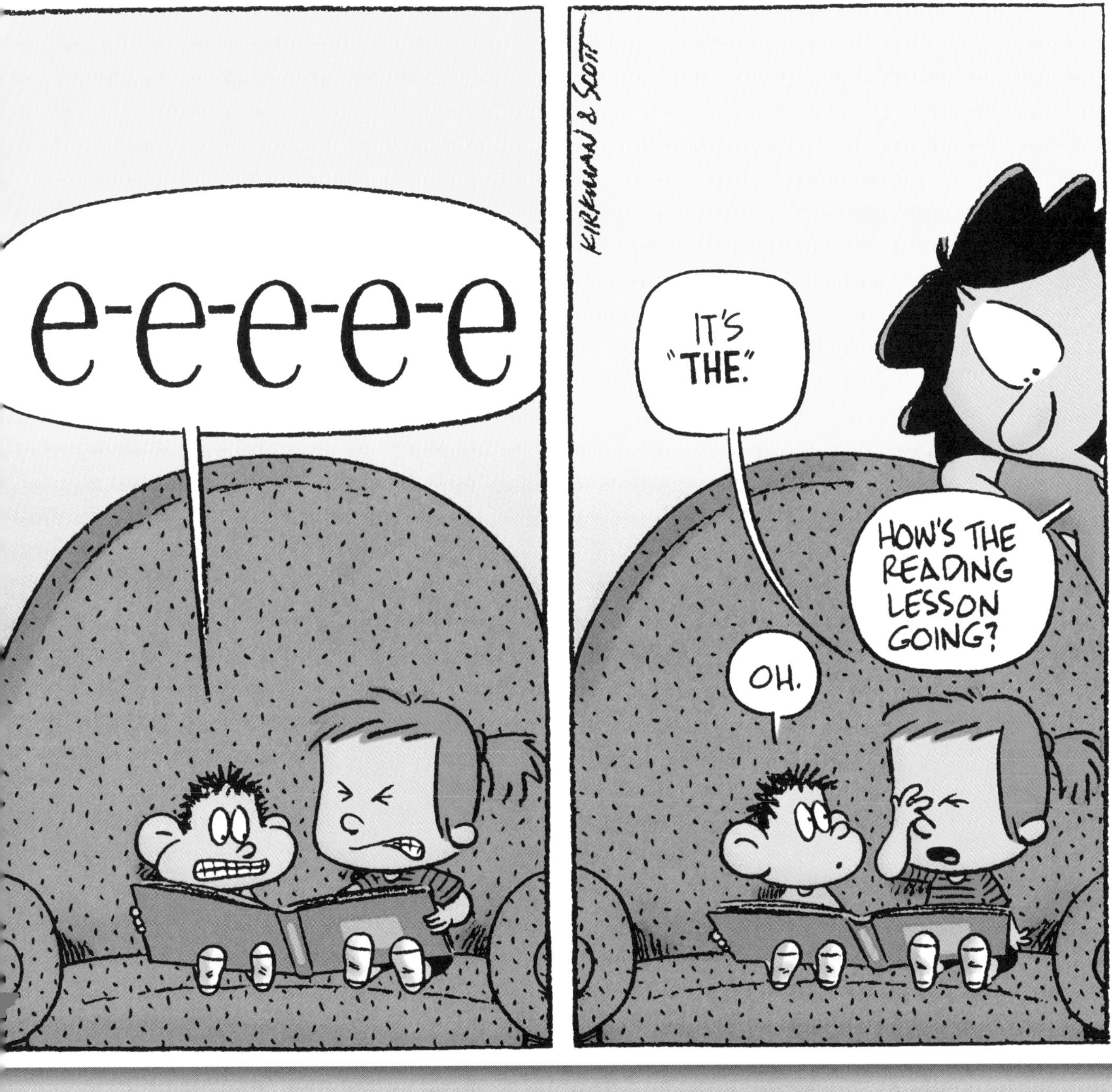

e-e-e-e-e
KIRKMAN & SCOTT
IT'S "THE."
HOW'S THE READING LESSON GOING?
OH.

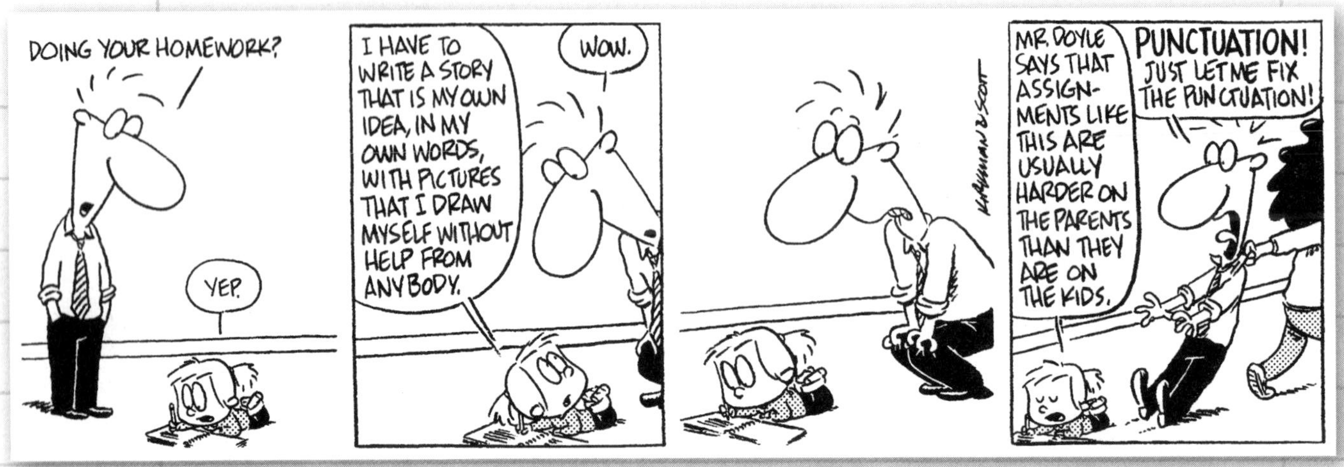
DOING YOUR HOMEWORK?
YEP.
I HAVE TO WRITE A STORY THAT IS MY OWN IDEA, IN MY OWN WORDS, WITH PICTURES THAT I DRAW MYSELF WITHOUT HELP FROM ANYBODY.
WOW.
MR. DOYLE SAYS THAT ASSIGN-MENTS LIKE THIS ARE USUALLY HARDER ON THE PARENTS THAN THEY ARE ON THE KIDS.
PUNCTUATION! JUST LET ME FIX THE PUNCTUATION!

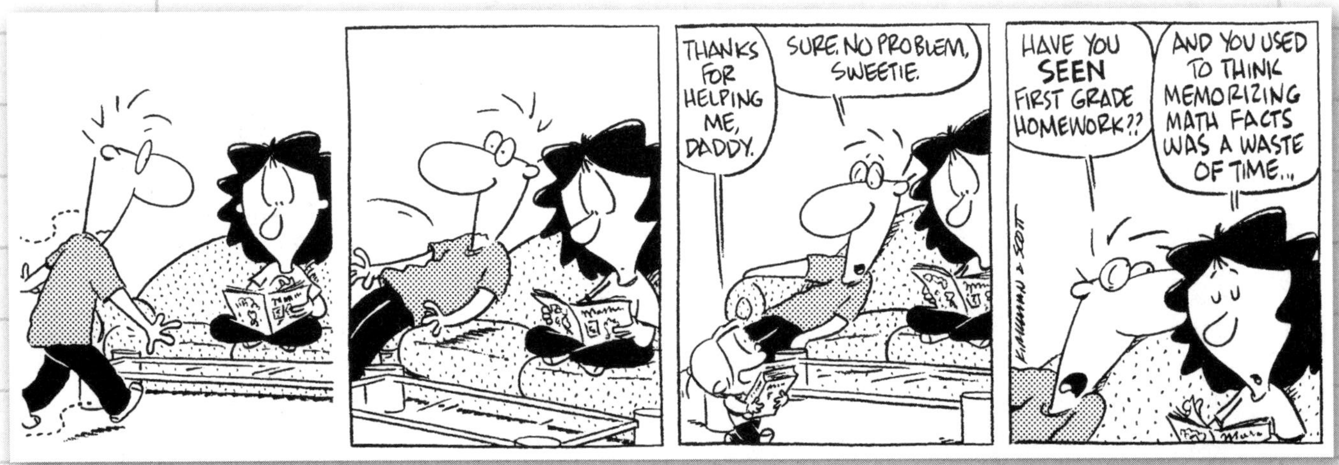
THANKS FOR HELPING ME, DADDY.
SURE. NO PROBLEM, SWEETIE.
HAVE YOU SEEN FIRST GRADE HOMEWORK??
AND YOU USED TO THINK MEMORIZING MATH FACTS WAS A WASTE OF TIME...

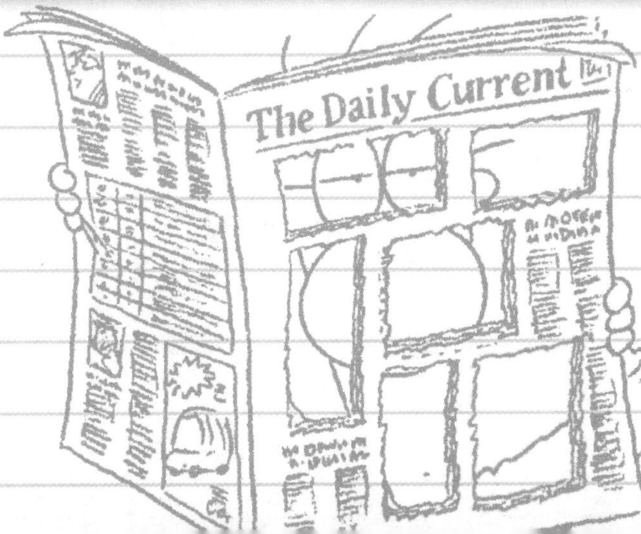
The Daily Current

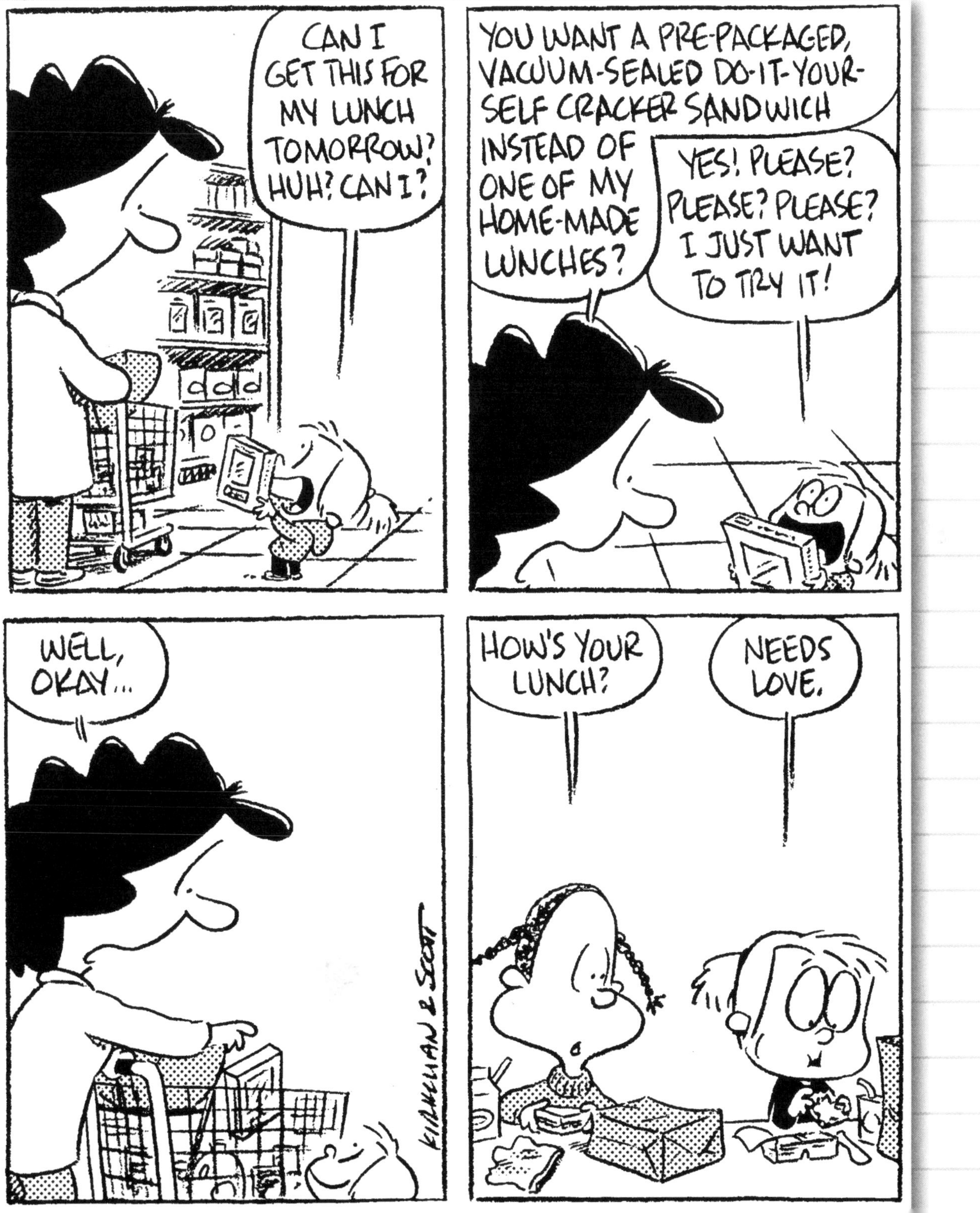
CAN I GET THIS FOR MY LUNCH TOMORROW? HUH? CAN I?
YOU WANT A PRE-PACKAGED, VACUUM-SEALED DO-IT-YOURSELF CRACKER SANDWICH INSTEAD OF ONE OF MY HOME-MADE LUNCHES?
YES! PLEASE? PLEASE? PLEASE? I JUST WANT TO TRY IT!
WELL, OKAY...
KIRKMAN & SCOTT
HOW'S YOUR LUNCH?
NEEDS LOVE.

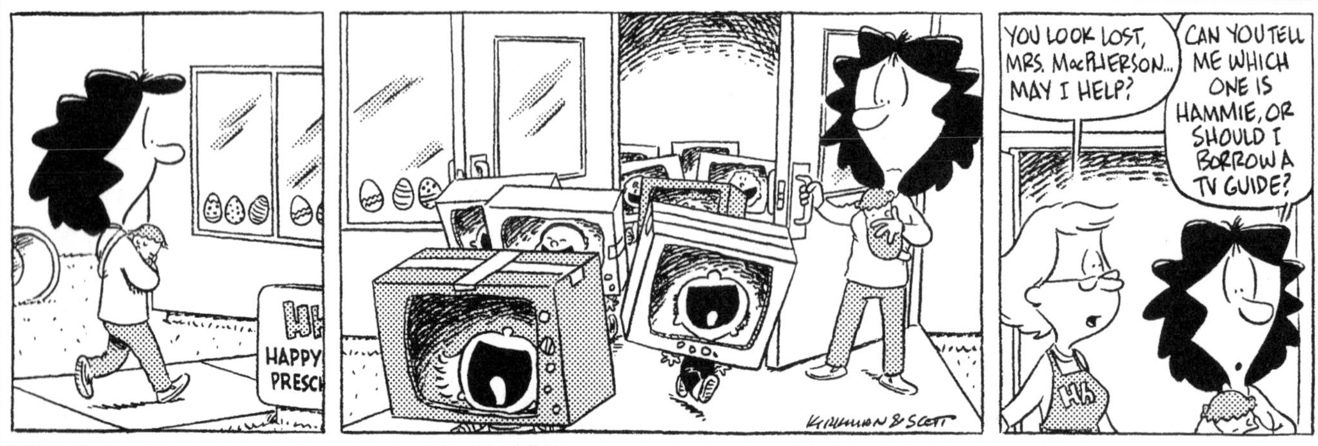
HAPPY
PRESCH
KIRKMAN & SCOTT
YOU LOOK LOST, MRS. MacPHERSON... MAY I HELP?
CAN YOU TELL ME WHICH ONE IS HAMMIE, OR SHOULD I BORROW A TV GUIDE?

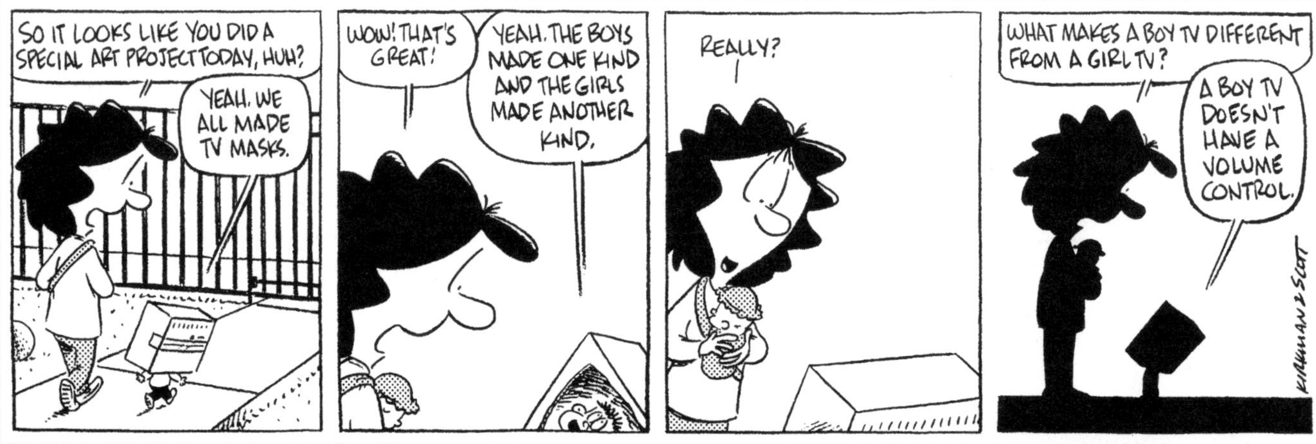
SO IT LOOKS LIKE YOU DID A SPECIAL ART PROJECT TODAY, HUH?
YEAH, WE ALL MADE TV MASKS.
WOW! THAT'S GREAT!
YEAH. THE BOYS MADE ONE KIND AND THE GIRLS MADE ANOTHER KIND.
REALLY?
WHAT MAKES A BOY TV DIFFERENT FROM A GIRL TV?
A BOY TV DOESN'T HAVE A VOLUME CONTROL.
KIRKMAN & SCOTT

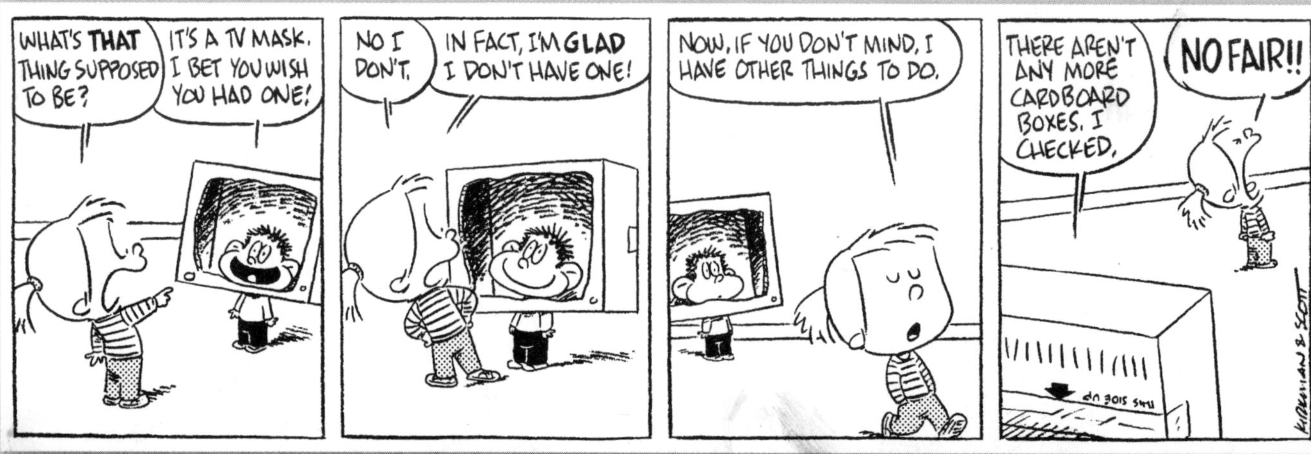
WHAT'S **THAT** THING SUPPOSED TO BE?
IT'S A TV MASK. I BET YOU WISH YOU HAD ONE!
NO I DON'T.
IN FACT, I'M **GLAD** I DON'T HAVE ONE!
NOW, IF YOU DON'T MIND, I HAVE OTHER THINGS TO DO.
THERE AREN'T ANY MORE CARDBOARD BOXES. I CHECKED.
NO FAIR!!
KIRKMAN & SCOTT

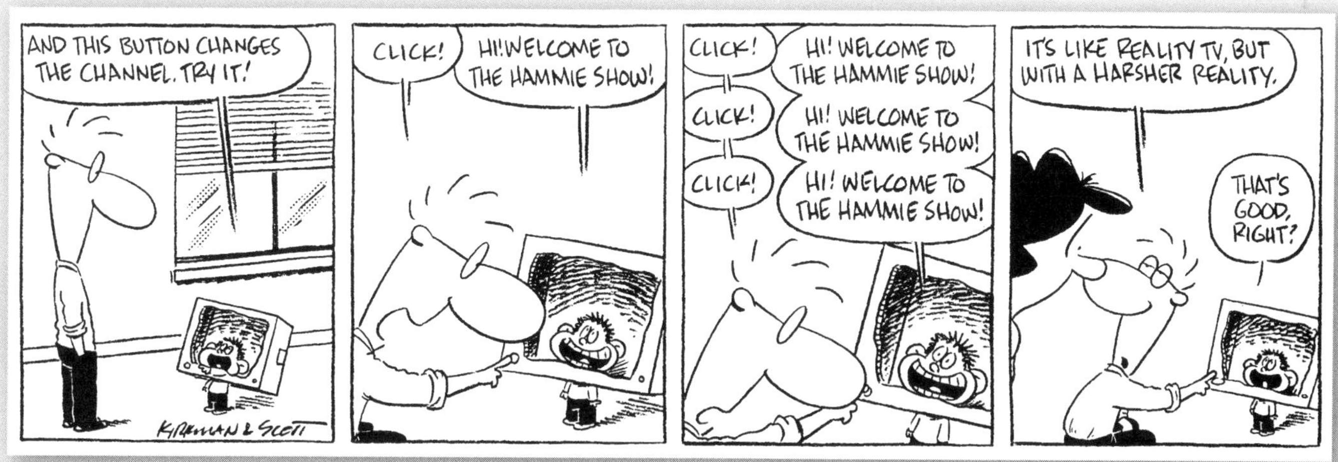
AND THIS BUTTON CHANGES THE CHANNEL. TRY IT!
KIRKMAN & SCOTT
CLICK!
HI! WELCOME TO THE HAMMIE SHOW!
CLICK!
HI! WELCOME TO THE HAMMIE SHOW!
CLICK!
HI! WELCOME TO THE HAMMIE SHOW!
CLICK!
HI! WELCOME TO THE HAMMIE SHOW!
IT'S LIKE REALITY TV, BUT WITH A HARSHER REALITY.
THAT'S GOOD, RIGHT?

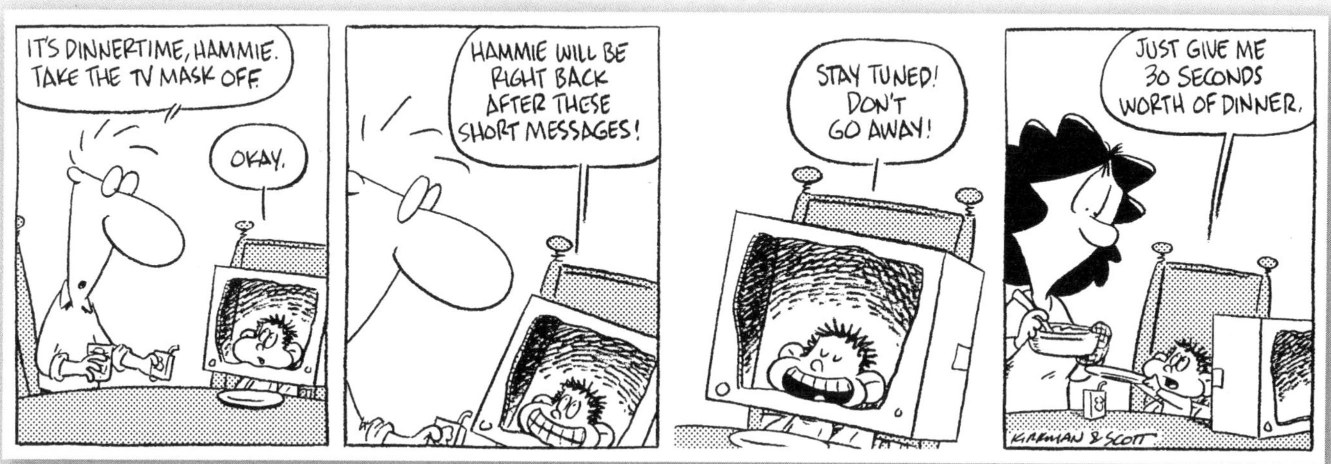
IT'S DINNERTIME, HAMMIE. TAKE THE TV MASK OFF.
OKAY.
HAMMIE WILL BE RIGHT BACK AFTER THESE SHORT MESSAGES!
STAY TUNED! DON'T GO AWAY!
JUST GIVE ME 30 SECONDS WORTH OF DINNER.
KIRKMAN & SCOTT

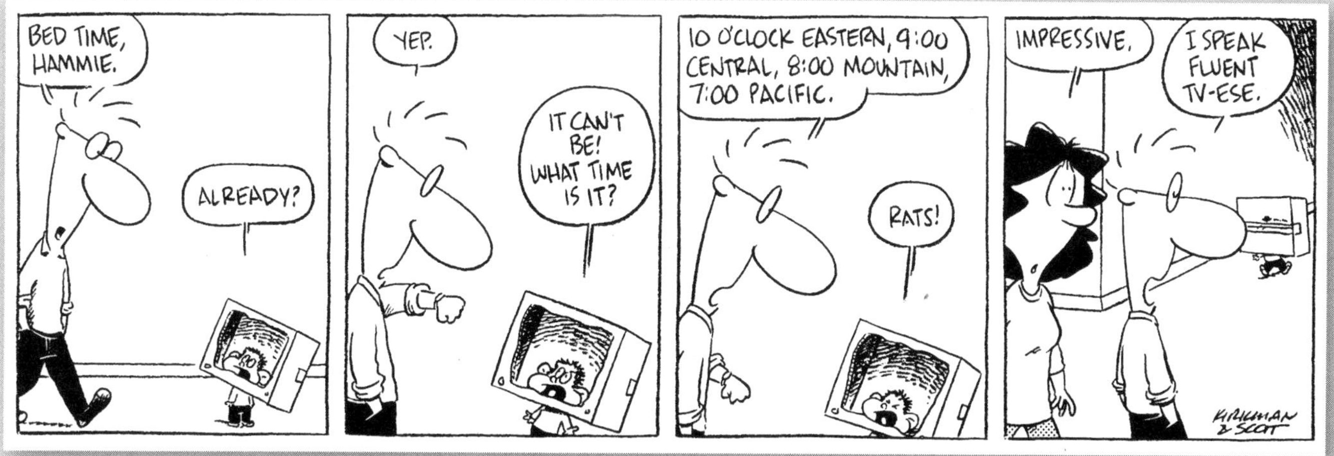
BED TIME, HAMMIE.
ALREADY?
YEP.
IT CAN'T BE! WHAT TIME IS IT?
10 O'CLOCK EASTERN, 9:00 CENTRAL, 8:00 MOUNTAIN, 7:00 PACIFIC.
RATS!
IMPRESSIVE.
I SPEAK FLUENT TV-ESE.
KIRKMAN & SCOTT

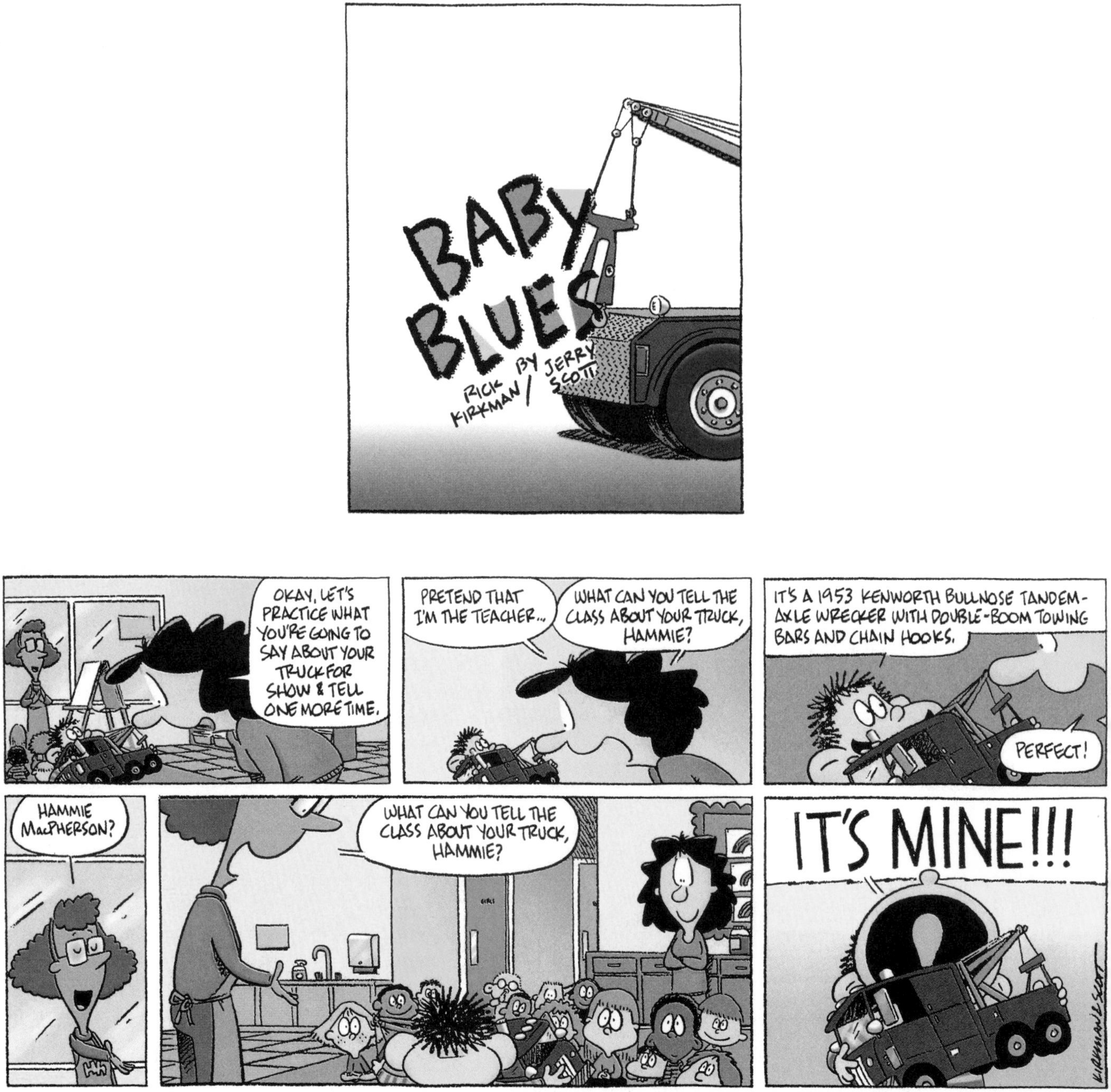
BABY BLUES
BY RICK KIRKMAN / JERRY SCOTT
OKAY, LET'S PRACTICE WHAT YOU'RE GOING TO SAY ABOUT YOUR TRUCK FOR SHOW & TELL ONE MORE TIME.
PRETEND THAT I'M THE TEACHER...
WHAT CAN YOU TELL THE CLASS ABOUT YOUR TRUCK, HAMMIE?
IT'S A 1953 KENWORTH BULLNOSE TANDEM-AXLE WRECKER WITH DOUBLE-BOOM TOWING BARS AND CHAIN HOOKS.
PERFECT!
HAMMIE MacPHERSON?
WHAT CAN YOU TELL THE CLASS ABOUT YOUR TRUCK, HAMMIE?
IT'S MINE!!!
KIRKMAN & SCOTT

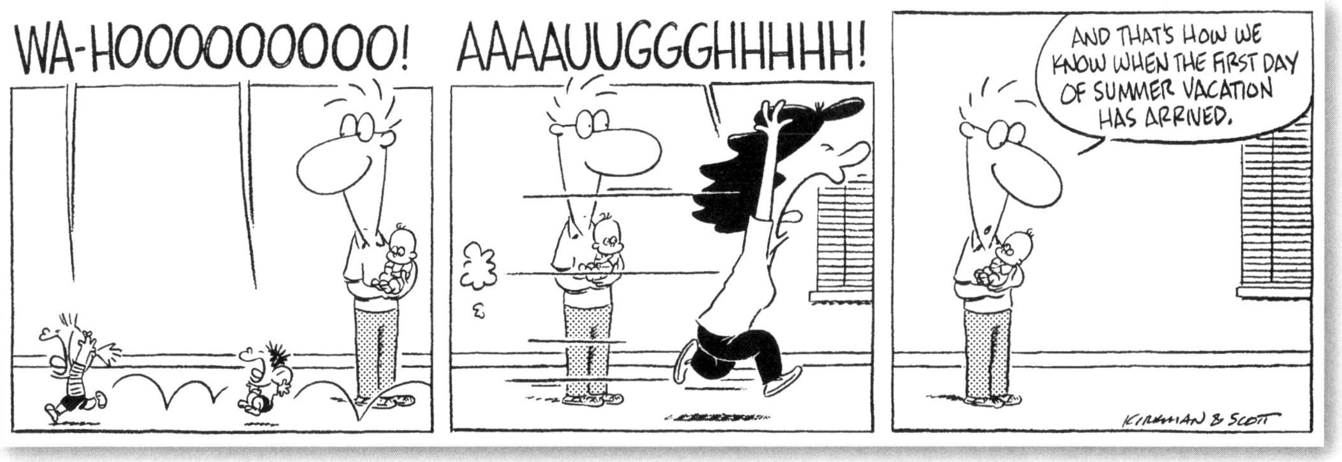
WA-HOOOOOOOOOO!
AAAAUUGGGHHHHH!
AND THAT'S HOW WE KNOW WHEN THE FIRST DAY OF SUMMER VACATION HAS ARRIVED.
KIRKMAN & SCOTT

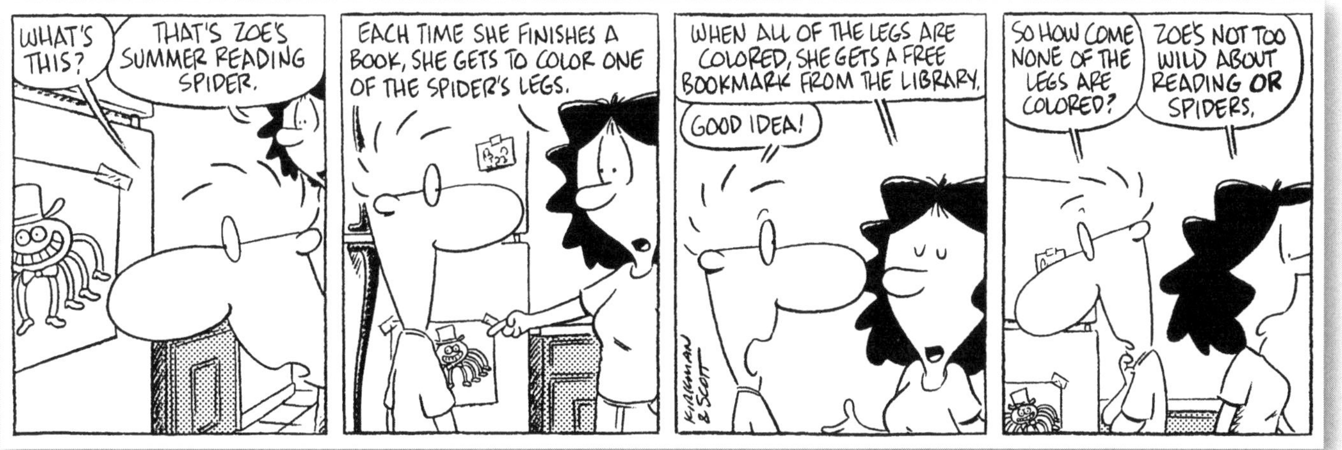
WHAT'S THIS?
THAT'S ZOE'S SUMMER READING SPIDER.
EACH TIME SHE FINISHES A BOOK, SHE GETS TO COLOR ONE OF THE SPIDER'S LEGS.
WHEN ALL OF THE LEGS ARE COLORED, SHE GETS A FREE BOOKMARK FROM THE LIBRARY.
GOOD IDEA!
KIRKMAN & SCOTT
SO HOW COME NONE OF THE LEGS ARE COLORED?
ZOE'S NOT TOO WILD ABOUT READING **OR** SPIDERS.

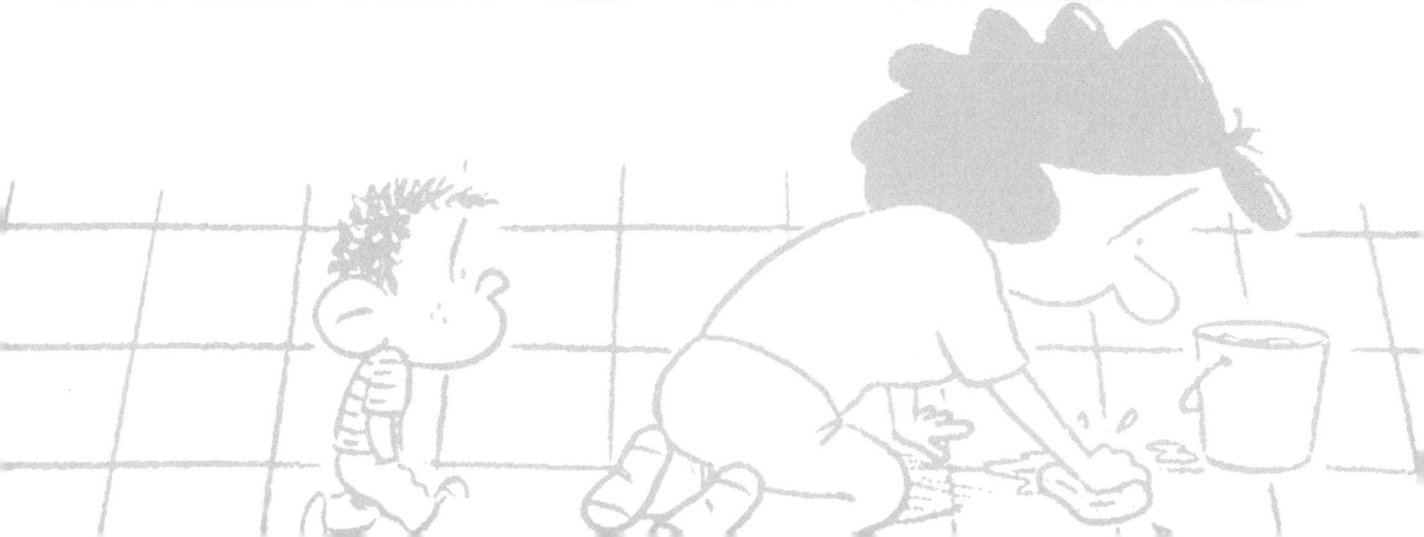

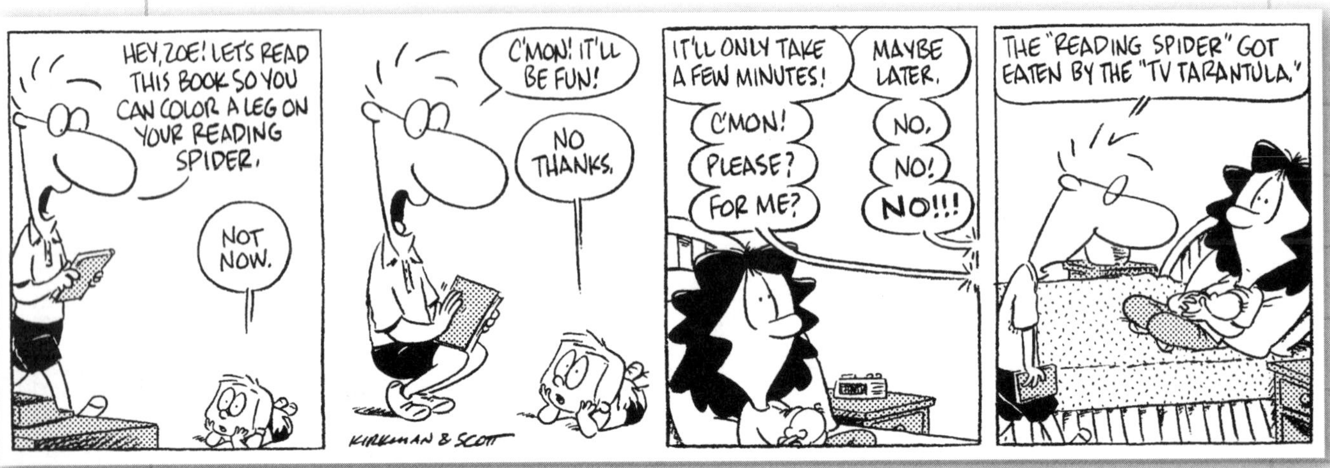
HEY, ZOE! LET'S READ THIS BOOK SO YOU CAN COLOR A LEG ON YOUR READING SPIDER.
NOT NOW.
C'MON! IT'LL BE FUN!
NO THANKS.
KIRKMAN & SCOTT
IT'LL ONLY TAKE A FEW MINUTES!
MAYBE LATER.
C'MON!
NO.
PLEASE?
NO!
FOR ME?
NO!!!
THE "READING SPIDER" GOT EATEN BY THE "TV TARANTULA."

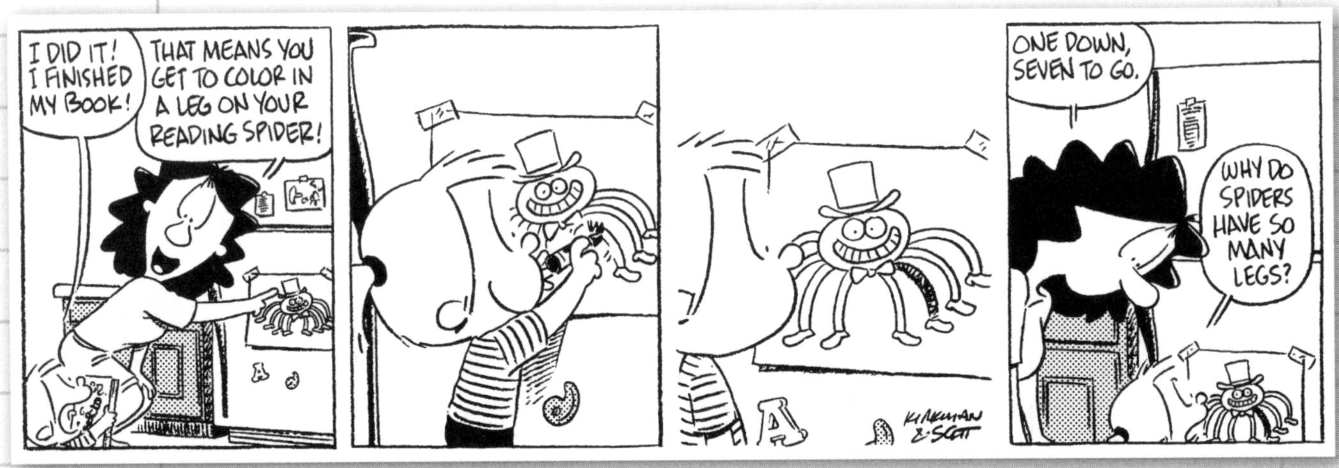
I DID IT! I FINISHED MY BOOK!
THAT MEANS YOU GET TO COLOR IN A LEG ON YOUR READING SPIDER!
KIRKMAN & SCOTT
ONE DOWN, SEVEN TO GO.
WHY DO SPIDERS HAVE SO MANY LEGS?

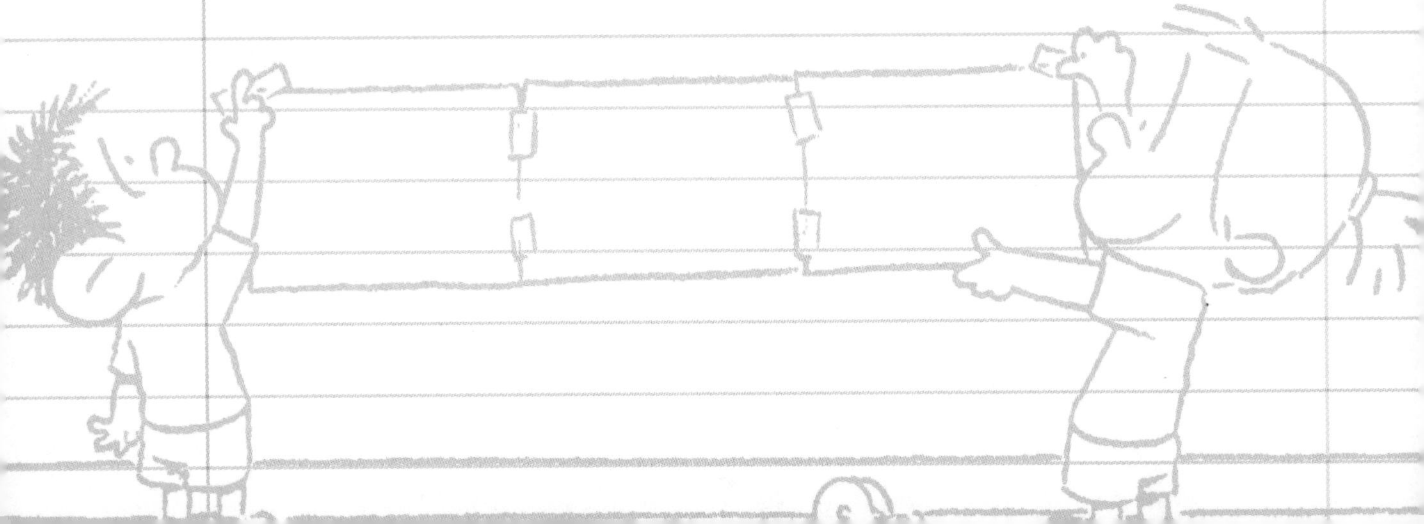

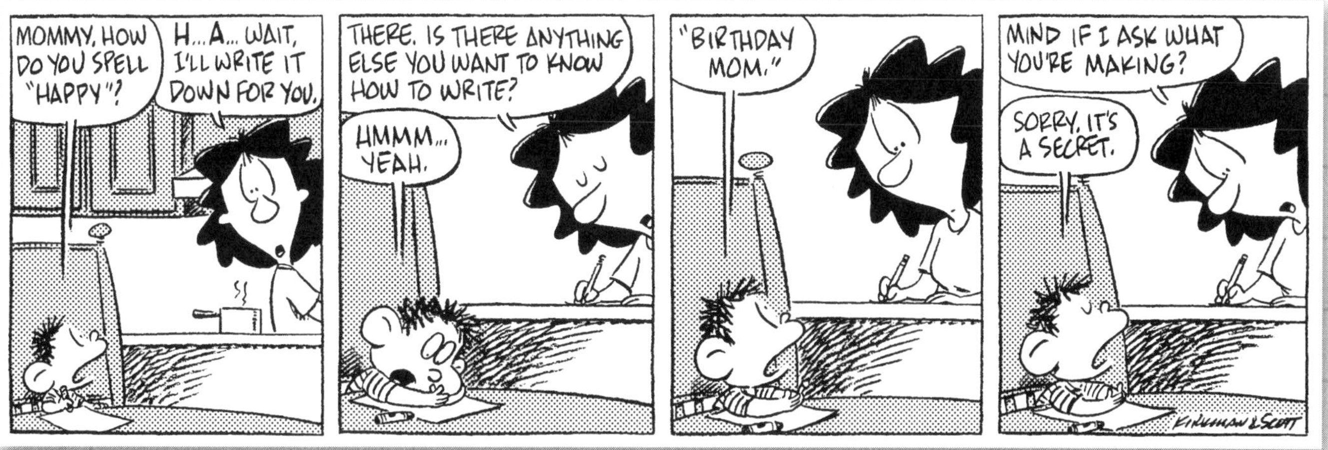
MOMMY, HOW DO YOU SPELL "HAPPY"?
H... A... WAIT, I'LL WRITE IT DOWN FOR YOU.
THERE. IS THERE ANYTHING ELSE YOU WANT TO KNOW HOW TO WRITE?
HMMM... YEAH.
"BIRTHDAY MOM."
MIND IF I ASK WHAT YOU'RE MAKING?
SORRY, IT'S A SECRET.
KIRKMAN & SCOTT

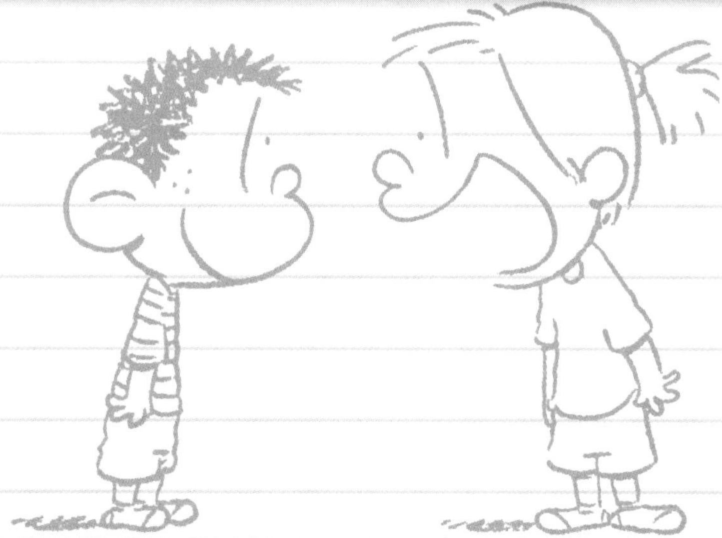

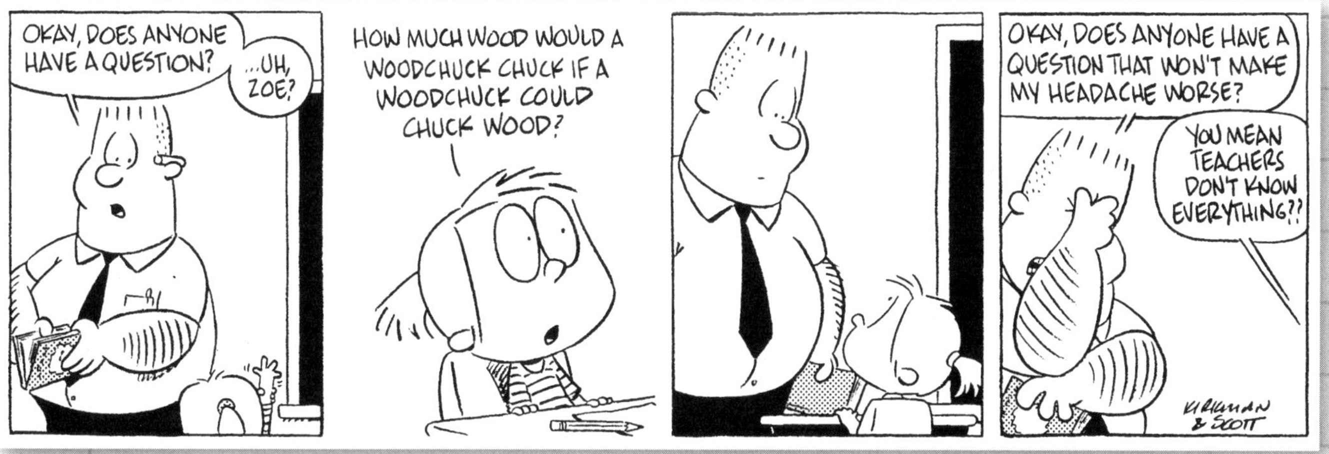
OKAY, DOES ANYONE HAVE A QUESTION?
...UH, ZOE?
HOW MUCH WOOD WOULD A WOODCHUCK CHUCK IF A WOODCHUCK COULD CHUCK WOOD?
OKAY, DOES ANYONE HAVE A QUESTION THAT WON'T MAKE MY HEADACHE WORSE?
YOU MEAN TEACHERS DON'T KNOW EVERYTHING??
KIRKMAN & SCOTT

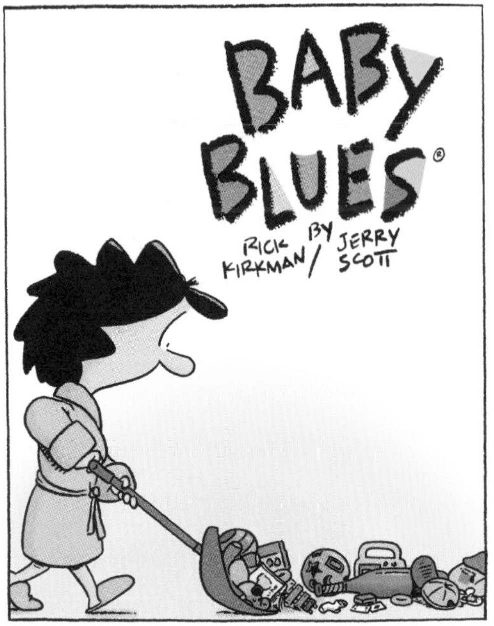
BABY BLUES®
BY RICK KIRKMAN / JERRY SCOTT

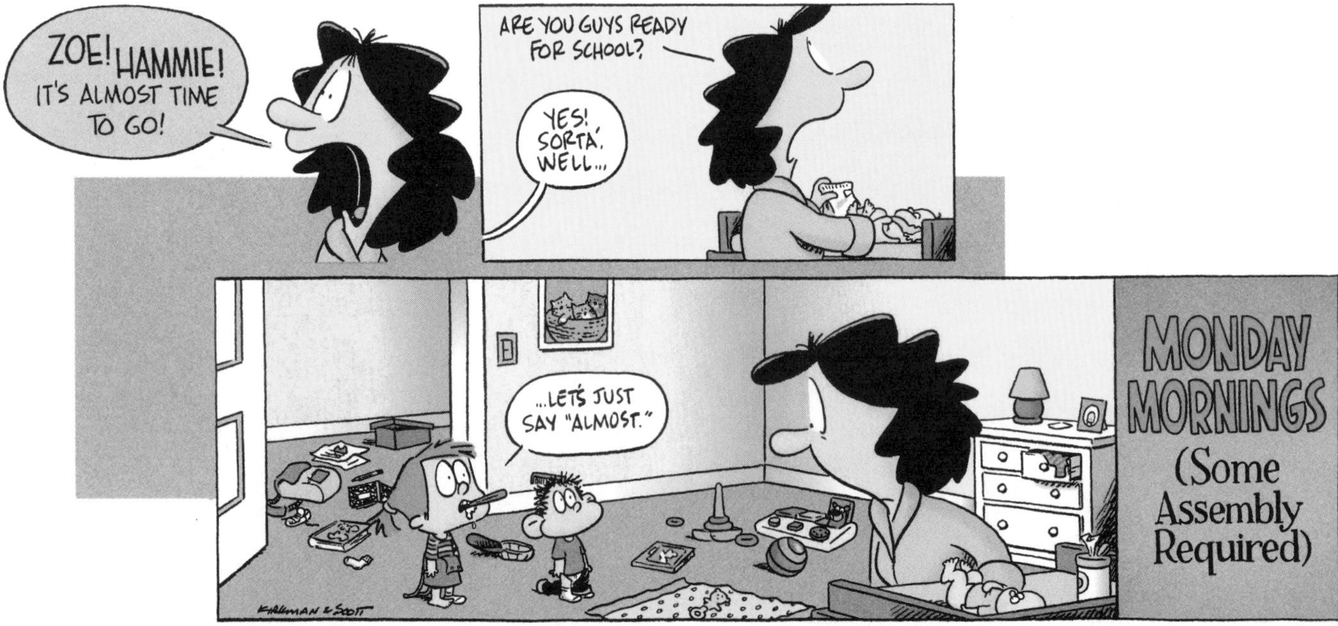
ZOE! HAMMIE! IT'S ALMOST TIME TO GO!
ARE YOU GUYS READY FOR SCHOOL?
YES! SORTA. WELL...
...LET'S JUST SAY "ALMOST."
MONDAY MORNINGS (Some Assembly Required)
KIRKMAN & SCOTT

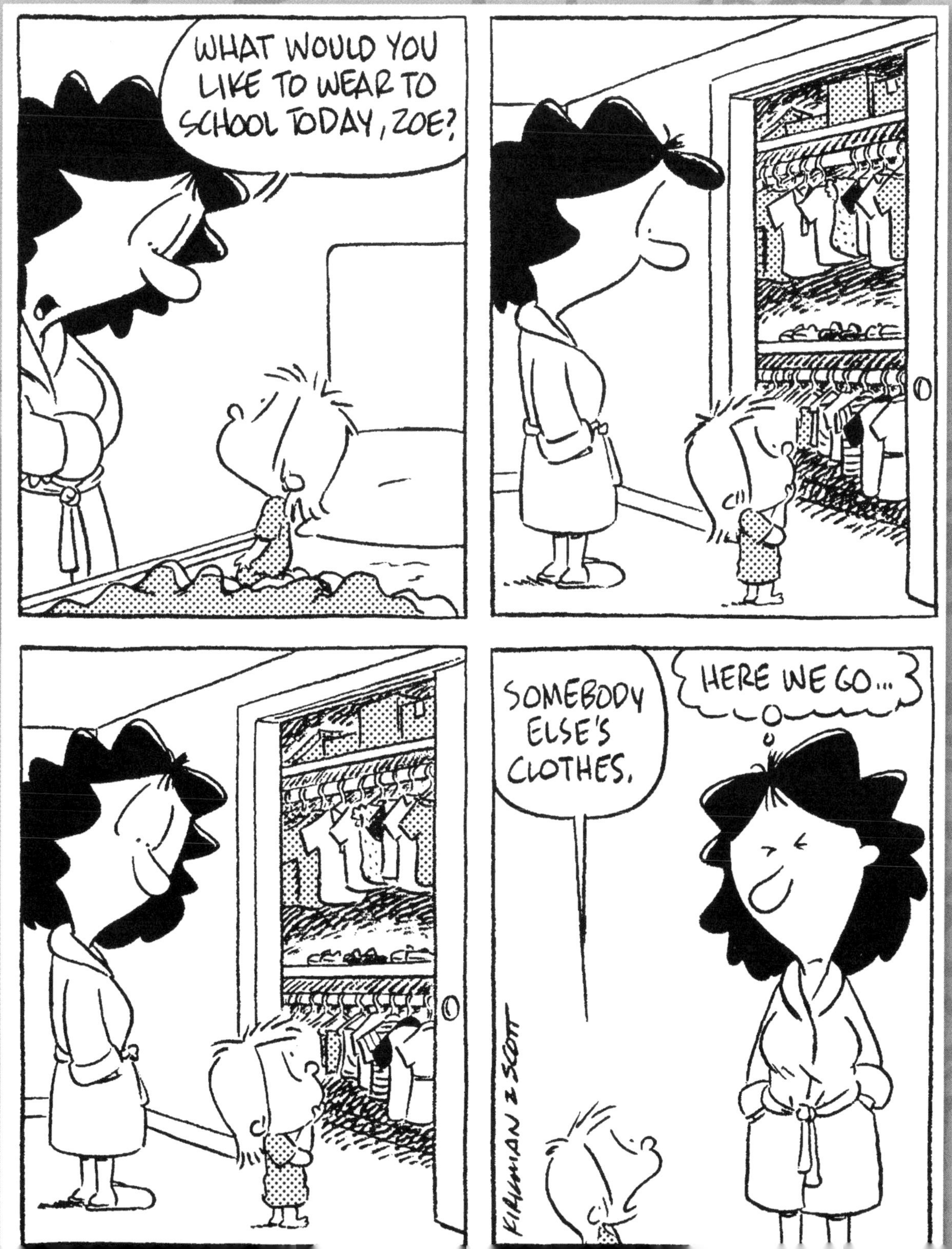
WHAT WOULD YOU LIKE TO WEAR TO SCHOOL TODAY, ZOE?
SOMEBODY ELSE'S CLOTHES.
HERE WE GO...
KIRKMAN & SCOTT

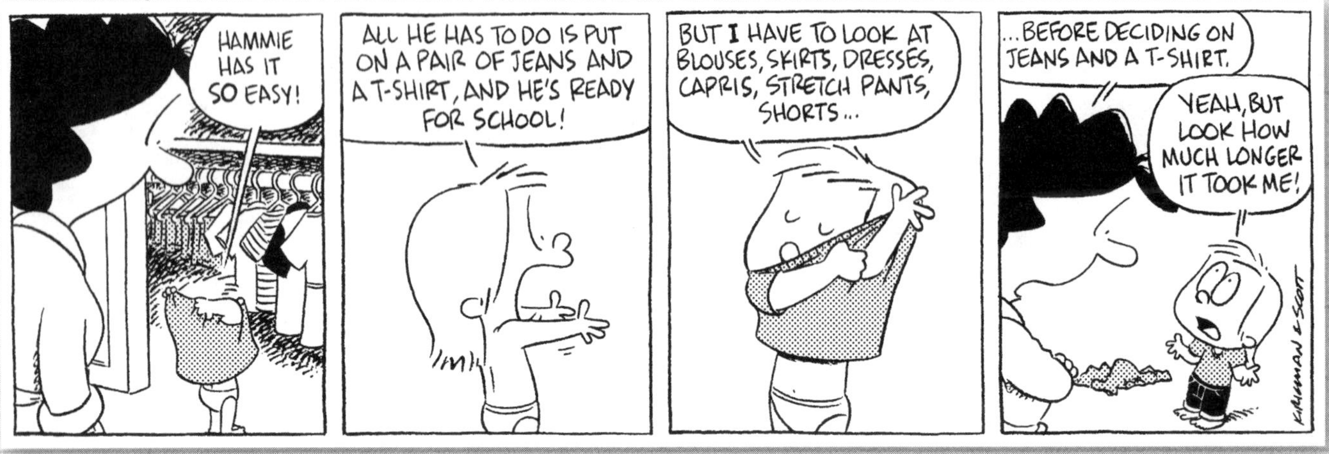
HAMMIE HAS IT SO EASY!
ALL HE HAS TO DO IS PUT ON A PAIR OF JEANS AND A T-SHIRT, AND HE'S READY FOR SCHOOL!
BUT I HAVE TO LOOK AT BLOUSES, SKIRTS, DRESSES, CAPRIS, STRETCH PANTS, SHORTS...
...BEFORE DECIDING ON JEANS AND A T-SHIRT.
YEAH, BUT LOOK HOW MUCH LONGER IT TOOK ME!
KIRKMAN & SCOTT

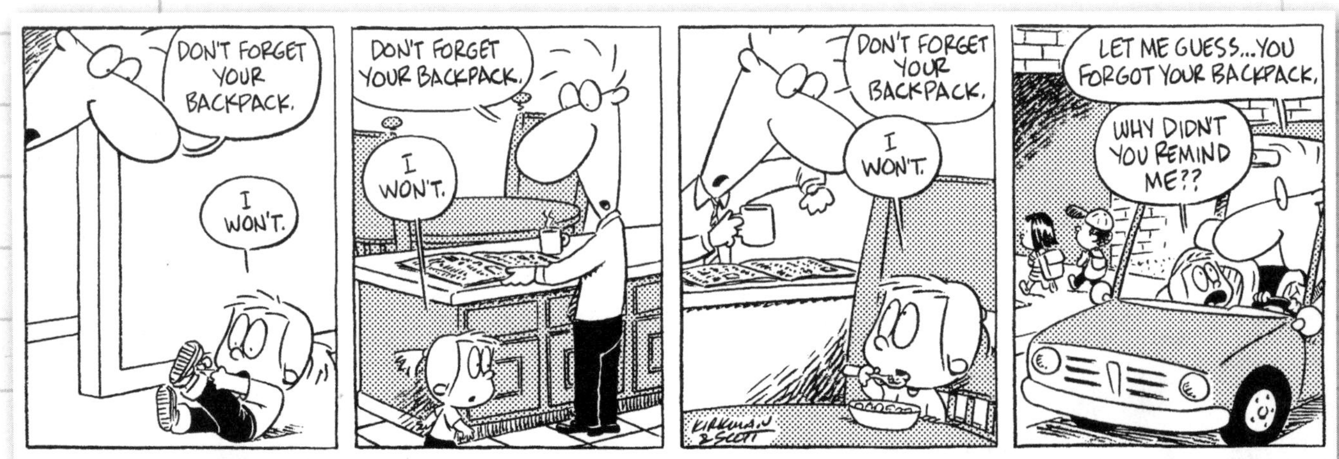
DON'T FORGET YOUR BACKPACK.
I WON'T.
DON'T FORGET YOUR BACKPACK.
I WON'T.
DON'T FORGET YOUR BACKPACK.
I WON'T.
KIRKMAN & SCOTT
LET ME GUESS...YOU FORGOT YOUR BACKPACK.
WHY DIDN'T YOU REMIND ME??

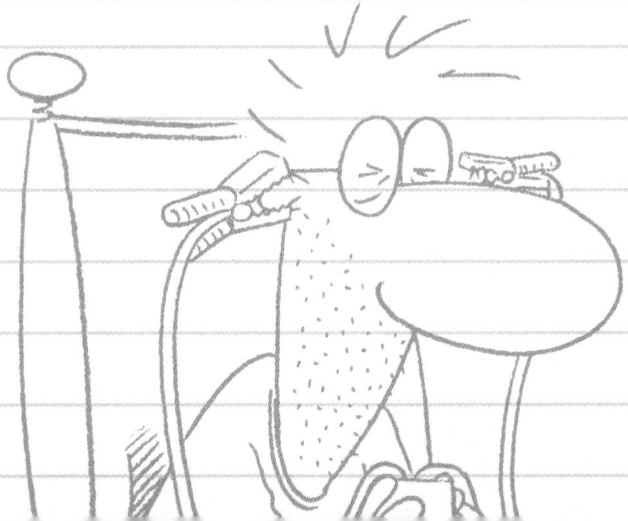

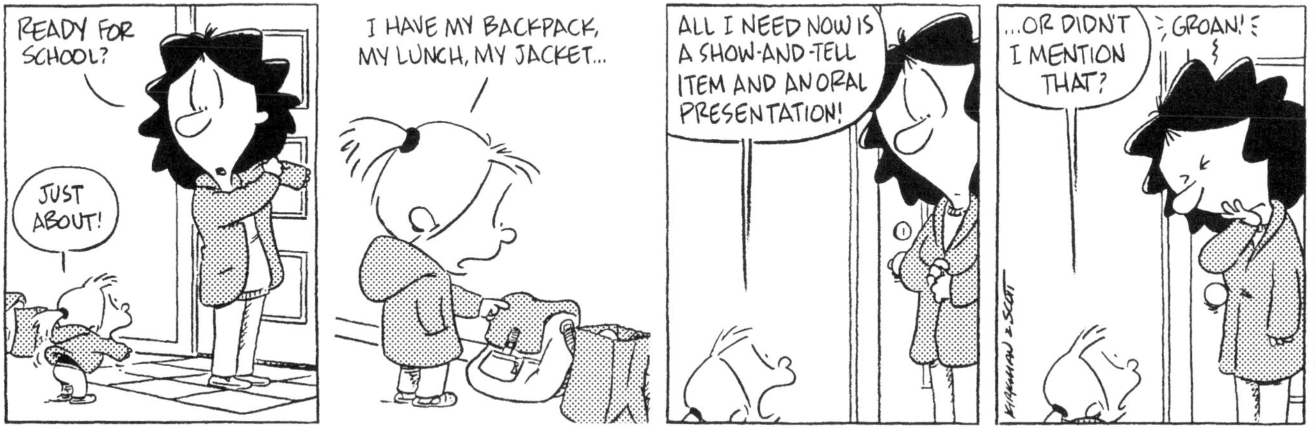
READY FOR SCHOOL?
JUST ABOUT!
I HAVE MY BACKPACK, MY LUNCH, MY JACKET...
ALL I NEED NOW IS A SHOW-AND-TELL ITEM AND AN ORAL PRESENTATION!
...OR DIDN'T I MENTION THAT?
GROAN!

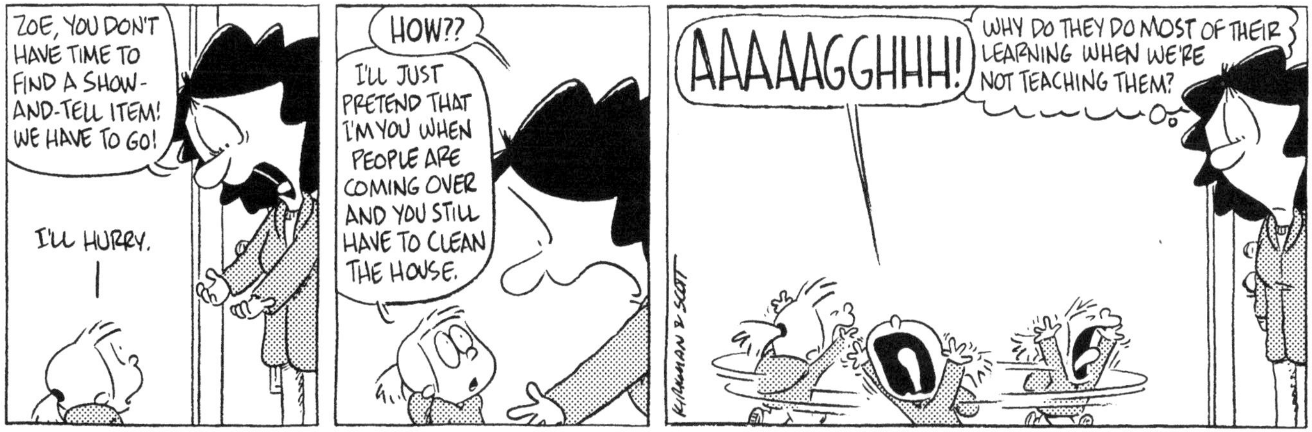
ZOE, YOU DON'T HAVE TIME TO FIND A SHOW-AND-TELL ITEM! WE HAVE TO GO!
I'LL HURRY.
HOW??
I'LL JUST PRETEND THAT I'M YOU WHEN PEOPLE ARE COMING OVER AND YOU STILL HAVE TO CLEAN THE HOUSE.
AAAAAGGHHH!
WHY DO THEY DO MOST OF THEIR LEARNING WHEN WE'RE NOT TEACHING THEM?

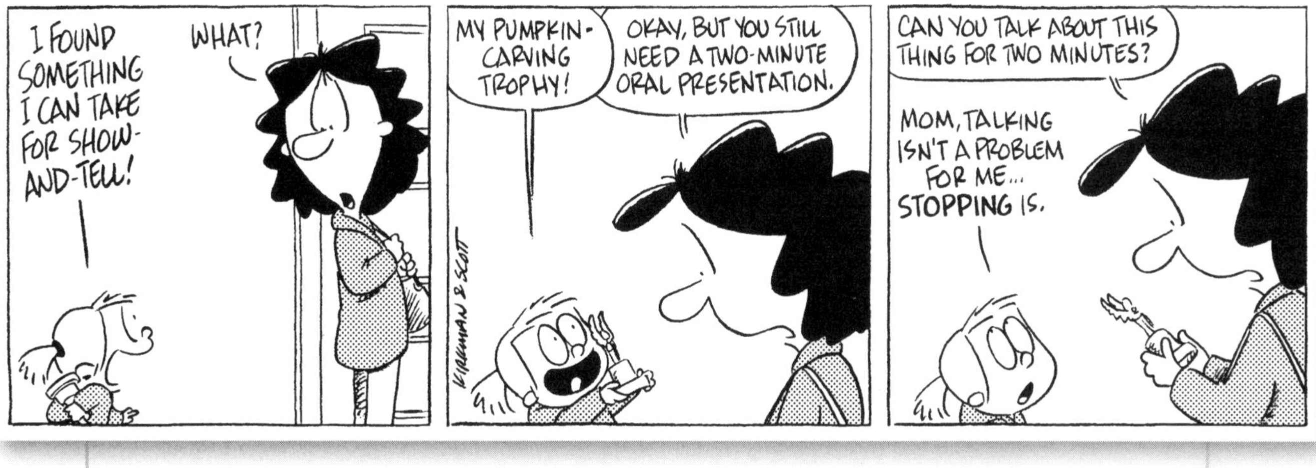
I FOUND SOMETHING I CAN TAKE FOR SHOW-AND-TELL!
WHAT?
MY PUMPKIN-CARVING TROPHY!
OKAY, BUT YOU STILL NEED A TWO-MINUTE ORAL PRESENTATION.
CAN YOU TALK ABOUT THIS THING FOR TWO MINUTES?
MOM, TALKING ISN'T A PROBLEM FOR ME... STOPPING IS.

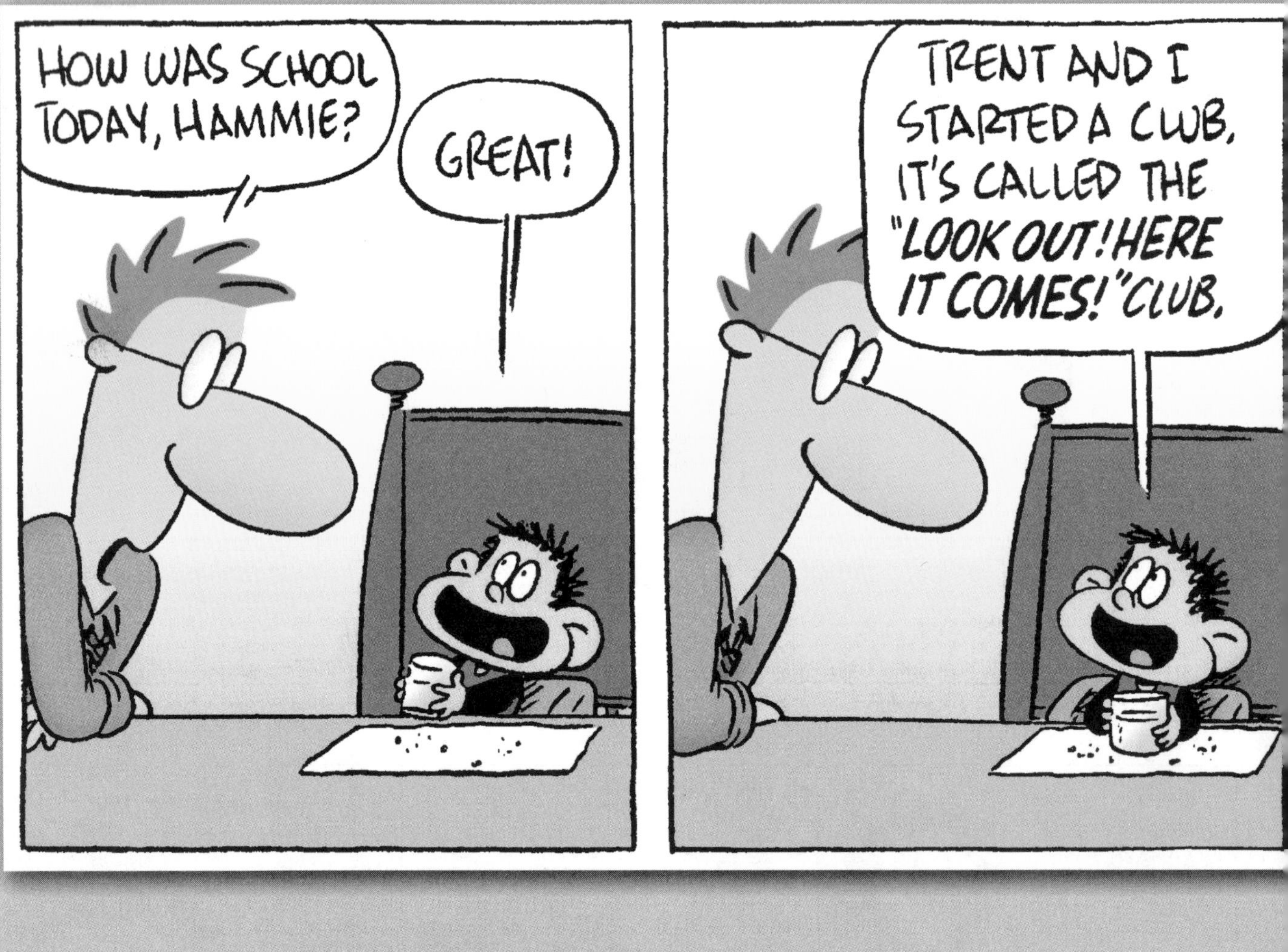
HOW WAS SCHOOL TODAY, HAMMIE?
GREAT!
TRENT AND I STARTED A CLUB. IT'S CALLED THE "LOOK OUT! HERE IT COMES!" CLUB.

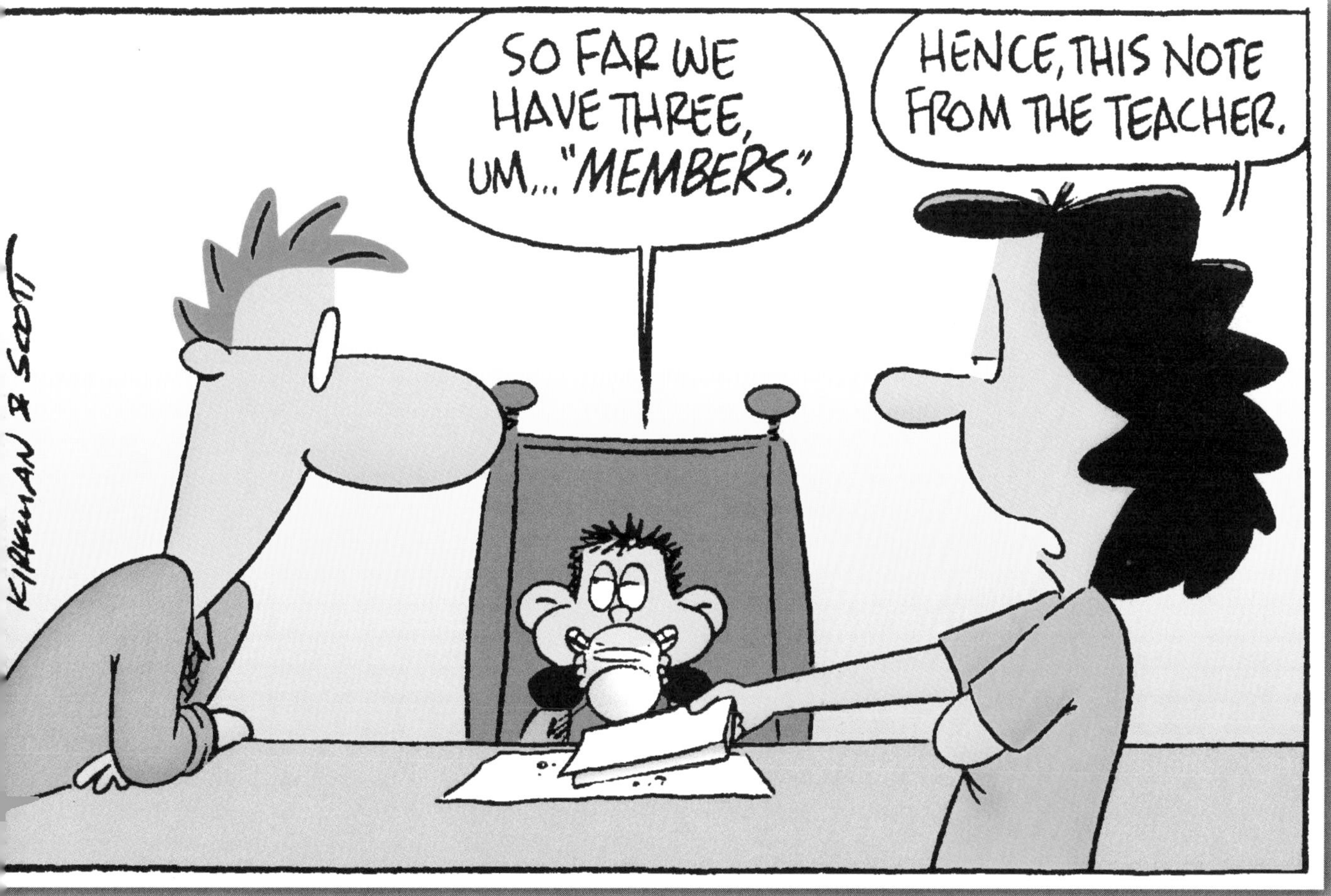
SO FAR WE HAVE THREE, UM..."MEMBERS."
HENCE, THIS NOTE FROM THE TEACHER.
KIRKMAN & SCOTT

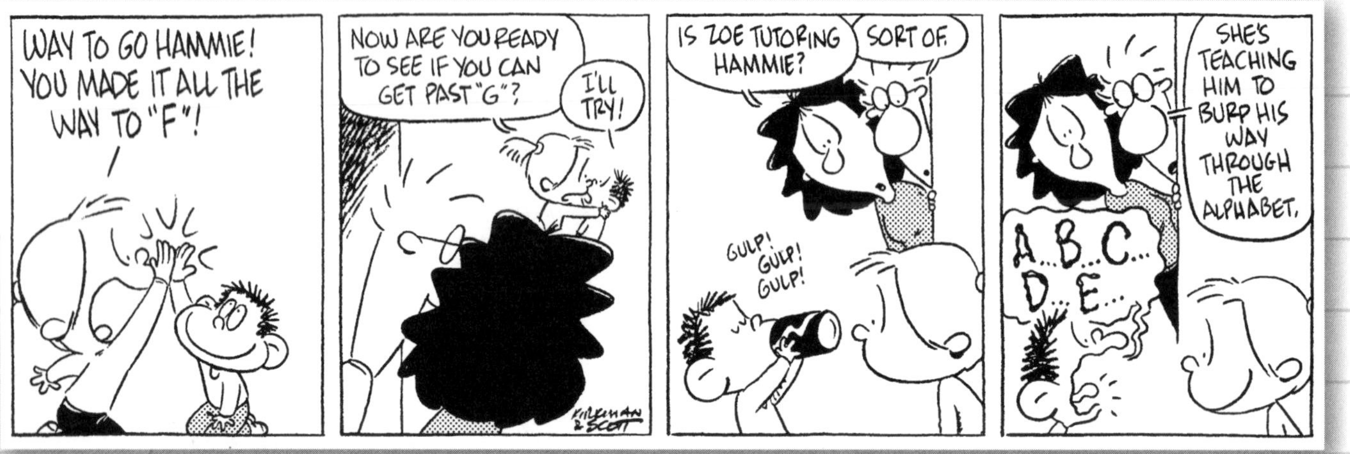
WAY TO GO HAMMIE! YOU MADE IT ALL THE WAY TO "F"!
NOW ARE YOU READY TO SEE IF YOU CAN GET PAST "G"?
I'LL TRY!
KIRKMAN & SCOTT
IS ZOE TUTORING HAMMIE?
SORT OF.
GULP! GULP! GULP!
SHE'S TEACHING HIM TO BURP HIS WAY THROUGH THE ALPHABET.
A...B...C... D...E...

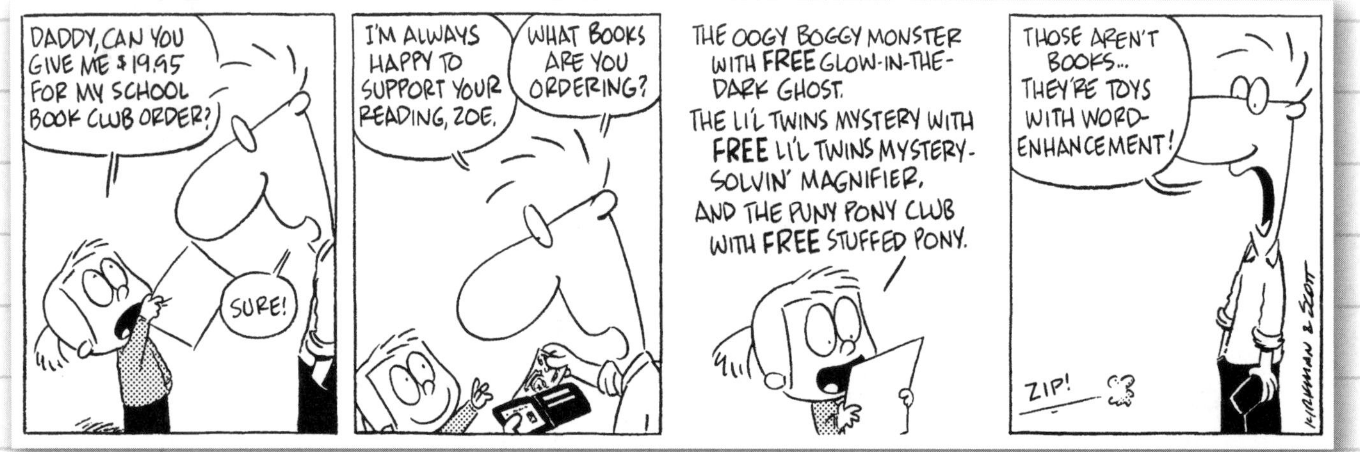
DADDY, CAN YOU GIVE ME $19.95 FOR MY SCHOOL BOOK CLUB ORDER?
SURE!
I'M ALWAYS HAPPY TO SUPPORT YOUR READING, ZOE.
WHAT BOOKS ARE YOU ORDERING?
THE OOGY BOGGY MONSTER WITH FREE GLOW-IN-THE-DARK GHOST.
THE LI'L TWINS MYSTERY WITH FREE LI'L TWINS MYSTERY-SOLVIN' MAGNIFIER,
AND THE PUNY PONY CLUB WITH FREE STUFFED PONY.
THOSE AREN'T BOOKS... THEY'RE TOYS WITH WORD-ENHANCEMENT!
ZIP!
KIRKMAN & SCOTT

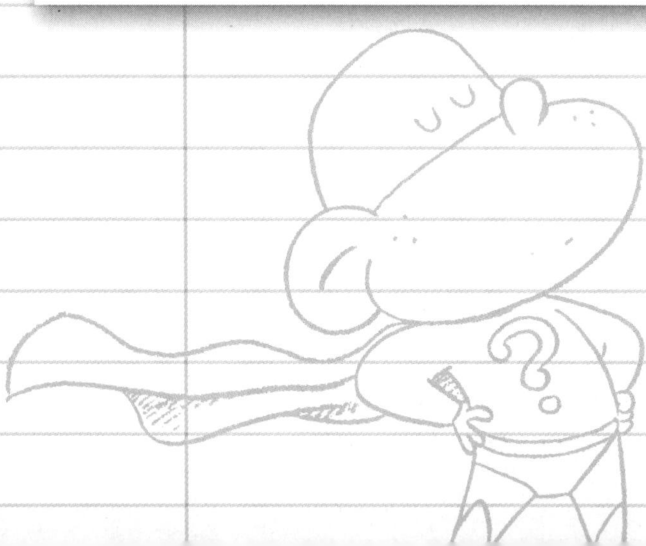

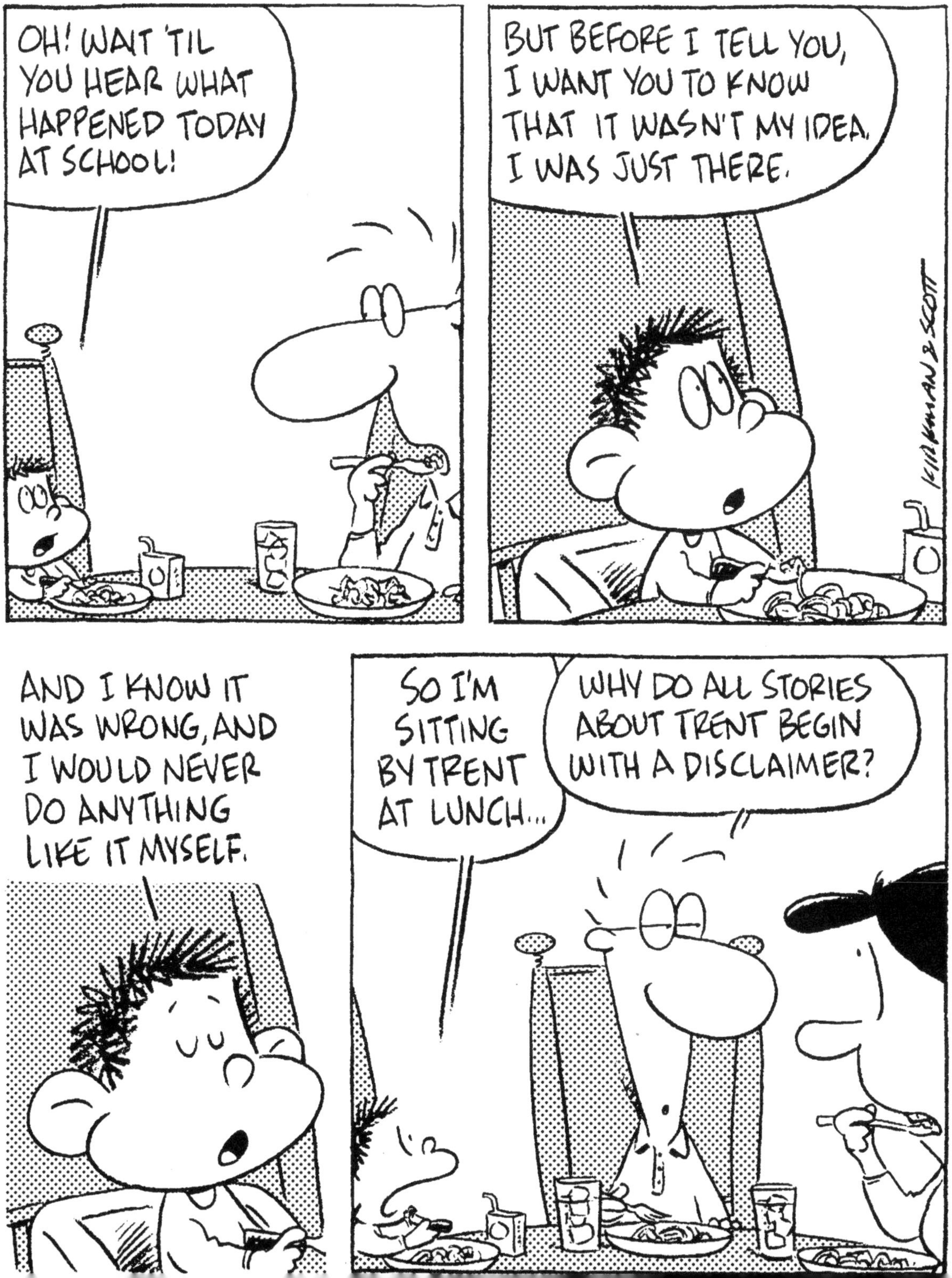
OH! WAIT 'TIL YOU HEAR WHAT HAPPENED TODAY AT SCHOOL!
BUT BEFORE I TELL YOU, I WANT YOU TO KNOW THAT IT WASN'T MY IDEA. I WAS JUST THERE.
KIRKMAN & SCOTT
AND I KNOW IT WAS WRONG, AND I WOULD NEVER DO ANYTHING LIKE IT MYSELF.
SO I'M SITTING BY TRENT AT LUNCH...
WHY DO ALL STORIES ABOUT TRENT BEGIN WITH A DISCLAIMER?

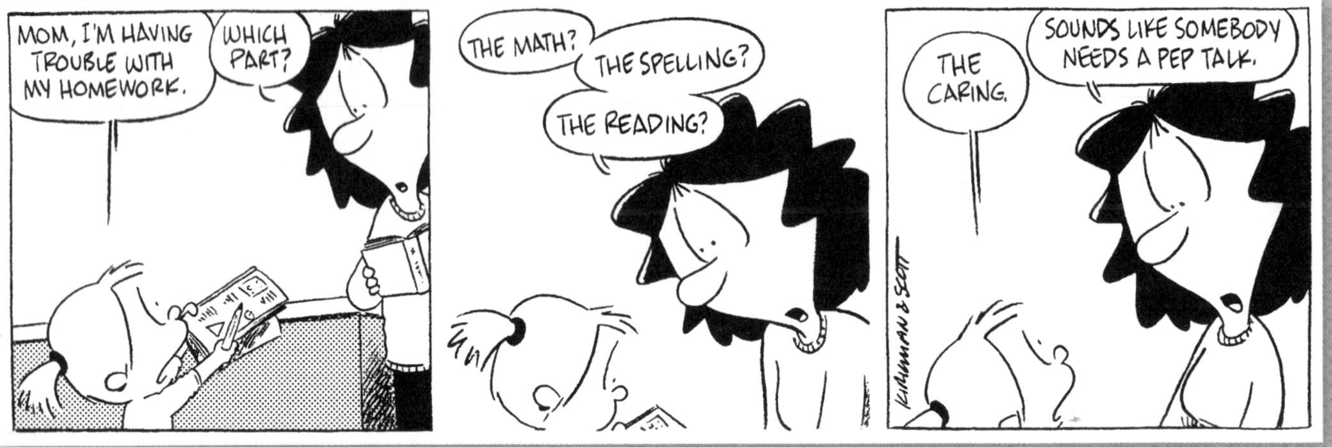
MOM, I'M HAVING TROUBLE WITH MY HOMEWORK.
WHICH PART?
THE MATH?
THE SPELLING?
THE READING?
THE CARING.
SOUNDS LIKE SOMEBODY NEEDS A PEP TALK.
KIRKMAN & SCOTT

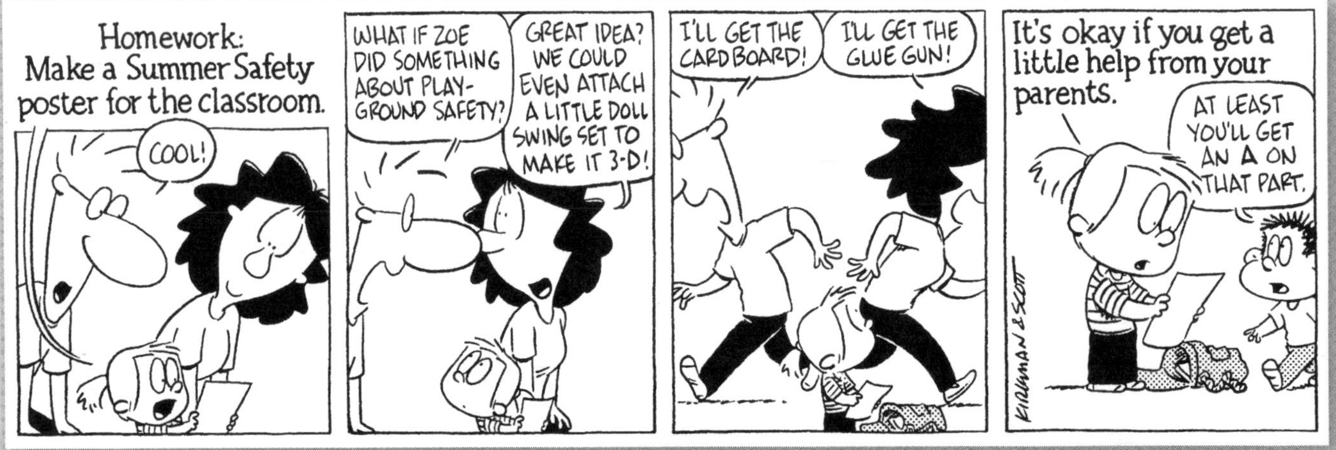
Homework: Make a Summer Safety poster for the classroom.
COOL!
WHAT IF ZOE DID SOMETHING ABOUT PLAY-GROUND SAFETY?
GREAT IDEA? WE COULD EVEN ATTACH A LITTLE DOLL SWING SET TO MAKE IT 3-D!
I'LL GET THE CARDBOARD!
I'LL GET THE GLUE GUN!
It's okay if you get a little help from your parents.
AT LEAST YOU'LL GET AN A ON THAT PART.
KIRKMAN & SCOTT

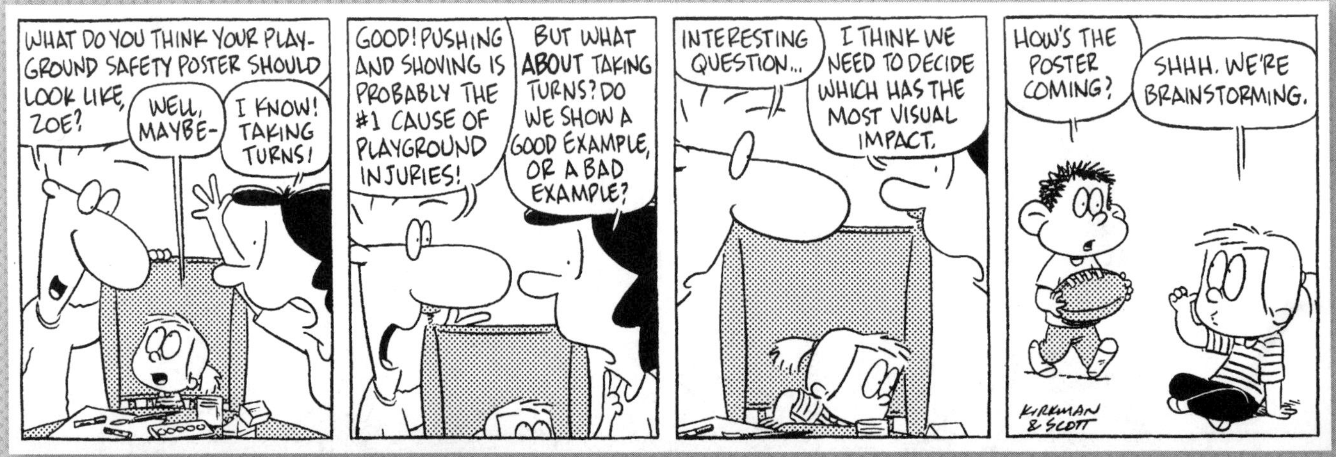
WHAT DO YOU THINK YOUR PLAY-GROUND SAFETY POSTER SHOULD LOOK LIKE, ZOE?
WELL, MAYBE-
I KNOW! TAKING TURNS!
GOOD! PUSHING AND SHOVING IS PROBABLY THE #1 CAUSE OF PLAYGROUND INJURIES!
BUT WHAT ABOUT TAKING TURNS? DO WE SHOW A GOOD EXAMPLE, OR A BAD EXAMPLE?
INTERESTING QUESTION...
I THINK WE NEED TO DECIDE WHICH HAS THE MOST VISUAL IMPACT.
HOW'S THE POSTER COMING?
SHHH. WE'RE BRAINSTORMING.
KIRKMAN & SCOTT

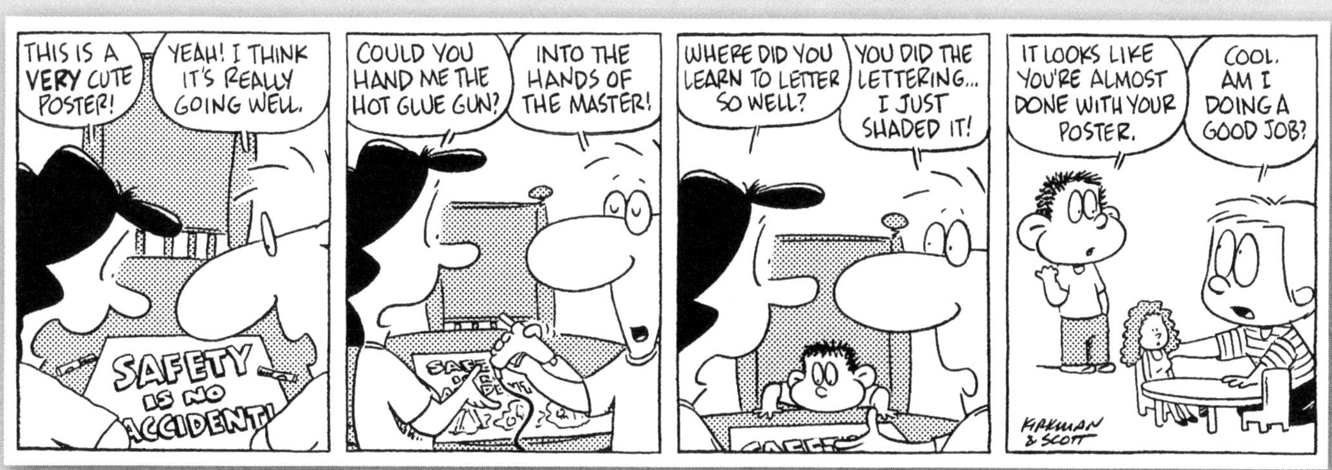
THIS IS A VERY CUTE POSTER!
YEAH! I THINK IT'S REALLY GOING WELL.
SAFETY IS NO ACCIDENT!
COULD YOU HAND ME THE HOT GLUE GUN?
INTO THE HANDS OF THE MASTER!
WHERE DID YOU LEARN TO LETTER SO WELL?
YOU DID THE LETTERING... I JUST SHADED IT!
IT LOOKS LIKE YOU'RE ALMOST DONE WITH YOUR POSTER.
COOL. AM I DOING A GOOD JOB?
KIRKMAN & SCOTT

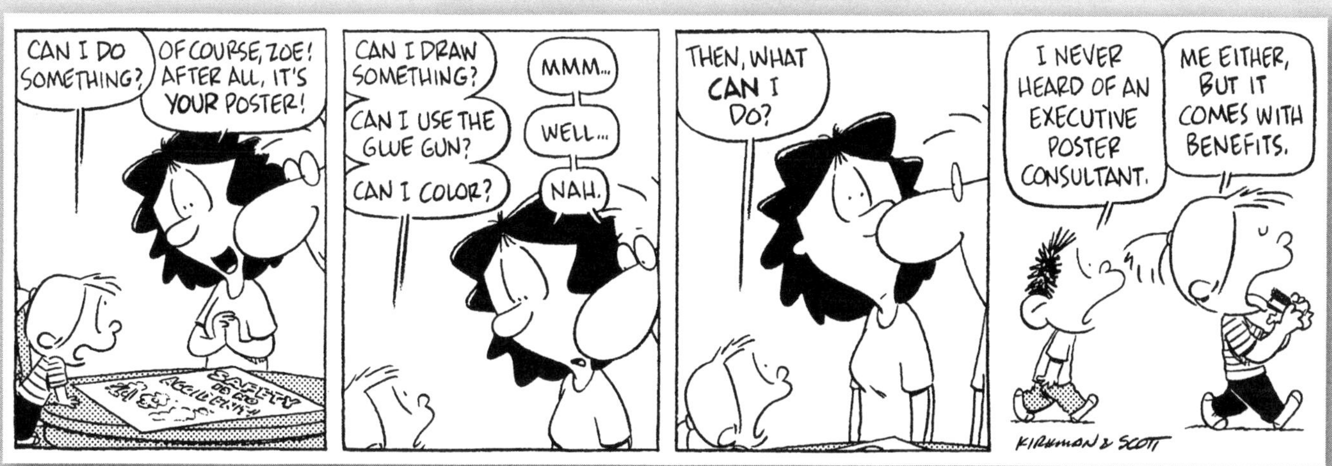
CAN I DO SOMETHING?
OF COURSE, ZOE! AFTER ALL, IT'S YOUR POSTER!
CAN I DRAW SOMETHING?
MMM...
CAN I USE THE GLUE GUN?
WELL...
CAN I COLOR?
NAH.
THEN, WHAT CAN I DO?
I NEVER HEARD OF AN EXECUTIVE POSTER CONSULTANT.
ME EITHER, BUT IT COMES WITH BENEFITS.
KIRKMAN & SCOTT

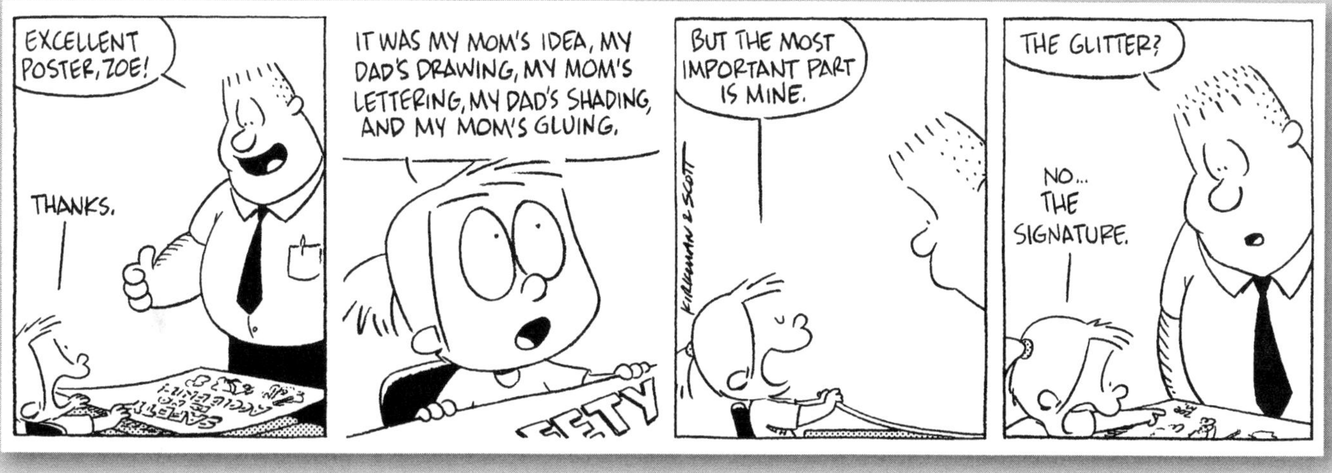
EXCELLENT POSTER, ZOE!
THANKS.
IT WAS MY MOM'S IDEA, MY DAD'S DRAWING, MY MOM'S LETTERING, MY DAD'S SHADING, AND MY MOM'S GLUING.
KIRKMAN & SCOTT
BUT THE MOST IMPORTANT PART IS MINE.
THE GLITTER?
NO... THE SIGNATURE.

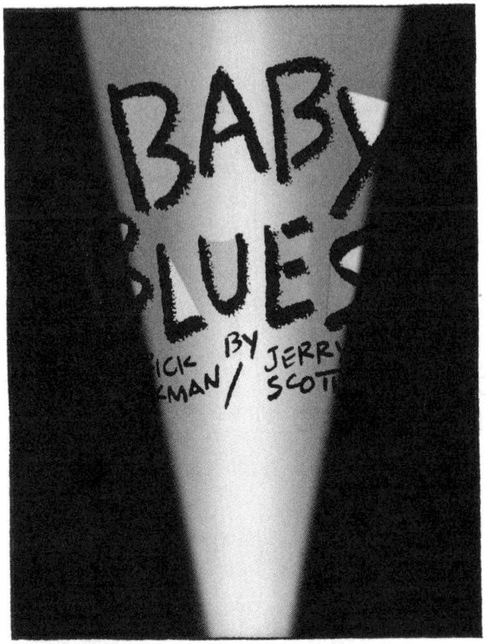
BABY BLUES
BY
RICK KIRKMAN/ JERRY SCOTT

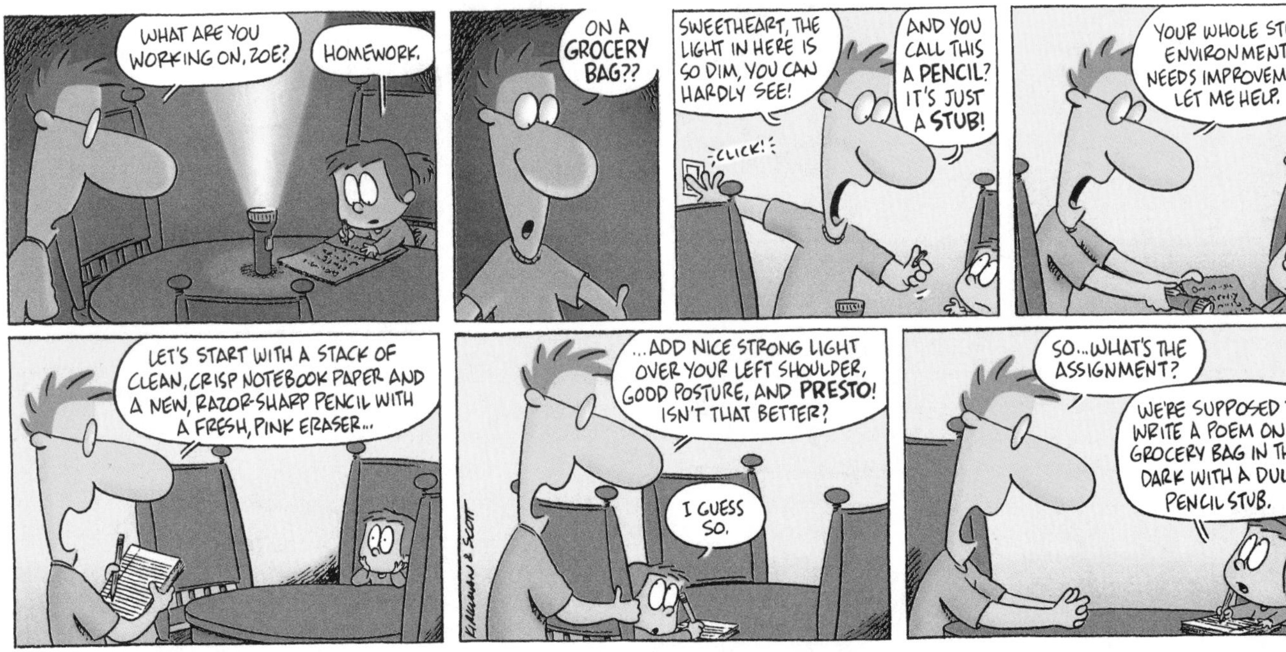
WHAT ARE YOU WORKING ON, ZOE?
HOMEWORK.
ON A GROCERY BAG??
SWEETHEART, THE LIGHT IN HERE IS SO DIM, YOU CAN HARDLY SEE!
CLICK!
AND YOU CALL THIS A PENCIL? IT'S JUST A STUB!
YOUR WHOLE STUDY ENVIRONMENT NEEDS IMPROVEMENT. LET ME HELP.
LET'S START WITH A STACK OF CLEAN, CRISP NOTEBOOK PAPER AND A NEW, RAZOR-SHARP PENCIL WITH A FRESH, PINK ERASER...
KIRKMAN & SCOTT
...ADD NICE STRONG LIGHT OVER YOUR LEFT SHOULDER, GOOD POSTURE, AND PRESTO! ISN'T THAT BETTER?
I GUESS SO.
SO...WHAT'S THE ASSIGNMENT?
WE'RE SUPPOSED TO WRITE A POEM ON A GROCERY BAG IN THE DARK WITH A DULL PENCIL STUB.

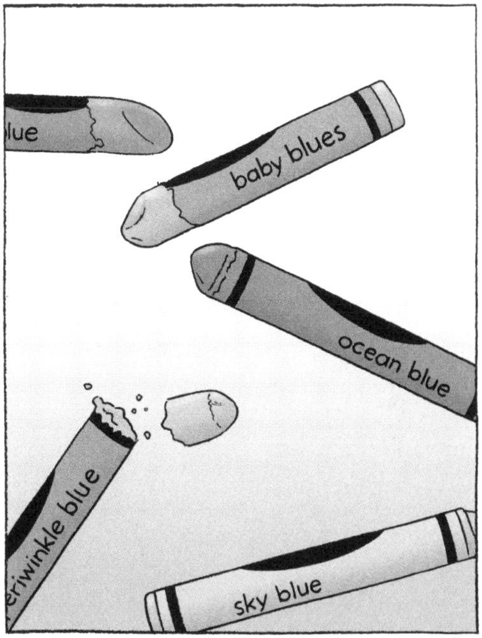
blue
baby blues
ocean blue
eriwinkle blue
sky blue

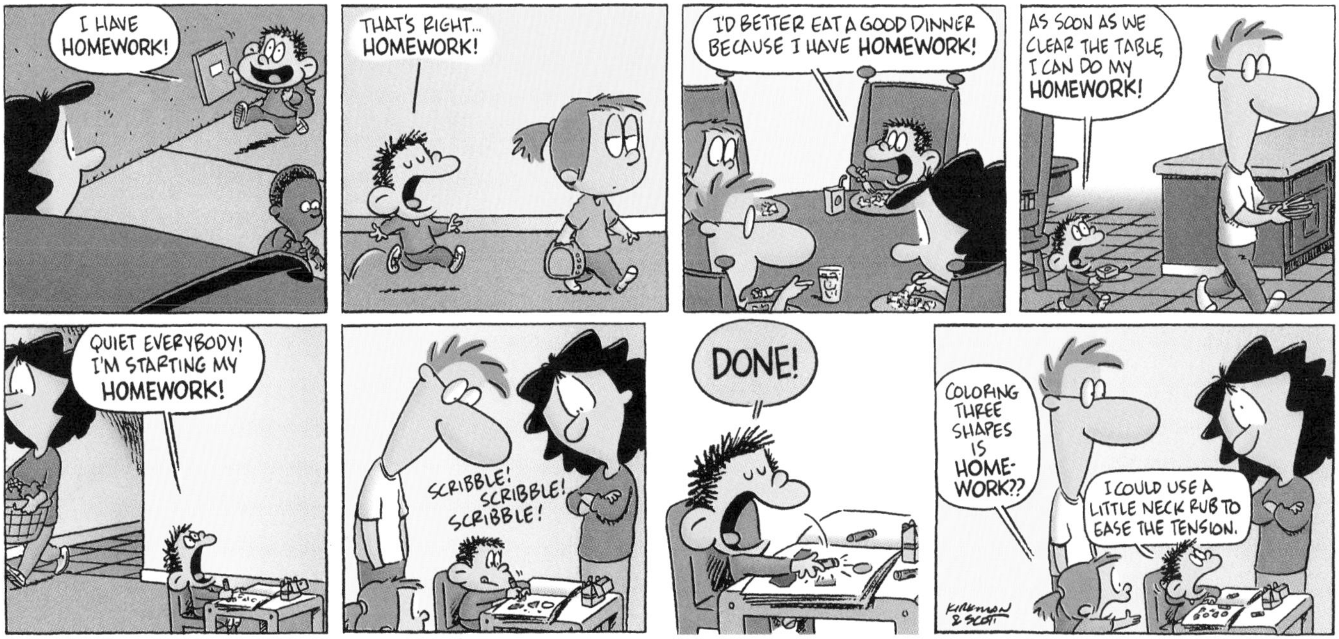
I HAVE HOMEWORK!
THAT'S RIGHT... HOMEWORK!
I'D BETTER EAT A GOOD DINNER BECAUSE I HAVE HOMEWORK!
AS SOON AS WE CLEAR THE TABLE, I CAN DO MY HOMEWORK!
QUIET EVERYBODY! I'M STARTING MY HOMEWORK!
SCRIBBLE! SCRIBBLE! SCRIBBLE!
DONE!
COLORING THREE SHAPES IS HOME-WORK??
I COULD USE A LITTLE NECK RUB TO EASE THE TENSION.
KIRKMAN & SCOTT

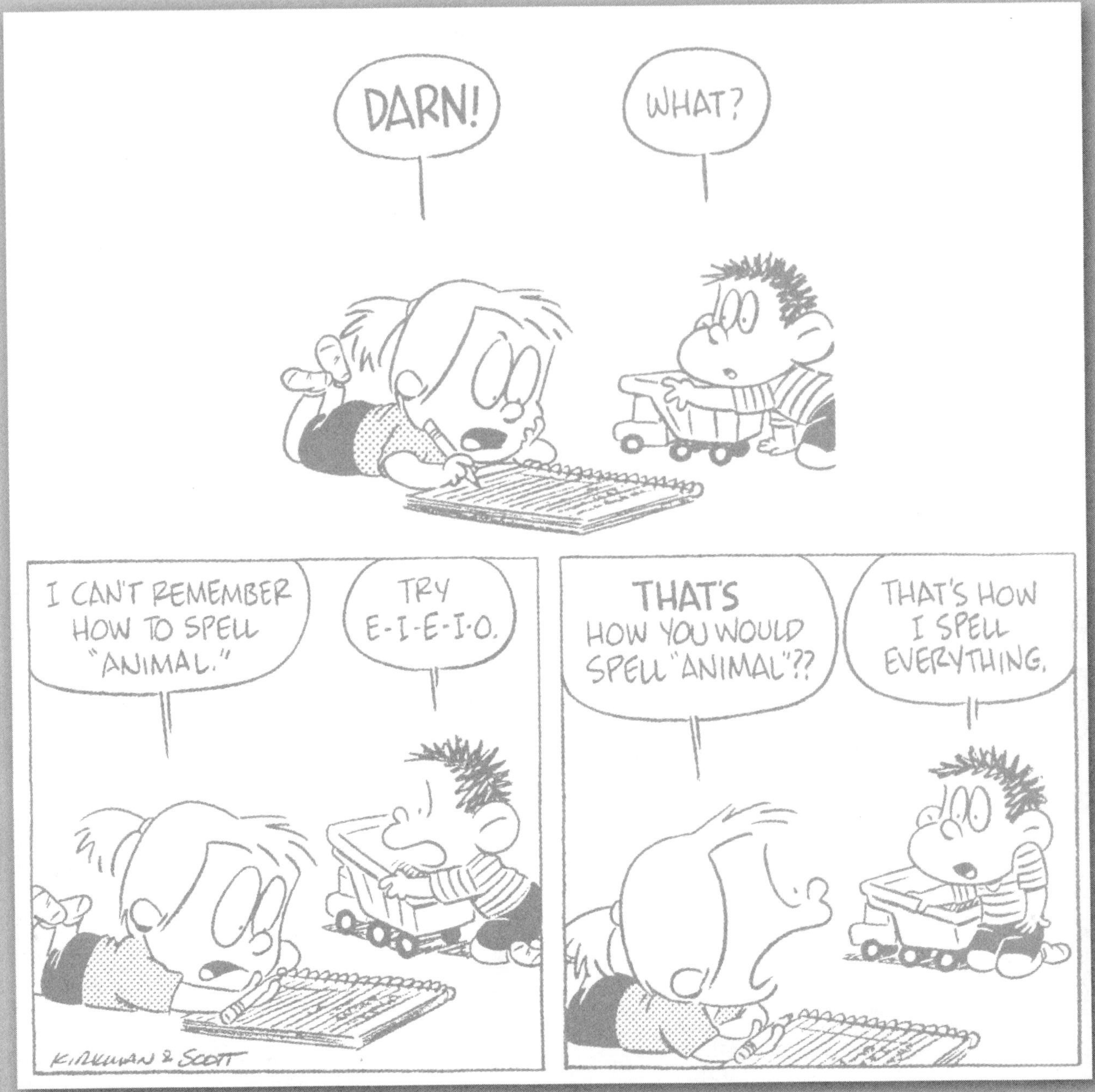
DARN!
WHAT?
I CAN'T REMEMBER HOW TO SPELL "ANIMAL."
TRY E-I-E-I-O.
THAT'S HOW YOU WOULD SPELL "ANIMAL"??
THAT'S HOW I SPELL EVERYTHING.
KIRKMAN & SCOTT

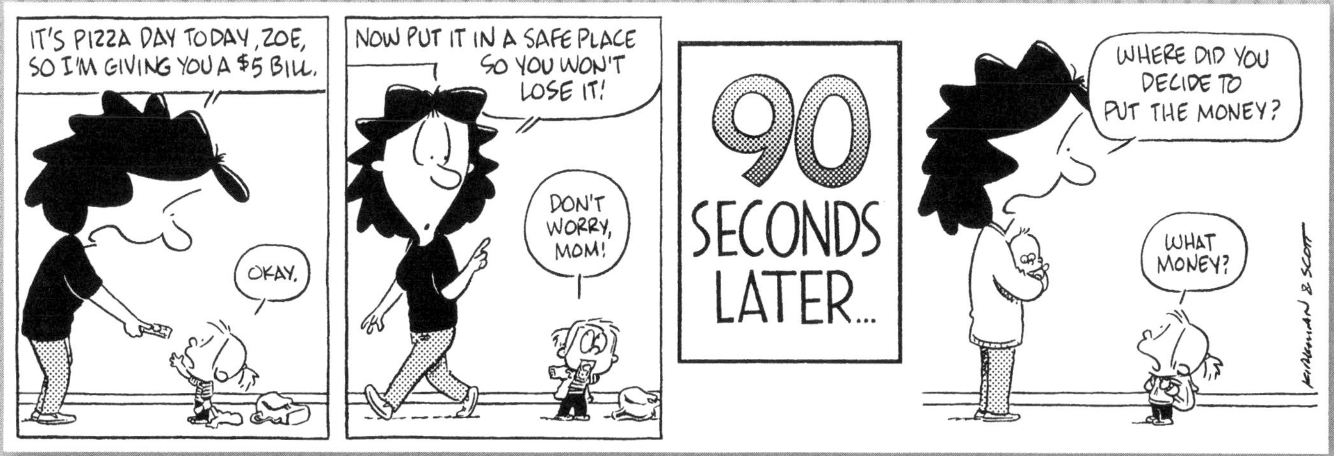

IT'S PIZZA DAY TODAY, ZOE, SO I'M GIVING YOU A $5 BILL.
OKAY.
NOW PUT IT IN A SAFE PLACE SO YOU WON'T LOSE IT!
DON'T WORRY, MOM!
90 SECONDS LATER...
WHERE DID YOU DECIDE TO PUT THE MONEY?
WHAT MONEY?
KIRKMAN & SCOTT

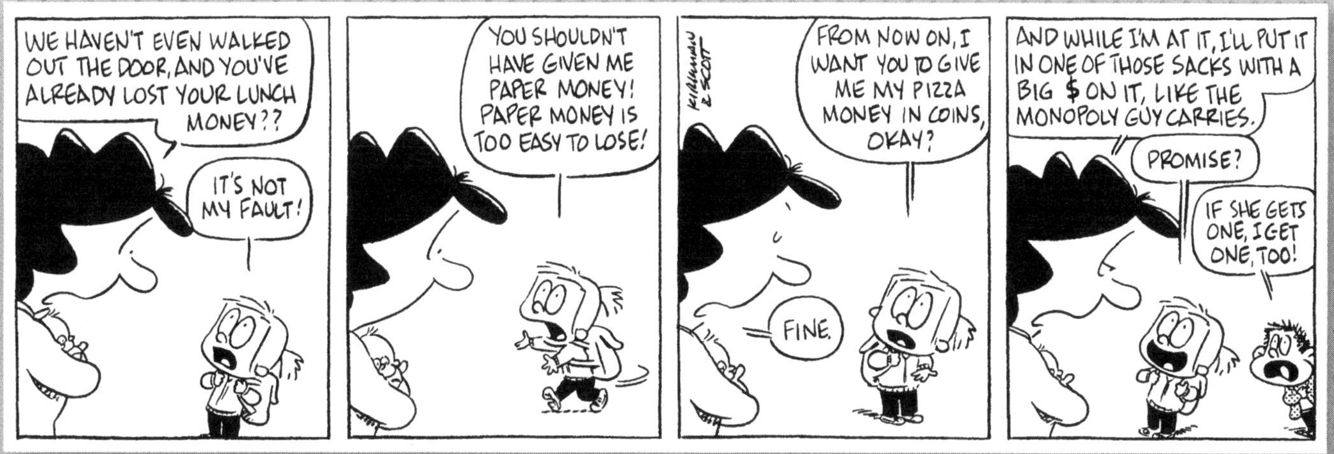

WE HAVEN'T EVEN WALKED OUT THE DOOR, AND YOU'VE ALREADY LOST YOUR LUNCH MONEY??
IT'S NOT MY FAULT!
YOU SHOULDN'T HAVE GIVEN ME PAPER MONEY! PAPER MONEY IS TOO EASY TO LOSE!
KIRKMAN & SCOTT
FROM NOW ON, I WANT YOU TO GIVE ME MY PIZZA MONEY IN COINS, OKAY?
FINE.
AND WHILE I'M AT IT, I'LL PUT IT IN ONE OF THOSE SACKS WITH A BIG $ ON IT, LIKE THE MONOPOLY GUY CARRIES.
PROMISE?
IF SHE GETS ONE, I GET ONE, TOO!

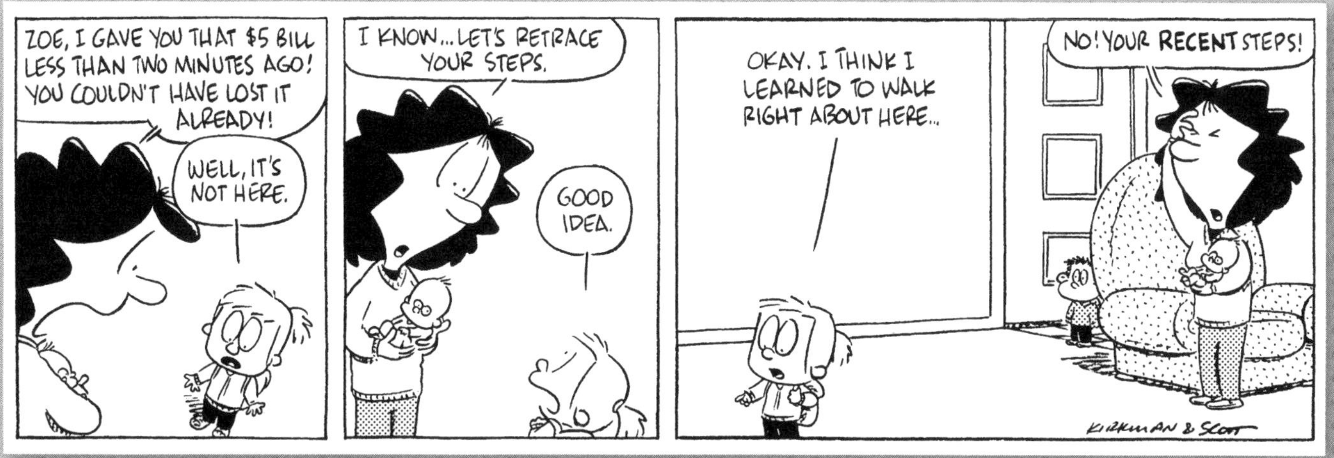

ZOE, I GAVE YOU THAT $5 BILL LESS THAN TWO MINUTES AGO! YOU COULDN'T HAVE LOST IT ALREADY!
WELL, IT'S NOT HERE.
I KNOW... LET'S RETRACE YOUR STEPS.
GOOD IDEA.
OKAY. I THINK I LEARNED TO WALK RIGHT ABOUT HERE...
NO! YOUR **RECENT** STEPS!
KIRKMAN & SCOTT

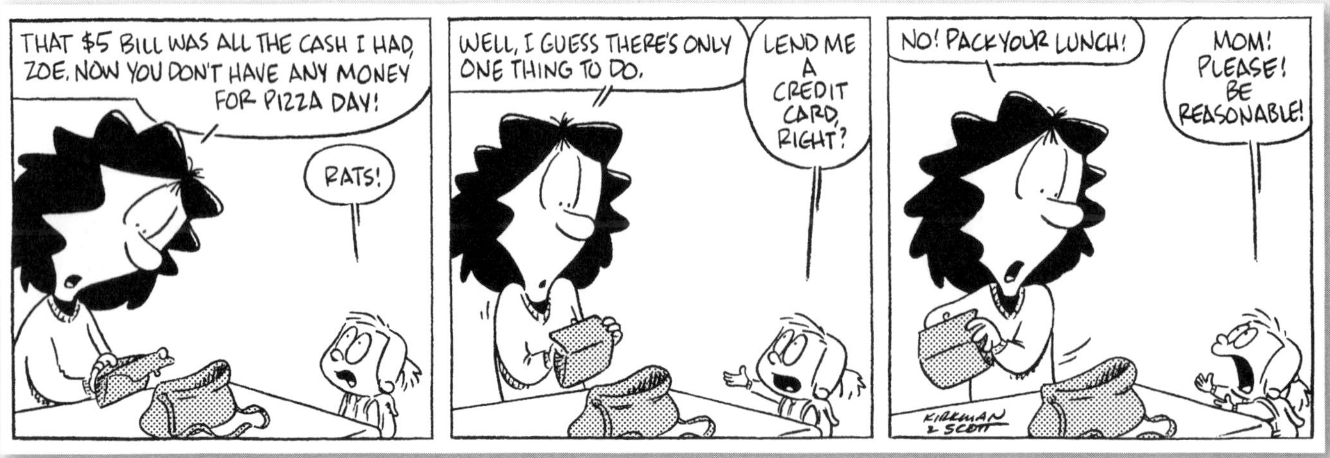
THAT $5 BILL WAS ALL THE CASH I HAD, ZOE. NOW YOU DON'T HAVE ANY MONEY FOR PIZZA DAY!
RATS!
WELL, I GUESS THERE'S ONLY ONE THING TO DO.
LEND ME A CREDIT CARD, RIGHT?
NO! PACK YOUR LUNCH!
MOM! PLEASE! BE REASONABLE!
KIRKMAN & SCOTT

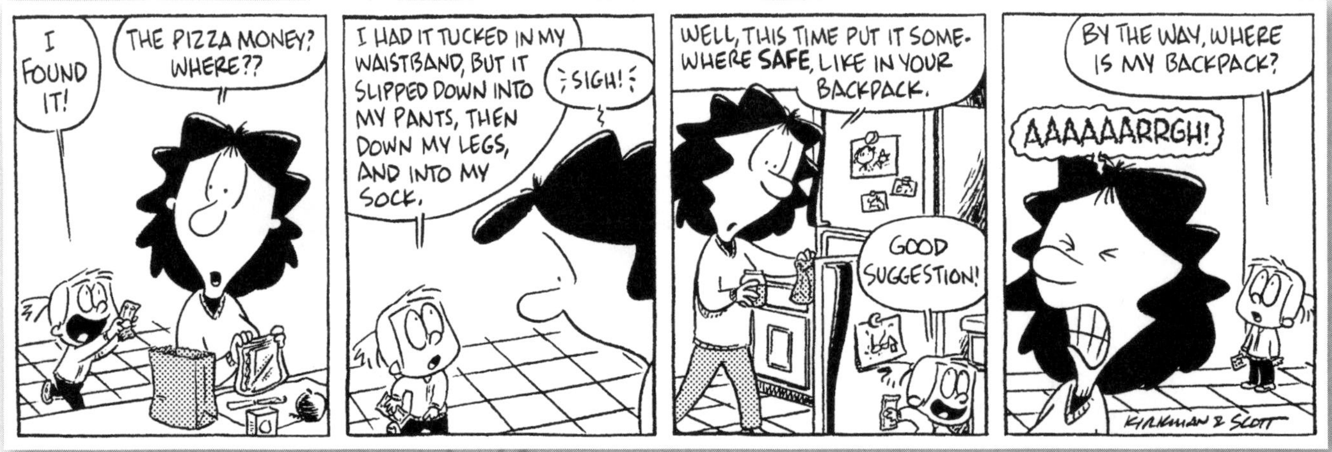
I FOUND IT!
THE PIZZA MONEY? WHERE??
I HAD IT TUCKED IN MY WAISTBAND, BUT IT SLIPPED DOWN INTO MY PANTS, THEN DOWN MY LEGS, AND INTO MY SOCK.
SIGH!
WELL, THIS TIME PUT IT SOMEWHERE SAFE, LIKE IN YOUR BACKPACK.
GOOD SUGGESTION!
BY THE WAY, WHERE IS MY BACKPACK?
AAAAAARRGH!
KIRKMAN & SCOTT

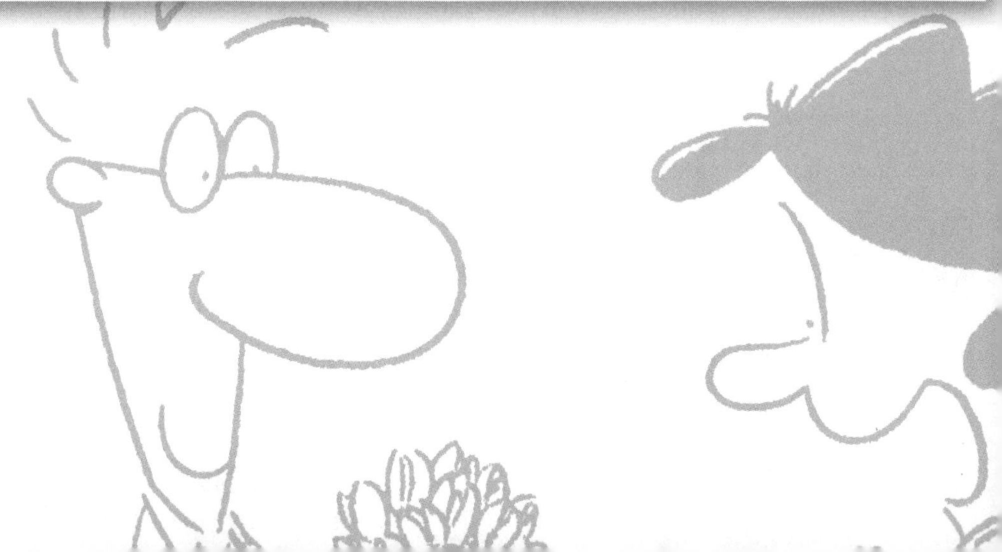

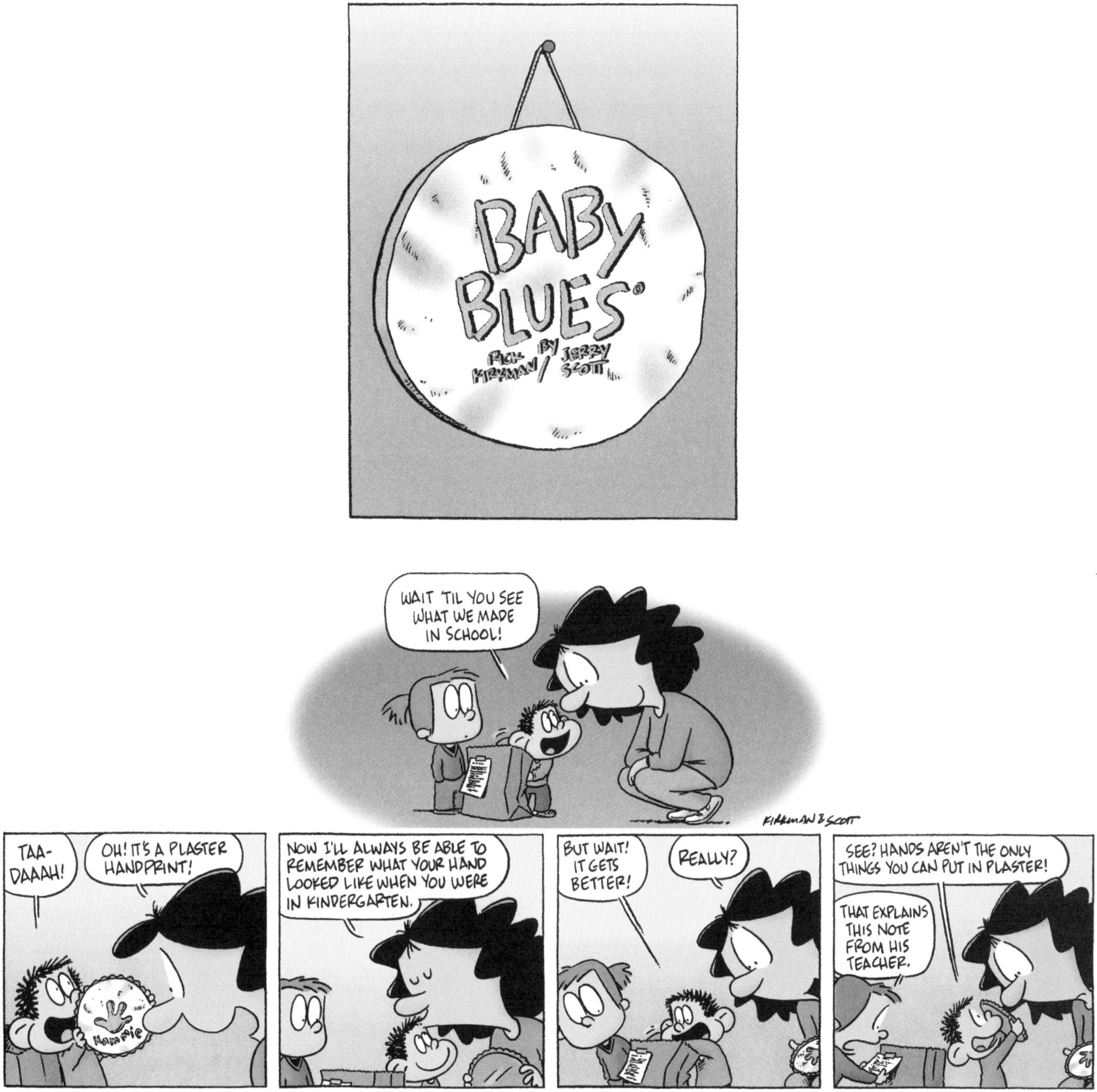

BABY BLUES®
BY RICK KIRKMAN / JERRY SCOTT
WAIT 'TIL YOU SEE WHAT WE MADE IN SCHOOL!
KIRKMAN & SCOTT
TAA-DAAAH!
OH! IT'S A PLASTER HANDPRINT!
Mommie
NOW I'LL ALWAYS BE ABLE TO REMEMBER WHAT YOUR HAND LOOKED LIKE WHEN YOU WERE IN KINDERGARTEN.
BUT WAIT! IT GETS BETTER!
REALLY?
SEE? HANDS AREN'T THE ONLY THINGS YOU CAN PUT IN PLASTER!
THAT EXPLAINS THIS NOTE FROM HIS TEACHER.

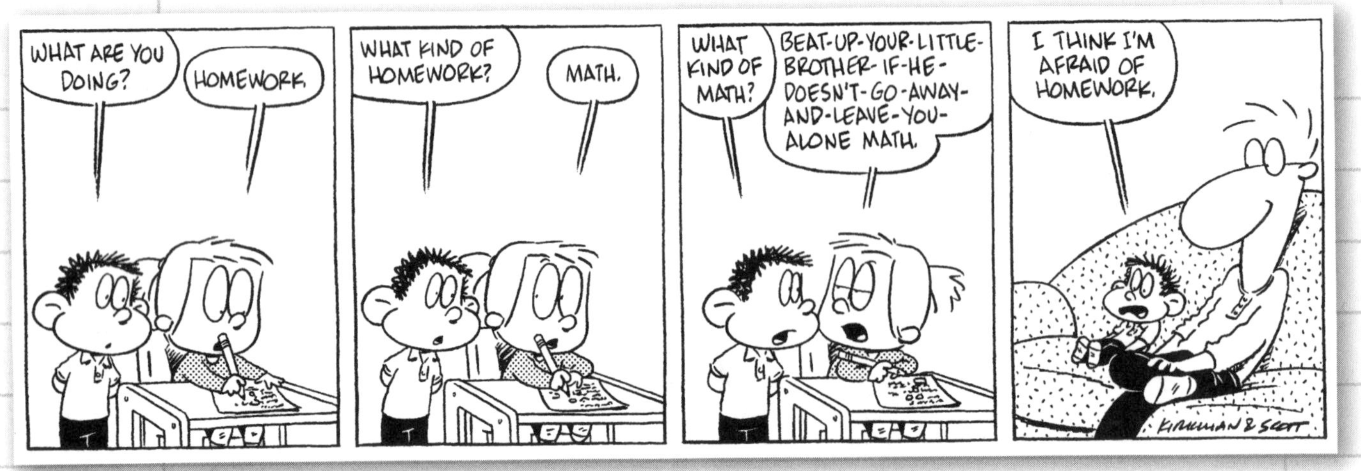
WHAT ARE YOU DOING?
HOMEWORK.
WHAT KIND OF HOMEWORK?
MATH.
WHAT KIND OF MATH?
BEAT-UP-YOUR-LITTLE-BROTHER-IF-HE-DOESN'T-GO-AWAY-AND-LEAVE-YOU-ALONE MATH.
I THINK I'M AFRAID OF HOMEWORK.
KIRKMAN & SCOTT

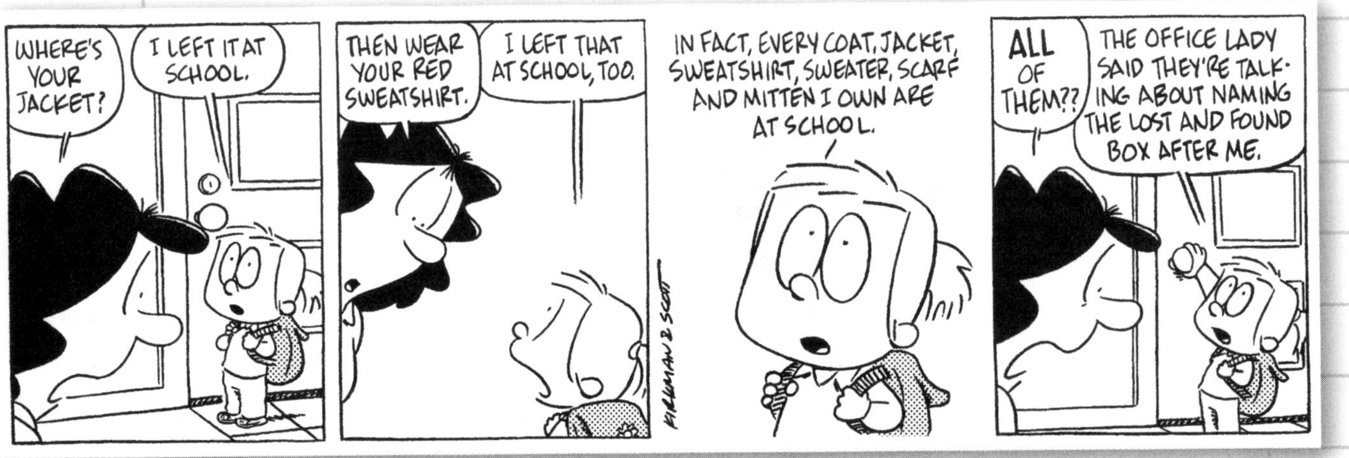
WHERE'S YOUR JACKET?
I LEFT IT AT SCHOOL.
THEN WEAR YOUR RED SWEATSHIRT.
I LEFT THAT AT SCHOOL, TOO.
KIRKMAN & SCOTT
IN FACT, EVERY COAT, JACKET, SWEATSHIRT, SWEATER, SCARF AND MITTEN I OWN ARE AT SCHOOL.
ALL OF THEM??
THE OFFICE LADY SAID THEY'RE TALKING ABOUT NAMING THE LOST AND FOUND BOX AFTER ME.

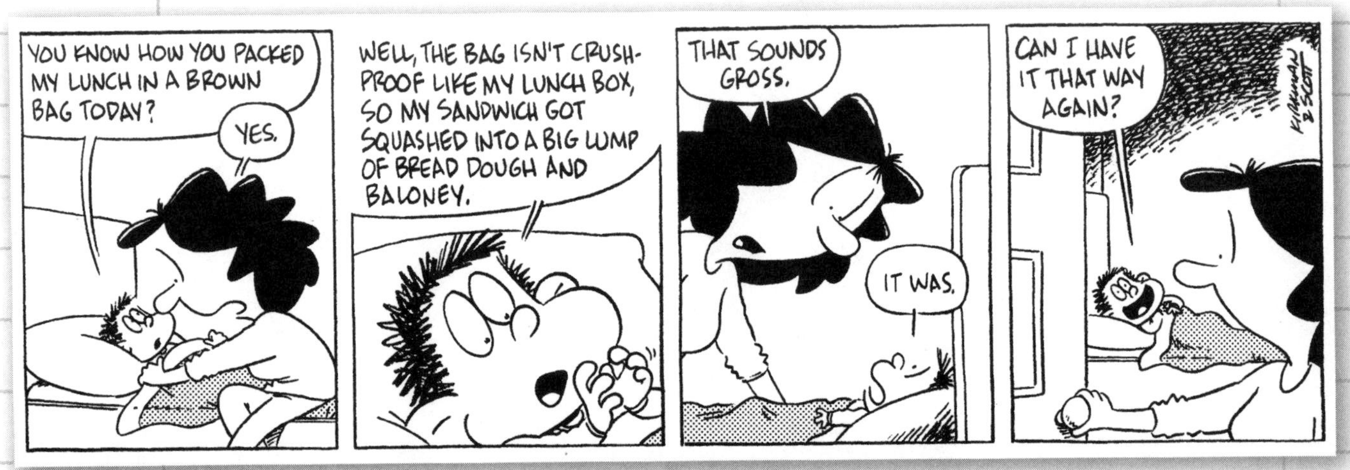
YOU KNOW HOW YOU PACKED MY LUNCH IN A BROWN BAG TODAY?
YES.
WELL, THE BAG ISN'T CRUSH-PROOF LIKE MY LUNCH BOX, SO MY SANDWICH GOT SQUASHED INTO A BIG LUMP OF BREAD DOUGH AND BALONEY.
THAT SOUNDS GROSS.
IT WAS.
CAN I HAVE IT THAT WAY AGAIN?
KIRKMAN & SCOTT

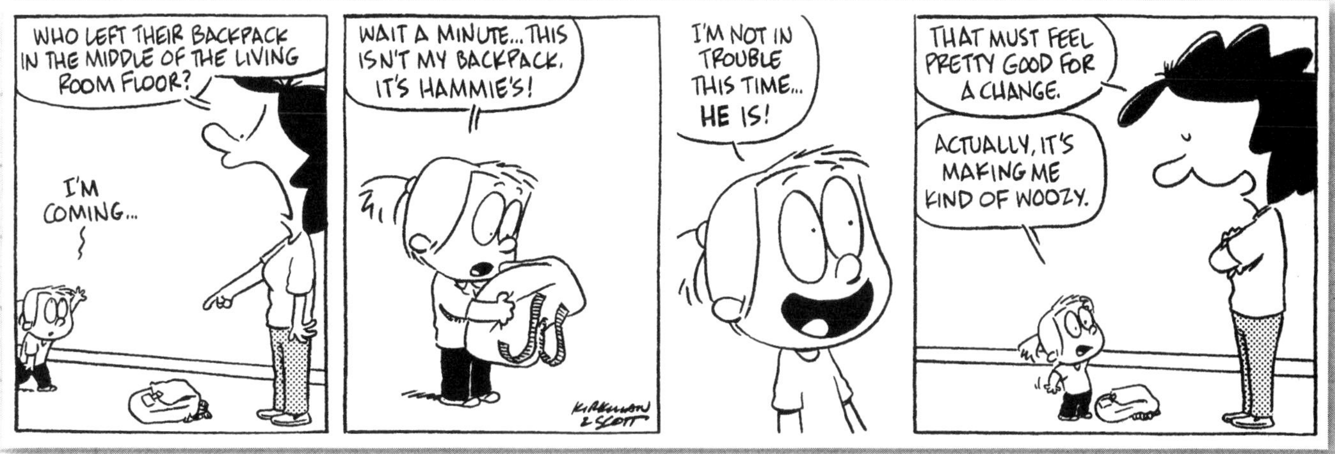
WHO LEFT THEIR BACKPACK IN THE MIDDLE OF THE LIVING ROOM FLOOR?
I'M COMING...
WAIT A MINUTE... THIS ISN'T MY BACKPACK. IT'S HAMMIE'S!
I'M NOT IN TROUBLE THIS TIME... HE IS!
THAT MUST FEEL PRETTY GOOD FOR A CHANGE.
ACTUALLY, IT'S MAKING ME KIND OF WOOZY.
KIRKMAN & SCOTT

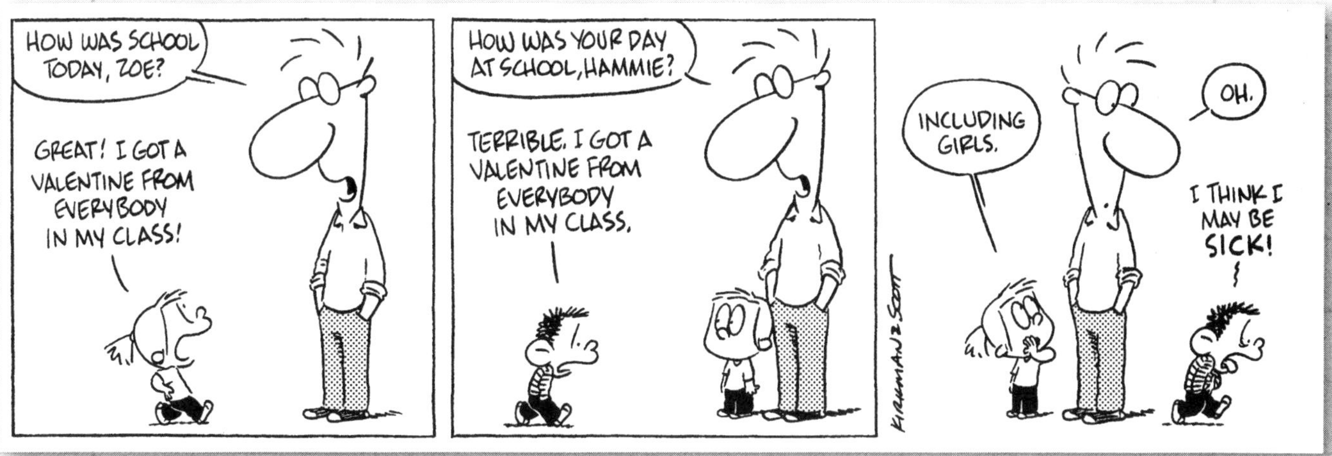
HOW WAS SCHOOL TODAY, ZOE?
GREAT! I GOT A VALENTINE FROM EVERYBODY IN MY CLASS!
HOW WAS YOUR DAY AT SCHOOL, HAMMIE?
TERRIBLE. I GOT A VALENTINE FROM EVERYBODY IN MY CLASS.
INCLUDING GIRLS.
OH.
I THINK I MAY BE SICK!
KIRKMAN & SCOTT

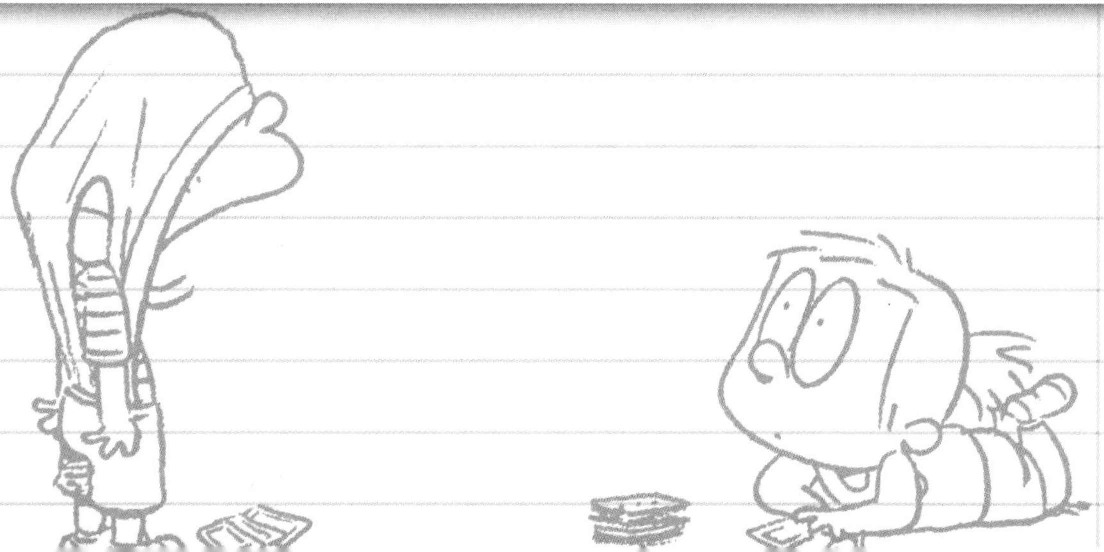

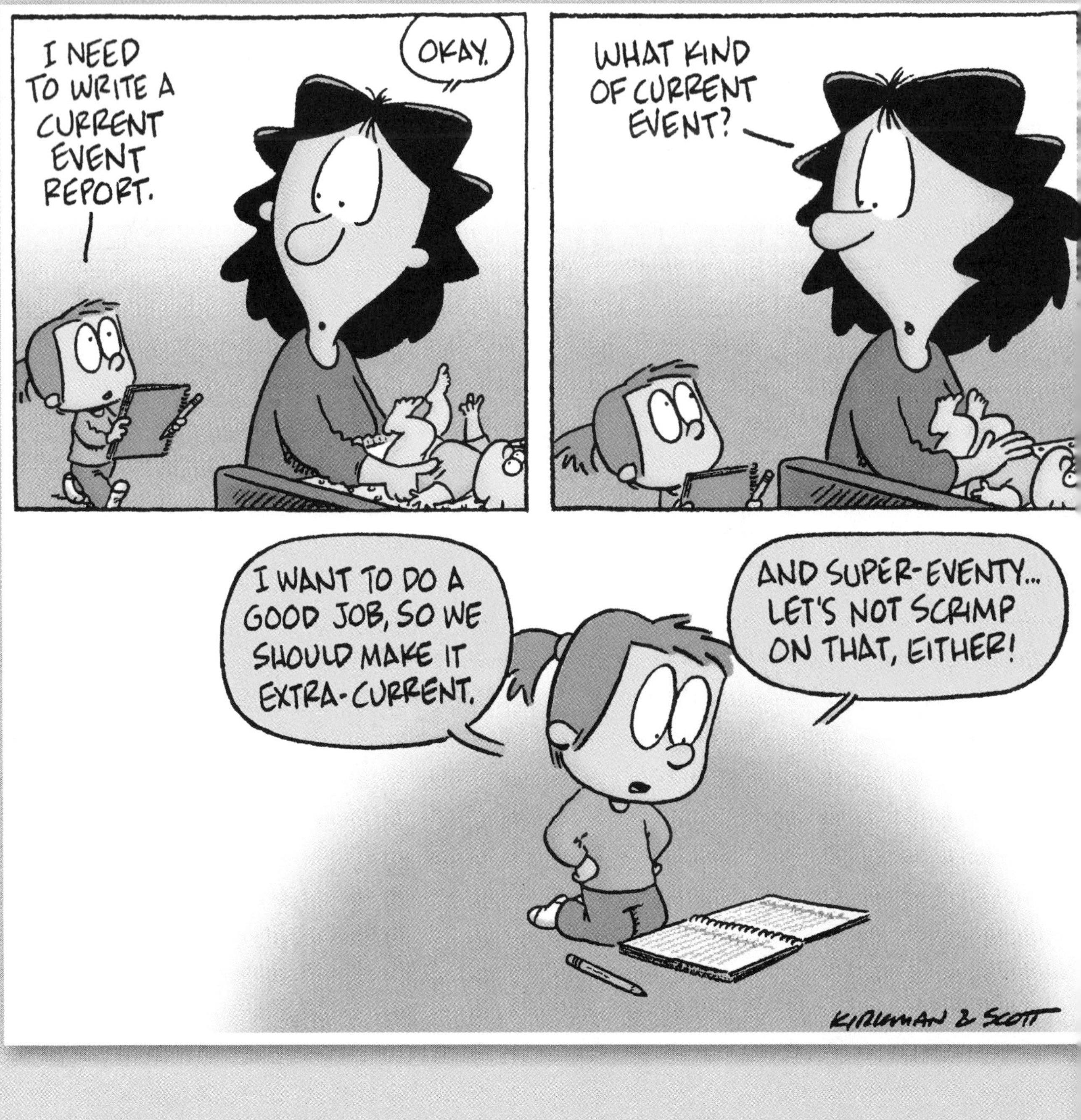
I NEED TO WRITE A CURRENT EVENT REPORT.
OKAY.
WHAT KIND OF CURRENT EVENT?
I WANT TO DO A GOOD JOB, SO WE SHOULD MAKE IT EXTRA-CURRENT.
AND SUPER-EVENTY... LET'S NOT SCRIMP ON THAT, EITHER!
KIRKMAN & SCOTT

I DON'T KNOW. THE REGULAR KIND, I GUESS.
JUST AS LONG AS IT'S CURRENT, AND AN EVENT.
YOU DON'T HAVE ANY IDEA WHAT A CURRENT EVENT IS, DO YOU?
DO YOU THINK THAT WILL AFFECT MY GRADE?

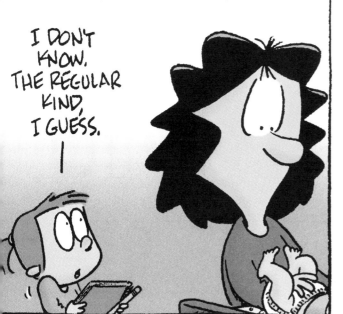

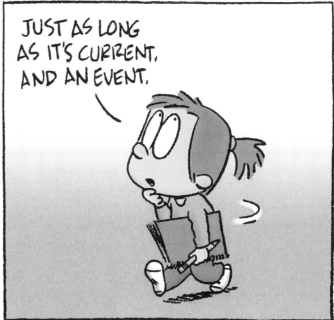

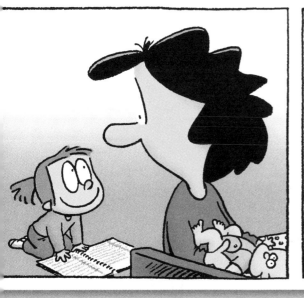

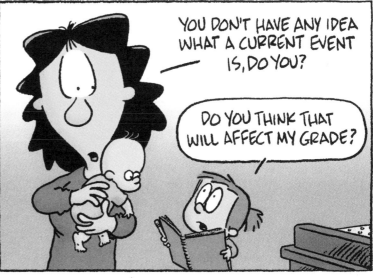

Panel 1: ALL RIGHT! MY SUBSCRIPTION TO "SOAP CARVERS' DIGEST" HAS EXPIRED! / FINALLY!

Panel 2: AND THE GOOD NEWS IS THAT ZOE'S SCHOOL ISN'T GOING TO SELL MAGAZINE SUBSCRIPTIONS AGAIN THIS YEAR. / HALLELUJAH!

Panel 3: WAIT— WHAT'S THE BAD NEWS? / GOOD AFTERNOON, SIR. WOULD YOU LIKE TO HELP ME RAISE MONEY FOR MY SCHOOL BY PURCHASING SOME DELICIOUS CANDY?

Panel 4: ZOE'S SCHOOL IS SELLING CANDY? / IT'S THEIR ANNUAL FUNDRAISER.

Panel 5: DON'T BE SO NEGATIVE ABOUT IT, DARRYL. / BUT CANDY??

Panel 6: WHY DON'T THEY SELL SOMETHING MORE USEFUL TO THE PARENTS OF SCHOOL-AGE KIDS? / LIKE WHAT?

Panel 7: LOTTERY TICKETS. / IF I DON'T SELL ALL 16 BOXES, YOU HAVE TO BUY THEM!

Panel 8: LOOK AT ALL THAT CANDY! / YOU CAN'T HAVE ANY. I'M SELLING IT FOR MY SCHOOL'S FUNDRAISER.

Panel 9: HOW MUCH ARE THEY? / THEY'RE SEVEN DOLLARS A BOX, OR TWO FOR TWELVE, WITH A TEN-PERCENT DISCOUNT FOR PURCHASES OVER FIFTY DOLLARS.

Panel 10: OH.

Panel 11: HOW MUCH FOR JUST A LICK?

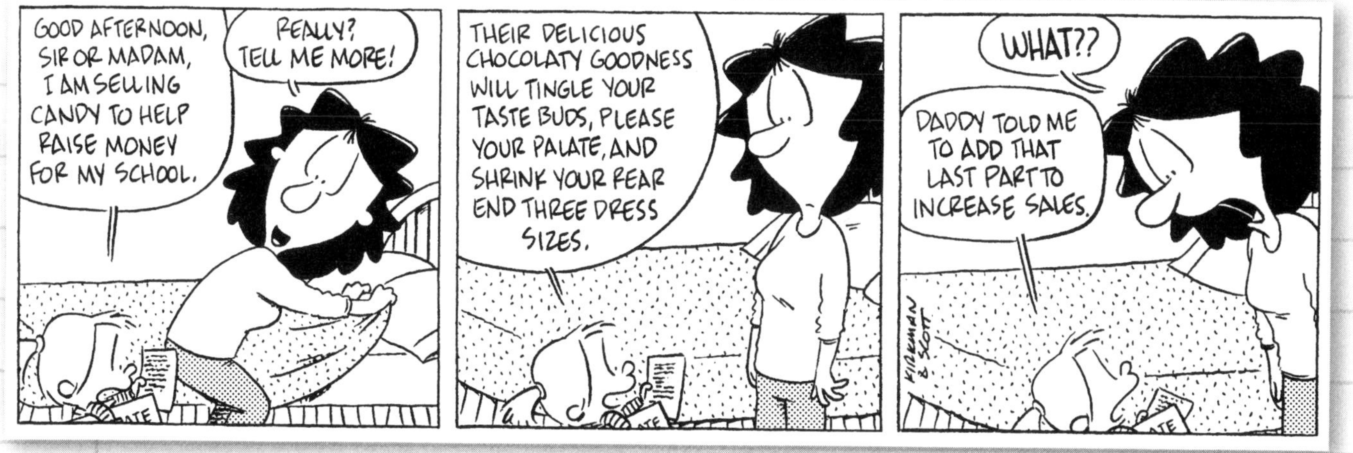
GOOD AFTERNOON, SIR OR MADAM, I AM SELLING CANDY TO HELP RAISE MONEY FOR MY SCHOOL.
REALLY? TELL ME MORE!
THEIR DELICIOUS CHOCOLATY GOODNESS WILL TINGLE YOUR TASTE BUDS, PLEASE YOUR PALATE, AND SHRINK YOUR REAR END THREE DRESS SIZES.
WHAT??
DADDY TOLD ME TO ADD THAT LAST PART TO INCREASE SALES.
KIRKMAN & SCOTT

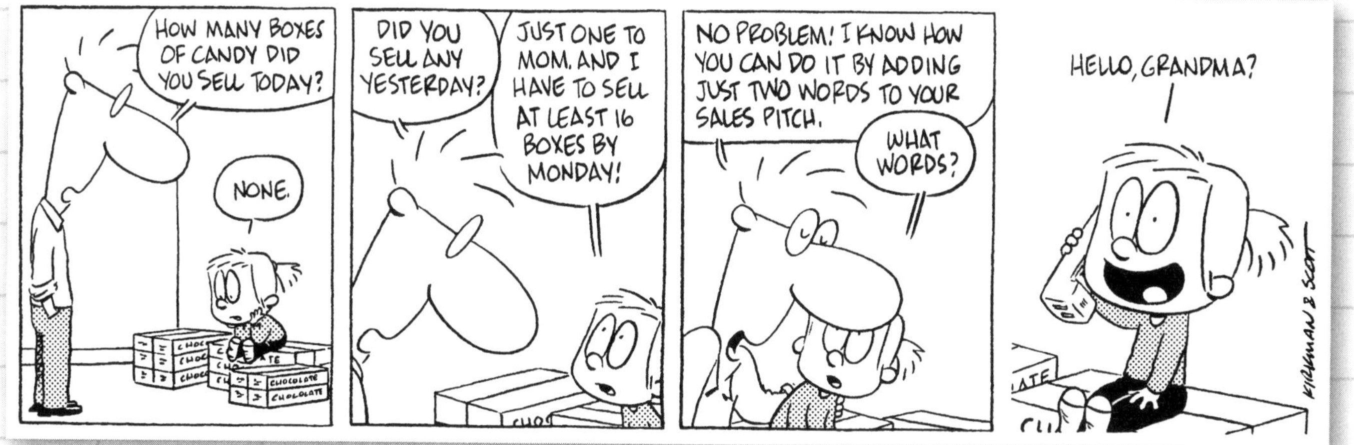
HOW MANY BOXES OF CANDY DID YOU SELL TODAY?
NONE.
DID YOU SELL ANY YESTERDAY?
JUST ONE TO MOM. AND I HAVE TO SELL AT LEAST 16 BOXES BY MONDAY!
NO PROBLEM! I KNOW HOW YOU CAN DO IT BY ADDING JUST TWO WORDS TO YOUR SALES PITCH.
WHAT WORDS?
HELLO, GRANDMA?
KIRKMAN & SCOTT

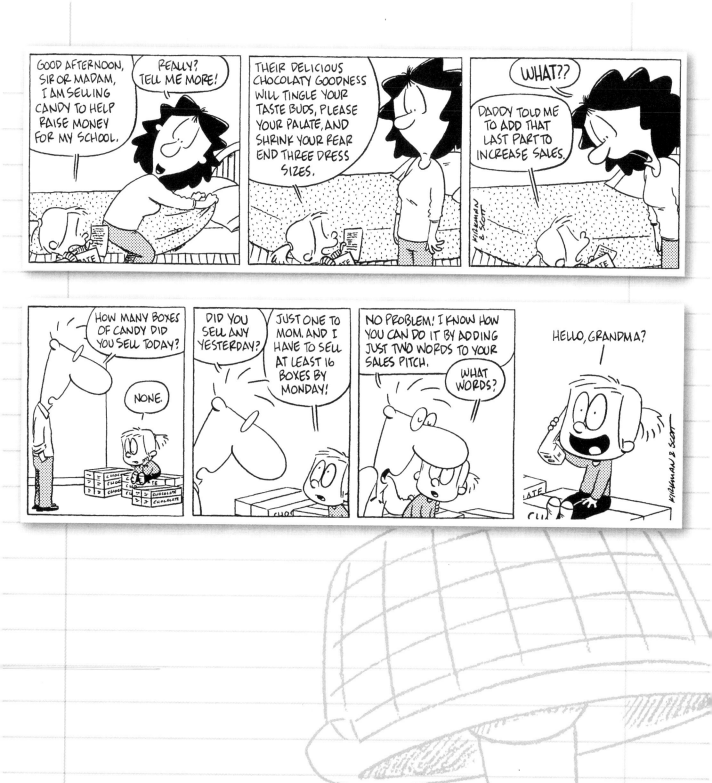

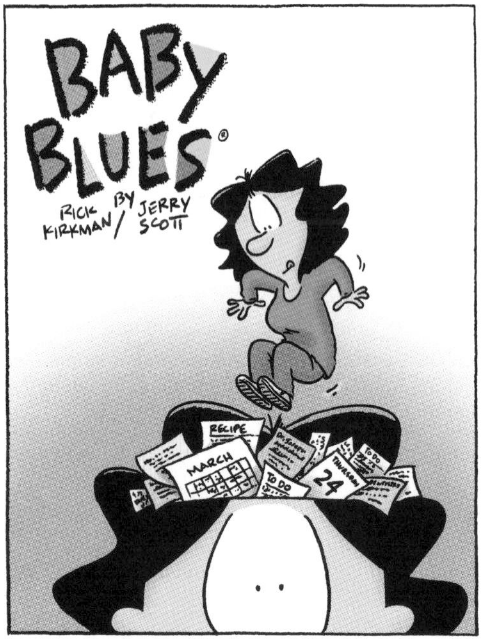
BABY BLUES®
BY RICK KIRKMAN / JERRY SCOTT
RECIPE
MARCH
TO DO
24
THURSDAY

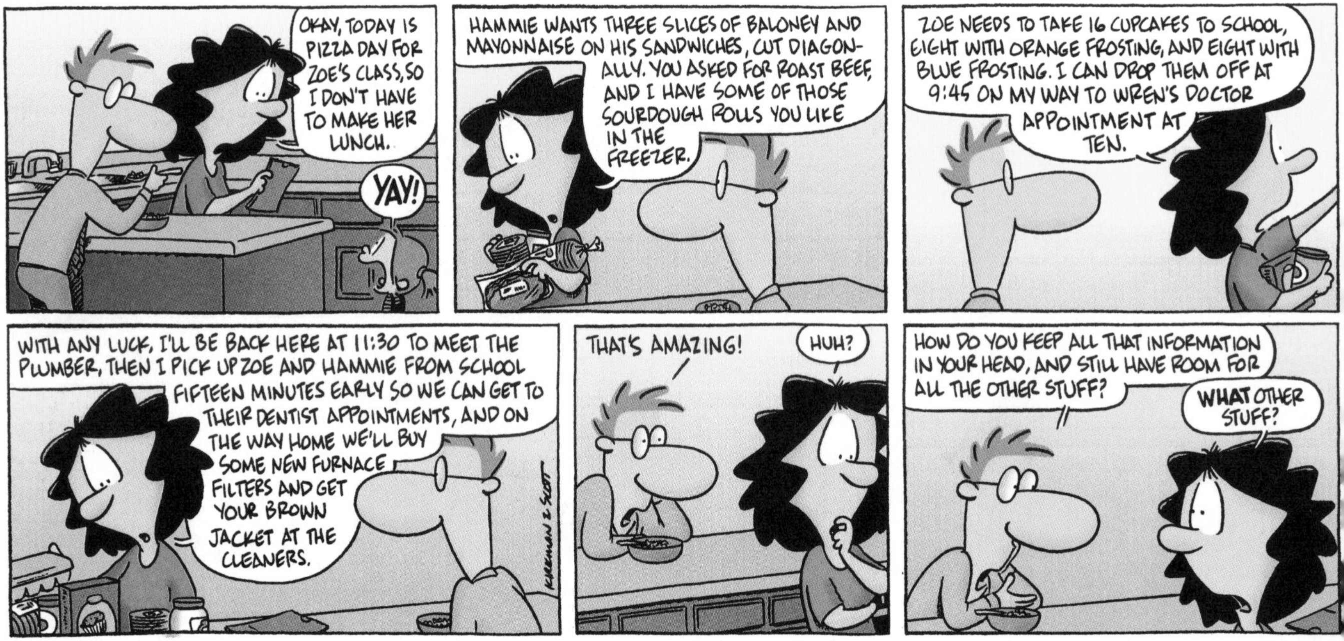
OKAY, TODAY IS PIZZA DAY FOR ZOE'S CLASS, SO I DON'T HAVE TO MAKE HER LUNCH.
YAY!
HAMMIE WANTS THREE SLICES OF BALONEY AND MAYONNAISE ON HIS SANDWICHES, CUT DIAGON-ALLY. YOU ASKED FOR ROAST BEEF, AND I HAVE SOME OF THOSE SOURDOUGH ROLLS YOU LIKE IN THE FREEZER.
ZOE NEEDS TO TAKE 16 CUPCAKES TO SCHOOL, EIGHT WITH ORANGE FROSTING, AND EIGHT WITH BLUE FROSTING. I CAN DROP THEM OFF AT 9:45 ON MY WAY TO WREN'S DOCTOR APPOINTMENT AT TEN.
WITH ANY LUCK, I'LL BE BACK HERE AT 11:30 TO MEET THE PLUMBER, THEN I PICK UP ZOE AND HAMMIE FROM SCHOOL FIFTEEN MINUTES EARLY SO WE CAN GET TO THEIR DENTIST APPOINTMENTS, AND ON THE WAY HOME WE'LL BUY SOME NEW FURNACE FILTERS AND GET YOUR BROWN JACKET AT THE CLEANERS.
KIRKMAN & SCOTT
THAT'S AMAZING!
HUH?
HOW DO YOU KEEP ALL THAT INFORMATION IN YOUR HEAD, AND STILL HAVE ROOM FOR ALL THE OTHER STUFF?
WHAT OTHER STUFF?

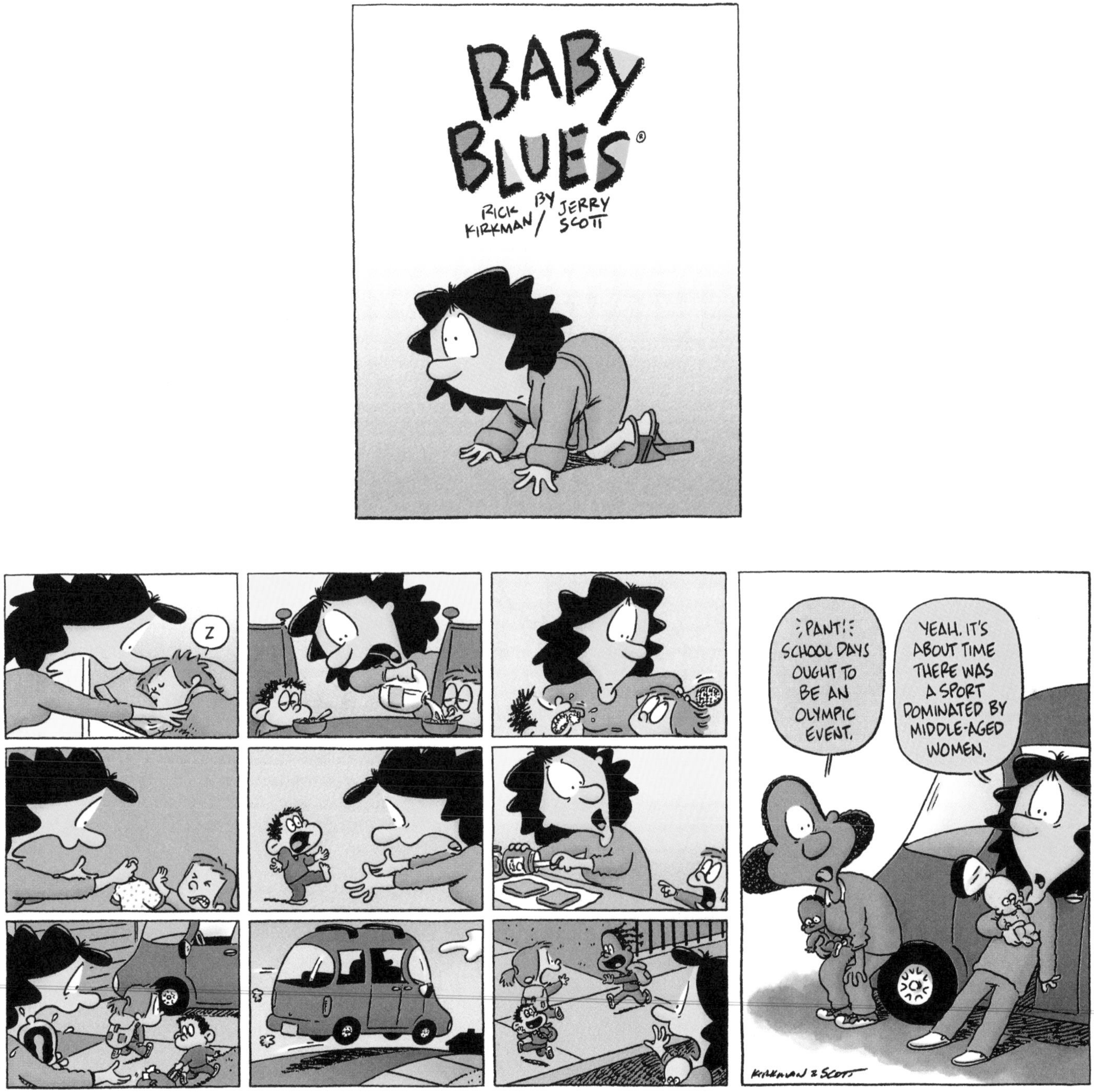
BABY BLUES®
BY RICK KIRKMAN / JERRY SCOTT
Z
PANT!
SCHOOL DAYS OUGHT TO BE AN OLYMPIC EVENT.
YEAH. IT'S ABOUT TIME THERE WAS A SPORT DOMINATED BY MIDDLE-AGED WOMEN.
KIRKMAN & SCOTT

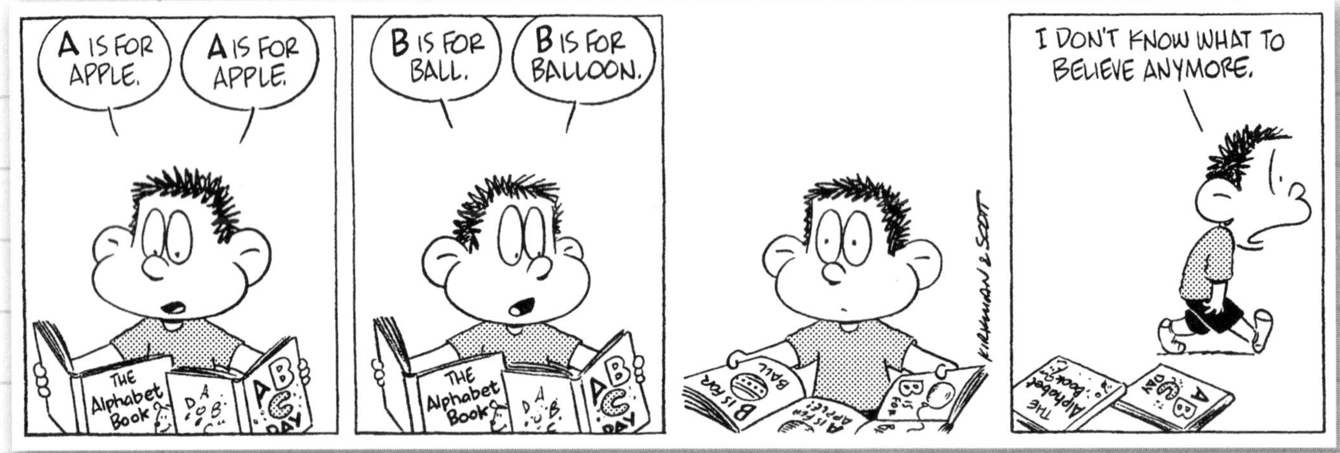
A IS FOR APPLE.
A IS FOR APPLE.
THE Alphabet Book
ABC DAY
B IS FOR BALL.
B IS FOR BALLOON.
B IS FOR BALL
KIRKMAN & SCOTT
I DON'T KNOW WHAT TO BELIEVE ANYMORE.

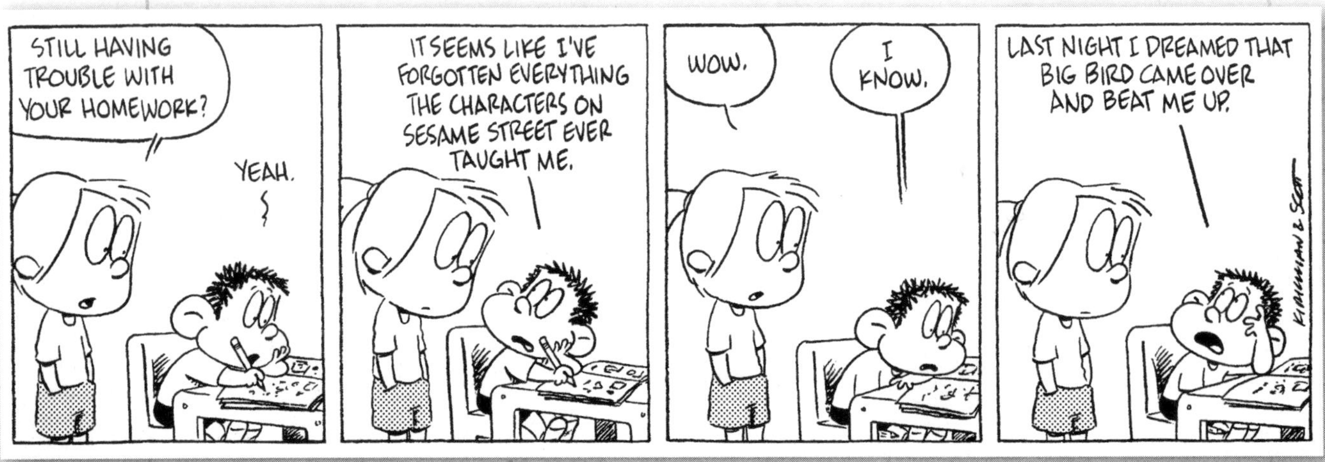
STILL HAVING TROUBLE WITH YOUR HOMEWORK?
YEAH.
IT SEEMS LIKE I'VE FORGOTTEN EVERYTHING THE CHARACTERS ON SESAME STREET EVER TAUGHT ME.
WOW.
I KNOW.
LAST NIGHT I DREAMED THAT BIG BIRD CAME OVER AND BEAT ME UP.
KIRKMAN & SCOTT

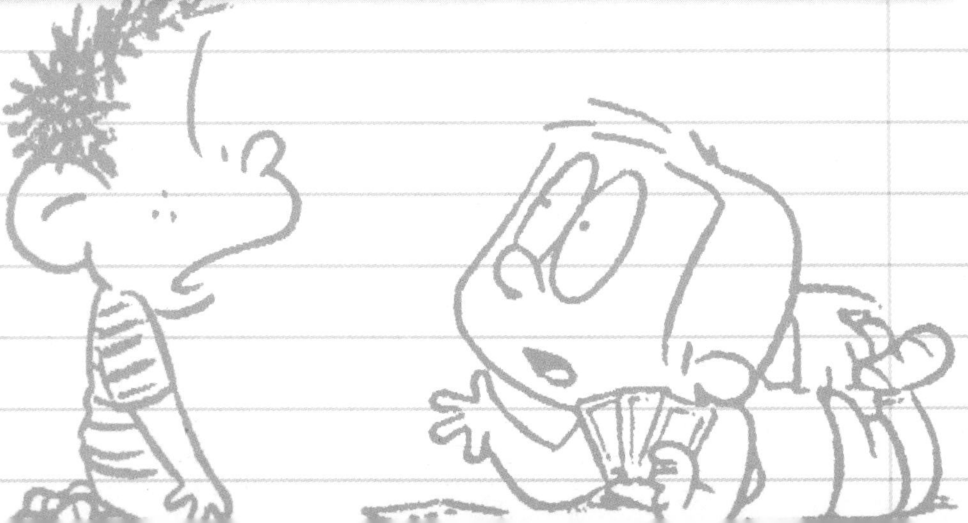

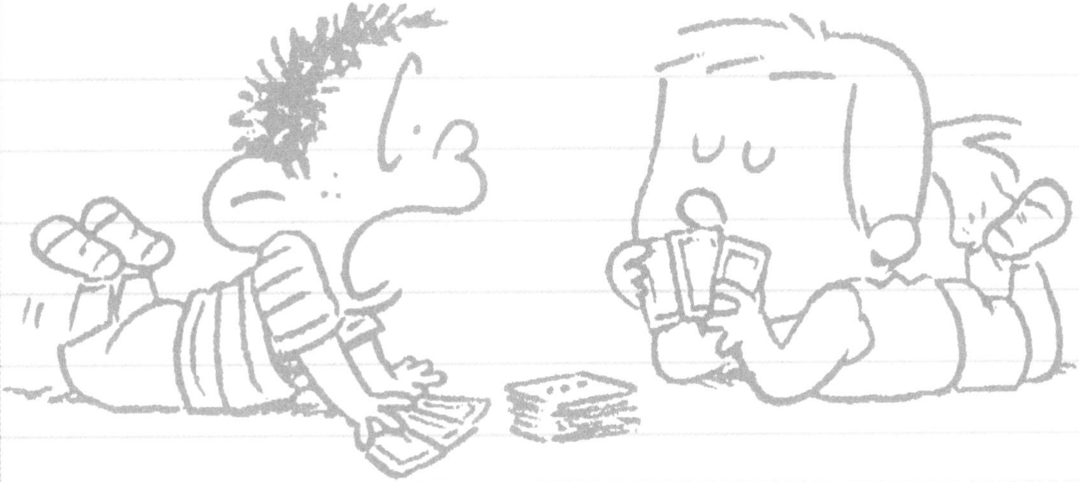

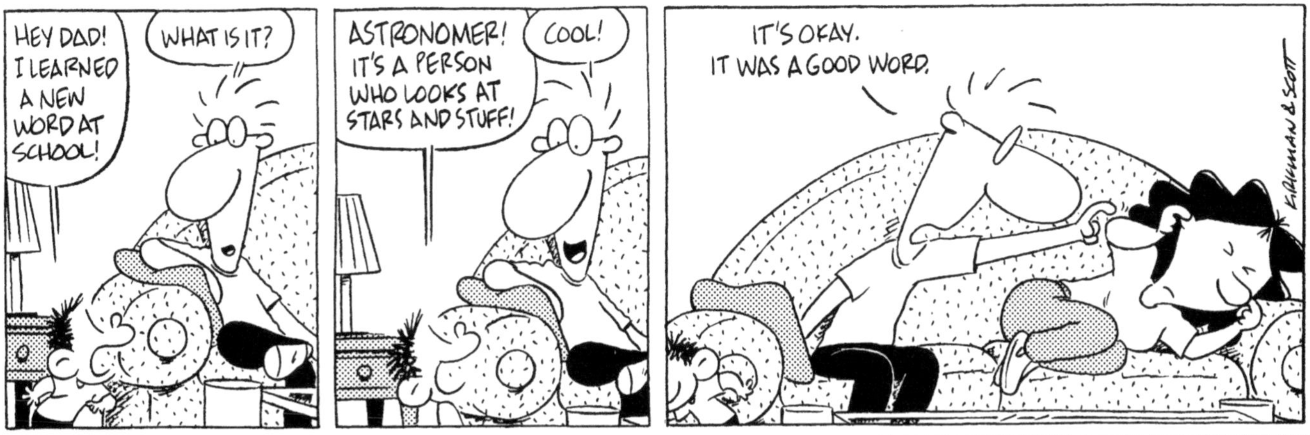
HEY DAD! I LEARNED A NEW WORD AT SCHOOL!
WHAT IS IT?
ASTRONOMER! IT'S A PERSON WHO LOOKS AT STARS AND STUFF!
COOL!
IT'S OKAY. IT WAS A GOOD WORD.
KIRKMAN & SCOTT

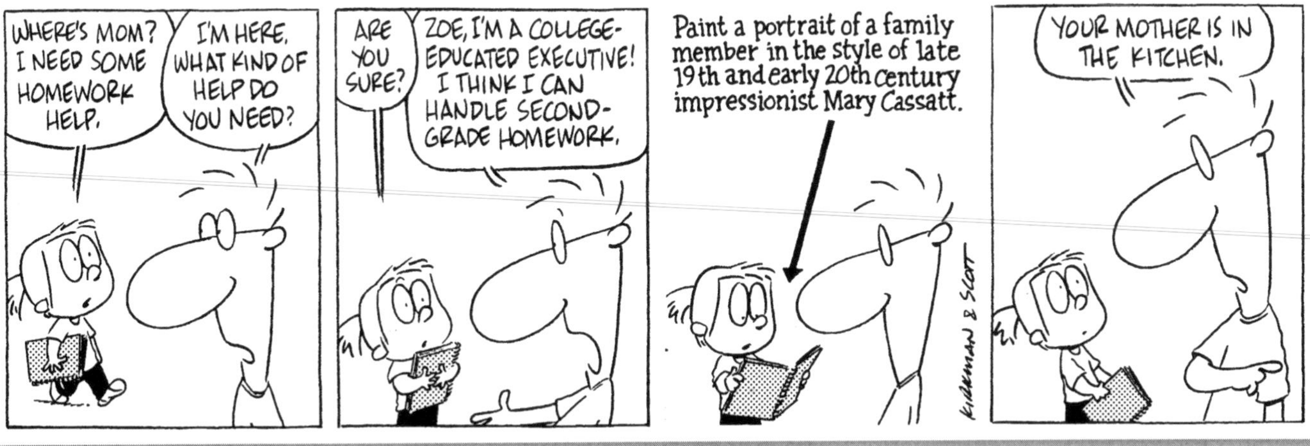
WHERE'S MOM? I NEED SOME HOMEWORK HELP.
I'M HERE. WHAT KIND OF HELP DO YOU NEED?
ARE YOU SURE?
ZOE, I'M A COLLEGE-EDUCATED EXECUTIVE! I THINK I CAN HANDLE SECOND-GRADE HOMEWORK.
Paint a portrait of a family member in the style of late 19th and early 20th century impressionist Mary Cassatt.
KIRKMAN & SCOTT
YOUR MOTHER IS IN THE KITCHEN.

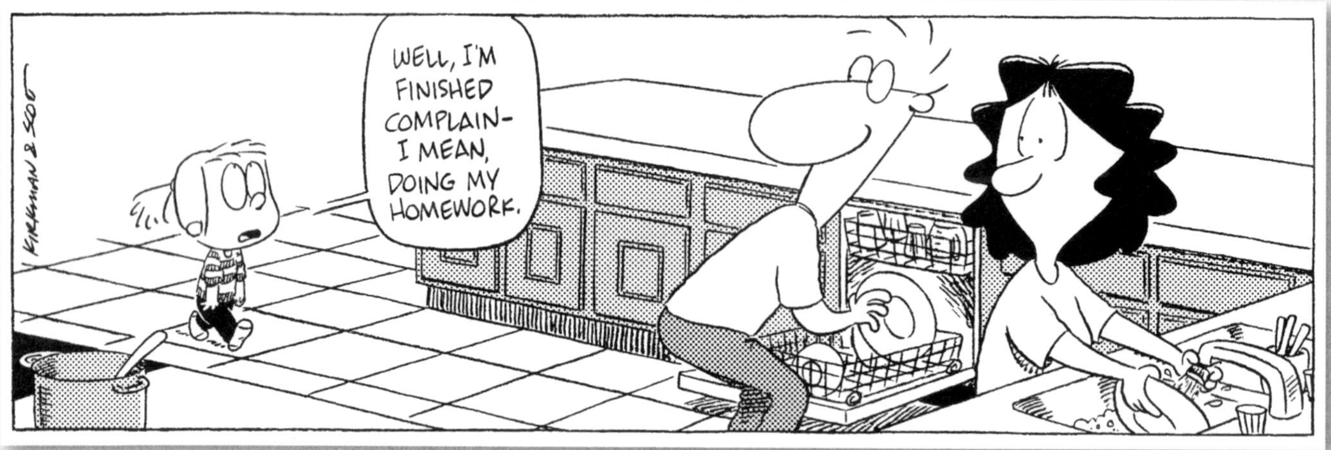
KIRKMAN & SCOTT
WELL, I'M FINISHED COMPLAIN- I MEAN, DOING MY HOMEWORK.

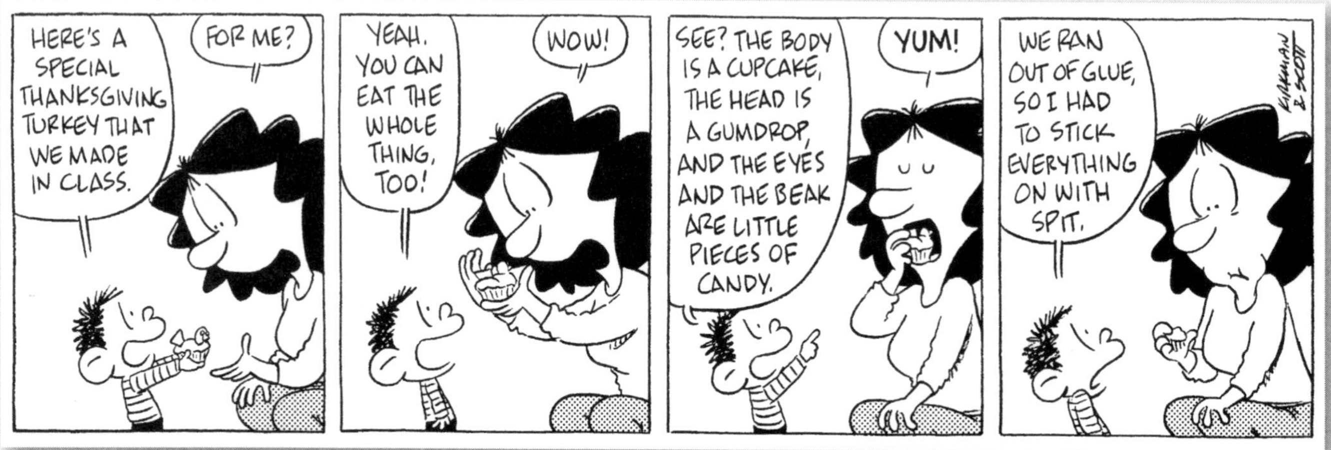
HERE'S A SPECIAL THANKSGIVING TURKEY THAT WE MADE IN CLASS.
FOR ME?
YEAH. YOU CAN EAT THE WHOLE THING, TOO!
WOW!
SEE? THE BODY IS A CUPCAKE, THE HEAD IS A GUMDROP, AND THE EYES AND THE BEAK ARE LITTLE PIECES OF CANDY.
YUM!
WE RAN OUT OF GLUE, SO I HAD TO STICK EVERYTHING ON WITH SPIT.
KIRKMAN & SCOTT

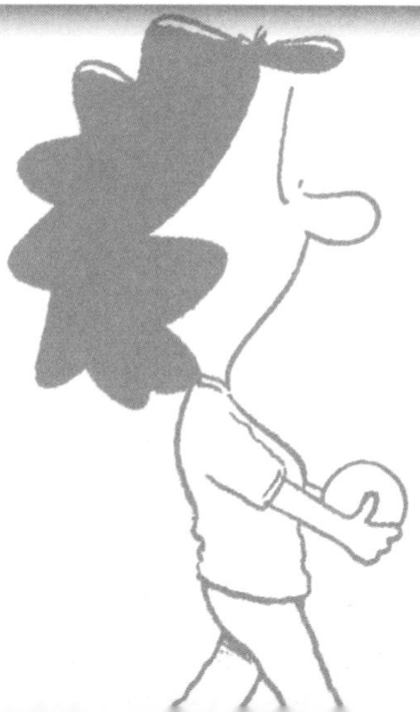

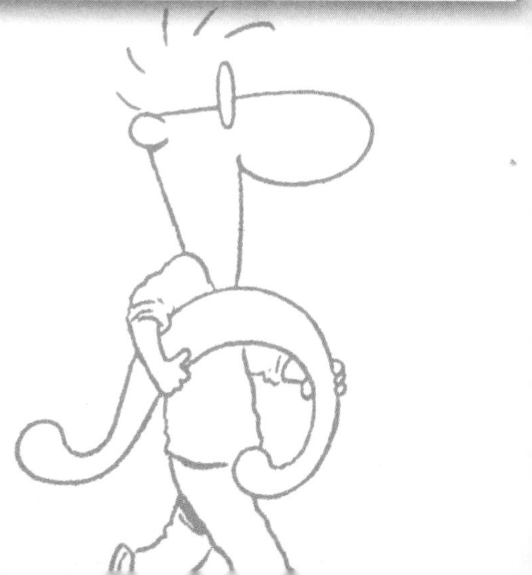

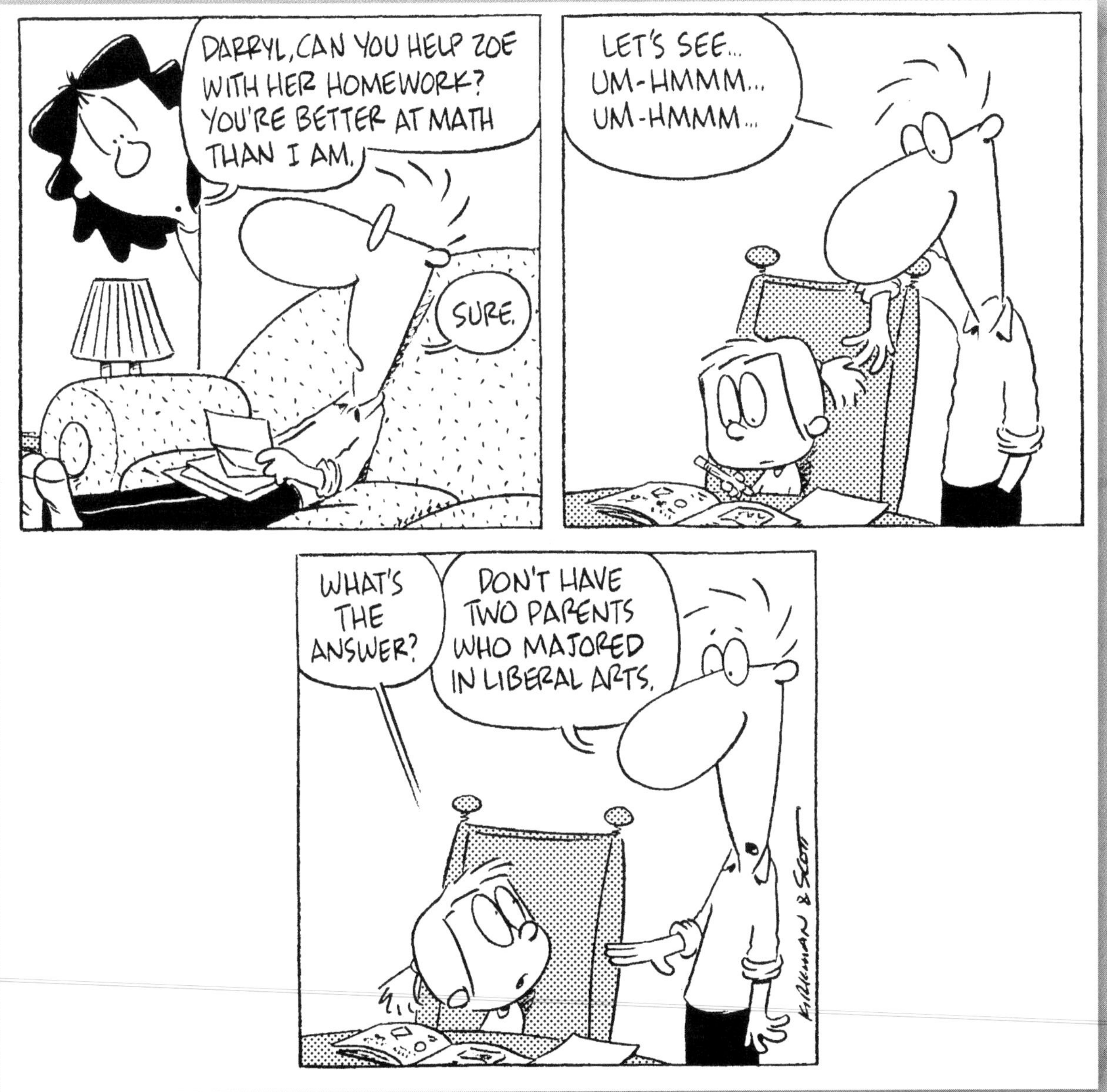
DARRYL, CAN YOU HELP ZOE WITH HER HOMEWORK? YOU'RE BETTER AT MATH THAN I AM.
SURE.
LET'S SEE... UM-HMMM... UM-HMMM...
WHAT'S THE ANSWER?
DON'T HAVE TWO PARENTS WHO MAJORED IN LIBERAL ARTS.
KIRKMAN & SCOTT

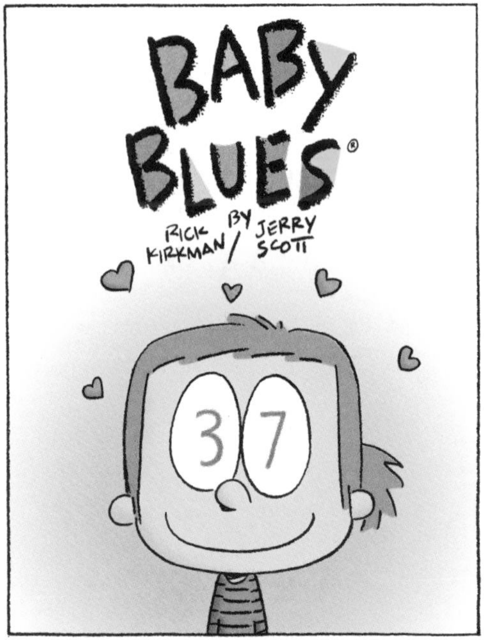
BABY BLUES®
RICK KIRKMAN / BY / JERRY SCOTT
37

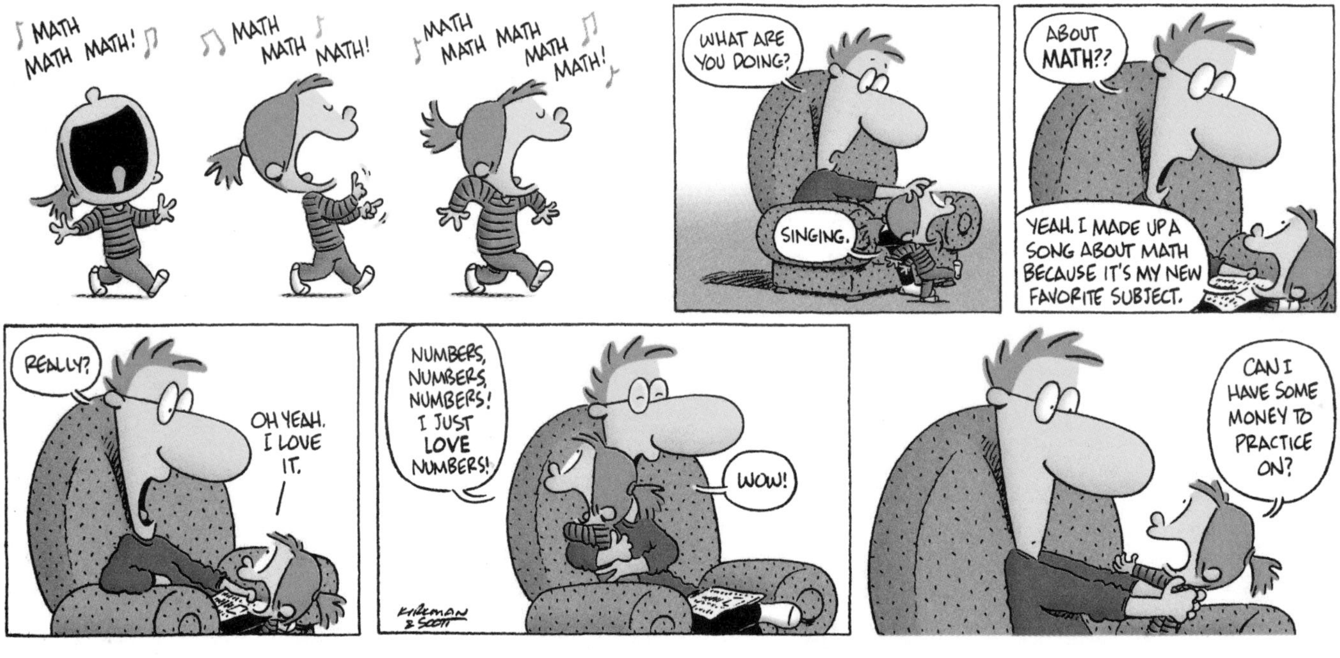
MATH MATH MATH!
MATH MATH MATH!
MATH MATH MATH MATH MATH!
WHAT ARE YOU DOING?
SINGING.
ABOUT MATH??
YEAH. I MADE UP A SONG ABOUT MATH BECAUSE IT'S MY NEW FAVORITE SUBJECT.
REALLY?
OH YEAH. I LOVE IT.
NUMBERS, NUMBERS, NUMBERS! I JUST LOVE NUMBERS!
WOW!
KIRKMAN & SCOTT
CAN I HAVE SOME MONEY TO PRACTICE ON?

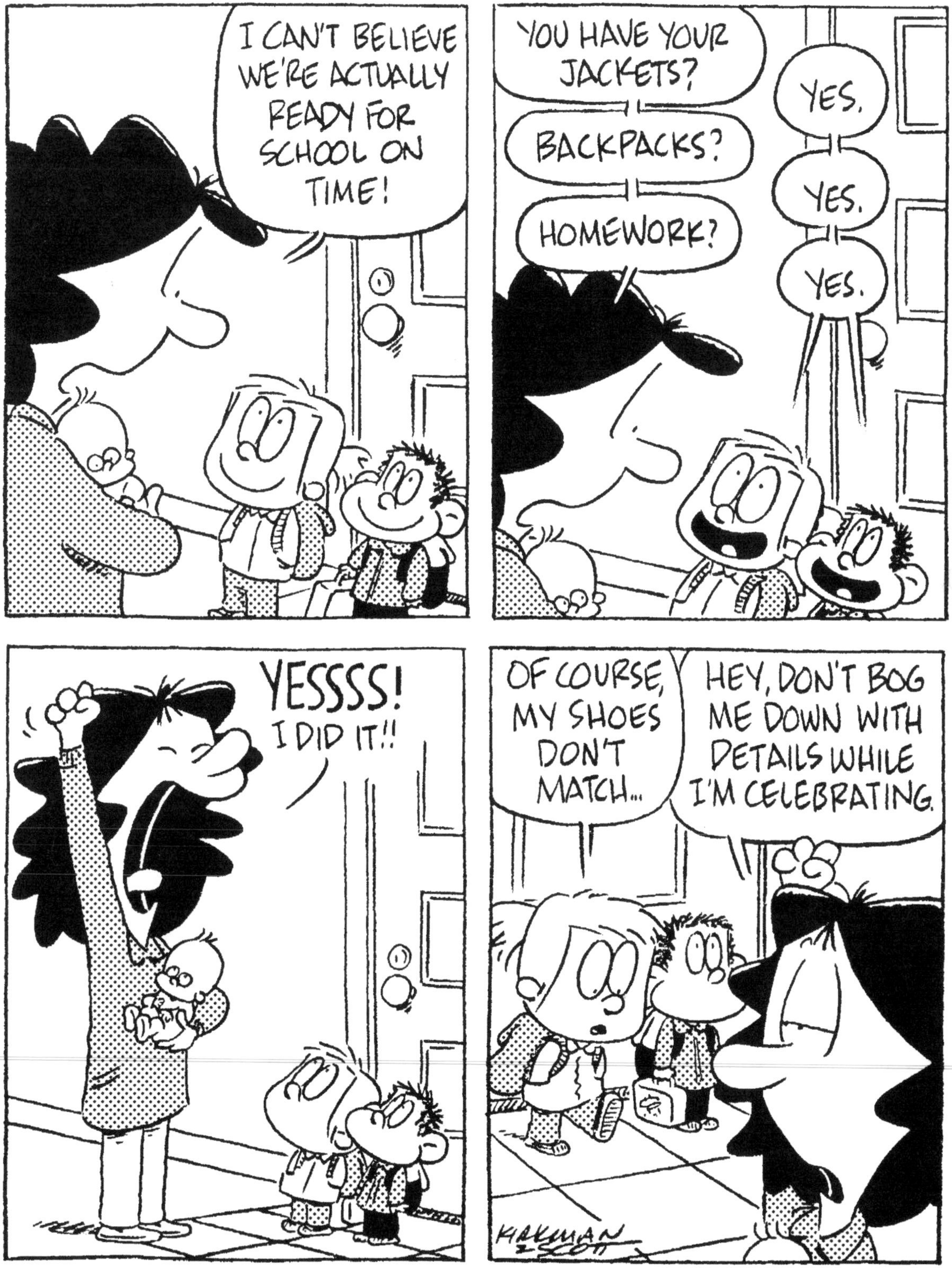
I CAN'T BELIEVE WE'RE ACTUALLY READY FOR SCHOOL ON TIME!
YOU HAVE YOUR JACKETS?
YES.
BACKPACKS?
YES.
HOMEWORK?
YES.
YESSSS! I DID IT!!
OF COURSE, MY SHOES DON'T MATCH...
HEY, DON'T BOG ME DOWN WITH DETAILS WHILE I'M CELEBRATING.
KIRKMAN & SCOTT

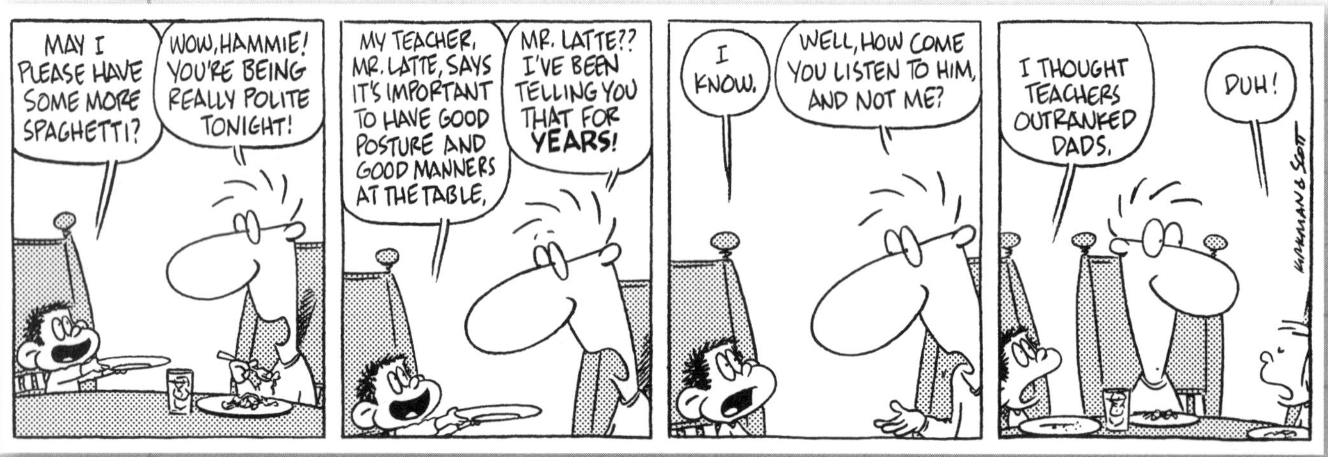
MAY I PLEASE HAVE SOME MORE SPAGHETTI?
WOW, HAMMIE! YOU'RE BEING REALLY POLITE TONIGHT!
MY TEACHER, MR. LATTE, SAYS IT'S IMPORTANT TO HAVE GOOD POSTURE AND GOOD MANNERS AT THE TABLE.
MR. LATTE?? I'VE BEEN TELLING YOU THAT FOR **YEARS!**
I KNOW.
WELL, HOW COME YOU LISTEN TO HIM, AND NOT ME?
I THOUGHT TEACHERS OUTRANKED DADS.
DUH!
KIRKMAN & SCOTT

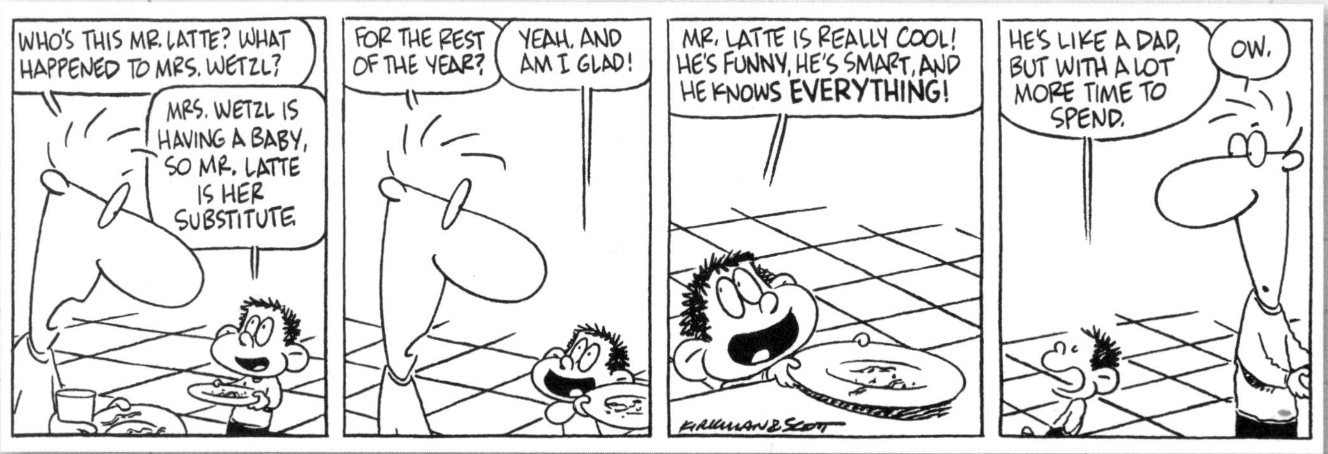
WHO'S THIS MR. LATTE? WHAT HAPPENED TO MRS. WETZL?
MRS. WETZL IS HAVING A BABY, SO MR. LATTE IS HER SUBSTITUTE.
FOR THE REST OF THE YEAR?
YEAH. AND AM I GLAD!
MR. LATTE IS REALLY COOL! HE'S FUNNY, HE'S SMART, AND HE KNOWS **EVERYTHING!**
HE'S LIKE A DAD, BUT WITH A LOT MORE TIME TO SPEND.
OW.
KIRKMAN & SCOTT

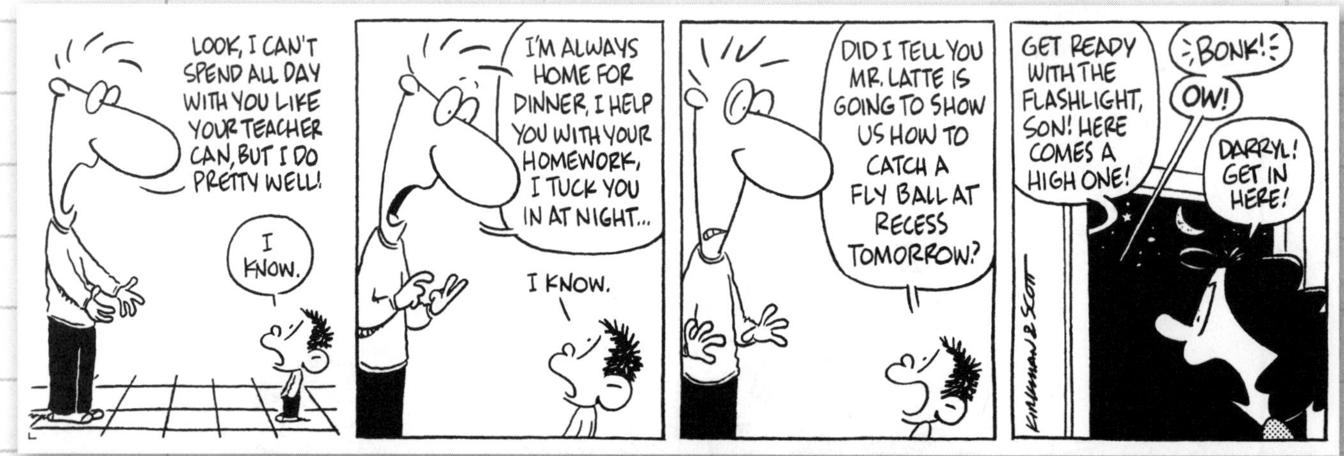
LOOK, I CAN'T SPEND ALL DAY WITH YOU LIKE YOUR TEACHER CAN, BUT I DO PRETTY WELL!
I KNOW.
I'M ALWAYS HOME FOR DINNER, I HELP YOU WITH YOUR HOMEWORK, I TUCK YOU IN AT NIGHT...
I KNOW.
DID I TELL YOU MR. LATTE IS GOING TO SHOW US HOW TO CATCH A FLY BALL AT RECESS TOMORROW?
GET READY WITH THE FLASHLIGHT, SON! HERE COMES A HIGH ONE!
BONK!
OW!
DARRYL! GET IN HERE!
KIRKMAN & SCOTT

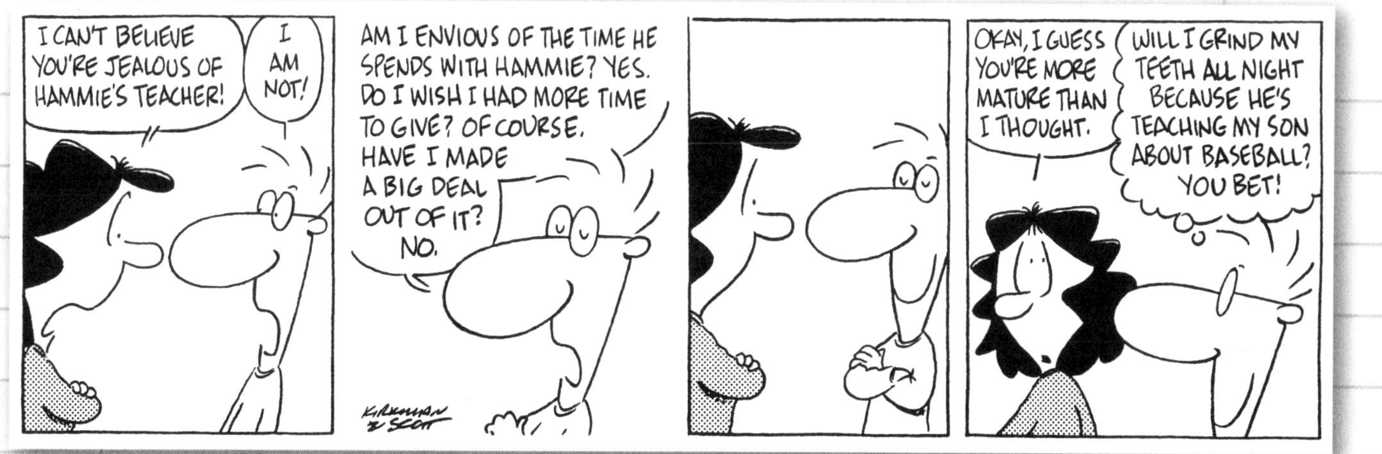
I CAN'T BELIEVE YOU'RE JEALOUS OF HAMMIE'S TEACHER!
I AM NOT!
AM I ENVIOUS OF THE TIME HE SPENDS WITH HAMMIE? YES. DO I WISH I HAD MORE TIME TO GIVE? OF COURSE. HAVE I MADE A BIG DEAL OUT OF IT? NO.
KIRKMAN & SCOTT
OKAY, I GUESS YOU'RE MORE MATURE THAN I THOUGHT.
WILL I GRIND MY TEETH ALL NIGHT BECAUSE HE'S TEACHING MY SON ABOUT BASEBALL? YOU BET!

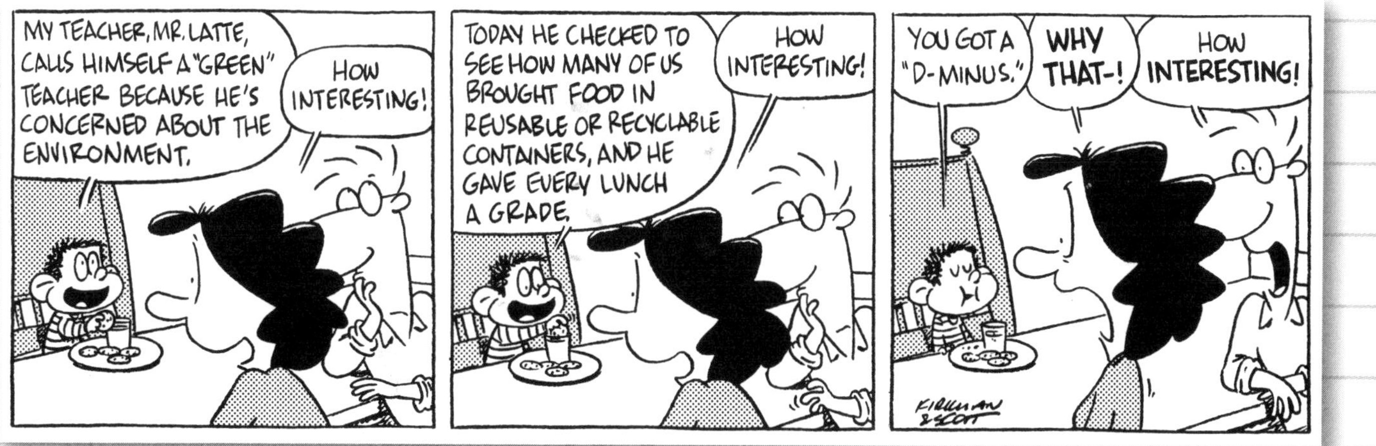
MY TEACHER, MR. LATTE, CALLS HIMSELF A "GREEN" TEACHER BECAUSE HE'S CONCERNED ABOUT THE ENVIRONMENT.
HOW INTERESTING!
TODAY HE CHECKED TO SEE HOW MANY OF US BROUGHT FOOD IN REUSABLE OR RECYCLABLE CONTAINERS, AND HE GAVE EVERY LUNCH A GRADE.
HOW INTERESTING!
YOU GOT A "D-MINUS."
WHY THAT-!
HOW INTERESTING!
KIRKMAN & SCOTT

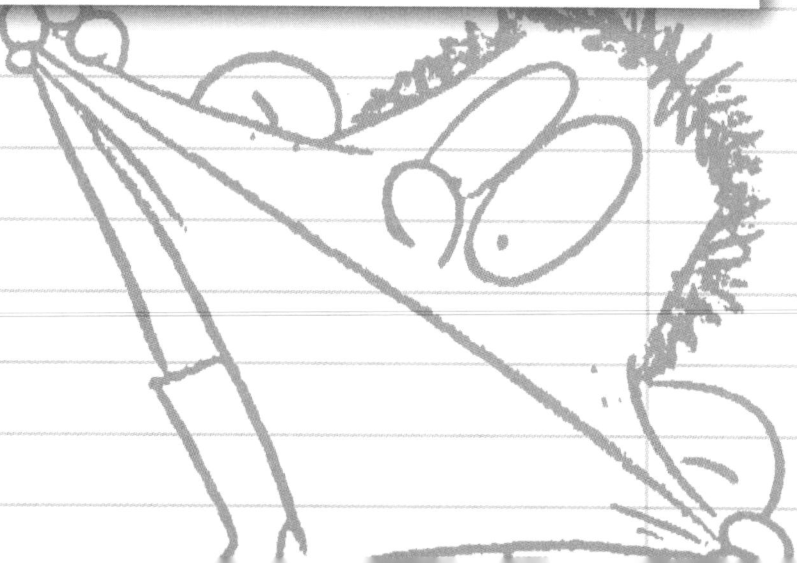

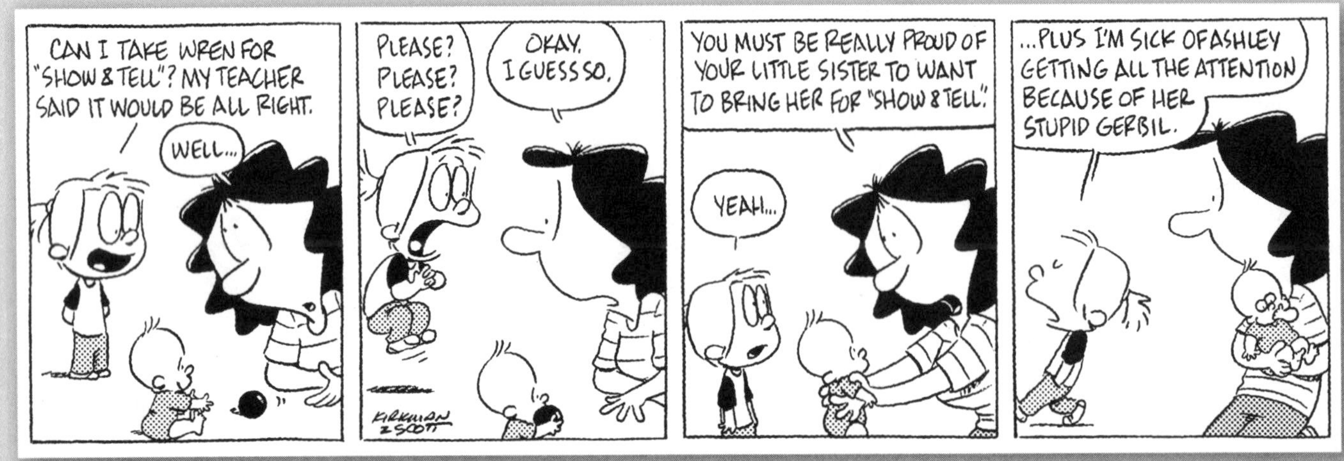
CAN I TAKE WREN FOR "SHOW & TELL"? MY TEACHER SAID IT WOULD BE ALL RIGHT.
WELL...
PLEASE? PLEASE? PLEASE?
OKAY. I GUESS SO.
KIRKMAN & SCOTT
YOU MUST BE REALLY PROUD OF YOUR LITTLE SISTER TO WANT TO BRING HER FOR "SHOW & TELL."
YEAH...
...PLUS I'M SICK OF ASHLEY GETTING ALL THE ATTENTION BECAUSE OF HER STUPID GERBIL.

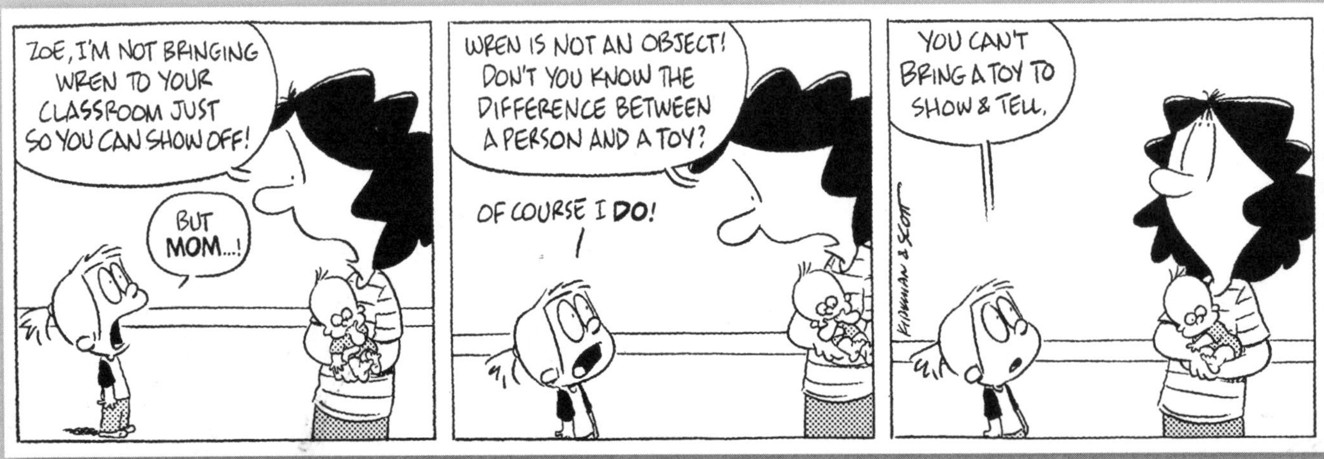
ZOE, I'M NOT BRINGING WREN TO YOUR CLASSROOM JUST SO YOU CAN SHOW OFF!
BUT MOM...!
WREN IS NOT AN OBJECT! DON'T YOU KNOW THE DIFFERENCE BETWEEN A PERSON AND A TOY?
OF COURSE I DO!
KIRKMAN & SCOTT
YOU CAN'T BRING A TOY TO SHOW & TELL.

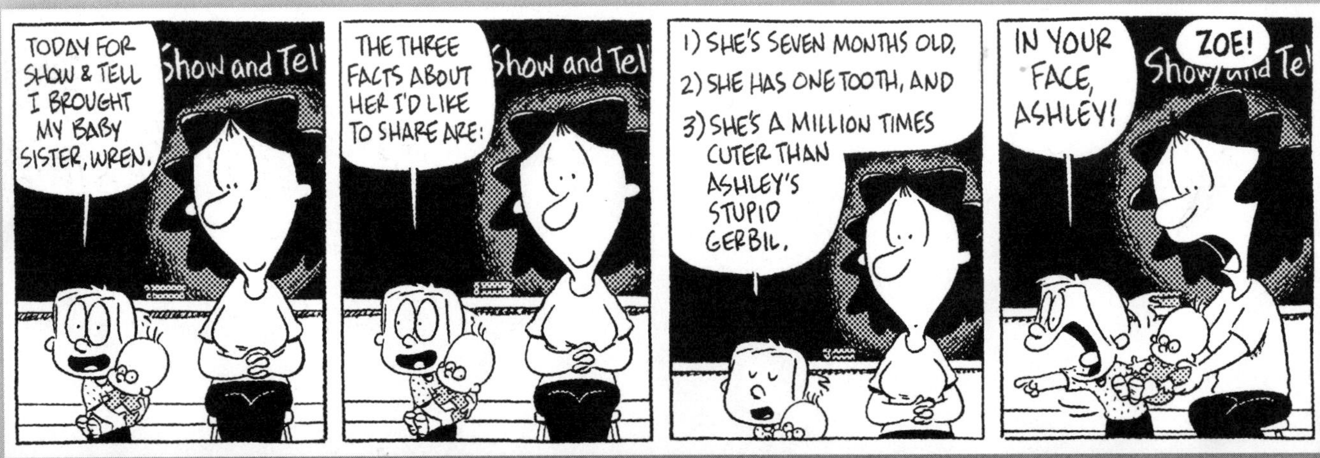
TODAY FOR SHOW & TELL I BROUGHT MY BABY SISTER, WREN.
Show and Tel
THE THREE FACTS ABOUT HER I'D LIKE TO SHARE ARE:
Show and Tel
1) SHE'S SEVEN MONTHS OLD,
2) SHE HAS ONE TOOTH, AND
3) SHE'S A MILLION TIMES CUTER THAN ASHLEY'S STUPID GERBIL.
IN YOUR FACE, ASHLEY!
ZOE!

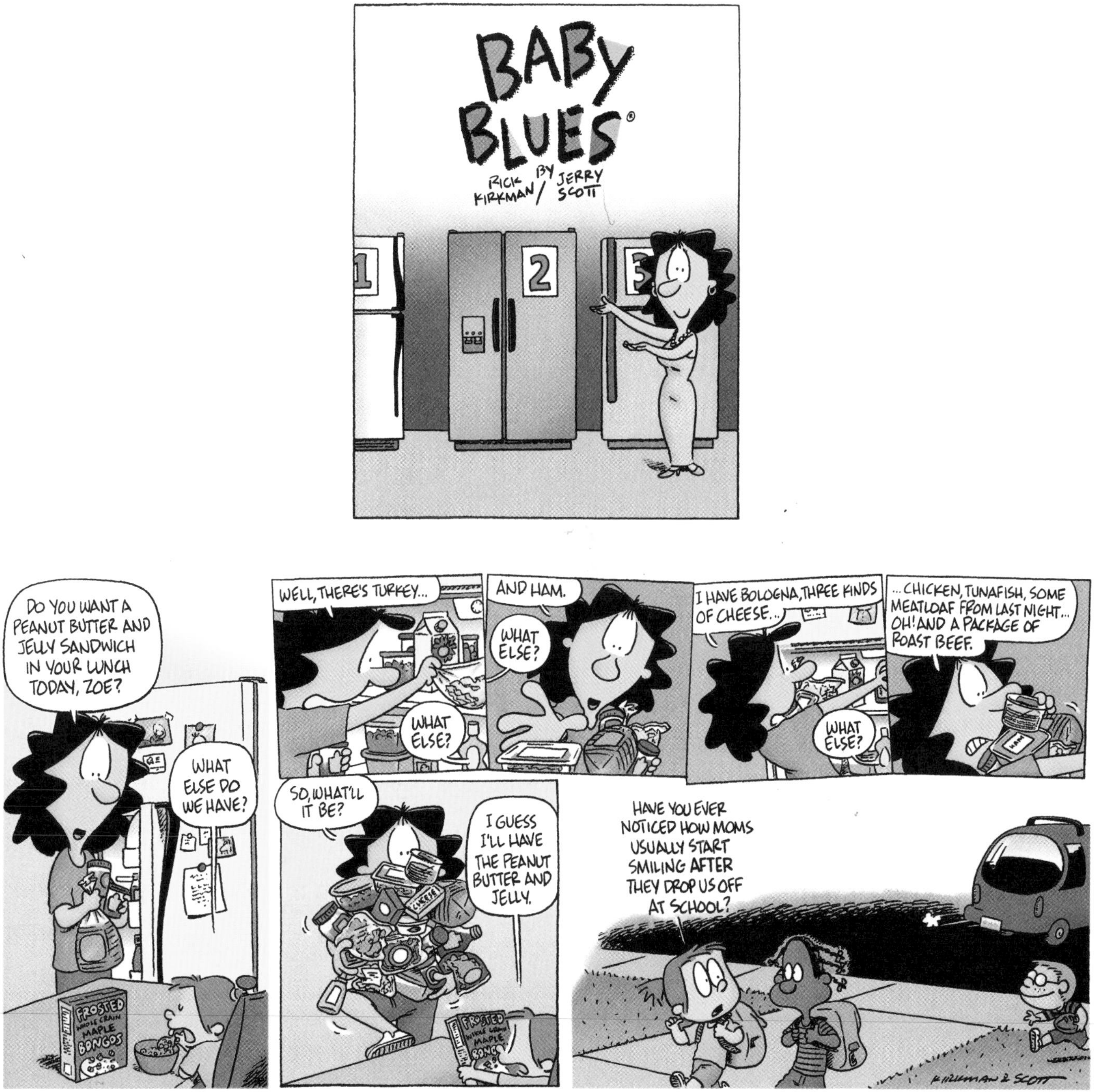
BABY BLUES®
BY RICK KIRKMAN / JERRY SCOTT
1
2
3
DO YOU WANT A PEANUT BUTTER AND JELLY SANDWICH IN YOUR LUNCH TODAY, ZOE?
WHAT ELSE DO WE HAVE?
WELL, THERE'S TURKEY...
WHAT ELSE?
AND HAM.
WHAT ELSE?
I HAVE BOLOGNA, THREE KINDS OF CHEESE...
WHAT ELSE?
...CHICKEN, TUNAFISH, SOME MEATLOAF FROM LAST NIGHT... OH! AND A PACKAGE OF ROAST BEEF.
SO, WHAT'LL IT BE?
I GUESS I'LL HAVE THE PEANUT BUTTER AND JELLY.
FROSTED WHOLE GRAIN MAPLE BONGOS
CHEESE
HAVE YOU EVER NOTICED HOW MOMS USUALLY START SMILING AFTER THEY DROP US OFF AT SCHOOL?
KIRKMAN & SCOTT

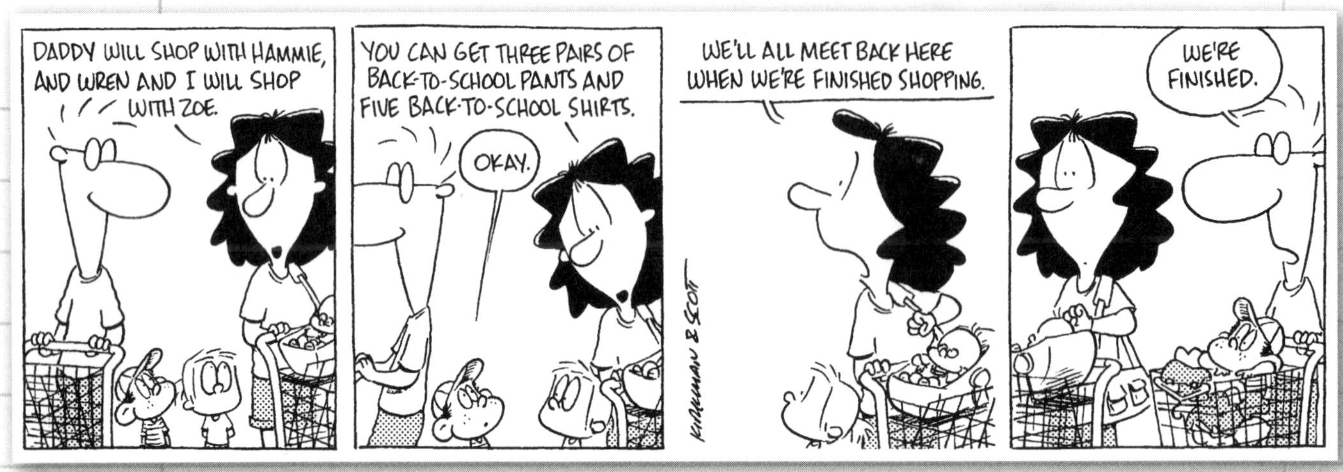
DADDY WILL SHOP WITH HAMMIE, AND WREN AND I WILL SHOP WITH ZOE.
YOU CAN GET THREE PAIRS OF BACK-TO-SCHOOL PANTS AND FIVE BACK-TO-SCHOOL SHIRTS.
OKAY.
KIRKMAN & SCOTT
WE'LL ALL MEET BACK HERE WHEN WE'RE FINISHED SHOPPING.
WE'RE FINISHED.

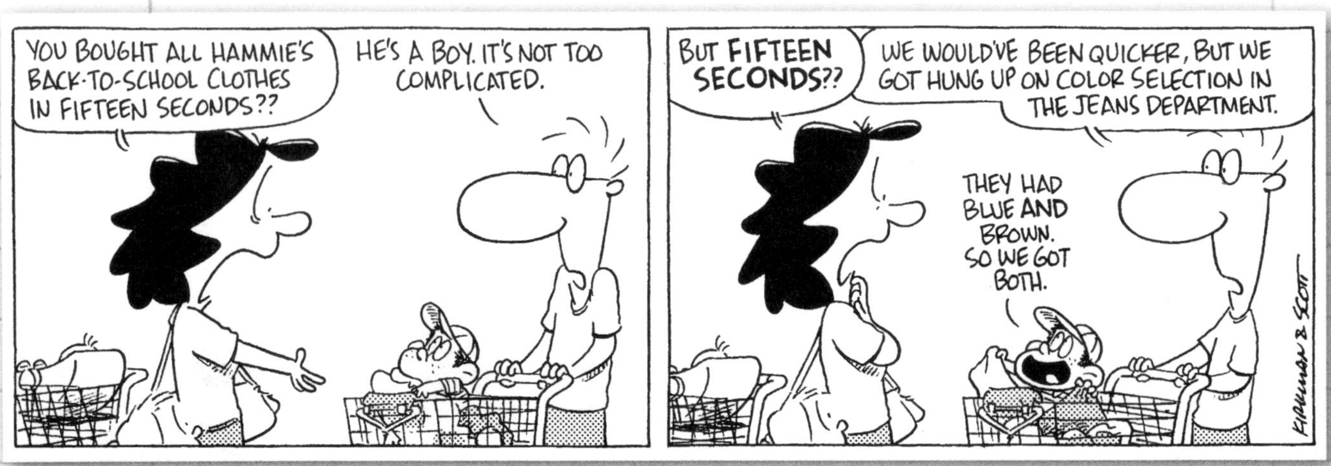
YOU BOUGHT ALL HAMMIE'S BACK-TO-SCHOOL CLOTHES IN FIFTEEN SECONDS??
HE'S A BOY. IT'S NOT TOO COMPLICATED.
BUT **FIFTEEN SECONDS**??
WE WOULD'VE BEEN QUICKER, BUT WE GOT HUNG UP ON COLOR SELECTION IN THE JEANS DEPARTMENT.
THEY HAD BLUE **AND** BROWN. SO WE GOT BOTH.
KIRKMAN & SCOTT

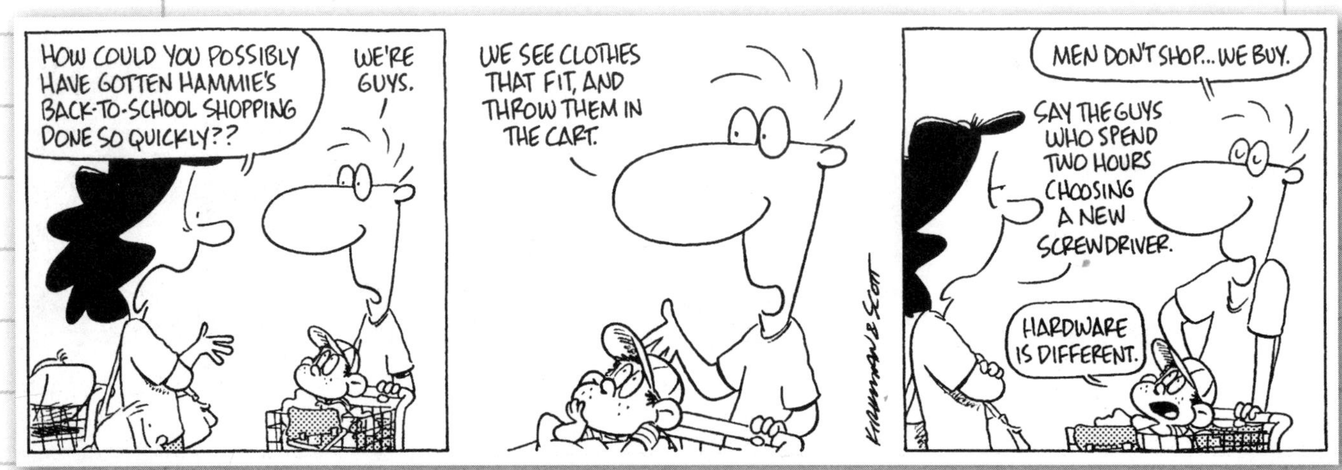
HOW COULD YOU POSSIBLY HAVE GOTTEN HAMMIE'S BACK-TO-SCHOOL SHOPPING DONE SO QUICKLY??
WE'RE GUYS.
WE SEE CLOTHES THAT FIT, AND THROW THEM IN THE CART.
KIRKMAN & SCOTT
MEN DON'T SHOP... WE BUY.
SAY THE GUYS WHO SPEND TWO HOURS CHOOSING A NEW SCREWDRIVER.
HARDWARE IS DIFFERENT.

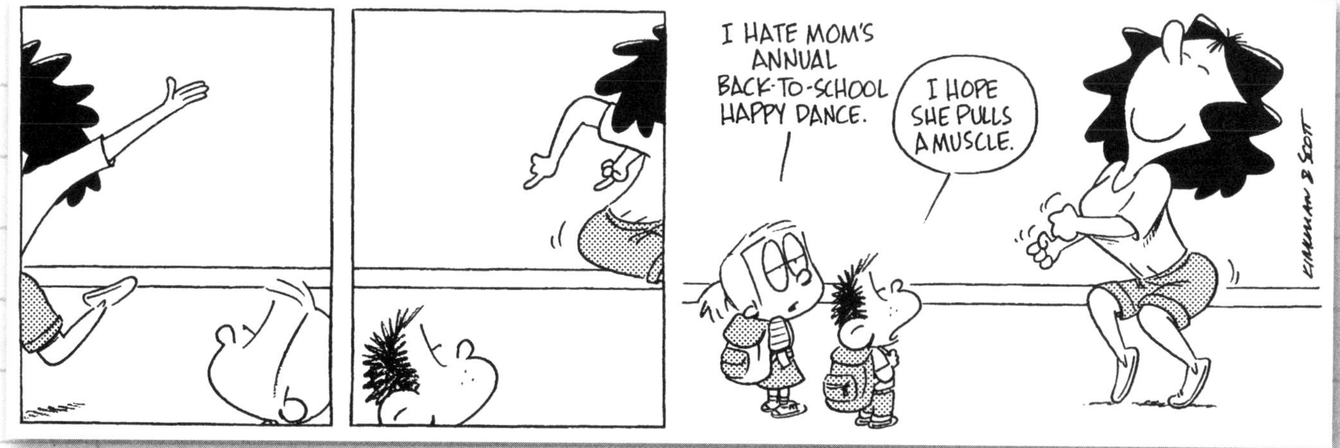
I HATE MOM'S ANNUAL BACK-TO-SCHOOL HAPPY DANCE.
I HOPE SHE PULLS A MUSCLE.
KIRKMAN & SCOTT

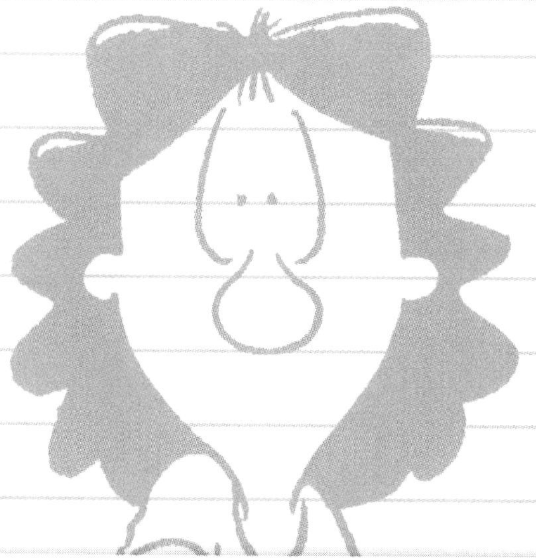

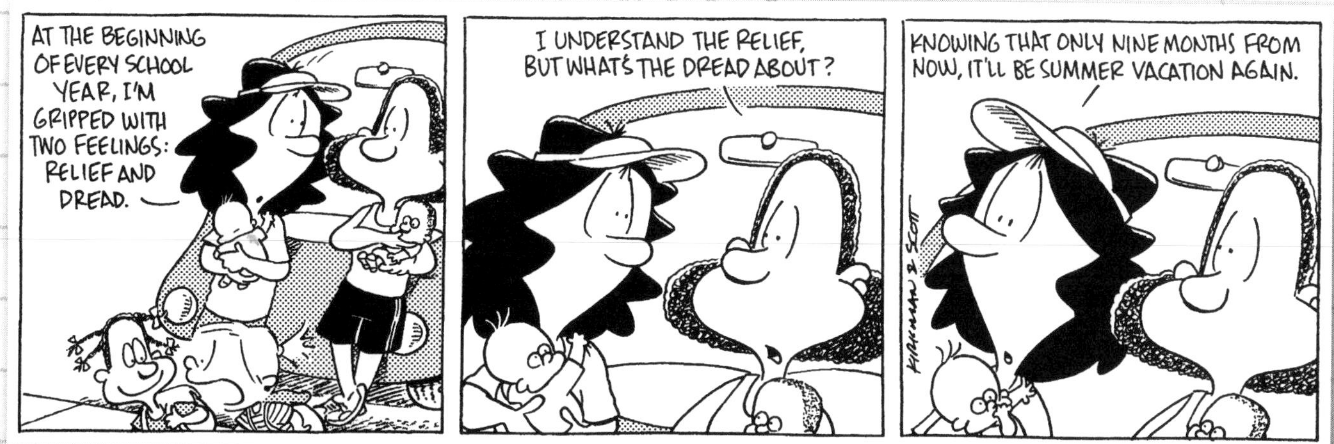
AT THE BEGINNING OF EVERY SCHOOL YEAR, I'M GRIPPED WITH TWO FEELINGS: RELIEF AND DREAD.
I UNDERSTAND THE RELIEF, BUT WHAT'S THE DREAD ABOUT?
KNOWING THAT ONLY NINE MONTHS FROM NOW, IT'LL BE SUMMER VACATION AGAIN.
KIRKMAN & SCOTT

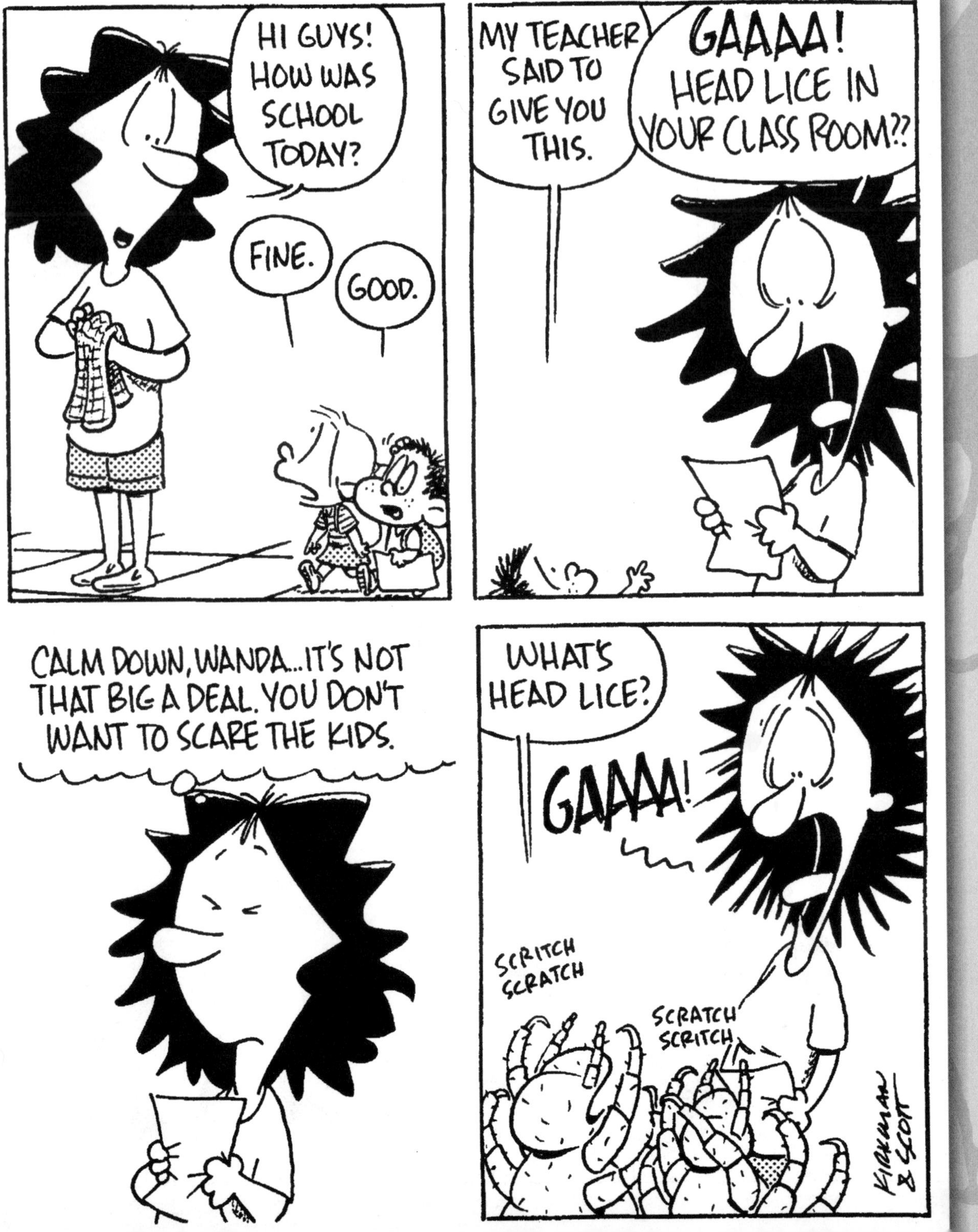
HI GUYS! HOW WAS SCHOOL TODAY?
FINE.
GOOD.
MY TEACHER SAID TO GIVE YOU THIS.
GAAAA! HEAD LICE IN YOUR CLASS ROOM??
CALM DOWN, WANDA...IT'S NOT THAT BIG A DEAL. YOU DON'T WANT TO SCARE THE KIDS.
WHAT'S HEAD LICE?
GAAAA!
SCRITCH SCRATCH
SCRATCH SCRITCH
KIRKMAN & SCOTT

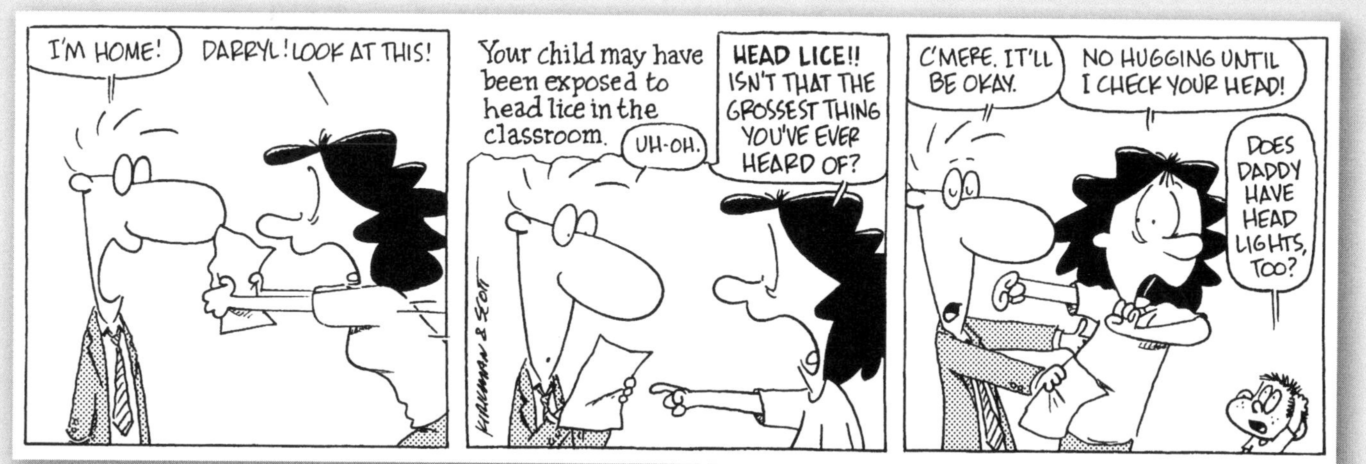
I'M HOME!
DARRYL! LOOK AT THIS!
Your child may have been exposed to head lice in the classroom.
UH-OH.
HEAD LICE!! ISN'T THAT THE GROSSEST THING YOU'VE EVER HEARD OF?
KIRKMAN & SCOTT
C'MERE. IT'LL BE OKAY.
NO HUGGING UNTIL I CHECK YOUR HEAD!
DOES DADDY HAVE HEAD LIGHTS, TOO?

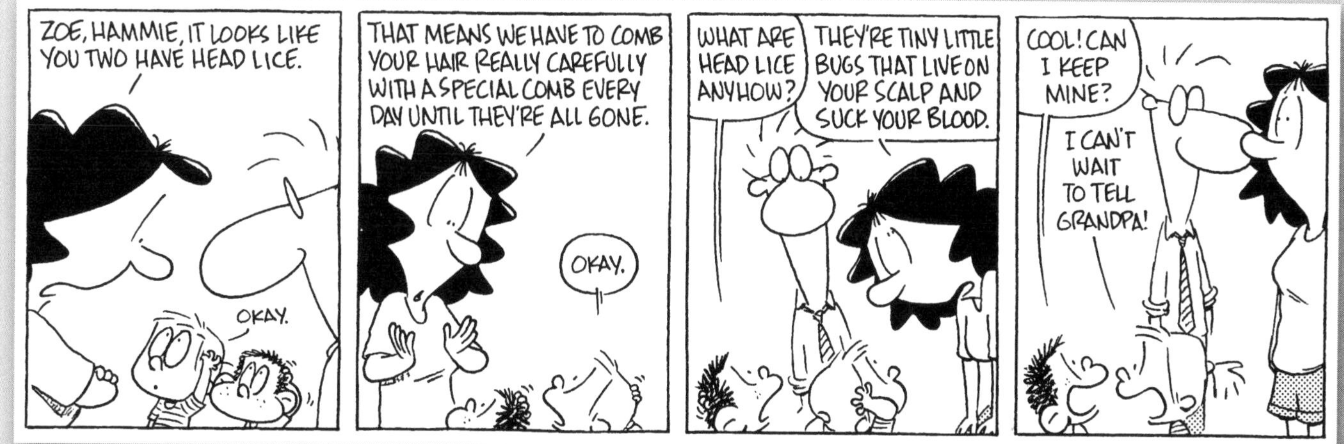
ZOE, HAMMIE, IT LOOKS LIKE YOU TWO HAVE HEAD LICE.
OKAY.
THAT MEANS WE HAVE TO COMB YOUR HAIR REALLY CAREFULLY WITH A SPECIAL COMB EVERY DAY UNTIL THEY'RE ALL GONE.
OKAY.
WHAT ARE HEAD LICE ANYHOW?
THEY'RE TINY LITTLE BUGS THAT LIVE ON YOUR SCALP AND SUCK YOUR BLOOD.
COOL! CAN I KEEP MINE?
I CAN'T WAIT TO TELL GRANDPA!

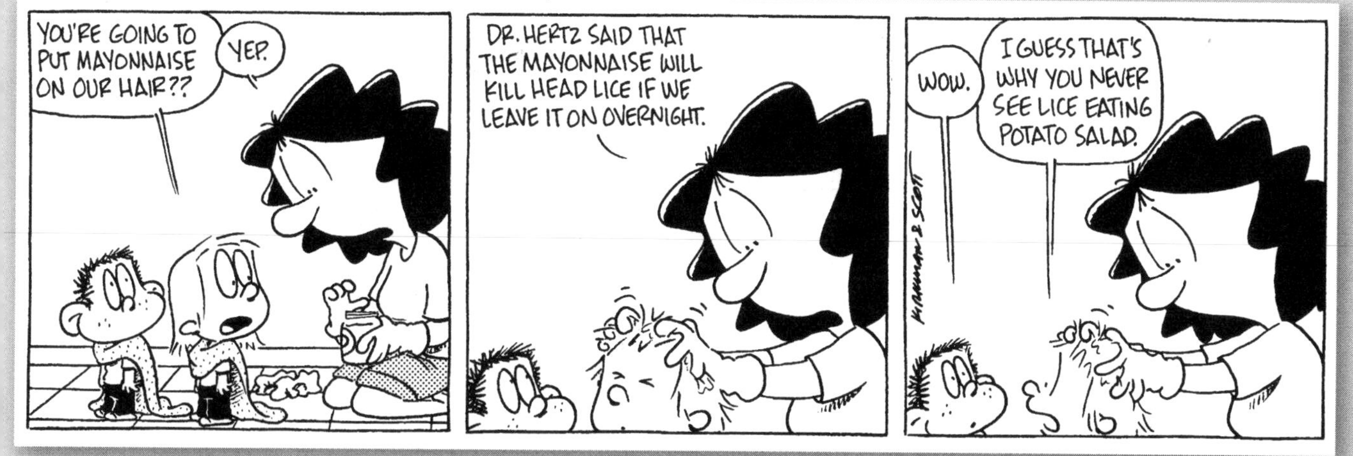
YOU'RE GOING TO PUT MAYONNAISE ON OUR HAIR??
YEP.
DR. HERTZ SAID THAT THE MAYONNAISE WILL KILL HEAD LICE IF WE LEAVE IT ON OVERNIGHT.
KIRKMAN & SCOTT
WOW.
I GUESS THAT'S WHY YOU NEVER SEE LICE EATING POTATO SALAD.

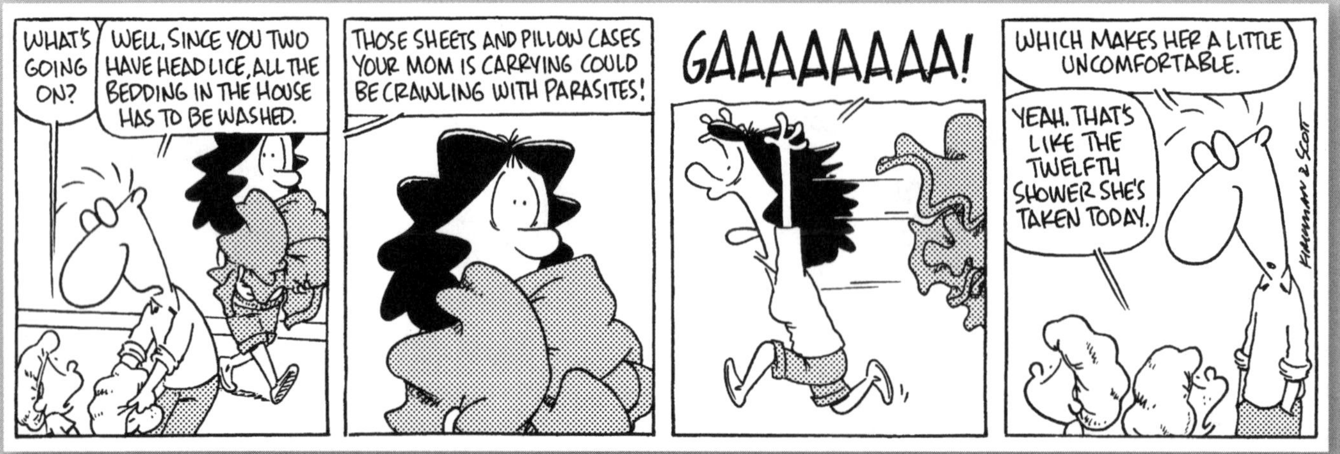
WHAT'S GOING ON?
WELL, SINCE YOU TWO HAVE HEAD LICE, ALL THE BEDDING IN THE HOUSE HAS TO BE WASHED.
THOSE SHEETS AND PILLOW CASES YOUR MOM IS CARRYING COULD BE CRAWLING WITH PARASITES!
GAAAAAAAA!
WHICH MAKES HER A LITTLE UNCOMFORTABLE.
YEAH. THAT'S LIKE THE TWELFTH SHOWER SHE'S TAKEN TODAY.
KIRKMAN & SCOTT

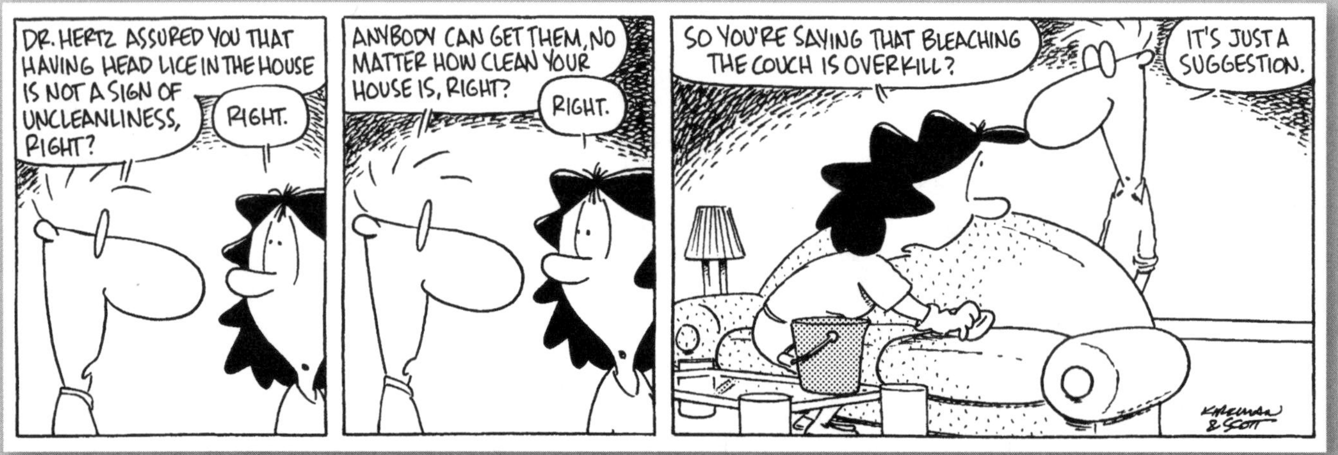
DR. HERTZ ASSURED YOU THAT HAVING HEAD LICE IN THE HOUSE IS NOT A SIGN OF UNCLEANLINESS, RIGHT?
RIGHT.
ANYBODY CAN GET THEM, NO MATTER HOW CLEAN YOUR HOUSE IS, RIGHT?
RIGHT.
SO YOU'RE SAYING THAT BLEACHING THE COUCH IS OVERKILL?
IT'S JUST A SUGGESTION.
KIRKMAN & SCOTT

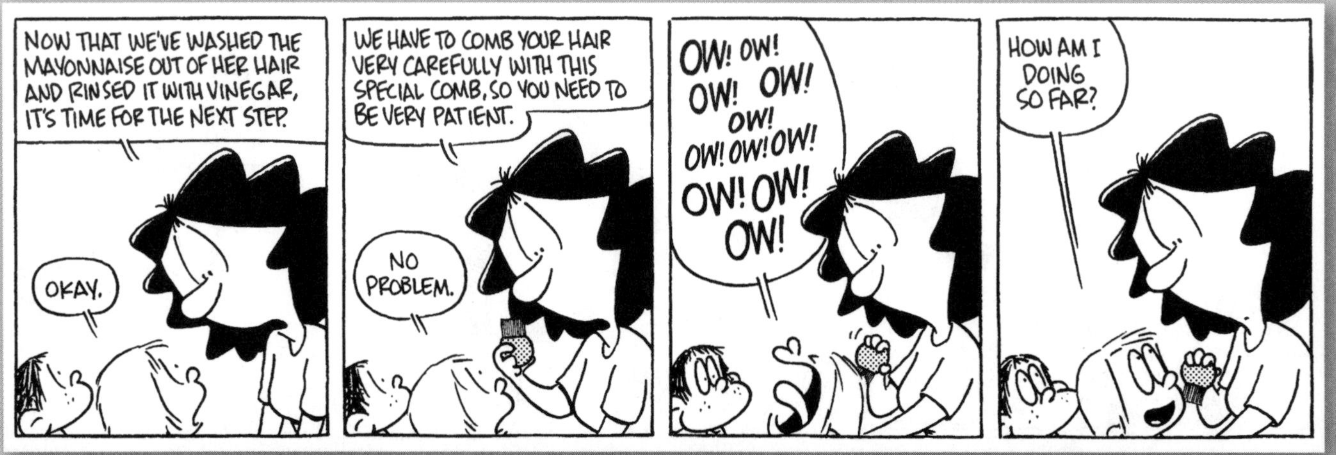
NOW THAT WE'VE WASHED THE MAYONNAISE OUT OF HER HAIR AND RINSED IT WITH VINEGAR, IT'S TIME FOR THE NEXT STEP.
OKAY.
WE HAVE TO COMB YOUR HAIR VERY CAREFULLY WITH THIS SPECIAL COMB, SO YOU NEED TO BE VERY PATIENT.
NO PROBLEM.
OW! OW! OW! OW! OW! OW! OW! OW! OW! OW! OW!
HOW AM I DOING SO FAR?

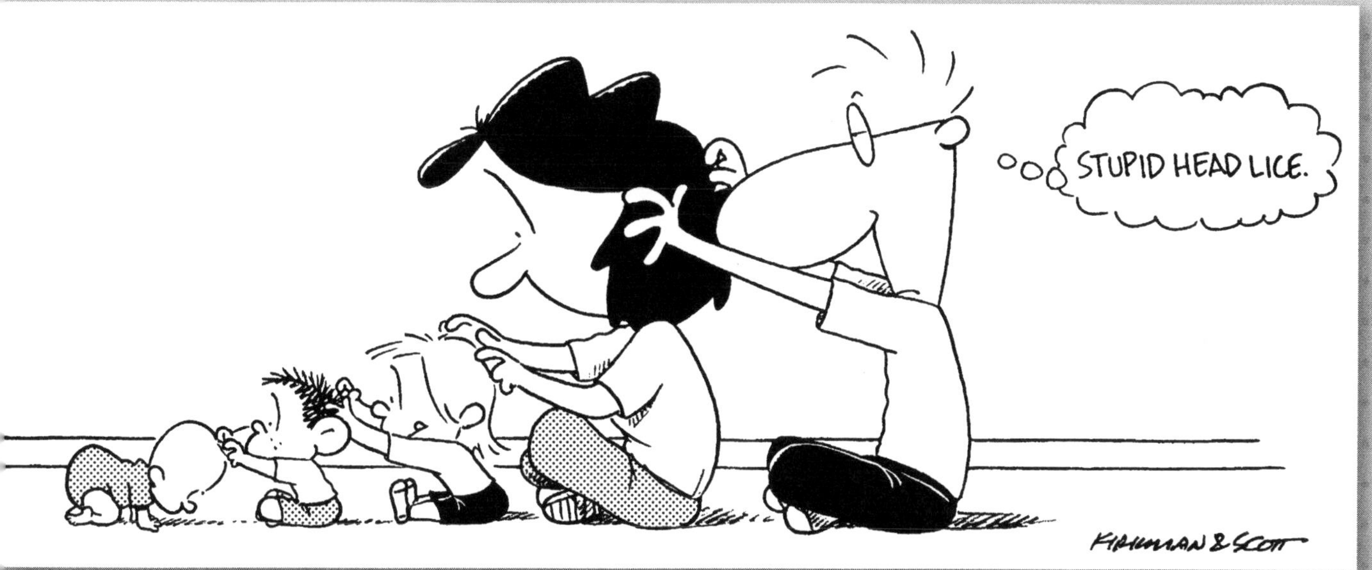
STUPID HEAD LICE.
KIRKMAN & SCOTT

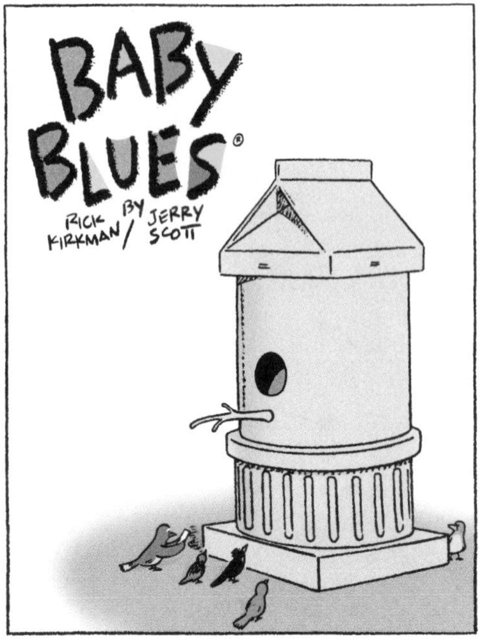
BABY BLUES®
RICK KIRKMAN / BY / JERRY SCOTT

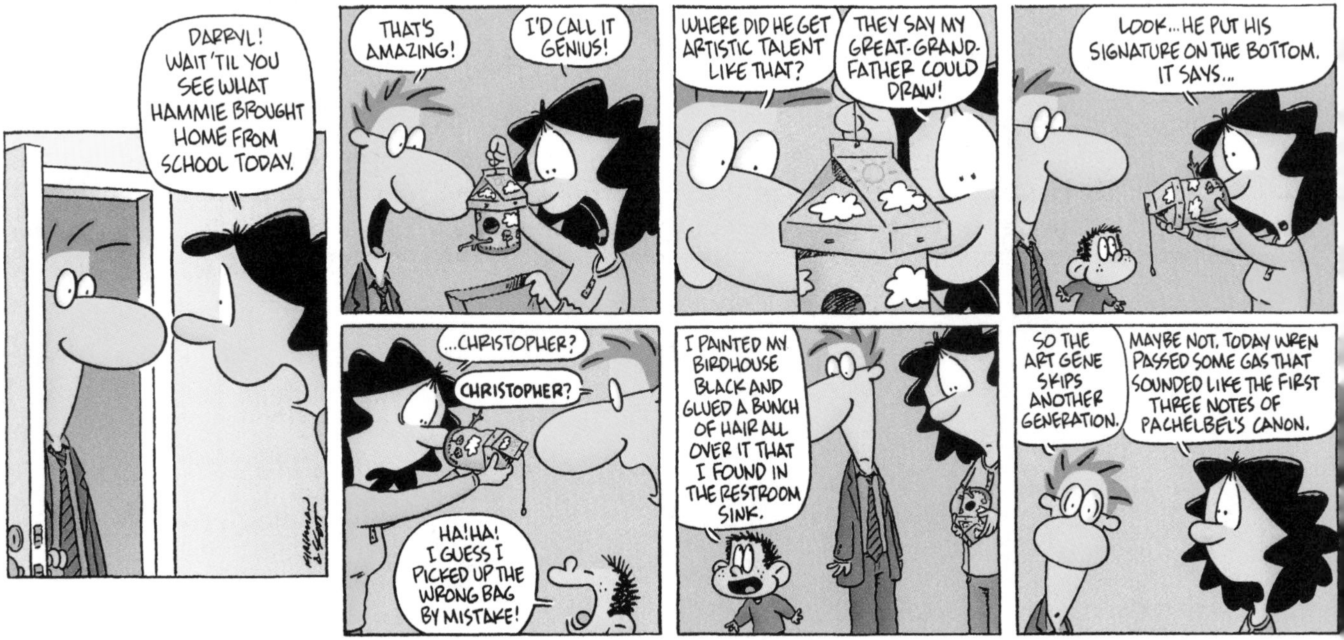
DARRYL! WAIT 'TIL YOU SEE WHAT HAMMIE BROUGHT HOME FROM SCHOOL TODAY.
THAT'S AMAZING!
I'D CALL IT GENIUS!
WHERE DID HE GET ARTISTIC TALENT LIKE THAT?
THEY SAY MY GREAT-GRAND-FATHER COULD DRAW!
LOOK... HE PUT HIS SIGNATURE ON THE BOTTOM. IT SAYS...
...CHRISTOPHER?
CHRISTOPHER?
HA! HA! I GUESS I PICKED UP THE WRONG BAG BY MISTAKE!
I PAINTED MY BIRDHOUSE BLACK AND GLUED A BUNCH OF HAIR ALL OVER IT THAT I FOUND IN THE RESTROOM SINK.
SO THE ART GENE SKIPS ANOTHER GENERATION.
MAYBE NOT. TODAY WREN PASSED SOME GAS THAT SOUNDED LIKE THE FIRST THREE NOTES OF PACHELBEL'S CANON.

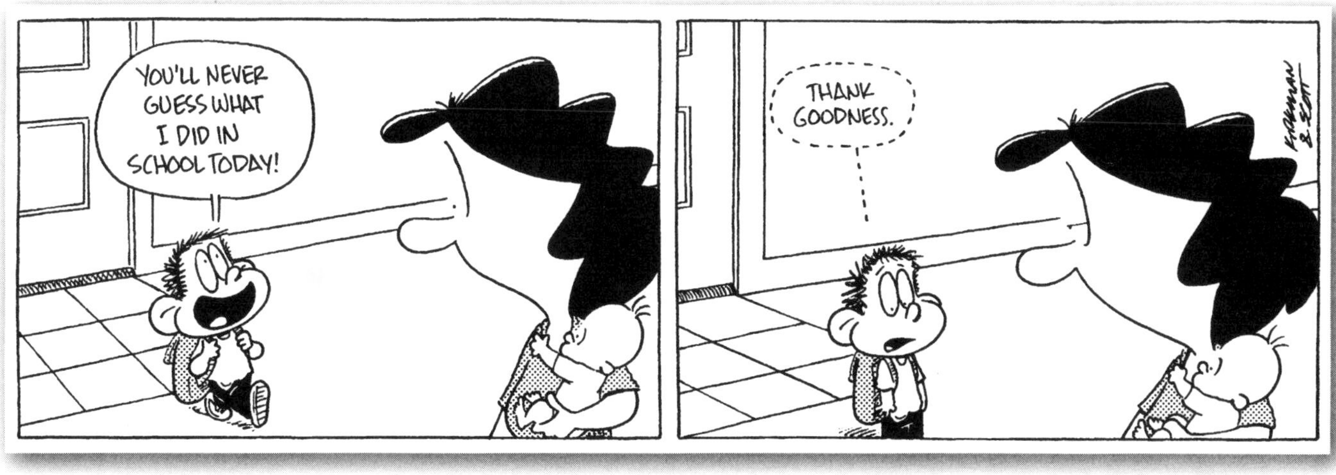
YOU'LL NEVER GUESS WHAT I DID IN SCHOOL TODAY!
THANK GOODNESS.
KIRKMAN & SCOTT

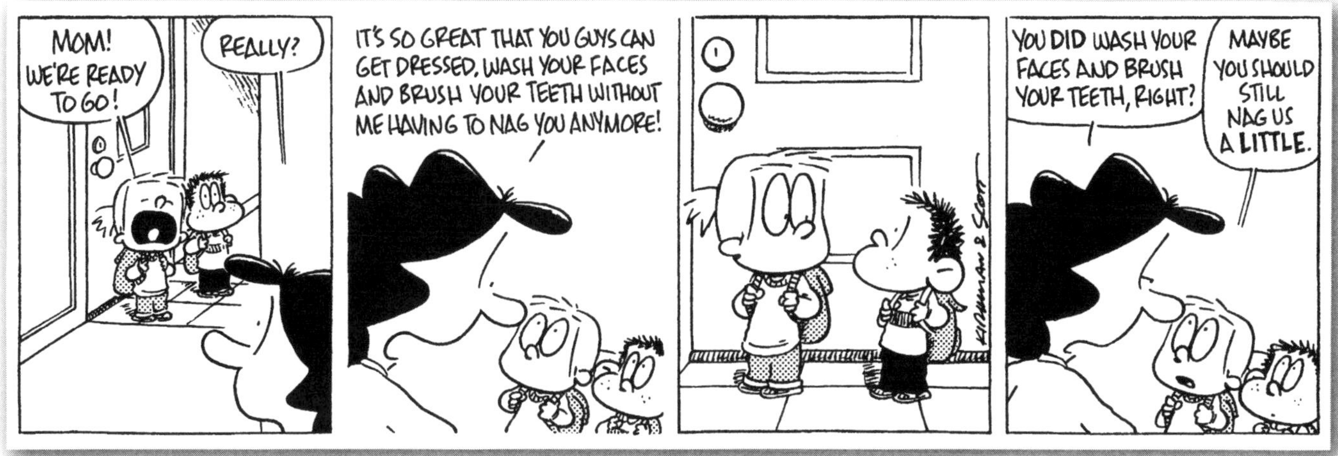
MOM! WE'RE READY TO GO!
REALLY?
IT'S SO GREAT THAT YOU GUYS CAN GET DRESSED, WASH YOUR FACES AND BRUSH YOUR TEETH WITHOUT ME HAVING TO NAG YOU ANYMORE!
KIRKMAN & SCOTT
YOU DID WASH YOUR FACES AND BRUSH YOUR TEETH, RIGHT?
MAYBE YOU SHOULD STILL NAG US A LITTLE.

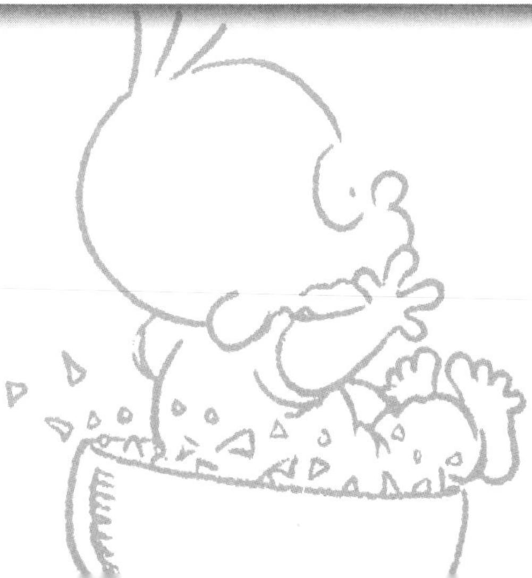

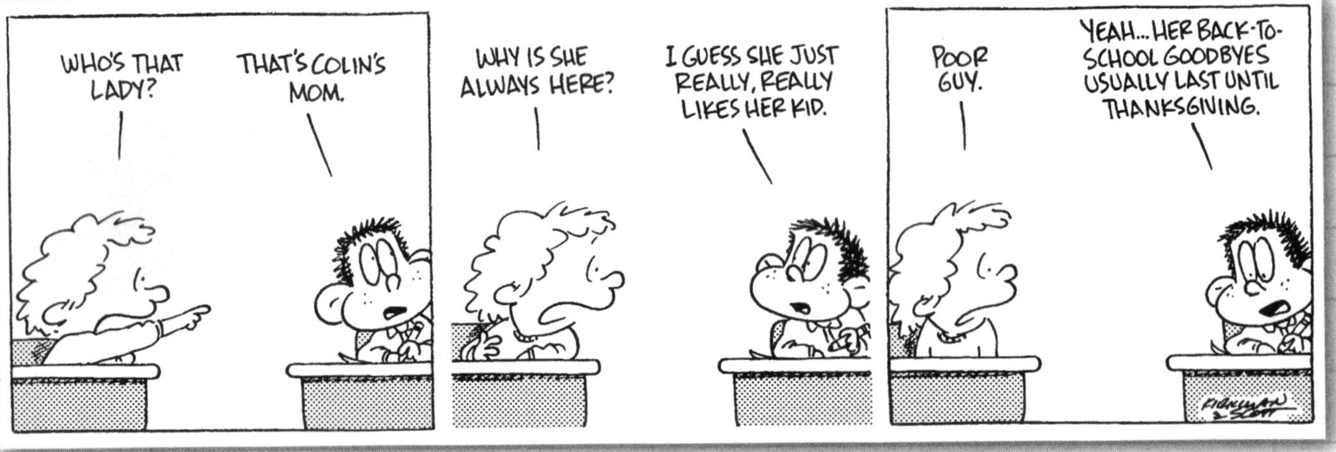
WHO'S THAT LADY?
THAT'S COLIN'S MOM.
WHY IS SHE ALWAYS HERE?
I GUESS SHE JUST REALLY, REALLY LIKES HER KID.
POOR GUY.
YEAH... HER BACK-TO-SCHOOL GOODBYES USUALLY LAST UNTIL THANKSGIVING.
KIRKMAN & SCOTT

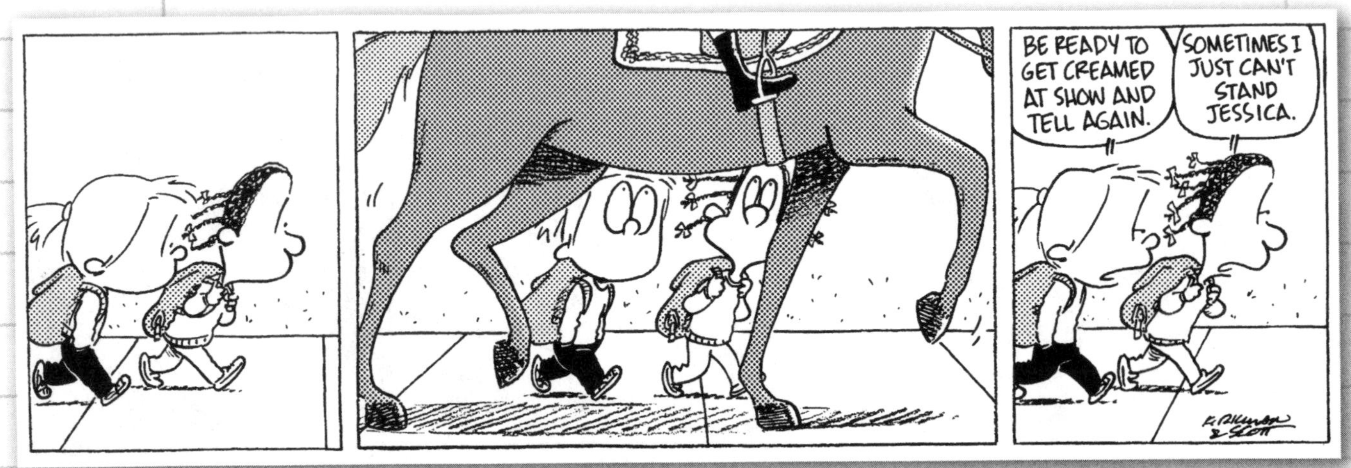
BE READY TO GET CREAMED AT SHOW AND TELL AGAIN.
SOMETIMES I JUST CAN'T STAND JESSICA.
KIRKMAN & SCOTT

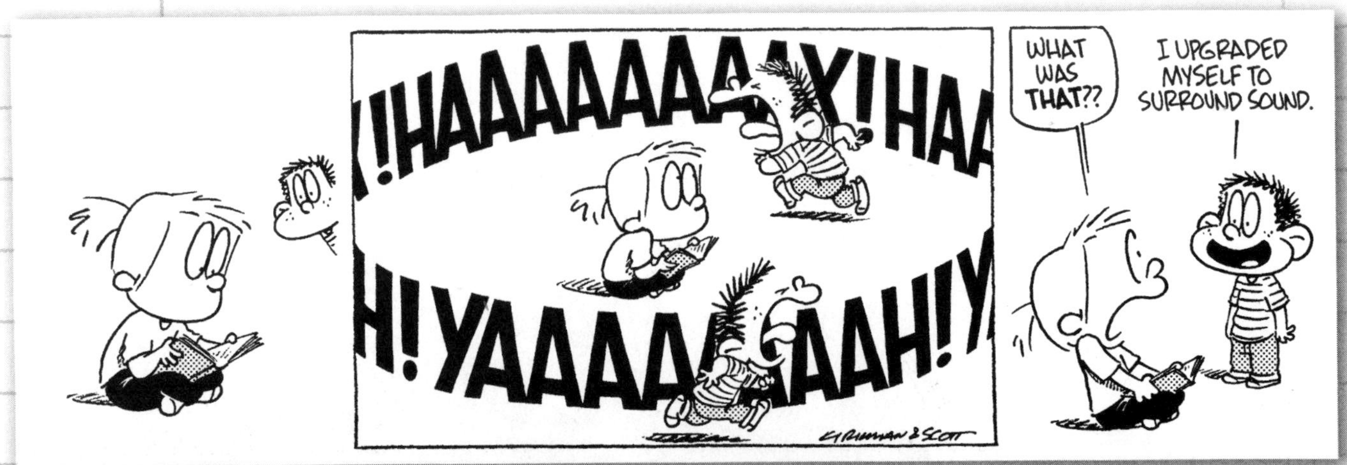
!HAAAAAAAAX!HAA
H!YAAAAAAAAH!Y
KIRKMAN & SCOTT
WHAT WAS THAT??
I UPGRADED MYSELF TO SURROUND SOUND.

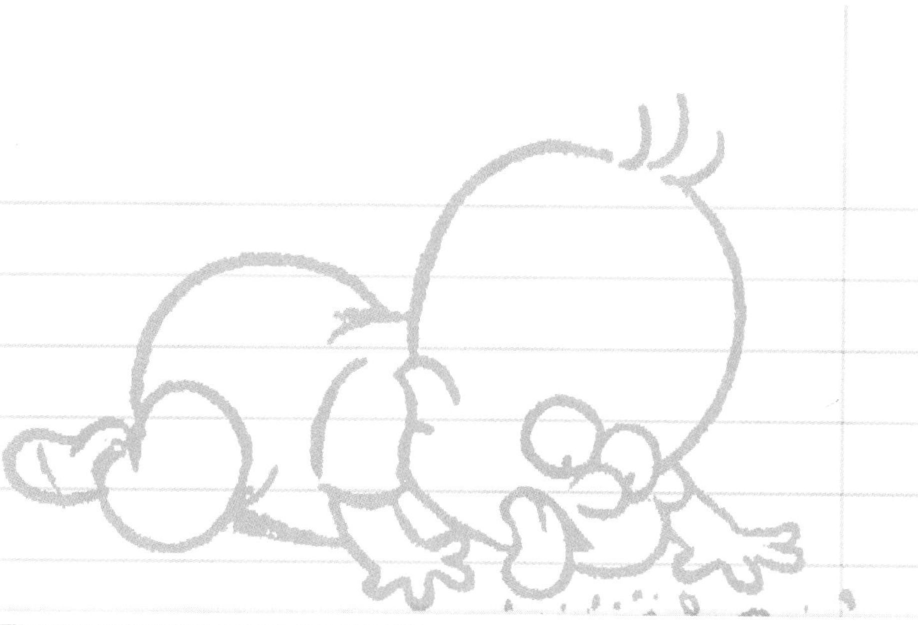

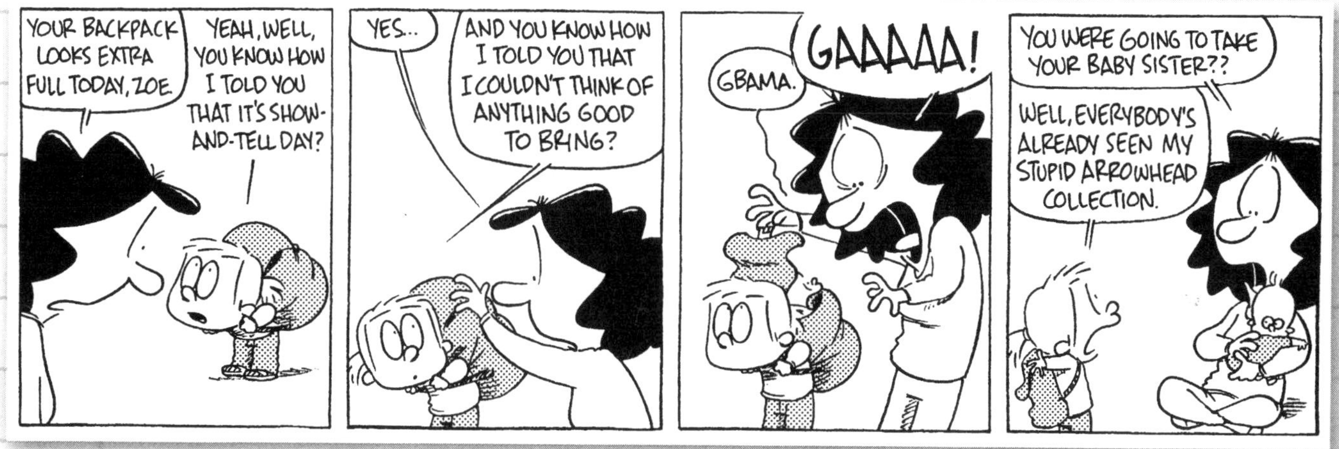
YOUR BACKPACK LOOKS EXTRA FULL TODAY, ZOE.
YEAH, WELL, YOU KNOW HOW I TOLD YOU THAT IT'S SHOW-AND-TELL DAY?
YES...
AND YOU KNOW HOW I TOLD YOU THAT I COULDN'T THINK OF ANYTHING GOOD TO BRING?
GBAMA.
GAAAAA!
YOU WERE GOING TO TAKE YOUR BABY SISTER??
WELL, EVERYBODY'S ALREADY SEEN MY STUPID ARROWHEAD COLLECTION.

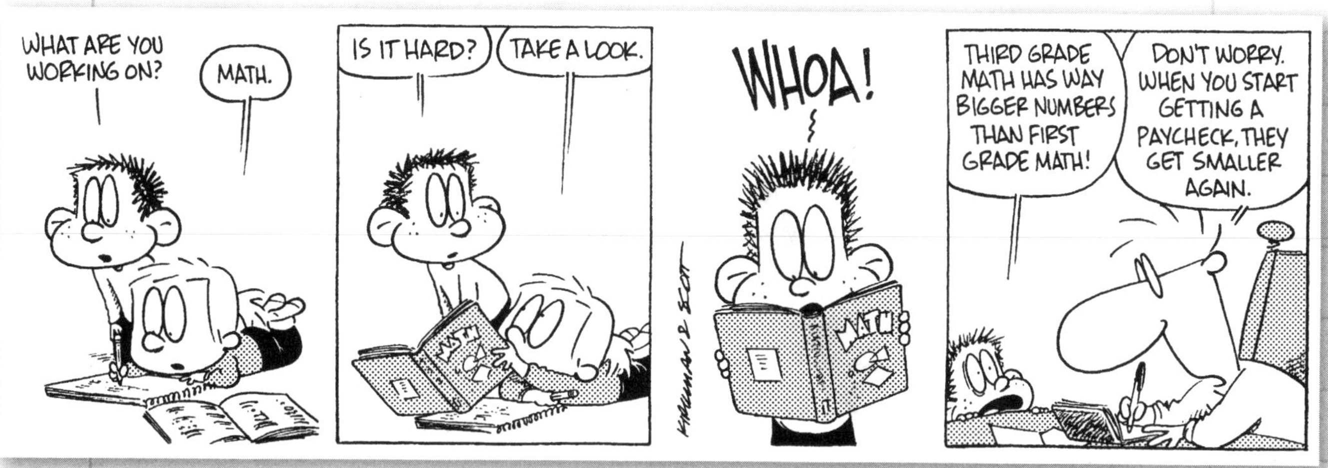
WHAT ARE YOU WORKING ON?
MATH.
IS IT HARD?
TAKE A LOOK.
WHOA!
THIRD GRADE MATH HAS WAY BIGGER NUMBERS THAN FIRST GRADE MATH!
DON'T WORRY. WHEN YOU START GETTING A PAYCHECK, THEY GET SMALLER AGAIN.

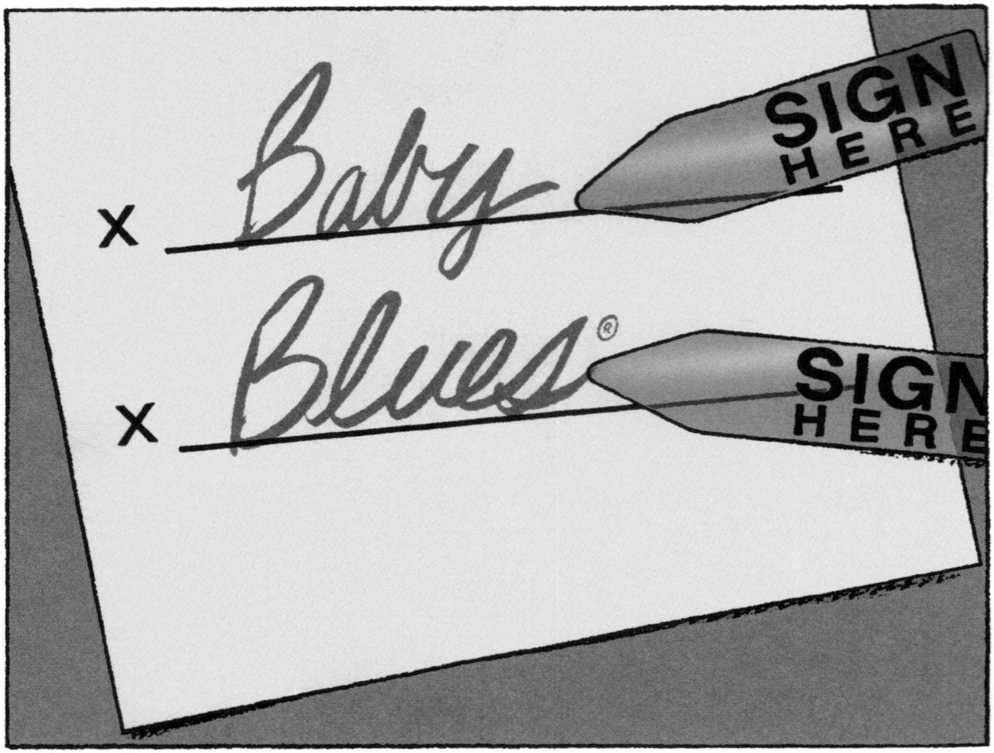
Baby Blues®
SIGN HERE
SIGN HERE
X
X

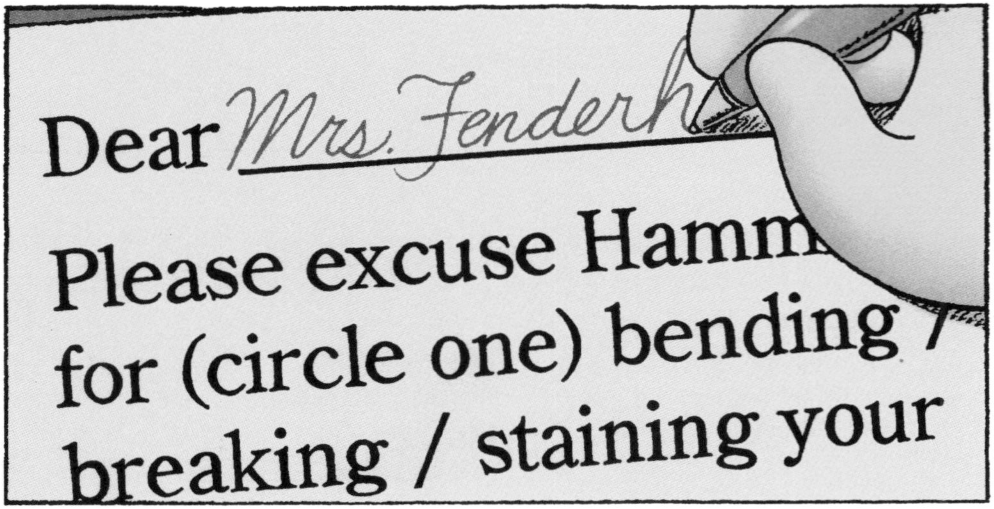
Dear Mrs. Fenderh
Please excuse Hamm
for (circle one) bending /
breaking / staining your

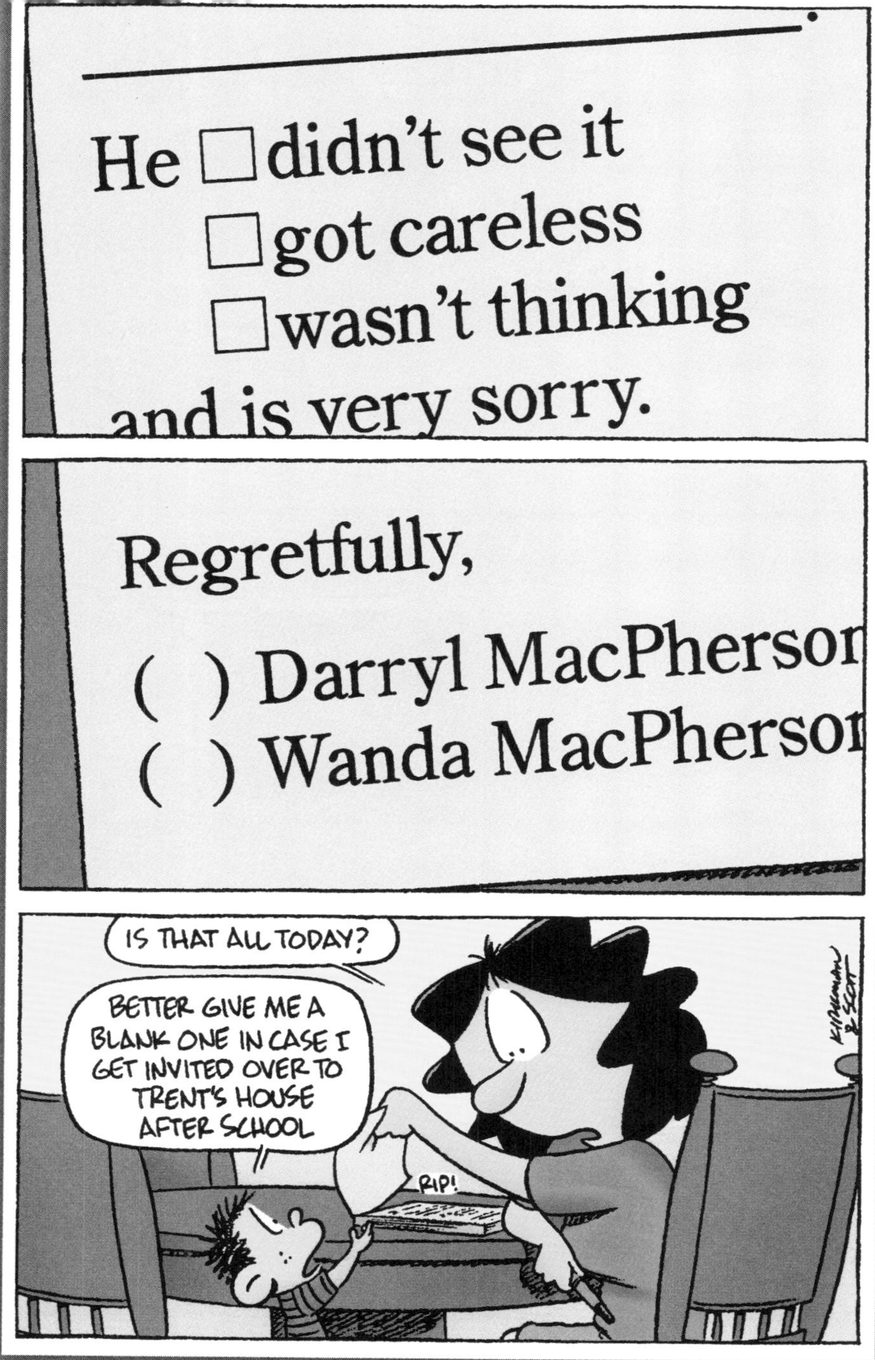
He didn't see it
got careless
wasn't thinking
and is very sorry.
Regretfully,
( ) Darryl MacPherson
( ) Wanda MacPherson
IS THAT ALL TODAY?
BETTER GIVE ME A BLANK ONE IN CASE I GET INVITED OVER TO TRENT'S HOUSE AFTER SCHOOL
RIP!

BABY BLUES®
BY RICK KIRKMAN / JERRY SCOTT
BABY
A
B
C
AAAAAGH!
IT'S QUARTER TO EIGHT!

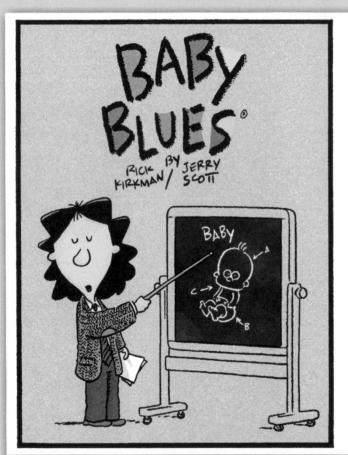

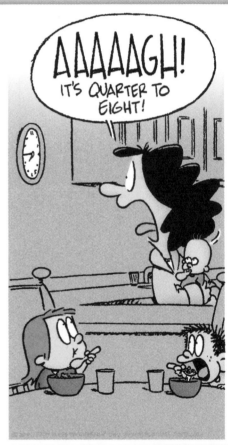

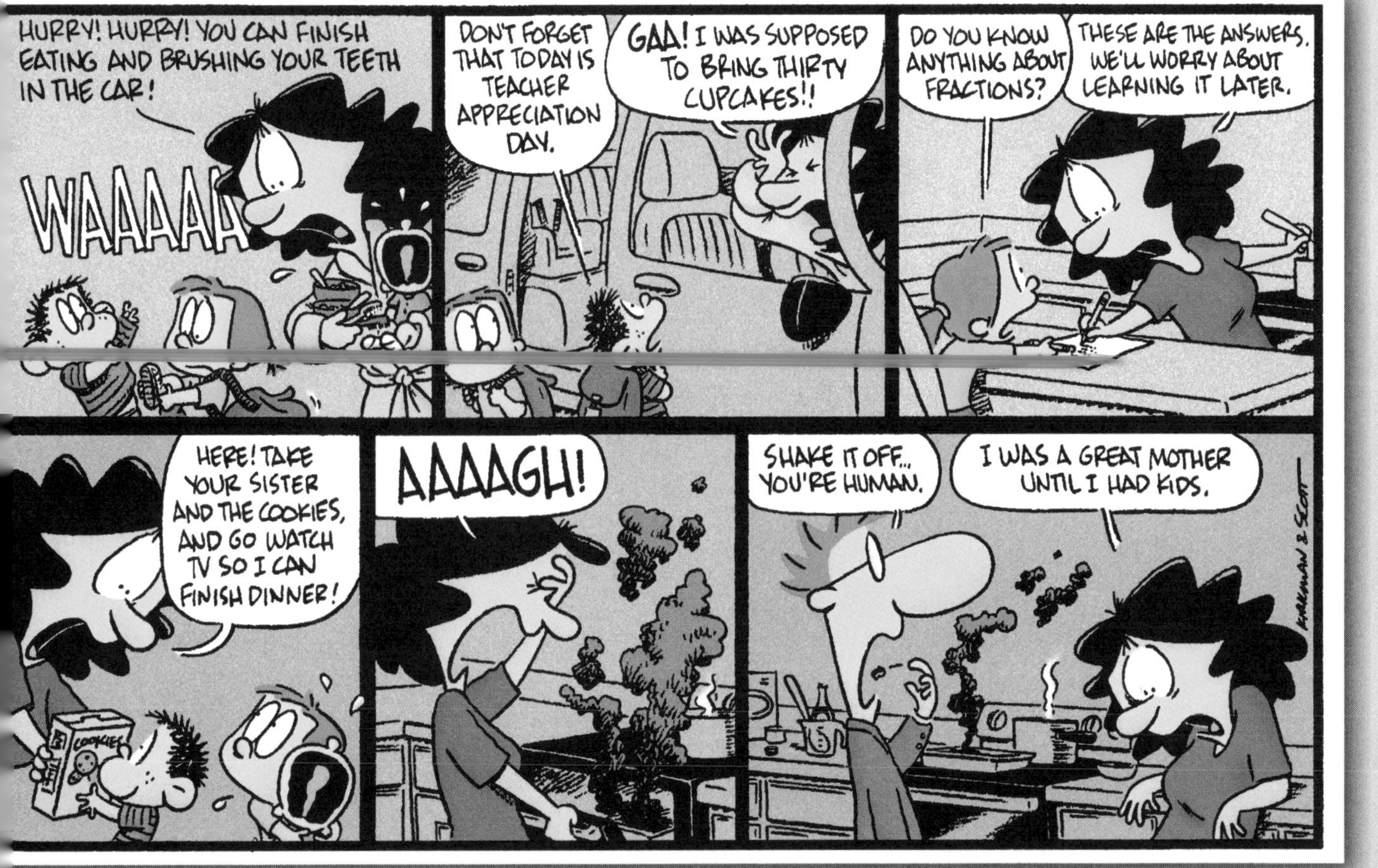

HURRY! HURRY! YOU CAN FINISH EATING AND BRUSHING YOUR TEETH IN THE CAR!
WAAAAAA
DON'T FORGET THAT TODAY IS TEACHER APPRECIATION DAY.
GAA! I WAS SUPPOSED TO BRING THIRTY CUPCAKES!!
DO YOU KNOW ANYTHING ABOUT FRACTIONS?
THESE ARE THE ANSWERS. WE'LL WORRY ABOUT LEARNING IT LATER.
HERE! TAKE YOUR SISTER AND THE COOKIES, AND GO WATCH TV SO I CAN FINISH DINNER!
COOKIES
AAAAGH!
SHAKE IT OFF... YOU'RE HUMAN.
I WAS A GREAT MOTHER UNTIL I HAD KIDS.
KIRKMAN & SCOTT

BABY BLUES®
BY RICK KIRKMAN / JERRY SCOTT
US MAIL
COME ON YOU GUYS! WE'RE GOING TO BE LATE FOR SCHOOL!

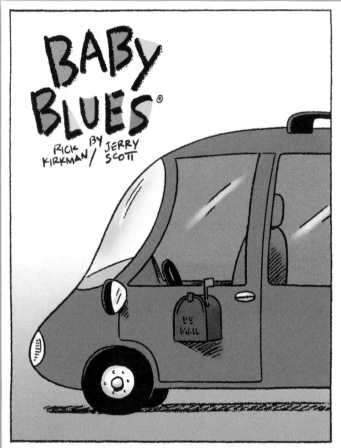

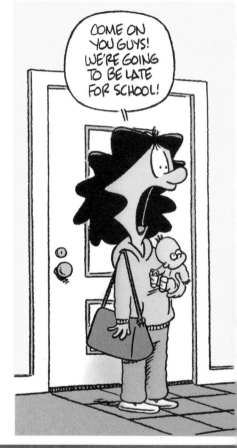

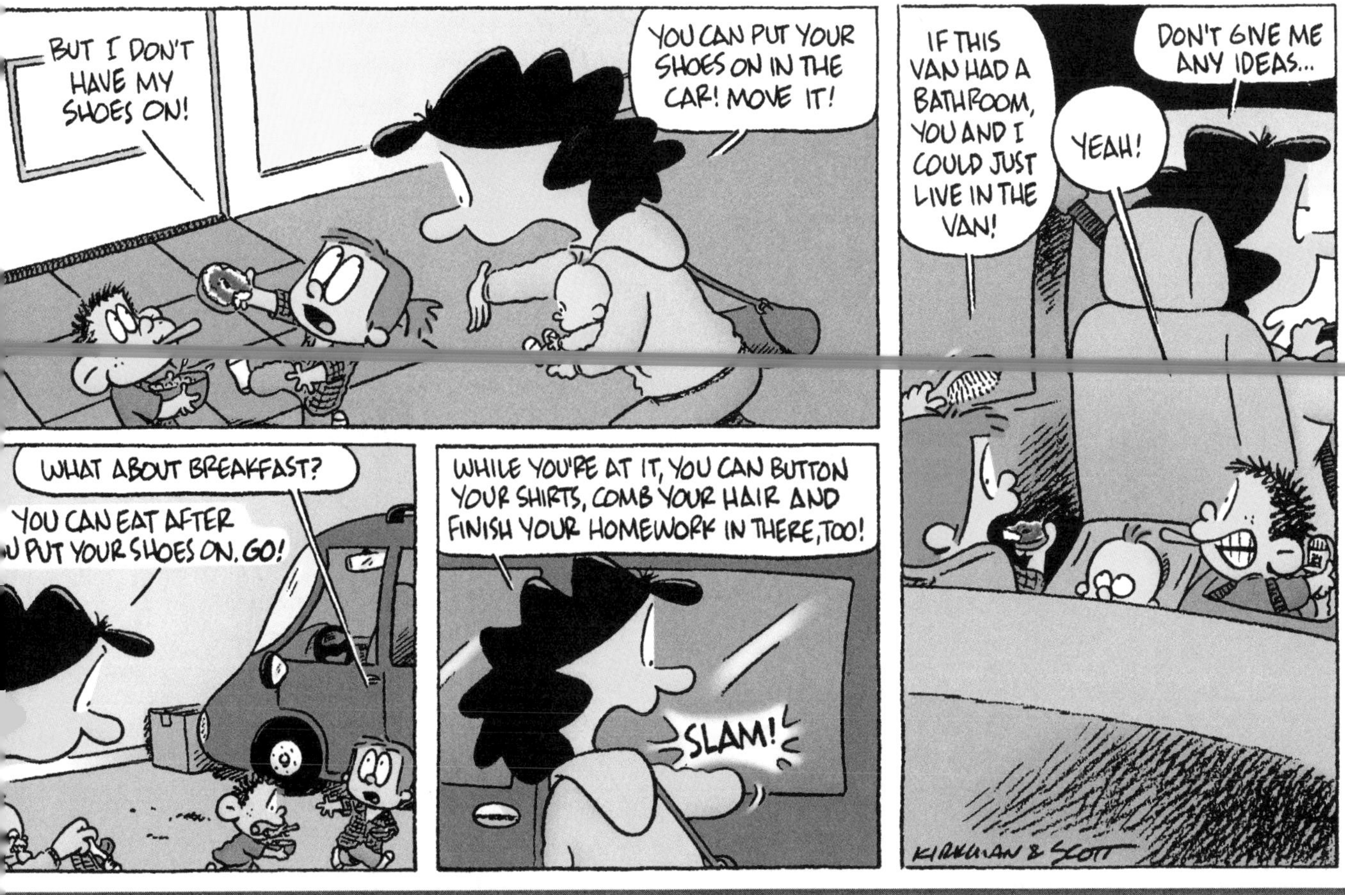
BUT I DON'T HAVE MY SHOES ON!
YOU CAN PUT YOUR SHOES ON IN THE CAR! MOVE IT!
WHAT ABOUT BREAKFAST?
YOU CAN EAT AFTER
U PUT YOUR SHOES ON. GO!
WHILE YOU'RE AT IT, YOU CAN BUTTON YOUR SHIRTS, COMB YOUR HAIR AND FINISH YOUR HOMEWORK IN THERE, TOO!
SLAM!
IF THIS VAN HAD A BATHROOM, YOU AND I COULD JUST LIVE IN THE VAN!
YEAH!
DON'T GIVE ME ANY IDEAS...
KIRKMAN & SCOTT

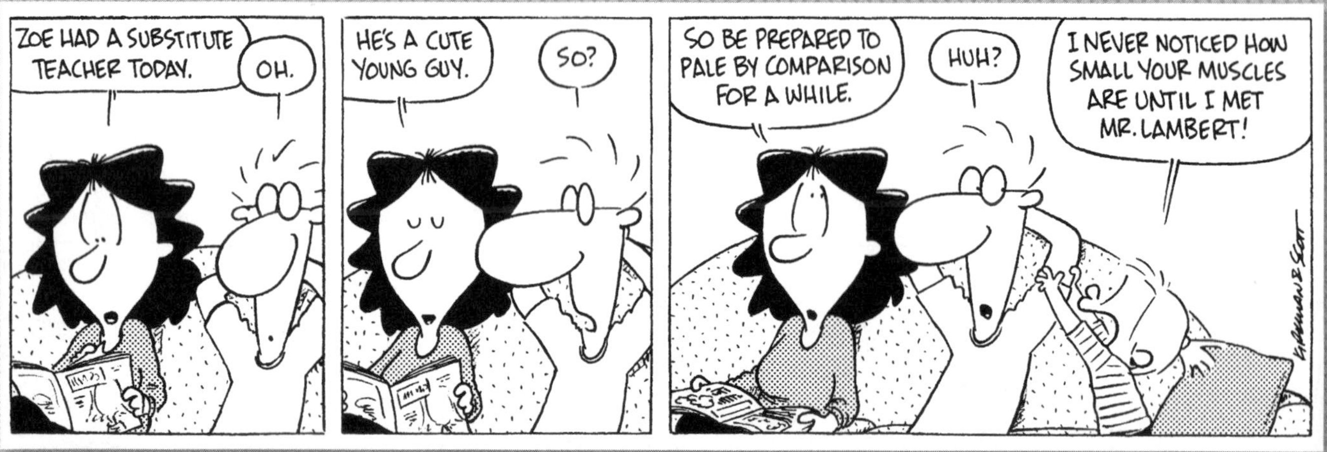
ZOE HAD A SUBSTITUTE TEACHER TODAY.
OH.
HE'S A CUTE YOUNG GUY.
SO?
SO BE PREPARED TO PALE BY COMPARISON FOR A WHILE.
HUH?
I NEVER NOTICED HOW SMALL YOUR MUSCLES ARE UNTIL I MET MR. LAMBERT!
KIRKMAN & SCOTT

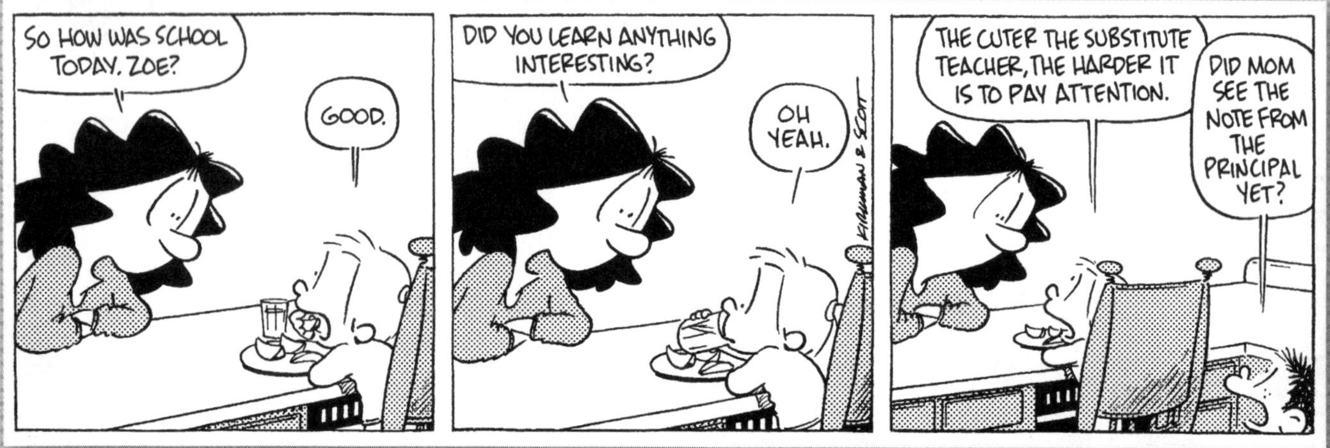
SO HOW WAS SCHOOL TODAY, ZOE?
GOOD.
DID YOU LEARN ANYTHING INTERESTING?
OH YEAH.
KIRKMAN & SCOTT
THE CUTER THE SUBSTITUTE TEACHER, THE HARDER IT IS TO PAY ATTENTION.
DID MOM SEE THE NOTE FROM THE PRINCIPAL YET?

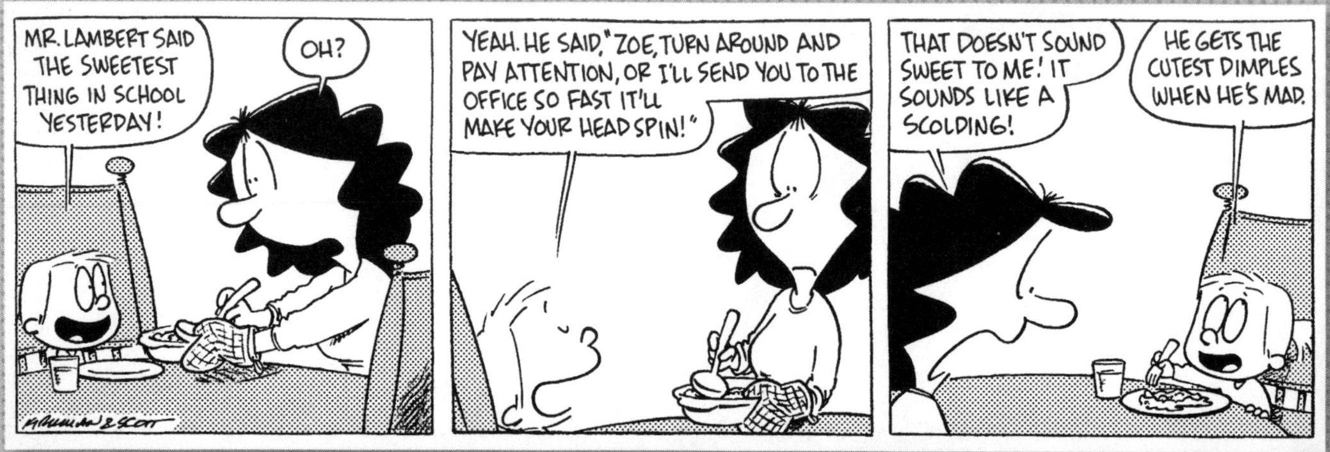
MR. LAMBERT SAID THE SWEETEST THING IN SCHOOL YESTERDAY!
OH?
KIRKMAN & SCOTT
YEAH. HE SAID, "ZOE, TURN AROUND AND PAY ATTENTION, OR I'LL SEND YOU TO THE OFFICE SO FAST IT'LL MAKE YOUR HEAD SPIN!"
THAT DOESN'T SOUND SWEET TO ME! IT SOUNDS LIKE A SCOLDING!
HE GETS THE CUTEST DIMPLES WHEN HE'S MAD.

Homework Pledge

When I help my child with homework:

☑ I will make sure my child completely understands the assignment.

☐ I w

the assignment.

☑ I will help my child develop a strategy for completing the assignment

☐ I will not blame the teacher school or the public education system when I find out my answers are wrong.

I'M NOT SIGNING THIS!!

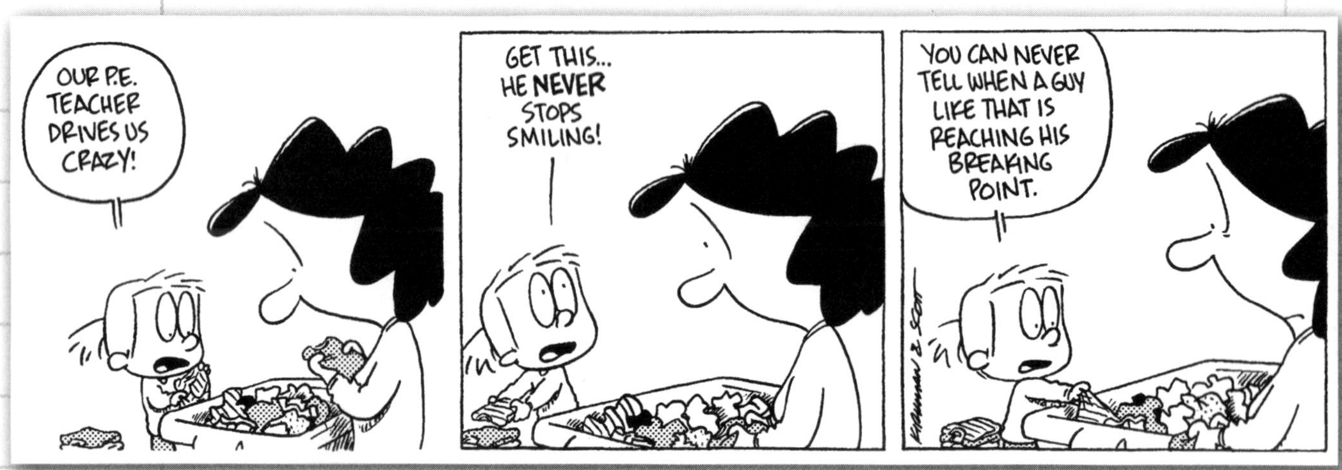
OUR P.E. TEACHER DRIVES US CRAZY!
GET THIS... HE **NEVER** STOPS SMILING!
YOU CAN NEVER TELL WHEN A GUY LIKE THAT IS REACHING HIS BREAKING POINT.

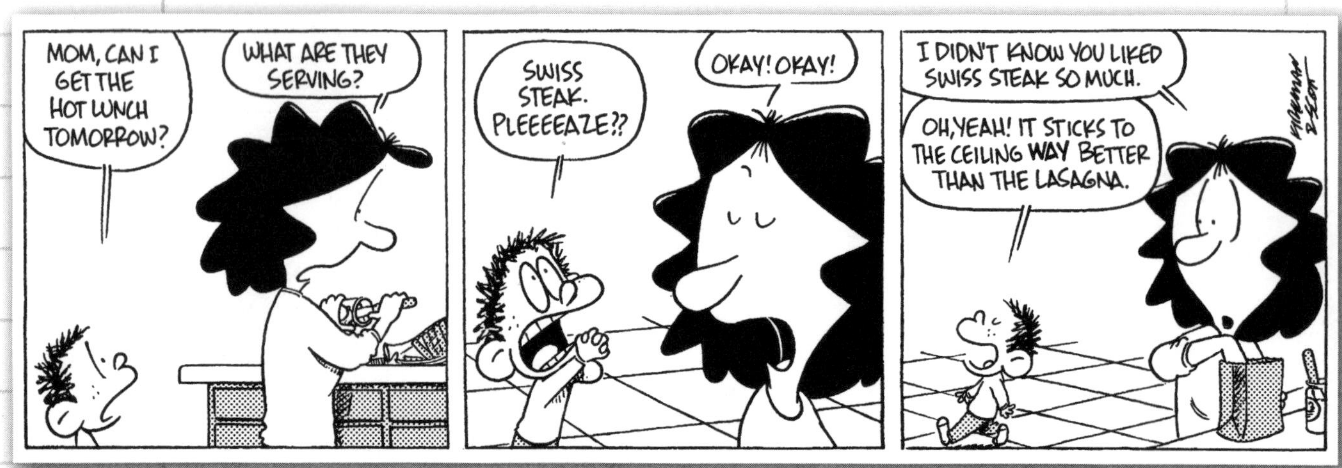
MOM, CAN I GET THE HOT LUNCH TOMORROW?
WHAT ARE THEY SERVING?
SWISS STEAK. PLEEEEAZE??
OKAY! OKAY!
I DIDN'T KNOW YOU LIKED SWISS STEAK SO MUCH.
OH, YEAH! IT STICKS TO THE CEILING **WAY** BETTER THAN THE LASAGNA.

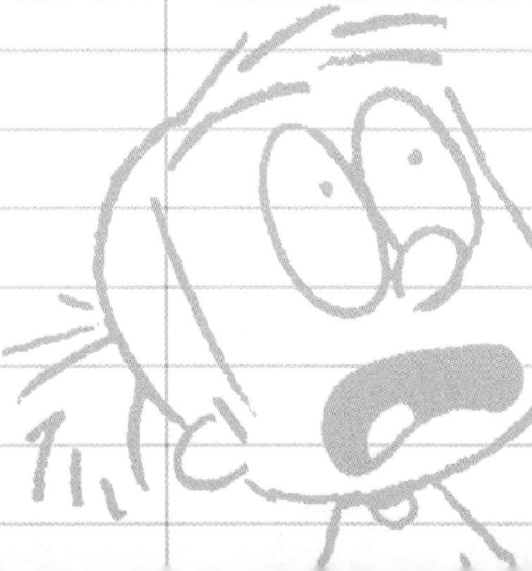

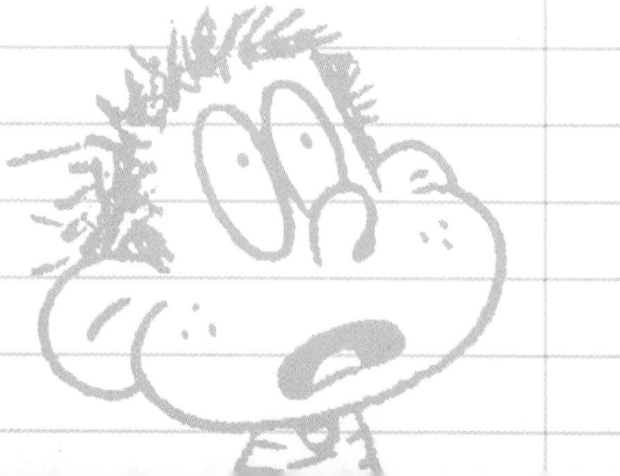

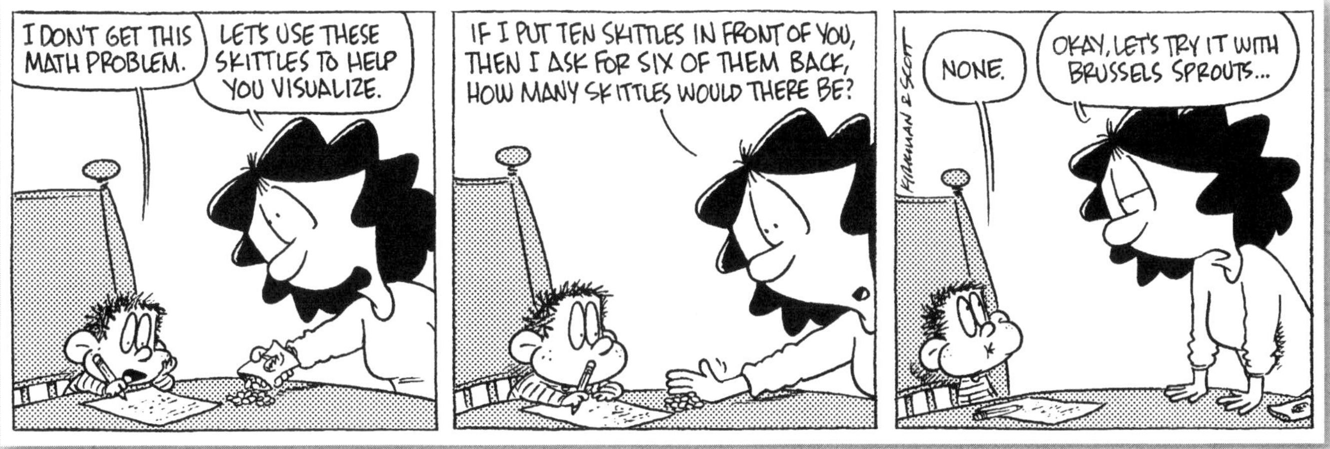
I DON'T GET THIS MATH PROBLEM.
LET'S USE THESE SKITTLES TO HELP YOU VISUALIZE.
IF I PUT TEN SKITTLES IN FRONT OF YOU, THEN I ASK FOR SIX OF THEM BACK, HOW MANY SKITTLES WOULD THERE BE?
NONE.
OKAY, LET'S TRY IT WITH BRUSSELS SPROUTS...
KIRKMAN & SCOTT

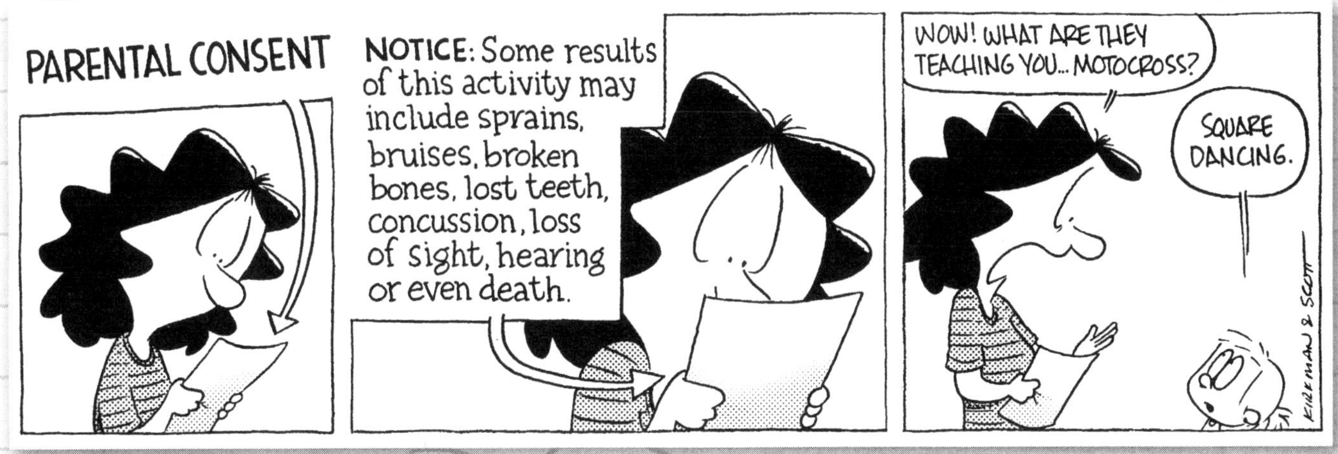
PARENTAL CONSENT
NOTICE: Some results of this activity may include sprains, bruises, broken bones, lost teeth, concussion, loss of sight, hearing or even death.
WOW! WHAT ARE THEY TEACHING YOU... MOTOCROSS?
SQUARE DANCING.
KIRKMAN & SCOTT

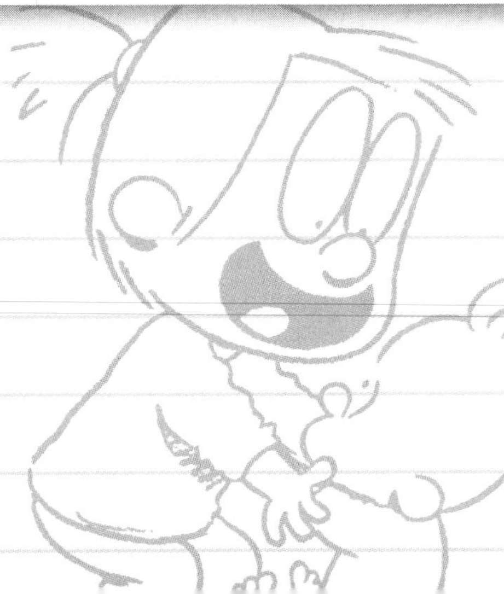

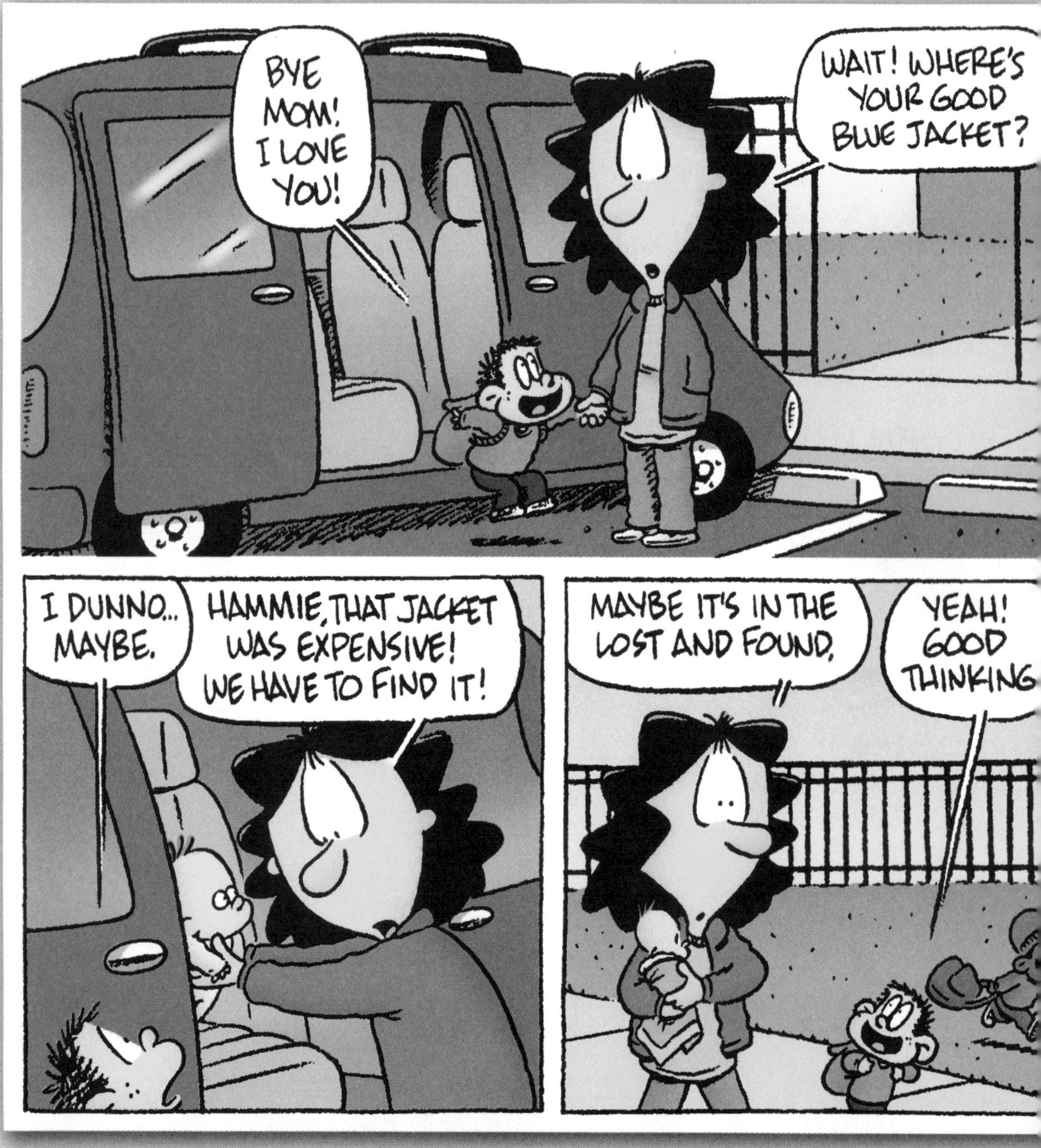
BYE MOM! I LOVE YOU!
WAIT! WHERE'S YOUR GOOD BLUE JACKET?
I DUNNO... MAYBE.
HAMMIE, THAT JACKET WAS EXPENSIVE! WE HAVE TO FIND IT!
MAYBE IT'S IN THE LOST AND FOUND.
YEAH! GOOD THINKING

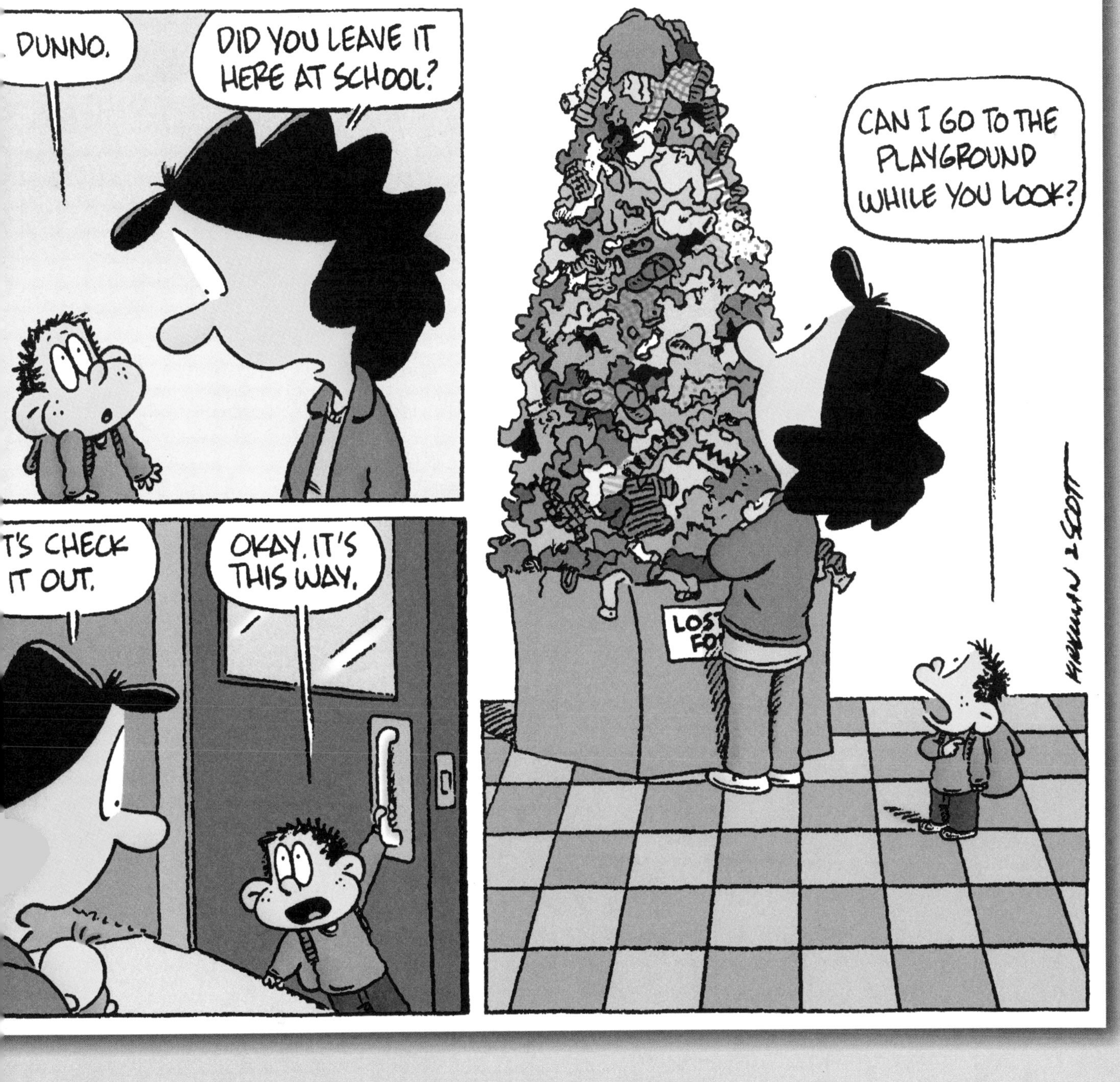
DUNNO.
DID YOU LEAVE IT HERE AT SCHOOL?
T'S CHECK IT OUT.
OKAY. IT'S THIS WAY.
CAN I GO TO THE PLAYGROUND WHILE YOU LOOK?
KIRKMAN & SCOTT

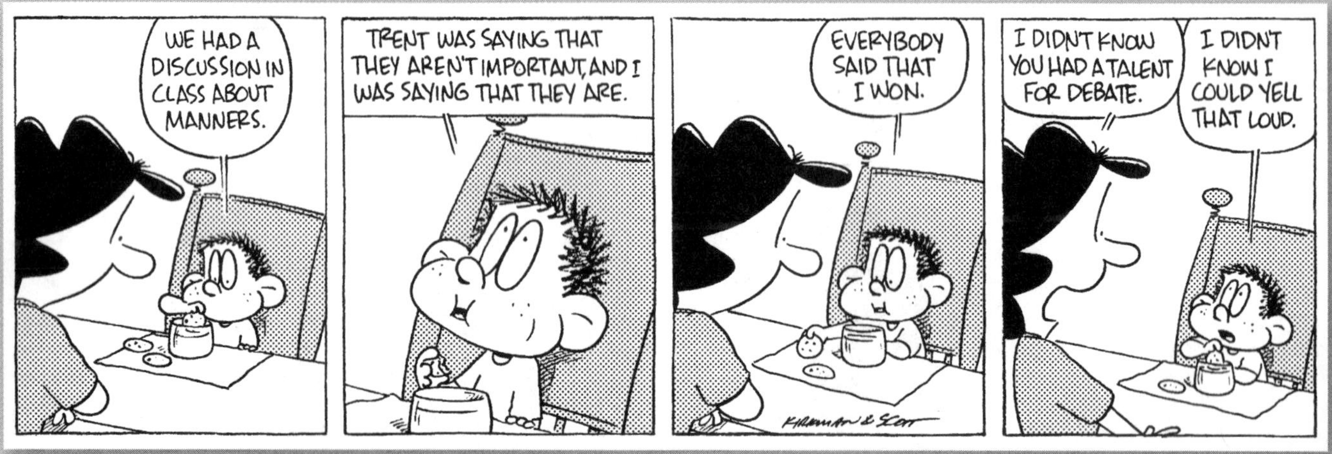
WE HAD A DISCUSSION IN CLASS ABOUT MANNERS.
TRENT WAS SAYING THAT THEY AREN'T IMPORTANT, AND I WAS SAYING THAT THEY ARE.
EVERYBODY SAID THAT I WON.
I DIDN'T KNOW YOU HAD A TALENT FOR DEBATE.
I DIDN'T KNOW I COULD YELL THAT LOUD.
KIRKMAN & SCOTT

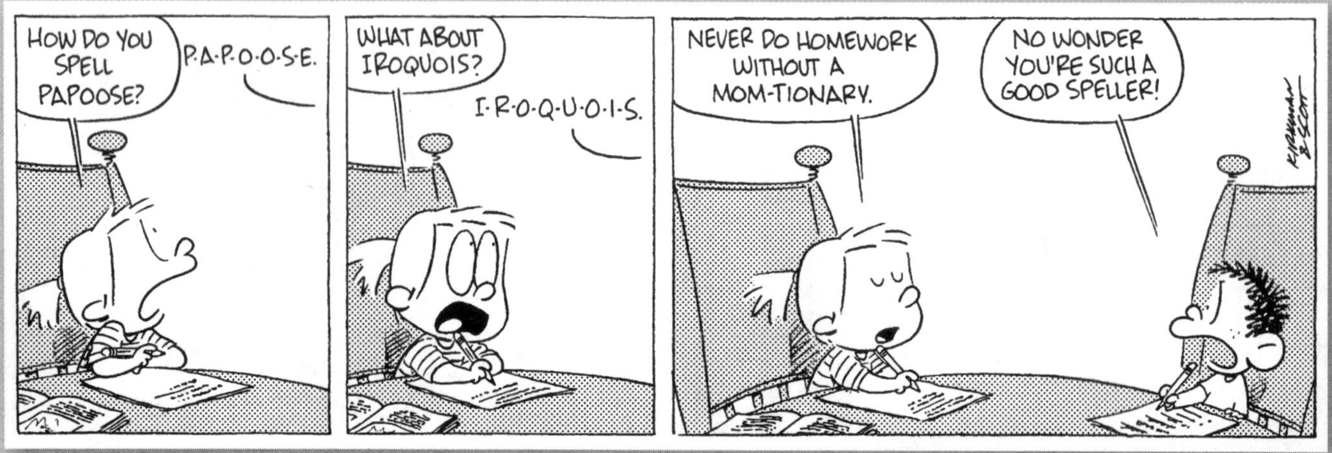
HOW DO YOU SPELL PAPOOSE?
P-A-P-O-O-S-E.
WHAT ABOUT IROQUOIS?
I-R-O-Q-U-O-I-S.
NEVER DO HOMEWORK WITHOUT A MOM-TIONARY.
NO WONDER YOU'RE SUCH A GOOD SPELLER!
KIRKMAN & SCOTT

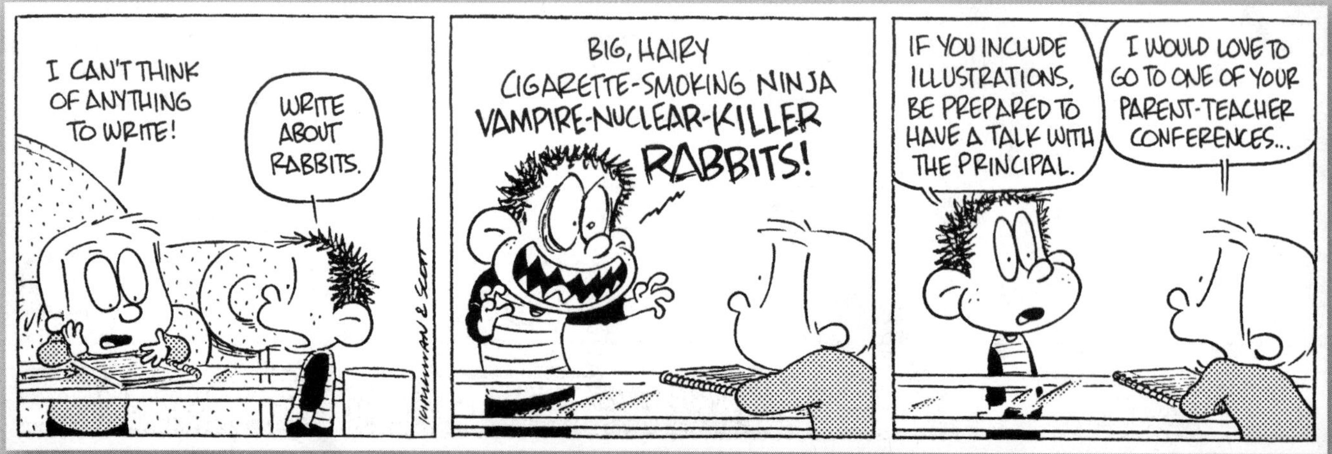
I CAN'T THINK OF ANYTHING TO WRITE!
WRITE ABOUT RABBITS.
KIRKMAN & SCOTT
BIG, HAIRY CIGARETTE-SMOKING NINJA VAMPIRE-NUCLEAR-KILLER RABBITS!
IF YOU INCLUDE ILLUSTRATIONS, BE PREPARED TO HAVE A TALK WITH THE PRINCIPAL.
I WOULD LOVE TO GO TO ONE OF YOUR PARENT-TEACHER CONFERENCES...

Panel 1: LOOK AT THE TRASH! — YEAH. THE PLAYGROUND IS LIKE THIS EVERY DAY.

Panel 2: THAT'S RIDICULOUS! FROM NOW ON, I'M GOING TO PACK YOU GUYS ZERO-WASTE LUNCHES IN REUSABLE CONTAINERS!

Panel 4: TRANSLATION: LEFTOVERS. — AAAGGHHH!

Panel 1: HERE ARE YOUR ZERO-WASTE LUNCHES!

Panel 2: EVERYTHING IN THEM IS REUSABLE, RECYCLABLE OR EDIBLE!

Panel 3: BIG WOOP. — I THINK GROWNUPS ARE CUTE WHEN THEY TRY TO MATTER.

Panel 1: WHAT DID YOU GET FOR LUNCH? — PEANUT BUTTER AND JELLY. WHAT ABOUT YOU?

Panel 2: MY MOM IS BEING ALL ENVIRONMENTAL, SO I HAVE LEFTOVERS PACKED IN RECYCLED MARGARINE TUBS.

Panel 3: TODAY IT'S A TUNA-NOODLE-MEATLOAF-CHICKEN SALAD MEDLEY.

Panel 4: NEEDLESS TO SAY, I'M WILLING TO TRADE. — I THINK I'LL GO SIT OVER THERE.

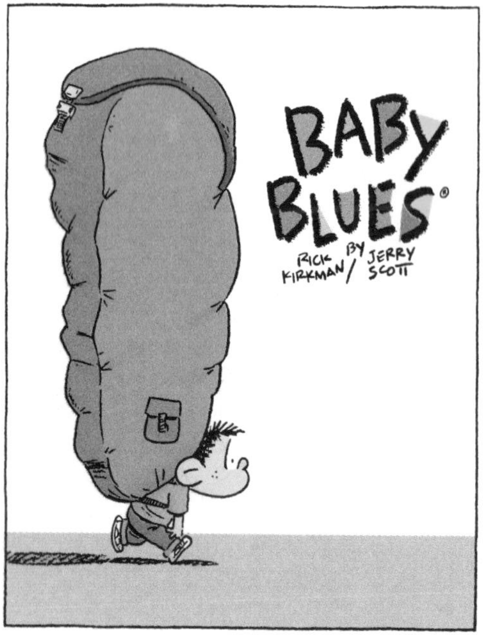
BABY BLUES®
BY RICK KIRKMAN / JERRY SCOTT

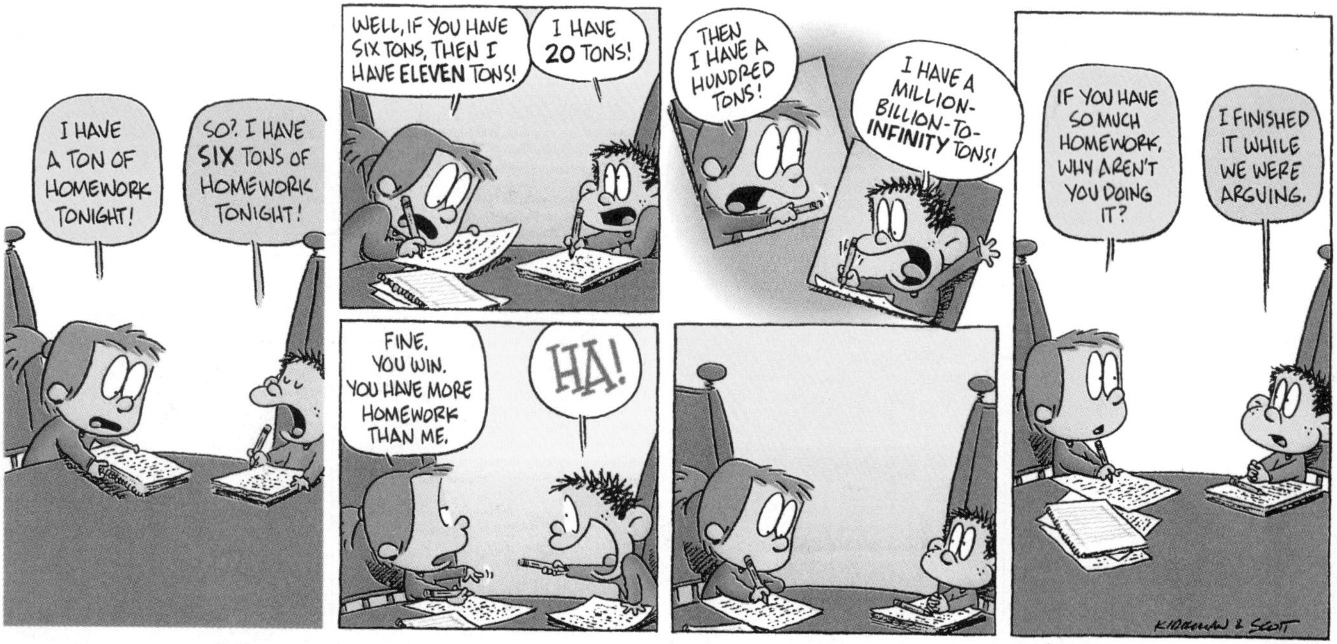
I HAVE A TON OF HOMEWORK TONIGHT!
SO? I HAVE SIX TONS OF HOMEWORK TONIGHT!
WELL, IF YOU HAVE SIX TONS, THEN I HAVE ELEVEN TONS!
I HAVE 20 TONS!
THEN I HAVE A HUNDRED TONS!
I HAVE A MILLION-BILLION-TO-INFINITY TONS!
FINE. YOU WIN. YOU HAVE MORE HOMEWORK THAN ME.
HA!
IF YOU HAVE SO MUCH HOMEWORK, WHY AREN'T YOU DOING IT?
I FINISHED IT WHILE WE WERE ARGUING.
KIRKMAN & SCOTT

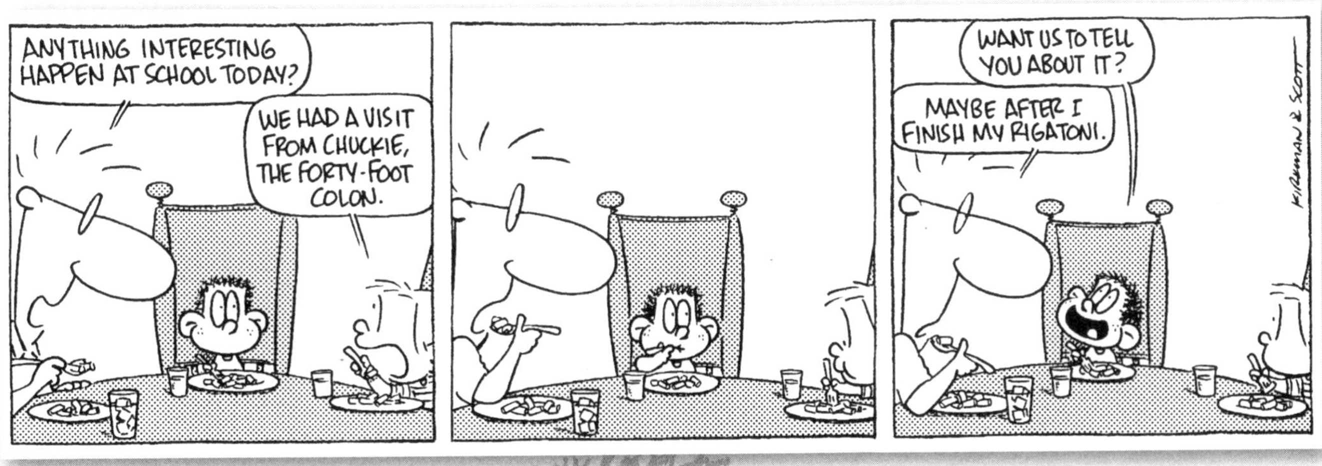
ANYTHING INTERESTING HAPPEN AT SCHOOL TODAY?
WE HAD A VISIT FROM CHUCKIE, THE FORTY-FOOT COLON.
WANT US TO TELL YOU ABOUT IT?
MAYBE AFTER I FINISH MY RIGATONI.
KIRKMAN & SCOTT

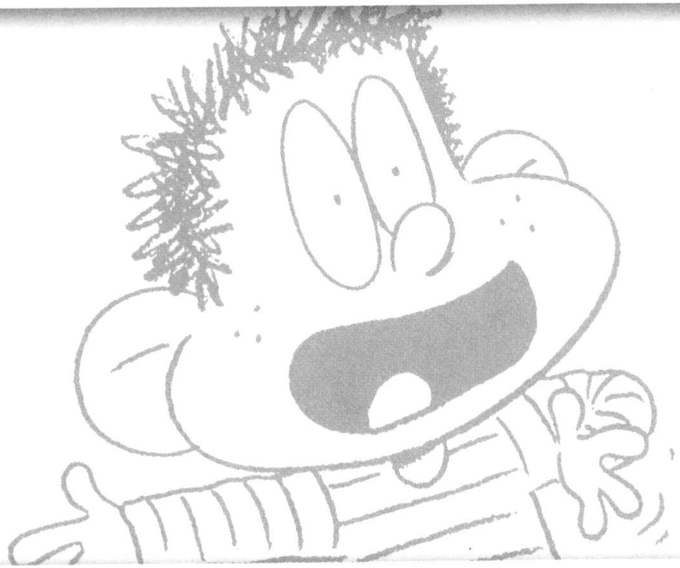

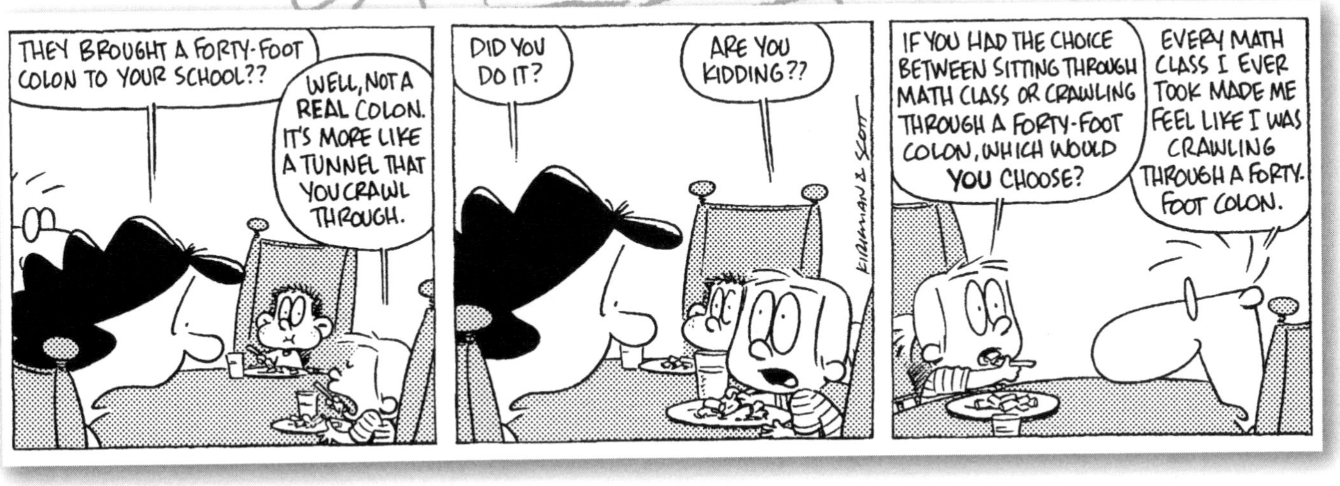
THEY BROUGHT A FORTY-FOOT COLON TO YOUR SCHOOL??
WELL, NOT A **REAL** COLON. IT'S MORE LIKE A TUNNEL THAT YOU CRAWL THROUGH.
DID YOU DO IT?
ARE YOU KIDDING??
KIRKMAN & SCOTT
IF YOU HAD THE CHOICE BETWEEN SITTING THROUGH MATH CLASS OR CRAWLING THROUGH A FORTY-FOOT COLON, WHICH WOULD **YOU** CHOOSE?
EVERY MATH CLASS I EVER TOOK MADE ME FEEL LIKE I WAS CRAWLING THROUGH A FORTY-FOOT COLON.

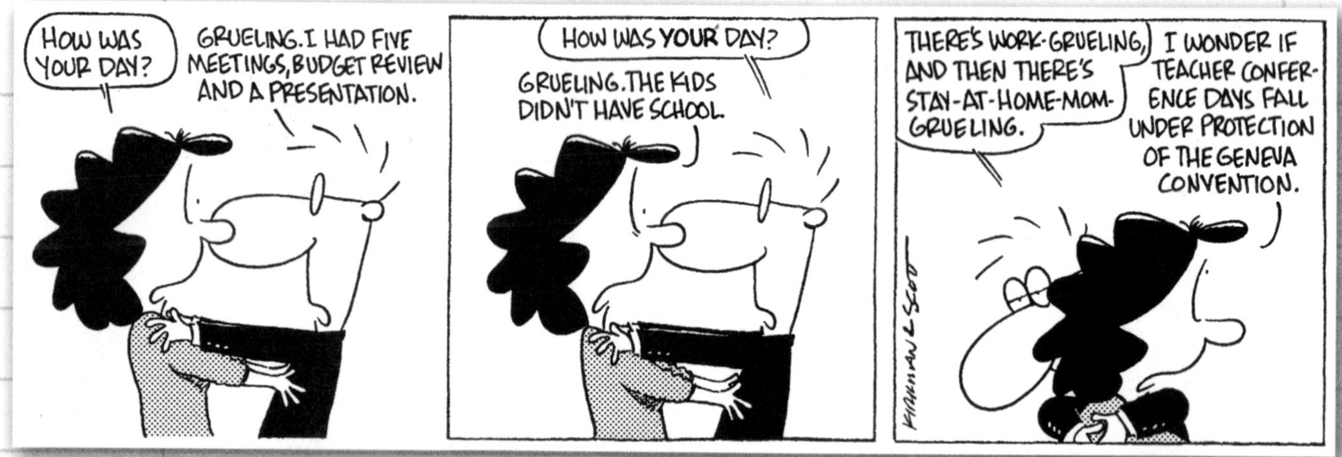
HOW WAS YOUR DAY?
GRUELING. I HAD FIVE MEETINGS, BUDGET REVIEW AND A PRESENTATION.
HOW WAS **YOUR** DAY?
GRUELING. THE KIDS DIDN'T HAVE SCHOOL.
THERE'S WORK-GRUELING, AND THEN THERE'S STAY-AT-HOME-MOM-GRUELING.
I WONDER IF TEACHER CONFERENCE DAYS FALL UNDER PROTECTION OF THE GENEVA CONVENTION.

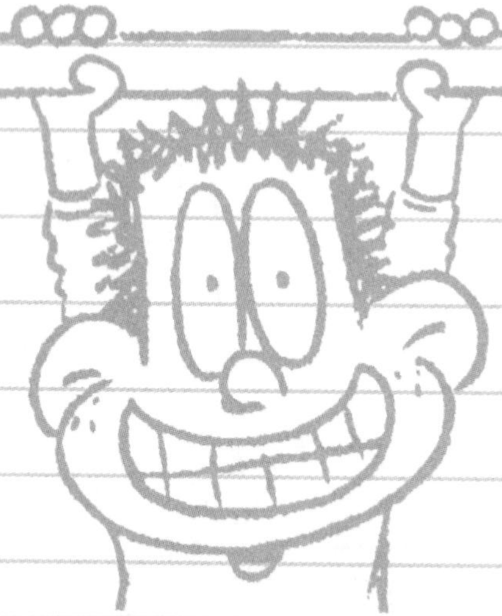

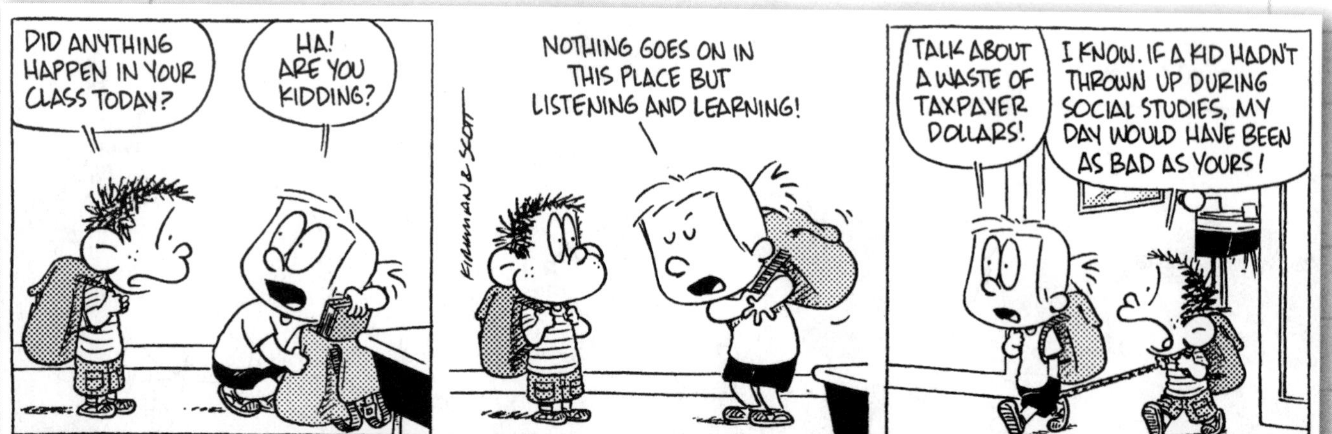
DID ANYTHING HAPPEN IN YOUR CLASS TODAY?
HA! ARE YOU KIDDING?
NOTHING GOES ON IN THIS PLACE BUT LISTENING AND LEARNING!
TALK ABOUT A WASTE OF TAXPAYER DOLLARS!
I KNOW. IF A KID HADN'T THROWN UP DURING SOCIAL STUDIES, MY DAY WOULD HAVE BEEN AS BAD AS YOURS!

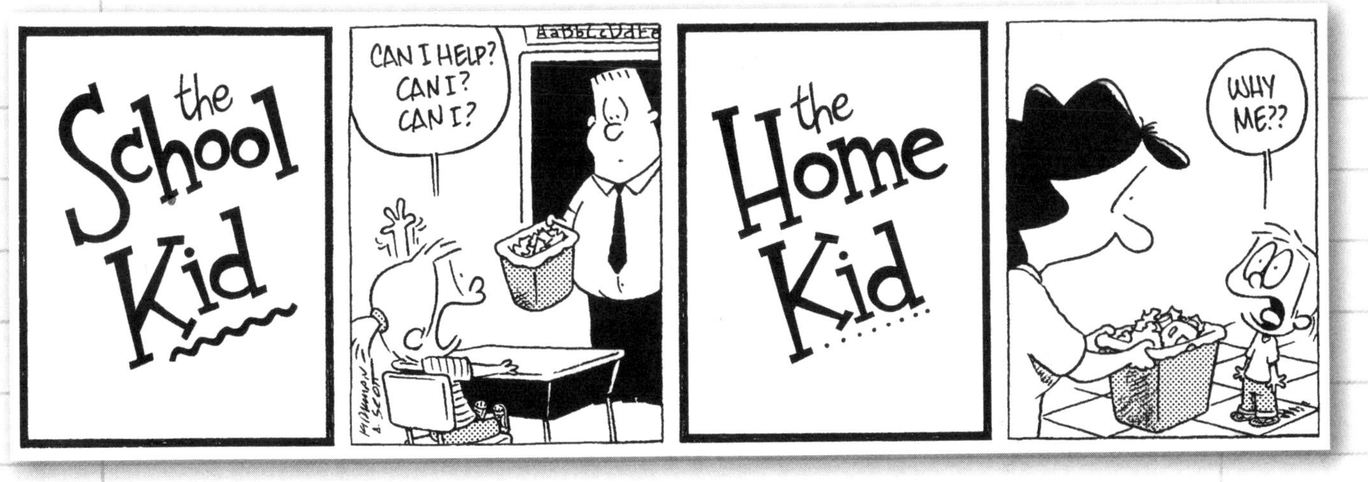
the School Kid
CAN I HELP? CAN I? CAN I?
the Home Kid
WHY ME??

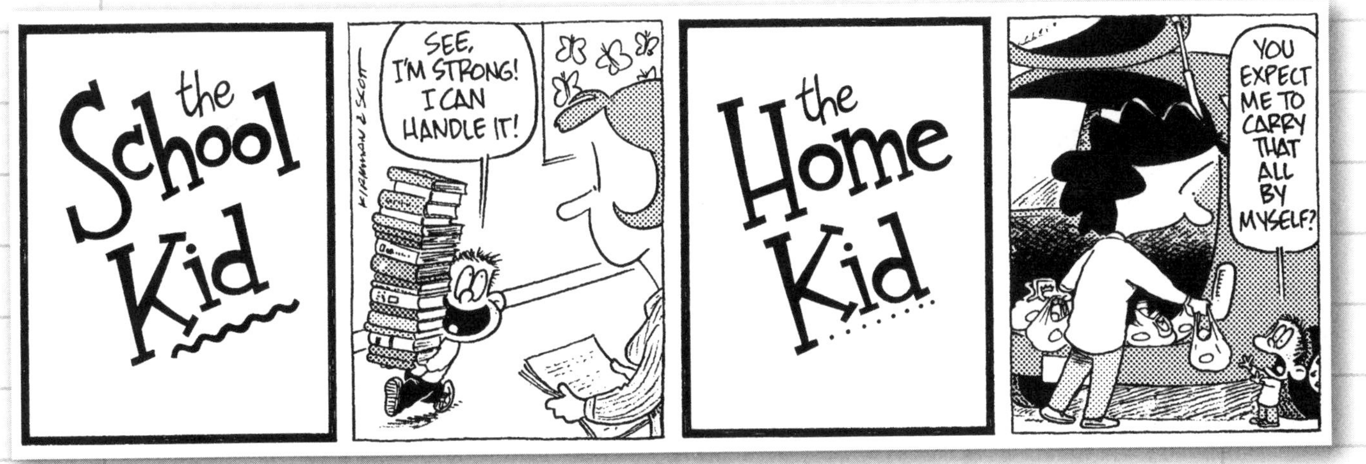
the School Kid
SEE, I'M STRONG! I CAN HANDLE IT!
the Home Kid
YOU EXPECT ME TO CARRY THAT ALL BY MYSELF?

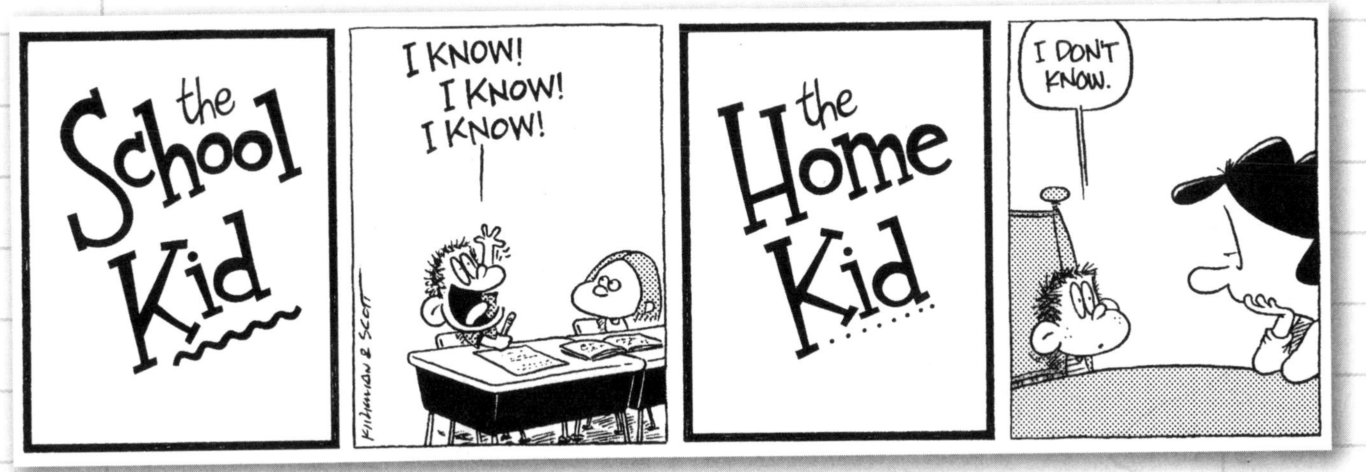
the School Kid
I KNOW! I KNOW! I KNOW!
the Home Kid
I DON'T KNOW.

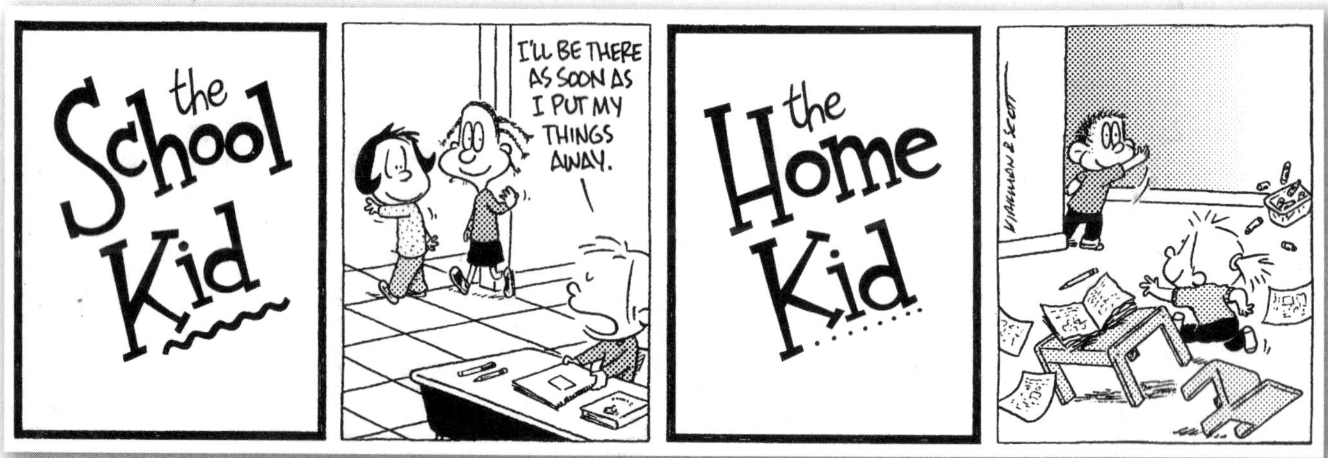
the School Kid
I'LL BE THERE AS SOON AS I PUT MY THINGS AWAY.
the Home Kid
KIRKMAN & SCOTT

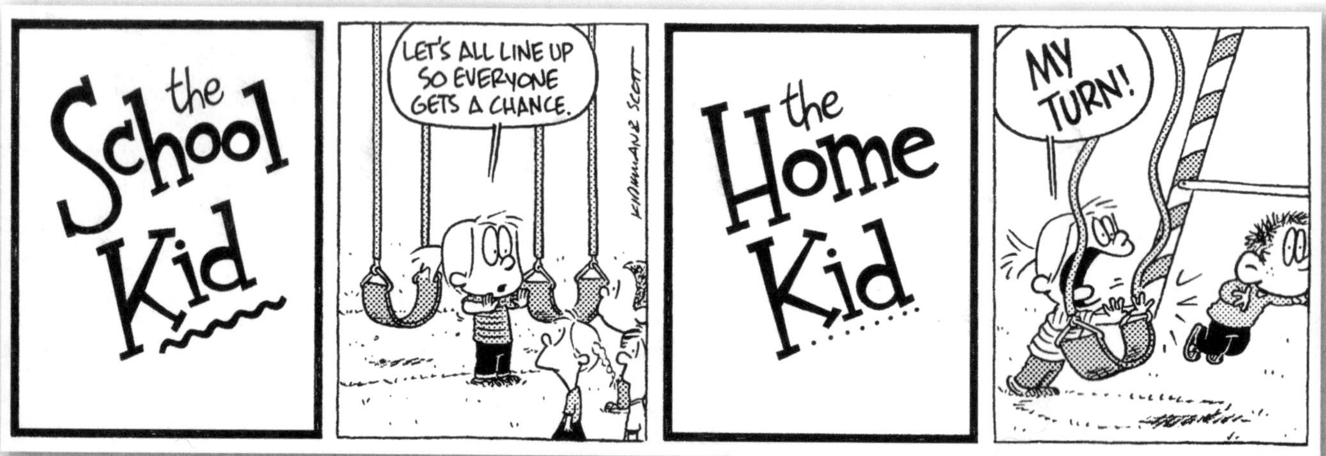
the School Kid
LET'S ALL LINE UP SO EVERYONE GETS A CHANCE.
KIRKMAN & SCOTT
the Home Kid
MY TURN!

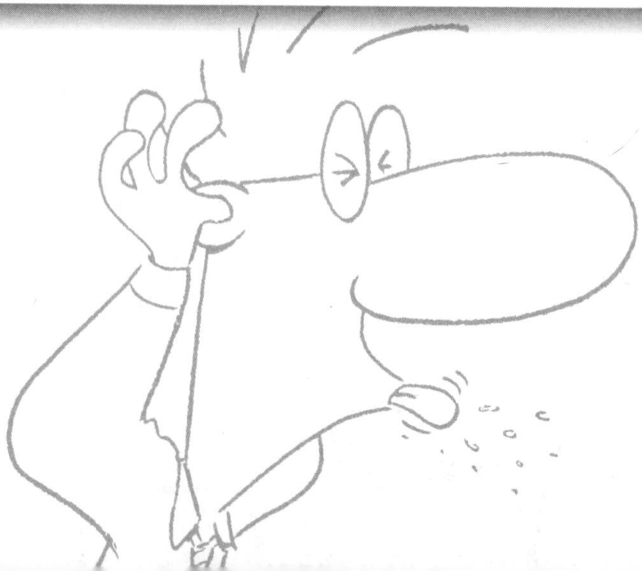